49

D0124738

THE APOCRYPHA

The Apocrypha

According to the Authorized Version

with an Introduction by
ROBERT H. PFEIFFER
Harvard University and Boston University

Her Majesty's Printers

LONDON: EYRE AND SPOTTISWOODE LIMITED
NEW YORK: HARPER & BROTHERS PUBLISHERS

PRINTED IN GREAT BRITAIN BY
EYRE AND SPOTTISWOODE LIMITED
HER MAJESTY'S PRINTERS, LONDON

TABLE OF CONTENTS

of

The Apocrypha

TABLE OF CONTENTS

of

The Apocrypha

INTRODUCTION

THE term "Apocrypha" is a Greek neuter plural adjective (erroneously used as a singular in English, like "data") meaning "hidden, spurious (books)". The Apocrypha of the Old Testament, according to the Protestants, are the books included in the Christian Greek and Latin Bibles but not found in the Hebrew Bible (which alone is generally regarded as canonical by the Protestants); Roman Catholics call these books "deuterocanonical", reserving the term "Apocrypha" for the books classed by the Protestants as "Pseudepigrapha".

In some early English Bibles, like the King James Version of 1611, the following books of the Apocrypha were collected at the end of the Old Testament: I and II Esdras, Tobit, Judith, the Rest of the Book of Esther, the Wisdom of Solomon, Ecclesiasticus, Baruch (including the Epistle of Jeremy as ch. 6), additions to Daniel (the Song of the Three Holy Children, the History of Susanna, the History of the Destruction of Bel and the Dragon), the Prayer of Manasses, I and II Maccabees. The standard printed editions of the Greek Bible (called the Septuagint) and of the Latin Bible (called the Vulgate, the official Roman Catholic Bible) vary slightly from the Authorized Version with respect to the Apocrypha. In the Septuagint II (or IV) Esdras never appears, but some manuscripts and editions contain III and IV Maccabees and Psalm 151; the Epistle of Jeremy is a separate book; the Prayer of Manasses is included among the *Odes* or *Cantica* which follow the Psalms in some manuscripts and editions. In the standard editions of the Vulgate the following books are placed in an appendix following the New Testament: the Prayer of Manasses, I (or III) Esdras, and II (or IV) Esdras. This last book, lost in the Greek text, is included among the English Apocrypha, but, being one of the latest apocalypses (dated about A.D. 90) and being supplied with Christian additions (chs. 1-2, 15-16), it really belongs among the Pseudepigrapha.

The Apocrypha in the Authorized Version were written by Jews during the last two centuries before the Christian Era, with the exception of I Esdras which is earlier and II Esdras which is later; all of them, however, were preserved by Christians after the Jewish biblical canon was fixed at Jamnia about A.D. 90, omitting the Apocrypha. With the exception of II

Esdras, they survived in the Greek Septuagint, the earliest Christian Bible. The authors of the books of the Apocrypha are unknown, with the exception of Jesus the son of Sirach (the author of Ecclesiasticus) and Jason of Cyrene, whose five books were summarized in II Maccabees.

Before the Council of Jamnia (A.D. 90) limited the Hebrew Bible to twenty-four books (five in the Pentateuch, eight in the Prophets, and eleven in the Writings or Hagiographa), the Christian Church had already received its Greek Bible from the Jews in Alexandria. Unfortunately we cannot be certain that the original (Jewish) Septuagint Bible was identical in contents and arrangement with the Christian Septuagint. With the exception of some small fragments unearthed in Egypt, dated by scholars in the second century B.C., all manuscripts of the Septuagint are Christian. We know that the Pentateuch was translated into Greek at Alexandria about 250 B.C., and that in 132, when the grandson of Sirach brought the Hebrew text of Ecclesiasticus to Egypt, the Former (Joshua, Judges, Samuel, and Kings) and Latter Prophets (Isaiah, Jeremiah, Ezekiel, and the Twelve Minor Prophets) had been translated into Greek: see the preface to the Greek version of Ecclesiasticus. But we do not know what Sirach's grandson meant when he added to the Law and the Prophets "the rest of the books". Scholars are not certain that all the Writings or Hagiographa (Psalms, Proverbs, Job; Song of Songs, Ruth, Lamentations, Ecclesiastes, Esther; Daniel; Ezra, Nehemiah, Chronicles) had been translated into Greek and were regarded as canonical at Alexandria before the Christian Era. And even more doubtful is the status of the Apocrypha among the Alexandrian Jews: for Josephus (died about A.D. 100) quoted from the Septuagint the Additions to Esther, I Esdras, and I Maccabees, wholly lacking in the Hebrew Bible, while Philo of Alexandria (died about A.D. 50) never alluded to the Apocrypha. But since the Apocrypha eventually found their way into the Greek Bible of the Christians (except II Esdras) it seems likely that at least a few Alexandrian Jews regarded them as canonical.

On the contrary the attitude of the Palestinian Jews with respect to the Apocrypha is clear: they were excluded from the canon of Scriptures without the slightest hesitation, in spite of the fact that Ecclesiasticus was more orthodox than Ecclesiastes and Judith more religious than Esther. Several reasons dictated this attitude at the Council of Jamnia (A.D. 90). At the time, the Palestinian Jews were certain that Ezra, during the reign of Artaxerxes I (465-424 B.C.), was the last of the inspired prophets; after him no Sacred Scripture could be written.

According to II (or IV) Esd. 14:45-46, all twenty-four books of the Hebrew Bible existed at the time of Ezra (cf. Josephus, *Against Apion* I:8). Ezra (Esdras, in Greek) is the latest alleged author of a Jewish apocalypse. In accordance with this dogma, which modern scholarship has proved to be questionable, no book known to be later than Ezra could be included in the canon of Scriptures: I and II Maccabees dealt with later history, Sirach (180 B.C.) appended his name to his book (Ecclesiasticus) instead of attributing it to Solomon; consequently these three books, though praiseworthy, were automatically excluded. Another reason militated against the canonization of II Maccabees: it was written in Greek and could not be included in the Hebrew Scriptures. The following books were likewise written in Greek: Wisdom of Solomon, III and IV Maccabees (the latter two, moreover, refer to events occurring long after Ezra). But the following books, written in Hebrew or Aramaic apparently before Ezra, seemed to have all the qualifications for canonical status—in fact more fitness for it than such books as Esther, Song of Songs, and Ecclesiastes: Tobit, Judith, Baruch, the Epistle of Jeremy, Additions to Daniel, the Prayer of Manasses. Manifestly the primary condition for canonization at Jamnia in A.D. 90 was survival in Hebrew or Aramaic. At that time, when books had to be copied laboriously by hand and public libraries preserving ancient manuscripts were unknown, survival depended on popularity, which, as every publisher knows, is capricious, unpredictable. For mysterious reasons, of all the Hebrew and Aramaic Apocrypha only Ecclesiasticus (quoted three times as Scripture in the Talmud and still copied in the Hebrew during the twelfth century) attained considerable popularity in Palestine; the others ceased to be copied, for lack of popular demand, soon after they were translated into Greek and were not accessible in the original languages when the Council of Jamnia met. While Ecclesiastes, Esther, and Song of Songs were canonized through popular demand in spite of the objections on the part of some learned men, books in the Apocrypha of similar merit had been inexplicably forgotten.

The Bible of St. Paul and of his Gentile converts was the Septuagint; thus the Apocrypha survived in Greek (except II or IV Esdras). Eighty per cent of the biblical quotations in the New Testament are not taken from the Hebrew text but from the Septuagint, although in most cases quotations are made from memory and do not reproduce the Greek text verbatim. Although the Apocrypha are never cited, the New Testament contains allusions to Ecclesiasticus (in Matthew and James), Wisdom of Solomon (in Matthew and in Paul's Epistles), II Maccabees (Heb. 11:35-36). Unmistakable references to some of the Pseudepigrapha are found in II Tim. 3:8; Heb. 11:37; Jude 9, 14, 15. Echoes of passages in the Apocrypha occur in early Christian literature. The Epistle of Barnabas quotes Wisdom, Ecclesiasticus, and II Esdras; I Clement likewise quotes Wisdom; Tertullian (died about 230) extols Judith and regards Ecclesiasticus as Scripture; Clement of Alexandria (died about 220), Origen (died about 250), and Cyprian (died about 260) recognize that the Apocrypha belong in the Christian Bible. Nevertheless Origen, as a scholar, knew that they were not part of the Hebrew Bible and therefore should not be accepted as God's Word. In other words Origen as a Christian minister used the Apocrypha for the edification of the Church but as a scholar denied their canonicity. Since Origen, many Christian leaders have been forced to tolerate such contradictions between faith and reason when no compromise was possible. Thus, for instance, Cyril of Jerusalem (died in 386) exhorted his pupils to disregard the Apocrypha, but he was forced to adhere to the general practice of the Church in accepting them. St. Jerome (died in 420) as a scholar relegated all books outside of the Hebrew Bible among apocryphal writings but as a churchman included the Apocrypha in his Latin Bible (the Vulgate), which became the official Roman Catholic Bible; and he even quoted Ecclesiasticus as Scripture.

Thus Christianity inherited from Judaism two contrasting attitudes toward the Apocrypha: their canonical status, recognized by some of the Alexandrian Jews, and their extra canonical status, tacitly assumed in Palestine. The earliest recorded discussion of these divergent views took place in 238: Julius Africanus of Emmaus wrote to Origen expressing astonishment at his reference to the Story of Susanna as Scripture. Origen could merely appeal to the authority of the Church, and quoted Prov. 22:28 in support of traditional views.

Few scholars took issue with the canonicity of the Apocrypha before the Reformation; in fact, some synods confirmed it. The African Council of Hippo (393) declared that Wisdom, Ecclesiasticus, Tobit, Judith, I and II Maccabees, and presumably the rest were canonical. The third (397) and sixteenth (419) Councils of Carthage confirmed this vote. The Council of Trent (1546) and the Vatican Council (1870) pronounced the anathema against whoever did not recognize as "sacred and canonical" all the books contained in the Vulgate, the Latin Bible of the Roman Catholic Church. The Clementine edition of the Vulgate (1592), which became the official text, added at the end of the New Testament I (or III) and II (or IV) Esdras; the Council of Trent, the decisions of which had been directed against the Protestant Reformers, had not mentioned these two books.

The Greek Orthodox Church at the Second Trullan Council (692) declared the Apocrypha (without II or IV Esdras) canonical; but the Council of Jerusalem (1672) recognized only Tobit, Judith, Ecclesiasticus, and Wisdom as canonical, besides the books of the Old Testament, among which I Esdras and the additions to Esther and Daniel were naturally included.

The Syriac Church, deeply influenced by Judaism at the beginning, accepted as canonical only the Hebrew Old Testament (without Chronicles, Ezra-Nehemiah, and Esther) and Ecclesiasticus. Gradually, however, the Septuagint prevailed over the Hebrew Bible, except among the Nestorians; the Ambrosian manuscript of the Syriac Bible (in Milan; sixth century) contains the Apocrypha, with the exception of I (or III) Esdras, the Prayer of Manasses, Tobit, and the additions to Esther; it even has III and IV Maccabees, II (or IV) Esdras, and Book VII of Josephus, *The Jewish War*.

But in the Syriac Church, as elsewhere, some scholarly objections were raised against the canonicity of the Apocrypha—notably at the theological school at Nisibis (northwest of Mosul). There, the admirable biblical studies previously flourishing at Antioch—the center for the earliest historical and critical interpretation of the Bible—were continued under excellent scholars. In 550 Junilius Africanus published in Latin translation the course of lectures of Paul the Persian to the first-year students at Nisibis. Biblical writings (omitting Ecclesiastes, which is not mentioned) are classed by Paul into three groups: those having perfect authority (the books of the Hebrew Old Testament, including Ecclesiasticus but omitting the books in the second group); those of qualified authority, which many would include in the first group (I-II Chronicles, Job, Tobit, Ezra, Nehemiah, Judith, Esther, I-II Maccabees); those having no authority (the remaining books), although Paul says that some regard Wisdom of Solomon and Song of Songs as canonical.

The Renaissance witnessed the revival of the study of ancient languages (Greek, Latin, Hebrew, etc.); the appearance of new trends in art, philosophy, and religion; the invention of printing; geographical discoveries; and other epoch-making changes. Nicholas of Lyra (died about 1340), a Franciscan monk whose parents were Jews, wrote a commentary on the "canonical" Old Testament (the Hebrew Bible) based on

Jewish commentaries and another one on the "uncanonical" books (the most important of the Apocrypha); in 1333 he even published a Latin treatise on "the difference between our version [i.e., the Vulgate] and Hebrew truth". His influence on Martin Luther (died in 1546) was decisive and eventually resulted in the exclusion of the Apocrypha from the Old Testament of the Protestant churches.

It was essential for the Reformers to determine the text and interpretation of the Scriptures, which they regarded as the supreme authority—in place of the Papacy for Roman Catholics—in matters of faith and conduct. The texts of the Vulgate and of the Septuagint were no longer regarded as the exact texts of God's Word, and vernacular translations from the original Hebrew Old Testament and Greek New Testament were now required for the guidance of Protestant Christians. In his great translation of the Bible into German (1534), Luther placed the Apocrypha (without I [III] and II [IV] Esdras) at the end of the Old Testament under this title: "Apocrypha. These books are not held equal to the sacred Scriptures, and yet are useful and good for reading". Coverdale (1535) in his English Bible likewise separated the Apocrypha from the Old Testament; following the Vulgate, however, he omitted the Prayer of Manasses and added the two Esdras books. All English editions of the Bible prior to 1629 included the bulk of the Apocrypha, either scattered among the Old Testament books, as in Wycliffe's Bible (1382, revised 1388), or placed together at the end, as in Coverdale's Bible. After 1629 some English Bibles were published without the Apocrypha; following some bitter attacks on the part of members of the Church of Scotland, after 1827 the British and Foreign Bible Society omitted the Apocrypha from all its English Bibles, with the exception of some pulpit Bibles. All the Bibles published by the American Bible Society omitted the Apocrypha.

The reluctance of the Reformers to recognize the canonicity of the Apocrypha was due not only to the fact that they were not included in the Hebrew Bible, which was regarded as the genuine, inspired Old Testament, but also to their dislike of some Roman Catholic doctrines for which proof texts were found in these books. The doctrine of merits acquired through good works—contrary to the principle of the Reformation, "The just shall live by faith" (Rom. 1:17; Gal. 3:11; cf. Hab. 2:4)—is supported by Tob. 12:9; Ecclus. 3:30; II Esd. 8:33; etc.; the merit of the saints for the benefit of sinners corresponds to the merit of the Patriarchs in the Prayer of Azarias 12;

the intercession of the living in behalf of the dead (II Macc. 12:43)—nay, their capacity to make expiation of the dead and thus deliver them from Purgatory (II Macc. 12:44-45)—caused Luther to regard II Maccabees as particularly obnoxious.

In contrast with the Roman Catholic assertion that the Apocrypha are canonical, no Protestant church regards them as the Word of God. But there are differences in the attitudes of the churches. The Lutheran, Anglican, Dutch, and Zurich Reformed Churches admit that they are instructive and edifying, without being inspired. The Church of England in its *Articles of Religion* (1553; 1563) declared: "The other Books (as Hierome saith [see Jerome's 'Preface to the Books of Samuel']) the Church doth read for example of life and instruction of manners; and yet doth not apply them to establish any doctrine". Conversely the *Westminster Confession* (article 3) stated that the Apocrypha were "of no authority in the Church of God, nor to be otherwise approved or made use of than other human writings". This severe verdict expresses the attitude of the Church of Scotland and of the various Calvinistic, Puritan, Evangelical, and Free Churches. Apart from these three views on the canonicity of the Apocrypha (full canonicity, usefulness without canonicity, and lack of any religious value), the Apocrypha are important for the history and thought of Judaism during the last two centuries before our era, and for an understanding of the origins of Christianity.

The books of the Apocrypha were originally written in Hebrew, Aramaic, or Greek, although they survive only in Greek, Latin (II or IV Esdras), and Syriac. The *Palestinian Apocrypha in Hebrew* include two types of poetry: psalms (Ecclus. 39:12-35; 42:15–43:33; 51:1-12; Tob. 13; Jth. 16; Bar. 4:5–5:9; the Prayer of Manasses; the Prayer of Azarias and the Song of the Three Holy Children were probably composed in Hebrew) and wise counsel (Ecclesiasticus; Bar. 3:9–4:4); and three types of prose: history (I Maccabees), legend (Bar. 1:1–3:8), and fiction (Judith). The *Palestinian literature in Aramaic* (the vernacular of the country after 400 B.C.) was more popular in character; it included fiction (the Story of the Three Youths in I or III Esd. 3:1–4:63 [the rest of this book is taken from Chronicles-Ezra-Nehemiah]; Tobit; Susanna, Bel and the Dragon; Esth. 11:2–12:6; 13:8-18; 14:1-19; 15:1-16; 10:4-13), legends (II Macc. 1:1-2:18; II or IV Esd. 14), apocalypse (II Esd. 3-13), and polemic against Babylonian idolatry (Epistle of Jeremy); the only poetry is the wise counsel in Tob. 4:3-21; 12:6-10.

The only *Alexandrian writings composed in Greek* which were included among the Apocrypha are the Wisdom of Solomon (popular philosophy), II Macc. 2:19–15:39 (legendary history), and the decrees of Ahasuerus in Esth. 13:1-7; 16:1-24.

This variety of literary types corresponds to the different kinds of religion which are stressed in the Apocrypha. In the *Palestinian writings* we note the nationalistic religion of the battlefield (Ecclus. 36:1-17; I Macc. 4:30-33; 5:62; 7:40-42); the ritualistic religion of the Temple (I Macc. 7:37; Tob. 1:4-8; 5:13; Ecclus. 7:31; 35:4-7; 50:1-21); the religion of observances, such as the dietary laws (Jth. 10:5; 12:2, 12, 19; Tob. 1:10-12), sabbath rest (I Macc. 2:34, 41), and circumcision (I Macc. 1:14, 48; 2:46); the religion of ethical conduct and good works (Tob. 4:3-19; 12:8-10; Ecclus. 2:1-18; 17:14; 22:27-23:27; etc.); the religion of personal piety (Ecclus. 17:24-18:14; 22:27–23:6; 32:14; 24; 40:26-27); and the hope in the vindication of the Jews and of the pious through the Messiah and the Final Judgment (II or IV Esd. 3–13).

In the *Alexandrian writings* (in Greek) we note two differences. In II Maccabees the enthusiasm for the Temple (3:39; 5:19; 14:13, 31, 35) and the zeal in observing the prescriptions of the Law of Moses (dietary laws, 6:18–7:1; sabbath rest, 6:11; 15:5; circumcision, 6:10) are more pronounced, more stressed, than in Palestine. The Wisdom of Solomon utilizes some of the teachings of Platonic and Stoic philosophy in the exposition and defense of Judaism (7:22-27; 8:7 [the four cardinal virtues]; 8:19-20; 9:15; 11:17; 14:3; 16:21; 17:2; 19:18); it teaches the immortality of the soul (1:5; 3:4; 5:15; 6:18; 8:17; 15:3) like the Greeks, instead of the resurrection of the body taught by another Alexandrian book, II Maccabees (7:11; 14:46); and it knows of the pre-existence of the soul (8:19-20), which becomes imprisoned in "the corruptible body", "the earthly tabernacle" (9:15; cf. II Cor. 5:1, 4; II Pet. 1:13-14).

The *Pseudepigrapha* are Jewish writings of the period 200 B.C.–A.D. 150 which were not included in the Septuagint and the Vulgate (and were not regarded as canonical in the Western Churches) but were preserved by Oriental Churches in various languages, such as Syriac, Ethiopic, Coptic, Georgian, Armenian, Slavonic, etc. The Psalms of Solomon, III and IV Maccabees, the Testament of Job, the Life of Adam and Eve, the Lives of the Prophets, the Letter of Aristeas, the Sibylline Oracles, and a few other writings survive in Greek; the Assumption of Moses and the Life of Adam and Eve are extant in Latin.

The *Palestinian Pseudepigrapha* written originally in *Hebrew* are the following: the Psalms of Solomon (about 40 B.C.); the Testaments of the Twelve Patriarchs (about 140 B.C.); the Lives of the Prophets (first century of our era). The following Palestinian works were written in *Aramaic*: Jubilees (about 150 B.C.); the Testament of Job (about 80 B.C.); the Book of Enoch (160-80 B.C.); legends from the first century of our era, with Christian additions (Martyrdom of Isaiah, the Paralipomena of Jeremiah, the Life of Adam and Eve, and the Assumption of Moses [A.D. 6-30]); apocalypses from about A.D. 90 (II or IV Esdras, in the Apocrypha; Syriac Baruch; Apocalypse of Abraham).

The *Alexandrian books*, written in Greek, are the following: the Letter of Aristeas (about 100 B.C.), Sibylline Oracles III:97-808 (about 140 B.C.); III Maccabees (about 50 B.C.); IV Maccabees (about A.D. 20); apocalypses with Christian additions (about A.D. 100 [Slavonic Enoch; Greek Baruch]); Sibylline Oracles IV (about A.D. 80) and V (about A.D. 125).

The only complete English text of the Pseudepigrapha, with introductions and notes, is to be found in Volume II of R. H. Charles (ed.), *The Apocrypha and Pseudepigrapha in English*, two vols., Oxford, at the Clarendon Press, 1913.*

I Esdras

This volume is not a complete book, as some scholars have claimed, but merely a small portion of the canonical books of Chronicles, Ezra, and Nehemiah: it presents merely some variations in diction, in order (Ezra 4:7-24 precedes Ezra 2:1), and in contents (Ezra 4:6; Neh. 1:1–7:5, 8:13b–13:31 are omitted; I Esd. 1:23-24, 3:1–5:6 have been added). It is a much clearer, more idiomatic Greek translation than the literal rendering in the Septuagint; and presumably it is earlier, since it is the text used by Josephus in the first century of our era; but it was eventually discarded in the Christian Church in favor of the canonical Greek version.

I Esdras begins with the celebration of the Passover by Josiah and ends with the reading of the Law in the days of Ezra, and thus includes the period 621-444 B.C. We may outline the contents as follows: the last kings of Judah, from Josiah to Zedekiah (ch. I; cf. II Chron. 35:1–36:21); a decree of Cyrus king of Persia allowing the Jewish exiles to return to Jerusalem and rebuild the Temple (2:1-15; cf. Ezra 1:1-11); the rebuilding

*For more details on the Apocrypha and Pseudepigrapha, and for bibliographical references, see R. H. Pfeiffer, *History of New Testament Times, with an Introduction to the Apocrypha.*
New York, Harper & Brothers, 1949.

of Jerusalem and its Temple forbidden by Artaxerxes (2:16-30; cf. Ezra 4:7-24); the Story of the Three Youths at the Court of Darius, who permits the rebuilding of the Temple (3:1–5:6; cf. Josephus, *Antiquities of the Jews* XI, 3); list of exiles returning with Zerubbabel (5:7-43; cf. Ezra 2:1-67; Neh. 7:6-69); the rebuilding of the Temple (5:44–7:15; cf. Ezra 2:68-4:5; 4:24–6:22); Ezra's journey to Jerusalem (8:1-67; cf. Ezra 7:1–8:36); Ezra's efforts to do away with marriages of Jews with Gentile women (8:68–9:36; cf. Ezra 9:1–10:44); the reading of the Law (9:37-55; cf. Neh. 7:73–8:13a).

This book, called III Esdras in the Latin Vulgate, was translated into Greek from a Hebrew-Aramaic text of Chronicles-Ezra-Nehemiah, which differed slightly from the canonical text, in the period 150 B.C.-A.D. 50. This fragment of the Chronicler's work was preserved by the Christians on account of the popularity of the Story of the Three Youths at the Court of Darius (3:1–4:42), the original ending of which was omitted in favor of 4:43-47 after the third youth was identified with Zerubbabel (4:13). Thus a story which had originally nothing to do with the Jews served to explain how Zerubbabel obtained from Darius the permission to lead back to Jerusalem a caravan of Jewish exiles and to rebuild the Temple (4:48–5:6). The original pagan story related that three pages of Darius I argued that the strongest thing in the world was wine, the king, or women, respectively. A Zoroastrian version added that "great is truth, and stronger than all things" (4:35; cf. 4:38, 41). The familiar aphorism "Great is truth, and it will prevail" is a rendering from the Latin mistranslation of 4:41, in the Vulgate. "Truth" is the Avestan *Asha*, the right cosmic and social order, the deity which directs the course of natural phenomena (4:34-36) and establishes justice among men (4:37–39), to whom consequently belong "the might, the kingdom, the power, and the majesty for ever and ever" (4:40; cf. Matt. 6:13). The original story may date back to the fifth century B.C., and the praise of Truth in 4:34-40 may be based on a Zoroastrian hymn in praise of Asha. Our Greek text was not translated from the Old Persian but from an Aramaic version made from it. In the Greek, and even in English (a fourth-hand version), the story preserves a sense of reality, a biting irony, a true eloquence, a religious feeling—in the speeches of the three youths—which give it a prominent place among ancient classical tales.

II Esdras

This pessimistic apocalypse was written in Aramaic about A.D. 90, but neither this text nor the Greek version made from it has survived: we have only an old Latin version from the Greek (called IV Esdras), which is printed in Latin Bibles after the New Testament, and some Oriental versions likewise based on the Greek text (except the Syriac, which goes back to the Aramaic original). The Jewish apocalypse, in the Latin text and in the English Authorized Version made from it (but not in the Oriental texts), is enclosed within two Christian prophecies: chs. 1-2 (about A.D. 150) denounce Israel for its sins and, after inviting the heathen to receive God's kingdom, announce the coming of the Son of God with the Christian martyrs; chs. 15-16 (about A.D. 250) announce the coming of the woes preceding the end of the world, notably dreadful wars, in which God's chosen "shall be tried as the gold in the fire. . . . Behold the days of trouble are at hand, but I will deliver you from the same" (16:73-74).

The original work consisted of six visions (chs. 3–13) of Salathiel (Shealtiel, in Hebrew), the father or uncle of Zerubbabel, identified with Ezra in 3:1 ("I, Salathiel, who am Esdras"; omitted in the Authorized Version), although Salathiel lived a century earlier. The book ended with the account of Ezra's restoration of the Scriptures (ch. 14).

The first vision (3:1–5:20). This vision vainly tries to explain why God, who did not remove from man the evil impulse transmitted by Adam to his descendants, allowed Nebuchadnezzar to destroy Jerusalem for its sins. The angel Uriel replies that man cannot understand God or defy the laws of nature: evil must produce evil. The new world will appear when the abode of the righteous dead is filled to capacity.

The second vision (5:21–6:34). Since the generation living at the end of this evil age is the most fortunate, why could not all generations have lived at that time? Because they must follow one another and, owing to the aging of the earth, become increasingly worse. After the signs of the end, the age to come will follow the present one without delay.

The third vision (6:35–9:25). The Vulgate, and therefore the Authorized Version, through some accident omits a long section after 7:35; this missing section in modern Bibles is numbered 7:36-105, while 7:36-70 in the Authorized Version is numbered 7:106-140. Owing to Adam's sin the Jews must reach the future world, which belongs to them, by difficult paths; the corruptible world belongs to the heathen. "My Son", the Messiah, will rule 400 years; then all men, including him, will die and silence will prevail during seven days; then will come the resurrection and the final judgment. [*The missing fragment*: Gehenna and Paradise will appear then, at the beginning of the new age. Only few are saved. After death the wicked are tormented while the righteous are at peace in their chambers.] Not Adam, but each individual is responsible for his damnation. God takes pleasure in the saved and forgets the evildoers.

The fourth vision (9:26–10:60). A woman (who represents Zion) mourns for her son (representing Jerusalem) and intends to starve herself. When the seer urges her to mourn for Zion instead, she disappears and the New Jerusalem appears.

The fifth vision (11:1–12:51). This is an allegorical dream. An eagle has twelve wings, three heads, and eight small wings. The twelve wings and two small ones rule in succession; two other small wings stay under one head, and two others are devoured by the heads, who rule next; finally two small wings rule. Following the sentence of a lion (representing the Messiah), the eagle is burned. The eagle is Daniel's fourth Kingdom (Dan. 7:7-8, 23), but it is no longer the Hellenistic Seleucid kingdom, but the Roman Empire. The first two wings are Caesar and Augustus; the three heads are Vespasian, Titus, and Domitian; during the latter's reign (81-96), the book was written.

The sixth vision (13:1-58). A human figure (the Messiah) rises from the sea and flies with the clouds of heaven (cf. Dan. 7:13). After destroying his enemies he gathers in Palestine the ten "lost" tribes of Israel, joining them to the Jews living there.

The restoration of the Scriptures (14:1-48; the Oriental versions add at the end an account of the ascension of Ezra to heaven). Withdrawing into the wilderness with five scribes, Ezra dictated to them ninety-four books: twenty-four (the Hebrew Old Testament) were to be published, but seventy (mostly apocalypses) were esoteric, available only to the wise among the Jews.

The first three visions deal with the miseries of the present age, the last three with the glorification of the pious Jews in the future world. The first part contains a searching discussion of the problem of evil, and especially of God's relation to it. The afflictions of all men, of the Jewish nation as a whole and of pious Jews in particular, and the triumphs of Babylon (meaning Rome) raise the question of God's justice in dealing with his people—a problem which cannot be solved rationally, but is rendered less acute in the second part of the book by the hope of salvation for the Jews in the future world. The extreme discouragement and pessimism of this brilliant author reflects the misery of the Jews following the destruction of Jerusalem in A.D. 70. He is not only a deep thinker, occasionally feeling pity for all men and not only for the Jews, but a greater writer, reaching a high level of eloquence and impressive beauty in such passages as 6:1-6; 7:6-8; 7:46-53; 8:34-36; 8:52-54. This book presents some close parallels with the Apocalypse of St. John, written about the same time, and it influenced the Apocalypse of Baruch. It marks the end of Jewish visions about the end of the world which had begun with Daniel in 164 B.C. The first and the last Jewish apocalypses, Daniel and II Esdras, were written by men of genius and are unsurpassed.

Tobit

This excellent short story was written in Aramaic about 190-170 B.C. but survives in three Greek texts. It illustrates, through precept (Tobit 4:3-21; 12:6-10) and example, the moral and religious ideals of the Jews living far from Jerusalem. Few moderns still believe that the events narrated are historical; the tale is manifestly fiction.

Tobit of the tribe of Naphtali was exiled to Nineveh where he continued to observe zealously the Law of Moses even after he became the purchasing agent of Shalmaneser. He fled when Sennacherib sought to kill him for burying the bodies of Jews executed by this king, but returned under Esarhaddon (1:1-22). He was blinded by birds' dung when he slept outdoors after burying a corpse, and became so depressed, particularly after a quarrel with his wife Anna, that he prayed for death (2:1-3:6). At the same moment in Ecbatana (Hamadan, Media), Sara, daughter of Raguel, whose seven husbands had been killed on the wedding night by the demon Asmodeus, likewise prayed for death when she was accused of murdering her husbands (3:7-15). God sent Raphael to help Tobit and Sara (3:16-17).

Tobit gave his son Tobias some wise counsel and sent him with Azarias (a disguise of the angel Raphael) to collect ten talents of silver (more than $20,000) which he had deposited with Gabael at Rages in Media (4:1-5:22). Tobias, on the advice of Azarias, took along the gall, heart, and liver of a fish he had caught in the Tigris (6:1-8). Azarias predicted that Tobias would marry Sara (6:9-17). When Tobias burned the liver and heart of the fish in the bridal chamber, Asmodeus was so nauseated by the smoke that he fled to Upper Egypt, where he was bound by Azarias-Raphael (7:1-8:3). While the wedding was celebrated, Azarias brought from Rages Gabael, with the ten talents of silver (8:4-9:6).

In Nineveh, Tobit and Anna were anxiously awaiting their son's return; Tobias hastened to depart from Ecbatana (10:1-11:1). He hurried ahead of his wife, and with the gall of the fish restored Tobit's sight (11:2-13). A second wedding was celebrated (11:14-19). Azarias refused a large sum, offered some

sound counsel, and ascended to heaven (12:1-22). Tobit sang a
psalm of thanksgiving (13:1-18), and before dying he advised
Tobias to leave Nineveh, which was to be destroyed—as
actually happened after Tobias and Sara had moved to Ecbatana (14:1-15).

Though the book is pure fiction, it gives a valuable picture of
Jewish piety and family life in the lands of their dispersion
about 190 B.C. These Jewish exiles or emigrants revered the
Temple in Jerusalem (3:11-12; 13:9-11; 14:5) and brought their
tithes there on the festivals (1:6-8; 5:13). But in general their
religious life consisted in the practice of those ordinances in the
Law of Moses which were not connected with the Temple worship: the prescriptions about food (1:10-12) and the prohibition
of mixed marriages (1:9; 3:15; 4:12-13; 6:11; 7:12-13) separated the Jews, as God's people, from the Gentiles (4:12; 14:7);
personal piety was particularly stressed (4:5) and found expres-
sion in prayer (3:1-6, 11-15), trust in God (5:16; 6:17), praise of
God (8:15-17; 11:14-15; 12:6-7; 13:1-18), fasting and alms-
giving (12:8). Moral life, summarized in the negative Golden
Rule (4:15), was inculcated through the counsels of Tobit and
Azarias (4:3-21; 12:6-10).

And yet, this thoroughly orthodox Jewish teaching is presented by the author in a tale utilizing heathen folklore, both
in motifs (such as the magical healing power of a fish's gall, the
demon Asmodeus, etc.) and in plot: the author combines the
folk tale of "The Grateful Dead" (in which a dead person
rewards whoever buries decently his corpse) and that of "The
Dangerous Bride" (Poison Maiden, Bride of the Monster, etc.).
It seems probable that the author was familiar with a heathen
tale joining both plots—they are ably combined in the story
of Tobit—and utilized it to encourage the Jews in lands far
from Palestine to rely on their God and obey his Law.

Judith

Judith, in contrast with Tobit which dealt with personal
vicissitudes, is a short story relating national events. It was
written in Palestine about 150 B.C., before the patriotic enthusiasm, aroused by the victories of Judas Maccabeus (168–161
B.C.), had lost its religious fervor: after the fervent faith of
Daniel (164) and before the secular nationalism of Esther (125).
The Hebrew original is lost, but we have a good Greek translation. The first part of the book describes the war of Holofernes
against the Jews (chs. 1–7); the second relates the deliverance wrought by Judith (chs. 8–16). The name "Judith"
(*Jehudith* in Hebrew) means "Jewess".

Nebuchadnezzar (Nabuchodonosor) summoned his subjects to supply troops for his war against Arphaxad (cf. Gen. 10:22), king of Media, and swore vengeance against those (including the Jews) who refused. He feasted 120 days to celebrate his victory (1:1-16). Nebuchadnezzar sent Holofernes to attack the nations that had refused their help; this general conquered all nations except the Jews, and ordered that Nebuchadnezzar alone be worshiped as God (2:1–3:9).

The Jews prepared to block the advance of Holofernes against Jerusalem from the north (4:1-15). The Ammonite Achior related to Holofernes the history of the Jews and declared them to be invincible unless their God was angry against them (5:1-21). In his rage the general delivered Achior in fetters to the Jews besieged in Bethulia (Shechem?); so Achior reported to Ozias (5:22–6:21). After a siege of thirty-four days, which cut off food supplies, the inhabitants of Bethulia decided to surrender after five days (7:1-32).

Judith rebuked the elders for agreeing to surrender in five days unless God delivered the city, for they had thus tempted God; but she assured them of God's intervention (8:1-36) and begged God to save his Temple (9:1-14). Attractively dressed, Judith went to the Assyrian camp accompanied by a maid and was assured by Holofernes that she had nothing to fear (10:1–11:4). Judith convinced Holofernes that he would conquer the Jews because they had provoked their God by proposing to eat the offerings set aside for the Temple (11:11-16). She planned to pray in the valley every night, and eventually would guide the general to victory (11:17-23).

Judith partook only of the food she had brought from Bethulia, in obedience to the Law of Moses, and three times, at night, she went to bathe and pray in the valley (12:1-9). On the fourth evening she dined with Holofernes (eating only her own food) and when he lay on his couch in a drunken stupor she cut off his head, which her maid took along as they calmly returned to Bethulia (12:10–13:10).

The people of Bethulia praised God when they saw the head of Holofernes and in the morning attacked the Assyrians, who fled in panic to Damascus; the Jews plundered the enemy's tents (13:11–15:7). The high priest Joakim blessed Judith, to whom the people donated the contents of the tent of Holofernes (15:8-13). Judith sang a psalm of thanksgiving (16:1-17) and lived peacefully ever after (16:18-25).

The Book of Judith is valuable for its literary and religious qualities but is worthless as a source of information about historical events. The plot—a woman kills treacherously the enemy general—may have been suggested by Jael's assassination of Sisera (Judg. 5:24-27); but the fictional situations and characters are described in an original and vivid manner. In spite of exaggerations and prolixity, typical of much of the Jewish and Greek literature of the time, the style of the Hebrew original, which can be detected without great difficulty underneath the almost literal Greek translation, was fairly good. The book teaches that for the Jews patriotism and religion are one: the nation can prosper and survive only through God's protection. God will defend the Jews if they observe his Law (5:21); otherwise he will allow their enemies to prevail (5:18, 20; 11:10-15). Typical of the period following the persecution by Antiochus IV Epiphanes (168-165 B.C.) and the victories of Judas Maccabeus (168-161) is the intense hatred of the heathen and the beginning of the Pharisaic punctiliousness in observing the oral law or "tradition of the elders" (Mark 7:3, 5, etc.; cf. Gal. 1:14) which was eventually preserved in writing in the Mishna (about A.D. 200). Tobit (13:11; 14:6) expected the conversion of the heathen, but Judith (16:17) anticipated their eternal punishment. Judith observed the dietary laws, fasted, prayed, performed ablutions, avoided ritual pollution; she even thought that God was pleased with her deceit and assassination, while he was "provoked to anger" if the tithes and offerings set aside for the Temple were used to feed starving Jews! The psalm in 16:2-17 is the noblest passage in the book, both for literary style and for religious faith.

The Rest of the Chapters of the Book of Esther

The Book of Esther in Hebrew—as in the Protestant English Bibles, which are generally translated from the Hebrew—became canonical despite its purely secular character. Although it aroused misgivings in some ancient rabbis, its immense popularity with the masses, which enjoyed the boisterous celebration of the festival of Purim inaugurated by this book (dated about 125 B.C.), prevented its omission from the canon of Scriptures.

The disturbing lack of religion in Esther was remedied in the Aramaic and Greek translations. In the Greek version, Esther has 270 verses, while the Hebrew canonical book has only 163. Professor C. C. Torrey, in contrast with most scholars, who regard the Hebrew text as the original, is convinced that a longer Aramaic original (substantially preserved in Greek, except for some Greek supplements) was shortened by omitting all religious matter so that the book could be used in the secular and hilarious celebration of Purim.

According to Esth. 11:1 (in the Apocrypha), the Greek version was made by Lysimachus son of Ptolemy in 114 B.C. (or, according to J. Cohen and E. J. Bickerman, in 78 B.C.). The Aramaic text from which the book was translated into Greek contained all the additions except 11:1 and the two decrees of Artaxerxes (13:1-7; 16:1-24), which were written in Greek. In Greek the additions are in their proper place, but in his Latin Vulgate Jerome placed them all after 10:3, following this note: "The contents of the Hebrew text I have rendered most faithfully. The following passages, however, I found written in the 'Vulgate Edition' [the Greek Bible]; they are couched in Greek language and letters. . . ." But Jerome placed the two final sections of the Greek book (10:4-13 and 11:1) immediately after the Hebrew book, so that in the Authorized Version, as in the Latin, the two final sections precede the others, and the interpretation of Mordecai's dream (10:4-13) precedes the account of the dream itself (11:2–12:6). In the following summary the correct arrangement, as given in the Greek text, is adopted (with the indication of the verses following each section in Greek and English given in *italics*).

1. Mordecai's dream (11:2–12:6). In his dream he saw two dragons, nations preparing for war, the Jews in grave danger, until a spring became a river and the Jews prevailed. Mordecai discovered and reported a conspiracy against Artaxerxes. *Esther 1:1–3:13 follows.*

2. The decree of Artaxerxes against the Jews (13:1-7). The king informed his 127 governors that on the 14th of Adar the Jews in the Persian Empire should be exterminated. *Esther 3:14–4:17 follows.*

3. The prayers of Mordecai (13:8-18) and of Esther (14:1-19). *Esther 15:1-16 follows.*

4. Esther's appearance before Artaxerxes (15:1-16). When, in her finest attire, Esther entered the throne hall, she fainted as the king looked at her with anger. God filled the king with mildness and concern, but despite his kind words she fainted again. *Esther 5:3–8:12 follows.*

5. The edict of Artaxerxes in favor of the Jews (16:1-24). Haman has conspired against the king, the queen, and the Jews in order to further Alexander's conquest of the Persian Empire. Haman's decree is abrogated; the Jews should be helped to avenge themselves against their enemies on the 13th of Adar. *Esther 8:13–10:3 follows.*

6. The interpretation of Mordecai's dream (10:4-13; cf. 11:2–12:6). The Jewish triumph was determined by God, for it had been predicted by Mordecai's dream, in which the spring was

Esther, the dragons were Mordecai and Haman, the nations were the enemies of the Jews. *Esther* 11:1 *follows.*

7. Colophon (11:1). The Greek translation of the Book of Esther, made by Lysimachus son of Ptolemy, was brought to Egypt from Jerusalem "in the fourth year of the reign of Ptolemy and Cleopatra" (114 or 78 B.C.).

The Wisdom of Solomon

This important book was written in Greek at Alexandria in the period 100-50 B.C. Some scholars have attempted to prove that all of it or parts of it were translated from the Hebrew, but Jerome recognized rightly that its "very style gives forth the aroma of Greek eloquence". Earlier and later dates have been proposed, but two quotations from the Greek version of Isaiah (Wisd. 2:12; 15:10) make a date earlier than 150 most unlikely while on the other hand its use of Greek philosophy to expound the tenets of Judaism is manifestly considerably earlier than Philo (who died about A.D. 50).

In form the book resembles a diatribe, or "soapbox" street address of Stoic and Cynic philosophers. The preacher, allegedly Solomon, exhorts an audience of Jews and Gentiles. He endeavors to kindle in the wealthy, worldly, and at times apostate Jews the zeal for God and his Law (chs. 1-5); to encourage the pious Jews, who were frequently poor and afflicted (chs. 10-12; 16-19); to prove to the heathen the truth of Judaism (chs. 6-9) and the foolishness of idolatry (chs. 13-15).

1. The eternal lot of the Jews dependent on their attitude to wisdom (chs. 1-5). Wisdom is attained through righteousness (1:1-5). Sin deprived man of immortality (1:6-15). Wicked Jews oppress the pious Jews (1:16-2:20) without realizing that the latter's hope is "full of immortality"; death came into the world through the envy of the devil (2:21-24; cf. Gen. 3). After death (3:1-9) and in this life (3:10-4:19) the lot of the righteous is preferable to that of the wicked; the latter will admit it at the Last Judgment (4:20-5:16). Eventually God will put on his whole armor and destroy the wicked (5:17-23; cf. Eph. 6:11-17).

2. The excellence of Wisdom and its attainments (chs. 6-9). Heathen kings may find Wisdom, which they need (6:1-16); others through Wisdom will rule over kingdoms (6:17-21). Solomon will explain the secrets of Wisdom to the other kings (6:22-25). He attained it through prayer (7:1-12; cf. ch. 9 and I Kings 3:9-12). Through Wisdom, which has twenty-one qualities, man attains friendship with God and scientific knowledge (7:13-23). Wisdom is an emanation of God's glory

(7:24-26; cf. Heb. 1:3; 4:12-13), inspires the prophets, and rules over the world (7:27-8:1). Solomon loved Wisdom for her qualities and her gifts (8:2-21), including the four cardinal virtues (8:7), and he prayed for Wisdom (9:1-18).

3. Wisdom's work in behalf of Israel (10:1-12:27). The wise men from Adam to Moses (10:1-11:1) and Israel in general (11:2-14) are contrasted with the wicked and with the Egyptians at the time of the Exodus (continued in 16:1-19:22). Men are punished through the things by which they sin (11:15-16), so notably the Egyptians (11:17-12:2) and the Canaanites (12:3-11). Israel enjoys God's mercy (12:12-22), but the heathen were afflicted to the utmost (12:23-27).

4. The foolishness of idolatry (13:1-15:19). The heathen worship natural phenomena and heavenly bodies, instead of their Creator (13:1-9); idols (13:10-14:11); divinized mortals, such as a dead son (14:12-16) or a remote king (14:17-21), according to the teaching of Euhemerus (about 275 B.C.). Idolatry (14:22-31; cf. Rom. 1:19-32), in contrast with the knowledge of God (15:1-5), destroys morality. Idol makers are evildoers (15:6-13); particularly foolish are the Egyptians, who worship not only foreign idols (15:15-17) but even ugly beasts (15:18-19).

5. Contrast between Israelites and Egyptians (16:1-19:22, concluding 11:2-14). Small beasts vexed the Egyptians, while quails nourished the Israelites (16:1-4; cf. Ex. 9:22-26; 16:14-34). Darkness and specters terrified the Egyptians (17:1-21; cf. Ex. 10:21-23), but the Israelites had light in Egypt (18:1-2; cf. Ex. 10:23) and a pillar of fire in the desert (18:3-4; cf. Ex. 13:21-22). Instead of slaying the Israelite infants, the Egyptians lost their firstborn sons and perished in the Red Sea, while the Israelites celebrated the Passover and were freed from the plague (18:5-19:9; cf. Ex. 11:4-7; 12:21-30, 33; 14:5-9, 21-30; 15:1-21; 18:20-25). Thus God, through nature, afflicts the wicked and blesses the righteous (19:10-22).

The author acquired in Alexandria a superficial knowledge of Greek philosophy, notably of the teachings of Plato and the Stoics (7:22, 24, 26-27; 8:7, 19-20; 9:15; 11:17; 14:3; 16:21; 17:2; 19:18), but remained more orthodox in his Judaism than Ecclesiastes. His influence in Judaism was not lasting, for Judaism after Philo tended more and more to reject Hellenism and other foreign ideas. Conversely the influence of this book was far-reaching in Christianity, beginning possibly with Matt. 27:39-42; Rom. 1:20-32; Eph. 6:13-17; Heb. 1:3; and reaching its climax with Clement of Rome, Clement of Alexandria,

Origen, Cyprian, Eusebius of Caesarea, and Augustine.

The Greek style is unusually good, and some passages, such as 3:1-8 and 5:7-16, are superb. As R. Reitzenstein said, this book is "the most beautiful" of all Jewish writings of the period 150 B.C.-A.D. 100.

The Wisdom of Jesus the Son of Sirach, or Ecclesiasticus

Aside from the prophetic books and the Memoirs of Nehemiah (those of Ezra are questionable), this is the only book in the Old Testament and the Apocrypha the name of whose real author is known; in the Greek text the name given in 50:27 is "Jesus [Hebrew, *Joshua*; Aramaic, *Jeshua*], the son of Sirach, of Jerusalem".

Sirach (or *Ben Sira*) as he is called, had a school in Jerusalem (51:23, 29, in the Hebrew text) and was an early "scribe" or student of the Bible (cf. 38:24–39:11, where he extols his profession). His summary of "the Law and the Prophets" (the Hagiographa were canonized later, in A.D. 90) is found in his "Hymn of the Fathers" (44:1–49:16; cf. Heb. 11). His book was published in two volumes (chs. 1–23 and 24–50) about 180 B.C.; it presumably contains the gist of his classroom lectures, couched in poetic meter, and was written in Hebrew, although Aramaic was then the vernacular of the Jews in Palestine. In 132 B.C. his grandson brought the Hebrew text to Egypt and translated it into Greek; see his preface preceding ch. 1 in the Greek and English versions. The Authorized Version also gives at the beginning "A Prologue made by an uncertain Author", taken from the Greek "Synopsis of Holy Scripture" wrongly attributed to Athanasius (who died in 373); this "Prologue" is filled with misinformation.

The text of Ecclesiasticus is preserved in a Greek and in a Syriac translation, both made from the original Hebrew text. In years 1896-1900 about two-thirds of the Hebrew text was recovered in four manuscripts dating from the eleventh and twelfth centuries, excavated from the *genizah* (synagogue repository for worn-out manuscripts) at Fostat (Old Cairo, Egypt). Although this text is corrupt, it not only contains some new poems but often enables us to improve the readings of the Greek and Syriac texts; it probably goes back ultimately to Sirach's original, although some scholars regard it as a translation from the Greek.

The contents of Ecclesiasticus may be condensed as follows:

The First Volume (1–23)

Introduction (1): the origin and nature of Wisdom; how it is attained.

1. Patience in affliction. One should be patient in affliction (2), honor one's parents (3:1-16), be humble (3:17-31), and help the needy courteously (4:1-10).

2. Wisdom's reward. Wisdom will reward her pupils after testing them (4:11-19); she warns against false shame (4:20-28) and various other unpleasant traits (4:29—5:8), notably wrong talk (5:9—6:4). True and false friends (6:5-17).

3. Strive after Wisdom (6:18-37); avoid wickedness (7:1-17).

4. On social intercourse. Be kind with friends, family, and unhappy persons (7:18-34); avoid the company of trouble makers (8:1-4); be considerate (8:5-7); learn from wise and aged men (8:8-9); avoid the wicked (8:10-11); make no loans (8:12-13), or lawsuits against judges (8:14); do not associate with angry and foolish people (8:15-17), or with strangers (8:18-19); be cautious in dealing with women (9:1-9); be true to a friend (9:10); be not envious (9:11-12); keep away from the mighty (9:13), but seek the company of the wise (9:14-16).

5. The upper classes; advice to rulers (9:17-11:1). Hasty opinions about people should be avoided (11:2-9). Wealth comes from God (11:10-28). Use discrimination in inviting guests to the house (11:29-34), in helping the needy (12:1-7), and in choosing friends (12:8—13:1). The poor should not associate with the upper classes (13:2-23). Wealth should be obtained honestly and used to make life pleasant (13:24—14:19).

6. On God and religion. The pious, not the wicked, attains Wisdom (14:20—15:10). God is not to be blamed for human sin (15:11-20). Wickedness may bring ruin to a people (16:1-10). God rewards and punishes men (16:11-23); he created the world (16:24-30) and man (17:1-24). Men should seek salvation from God (17:25—18:14, a psalm).

7. On various virtues: kindness (18:15-18), prudence (18:19-29), self-control (18:30—19:17), piety with wisdom (19:18-30), gentleness in correcting (20:1-17), restraint in speech (20:18-26).

8. Wisdom and foolishness, piety and sin. Bribes should not influence the wise (20:27-31). "Flee from sin" (21:1-10). A contrast between the wise and the fool (21:11—22:18). Behaviour with a true friend (22:19-26). The sins of speech (22:27—23:15) and of sex (23:16-28).

The Second Volume (24–50)

Introduction. Personified Wisdom (24:1-2) declares that her origin is divine (24:3), that she rules creation and all nations (24:4-6), and is flourishing in Jerusalem (24:7-22), being the Law of Moses (24:23-29). Sirach, a rivulet out of this great stream, has prepared his second volume (24:30-34).

1. Marriage; contrast between good and bad wives (25:1–26:27).

2. Commerce and speech. Merchants should be honest (26:28–27:10). Sins of speech should be avoided (27:11–28:26). One should lend to a neighbor and guarantee the payment of his debts (29:1-20). Foreign travel is unpleasant (29:21-28).

3. Family and society. Children should be brought up strictly (30:1-13). Good health is better than wealth (30:14–31:11). Good table manners (31:12-24) and moderation in drinking (31:25-30) are commended; at banquets one should be careful about one's speech (31:31–32:13).

4. Teachers. The pious man gains true understanding (32:14-18) and is divinely protected from trouble (33:1-3). Contrast between a good and bad teacher (33:4-6). Just as holidays are distinguished from other days, so God exalted the Israelites above the Canaanites (33:7-15). Sirach, the last of the teachers, has collected wisdom (33:16-18).

5. The head of the family should keep his property (33:19-23) and discipline servants (33:24-31).

6. True knowledge and piety. True knowledge does not come from dreams or divination (34:1-8) but through practical experiences (34:9-17). True piety does not consist in rituals (34:18-26) but in right living (35:1-3); but one must bring one's offering to the altar (35:4-11), although it will not bribe God (35:12-20). A psalm imploring the deliverance of Israel (36:1-17).

7. Friends indeed: a good wife (36:18-26), a true friend (37:1-6), a wise counselor (37:7-18), a wise public servant (37:19-26), a physician (37:27–38:15). Mourning should be limited to a day or two (38:16-23).

8. The calling of the scholar (the scribe) is the highest. It cannot be attained, for lack of leisure (38:24), by the farmer (38:25-26), the engraver (38:27), the smith (38:28), the potter (38:29-30). These perform useful work but are not educated for positions in the government, in the synagogue, and in schools (38:31-34). The scribe is a biblical scholar (39:1-3) who can advise rulers and teach (39:4-11).

9. A psalm in praise of the Creator (39:12-15, 16-35).

10. Suffering and death. Suffering is common to all men (40:1-10). The earthly perishes, the heavenly is eternal (40:11-17). The fear of the Lord is the best thing (40:18-27). A beggar's life is worse than death (40:28-30), which is bitter to the happy man but welcome to the desperate wretch (41:1-2). In any case death should be faced fearlessly (41:3-4). The ungodly's death marks his utter end, but the good name of the pious is imperish-

able (41:5-13). Wisdom should not be hidden (41:14-15; the same as 20:30-31).

11. Right and wrong shame. One should be ashamed of twenty situations (41:16-24) but not of what is right (42:1-8). Daughters may cause great anxiety to their fathers (42:9-14).

12. Hymns of praise. God should be praised for his visible works in nature, and even more for his invisible works (42:15–43:33). "Praise of the fathers of old" (title in the Hebrew text) from Adam, Enoch, and Noah to Zerubbabel, Joshua, and Nehemiah (chs. 44–49). Praise of the high priest Simon II (50).

13. Three detestable peoples: the Edomites or Idumeans, the Philistines, and the Samaritans (50:25-26).

14. Colophon. The author (Jesus the son of Sirach) commends his book to the reader (50:27-29).

15. Appendix. A psalm of thanksgiving (51:1-12). An alphabetic acrostic poem summarizing the author's life (51:13-30).

Ecclesiasticus is the longest, earliest (with the exception of I Esdras and perhaps of Tobit), and most important book in the Apocrypha. There is no better source of information on the religion and morality of the educated middle class in Jerusalem about 180 B.C. Sirach was familiar with "the Law and the Prophets" as well as with Psalms, Proverbs, and Job; his book contains many echoes of biblical passages. In a general way Ecclesiasticus resembles Proverbs but is nevertheless highly original and personal. The following literary types are used by the author: the single-verse proverb (3:25, 30; 4:30, 31; etc.), questions which resemble riddles (17:31; 22:14), numerical proverbs (23:16-17; 25:7-11; 25:5-6, 28; 50:25-26), psalms (23:4-6; 36:1-17; 39:16-20, 32-35; 42:15-25; 43:1-33; 51:1-12), a eulogy of "the fathers of old" and of the high priest Simon (chs. 44–49; 50) and other poems (16:24–18:14). The proverbs vary considerably in contents: they include exhortations (4:7-8), prohibitions (4:1-4), both of them together (4:25), common-sense truths (6:5, 14-16), contrasts (10:30), beatitudes (14:1-2, 20-27; 25:8-9; 28:19), woes (2:12-14; 41:8), and numerous similes, which are probably the most original and most brilliant literary productions of the author (3:15, 30; 9:10b; 13:1; 14:18; 18:10; 21:2-3, 8, 14, 18, 19, 21; 22:20; 25:20; 28:17).

Sirach apparently regarded the Temple services (50:4-24) and other national aspects of Judaism as valuable primarily in preserving the Jews as a separate nation, free from the contamination of Hellenism, which he manifestly abhorred. But he stressed primarily personal piety, obedience to the Law of Moses including some early precepts of the oral law: in 42:4a

(Hebrew text) he demands that a merchant dust his scales and wipe off the weights, anticipating this precept in the Mishna: "A shopkeeper must wipe his measures twice a week, and wipe off his weights once a week, and wipe his scales every time he uses them". He emphasized the moral law, which he summed up as follows: "And he [God] said unto them, 'Beware of all unrighteousness'; and he gave them a commandment, to each one concerning his neighbor [see Lev. 19:18; cf. Matt. 7:12]" (17:14). Much of his counsel deals with practical affairs, ordinary daily life in the family, in business, among friends (see, on friends, Joseph Addison, *The Spectator*, Vol. I, No. 68, May 18, 1711), at banquets, and the like. Sirach's advice is a mixture of common sense and moral ideals and was particularly adapted to the well-to-do pupils who attended his school; much of his advice is, however, still valuable in our time.

Baruch

This is the earliest of the books attributed to Baruch the son of Neriah, who was Jeremiah's secretary. Aside from his own contributions, contained in the Book of Jeremiah, he has, however, left no writings that still survive. This book was originally written in Hebrew but is extant in a Greek version. The book, though small, is not a unit: each one of its two parts has two subdivisions, and scholars have suggested that one, two, three, or four authors composed Baruch; the attribution to three authors seems the most probable. In Latin and English, the Epistle of Jeremy is wrongly included as ch. 6.

Part I. The Jews confess their sins after the destruction of Jerusalem in 586 B.C. (1:1–3:8)

1. Baruch read his book to the Babylonian exiles, who sent some money (1:1-7) and the silver Temple vessels (1:8-9) to the high priest Joakim. The priests were asked to pray for Nebuchadnezzar, his son Belshazzar (cf. Dan. 5:2, 13, 18, 22; Belshazzar was really the son of Nabonidus), and the exiles (1:10-13); they should read this book on holidays (1:14).
2. The Jews in Jerusalem confessed their sins (1:15-2:10), and the exiles begged God to have mercy on Israel (2:11-3:8).

Part II. Praise of Wisdom (3:9–4:4); *the future salvation of Israel* (4:5–5:9)

1. Israel was exiled because it forsook Wisdom (3:9-12), with whom is life (3:13-14). Neither the heathen rulers nor the sages

of Edom found Wisdom (3:15-23). The universe is immense (3:24-25). The giants perished for lack of Wisdom (3:26-28), which no one discovered (3:29-31) except God (3:32-36; cf. Job 28:12-27); he gave it to Israel as the Law of Moses (3:37-4:4).

2. Jerusalem saw the captivity of her sons and daughters (4:5-20), but they will be led back by God (4:21-29). Jerusalem should rejoice because Babylon will be destroyed (4:30-35) and the Jewish exiles will be brought back by God (4:36-5:9).

There are no valid reasons for attributing the first part of the book (1:1-3:8) to more than one author. Most of it (thirty-three out of fifty-one verses) contains reminiscences of biblical expressions, twenty-two from Jeremiah, five from Deuteronomy; there are numerous parallels between 1:15-3:8 and the prayer in Dan. 9:4-19. The first part of the book seems to have been written by a single author in the period 150-100 B.C.

While the first part of the book is in prose, the second part consists of two poems. The praise of Wisdom (3:9-4:4) alludes to the sages of Edom (3:22-23) like Jer. 49:7 and Obad. 8. Metaphysical Wisdom known only to God (Job 28), moral wisdom which secures wealth and happiness (Prov. 8), and Israel's own wisdom which is identified with the Law of Moses (as in Ecclus. 24) are somewhat combined here, without attaining the literary quality and the originality of thought of the poem's sources. The author is later than Sirach and probably wrote in the period 150-100 B.C.

The final poem (4:5-5:9), inspired by Is. 40-55, is a comforting conclusion to the pessimistic laments in 1:1-3:8; it was written by a later author about 100 B.C.

THE EPISTLE OF JEREMY

This sarcastic attack against Babylonian idolatry is neither a letter nor was it sent by Jeremiah to the Babylonian exiles, as verse 1 asserts. In the Greek Bible it is a separate book, but in the Vulgate, the Authorized Version, and Luther's Bible it is ch. 6 of Baruch. The author seems to have regarded Jeremiah's letter in Jer. 29:1-23 as commonplace, and proceeded to supply the kind of letter that Jeremiah should have written—that is, in this author's opinion. He was familiar with the sarcastic identification of foreign gods with idols devoid of life in Is. 40:18-20; 41:6-7; 44:9-20 (imitated in Jer. 10:1-16).

While it is certain that Jeremiah was not the author, as Jerome realized long ago, it is difficult to fix the date of this pamphlet in the absence of definite clues. It seems fairly certain that it was written during the period 300-100 B.C., probably about 150 B.C. The book was apparently written in Aramaic, but we have only a translation in good Hellenistic Greek.

Following an introduction, warning the Jewish exiles to beware of worshiping idols (1-7), the author variously describes the helplessness, lifelessness, uselessness, and destructibility of heathen divine images (8-73).

The Song of the Three Holy Children

The Greek Bible (followed by the Latin Vulgate) contains the following additions to the Book of Daniel: the Song of the Three Children including the Prayer of Azarias (following Dan. 3:23), the History of Susanna (placed at the beginning of Daniel in the Greek, and after ch. 12 [as ch. 13] in the Vulgate), and Bel and the Dragon (at the end; ch. 14 in the Vulgate). The English versions, beginning with the Authorized Version, translate the "Theodotion" text printed in the Greek Bibles. The original "Septuagint" Greek version, which is older and preferable, survives in a single manuscript; an English version is published in R. H. Charles, *Apocrypha and Pseudepigrapha*, Vol. I; the Greek text is included in A. Rahlfs, *Septuaginta*.

The Song of the Three Holy Children contains the following pieces: (1) the Prayer of Azarias (1-22), praising God, confessing Israel's sins, and imploring Israel's deliverance; (2) Details about the heating of the fiery furnace (23-28); (3) the Song of the Three Children (29-68): "Blessed art thou, O Lord" (29-34), "O all ye works of the Lord, bless ye the Lord" (35-68).

The second poem (29-34) is a liturgy in praise of God; the second half of all verses ("and to be praised and glorified above all forever") looks like a response of the congregation. The third poem (35-65, with a supplement in 66-68 in which v. 67 is identical in Greek with Ps. 136:1) is likewise an antiphonal liturgy similar to Psalms 136 and 148; it is the *Benedicite* (Bless ye!) of the Prayer Book, and was used in the liturgy from early times in Eastern and Western Christian Churches.

The narrative portions (1-2, 23-28 [in some editions 22-27]) were probably written in Aramaic; but the poems, like Jewish prayers in general, were composed in Hebrew—the sacred language—presumably in the period 200-100 B.C. These psalms were not written specifically for the Book of Daniel but were inserted into it from an anthology between 150 and 100 B.C.

The History of Susanna

This famous tale, added to the Book of Daniel and extant in Greek, is one of the earliest detective stories known, as is the following story of Bel. It has often inspired painters and writers, including Shakespeare in *The Merchant of Venice* ("a Daniel come to judgment").

The virtuous and attractive Susanna, whose name in Hebrew means "lily", lived in Babylonia with her prosperous husband Joakim (1-4). Two aged judges fell in love with Susanna (5-14) and, surprising her as she prepared to bathe in her garden pool, threatened to accuse her of adultery if she did not lie with them; but she refused (15-23). When the servants came running from the house at her cries, the elders accused her of adultery with a young man, and repeated the accusation the following day in Joakim's house (24-40). She was condemned to death, but Daniel accused the elders of false testimony and proved it when they disagreed about the tree under which the adultery had allegedly been committed (41-59). The elders were executed in accordance with Deut. 19:18-19; God and Daniel were praised for Susanna's deliverance (60-64).

Like Tobit, this story combines two plots derived from Oriental folklore: the "Genoveva" motif of a wife falsely accused by an unsuccessful suitor (the counterpart of the story of Potiphar's wife, Gen. 39:7-20) and the story of a young judge or friend saving from death a person falsely accused. Daniel was an ancient legendary character: he was wise (Ezra 14:14, 20; 28:3) and the protector of widows and orphans (in the Ugaritic poem *Danel*). The story was written in Aramaic, in spite of the fact that Daniel's puns on the Greek names of trees (54-55, 58-59) were adduced by Africanus, in a letter to Origen (A.D. 238), as proof that Susanna was written in Greek. Such puns are conceivable in a Semitic language, as also in English: mastic tree—you will be masticated.

The story of Susanna (written about 150 B.C.) illustrates, like Tobit and Judith, God's intervention in behalf of his faithful who pray unto him in their affliction (42-44).

The History of the Destruction of Bel and the Dragon

1. *The Story of Bel*, like the Epistle of Jeremy, ridicules Babylonian idolatry; like the other additions to Daniel it is pure fiction. Jerome called it a "fable".

The Babylonians presented to the image of their god Bel (Marduk) great quantities of food daily, but Daniel assured Cyrus that the idol could eat nothing (1-7). The king decreed that unless the seventy priests of Bel proved that their god ate the food they would be executed; if Daniel were proved wrong he would be killed (8-10). The doors of the temple were sealed after the food was placed on the table; but Daniel had scattered ashes on the floor, before the priests and their families entered the temple through a secret trap door to partake of the food (11-15). In the morning, when the king saw the footprints in the ashes and was shown the concealed entrance, he slew the priests and destroyed the temple (16-22).

2. *The Story of the Dragon* is likewise imaginary. When Cyrus asked Daniel to worship the dragon, who really ate, Daniel asked permission to slay it "without sword and staff" (23-26). Daniel fed the beast lumps of pitch, fat, and hair; so the dragon burst asunder (27). Threatened by the Babylonians, the king allowed Daniel to be cast into the den of lions (28-32). Habakkuk, however, was brought by an angel to Daniel from Judea and gave him the food he was to deliver to the reapers (33-39). After seven days the king found Daniel alive and fed his enemies to the hungry lions (40-42).

Both stories were written in Aramaic in the period 150–100 B.C. They are religiously insignificant but are valuable as rare specimens of popular Jewish fiction, which differs considerably from literary fiction, such as Tobit and Judith.

The Prayer of Manasses

This prayer for forgiveness, or penitential psalm, without reaching the spiritual level of Ps. 51 expresses repentance in time of trouble. It was composed in Hebrew shortly before the beginning of our era. According to II Chron. 33:11-13 King Manasseh repented from his sins when he was taken to Babylonia in fetters: this prayer was composed for that occasion. It survives in Greek among the *Odes* or *Cantica* appended to the Psalms in some manuscripts of the Greek Bible and is printed after the New Testament in the Vulgate. It is also included in the Christian *Didascalia* (third century), inserted into the *Apostolic Constitutions*. It may be summarized as follows:

Repentance was decreed by the Creator for sinners like Manasseh, not for the righteous. Aware of his sins, bound in chains, he implores forgiveness. If God in his mercy saves him, despite his unworthiness, he will always praise God.

The First Book of the Maccabees

Four books extant in Greek are entitled "Maccabees", from the surname of Judas "called Maccabeus" (I Macc. 2:4; 3:1). The meaning of this word (usually derived from the Hebrew *maqqabeth*, "small hammer", and interpreted "the Hammerer") is unknown. It is not found in Hebrew writings before the Middle Ages, the term "Hasmoneans" being used in its place.

I Maccabees is the most valuable of these four books, being

the most reliable account extant of the history of the Jews from 175 to 135 B.C. In brief, its contents are as follows:

1. Introduction. The conquests of Alexander and the division of his empire at his death in 323 B.C. (1:1-9).

2. The measures taken by Antiochus IV Epiphanes (175-164 B.C.) against the Jews (1:10-64). Hellenism in Jerusalem (1:10-15). Antiochus plundered the Temple in 171 B.C. (1:16-24). A lamentation in verse (1:25-28). In 168 Jerusalem was plundered again (1:29-32) and a garrison was stationed in Zion (1:33-36). Another lamentation in verse (1:37-40). The practices of Judaism were forbidden (1:41-53) and on December 25 of 168 the "abomination of desolation" (an altar dedicated to the Olympian Zeus) was erected over the Temple altar (1:54-64).

3. The outbreak of the Maccabean rebellion (2:1-70). The priest Mattathias was the father of John, Simon, Judas, Eleazar, and Jonathan; he lamented the profanation of the Temple (2:1-14, of which 8-13 are in verse) and by slaying a royal officer and an apostate Jew he started the rebellion (2:15-28). Many pious (Hasidim) were slain on the sabbath without defending themselves (2:29-38), but Mattathias induced even the pious to repel attacks on the sabbath (2:39-41). The Maccabees collected an army and forcibly prevented the apostasy of the Jews (2:42-48). On his deathbed Mattathias appointed Judas as his successor (2:49-70).

4. Poem in praise of Judas Maccabeus (3:1-9).

5. War for religious liberty (3:10-4:61). Judas defeated Apollonius (3:10-12) and Seron (3:13-26). Antiochus left Lysias in command during his campaign in Persia (3:27-37). Judas defeated Gorgias (3:38-4:25) and Lysias (4:26-35). On December 25 of 165 he rededicated the Temple—an event commemorated annually in the feast of Hanukkah or Dedication (see John 10:22); then he fortified Bethsura (4:36-61).

6. Wars against the heathen (5:1-68). Judas defeated the Idumeans (5:1-3), the "Children of Bean" (5:4-5), and the Ammonites (5:6-8). In answer to appeals for help (5:9-15) Judas sent Simon to Galilee while he campaigned east of the Jordan (5:16-17). Joseph and Azarias were left in command of Judea (5:18-19). Simon (5:20-23) and Judas were successful. Judas slew Timotheus at Carnaim (5:24-44), destroyed Ephron (5:45-51), and returned to Jerusalem (5:52-54). Joseph and Azarias, however, were defeated at Jamnia (5:55-64) because they "came not of the seed of those, by whose hand deliverance was given unto Israel" (5:62). Judas was successful at Hebron (5:65), suffered some losses at Marisa (erroneously "Samaria"

in the Authorized Version; 5:66-67), and burned the idols of Ashdod (5:68).

7. Death of Antiochus Epiphanes in 164; campaign of Lysias against the Jews (6:1-63). When Antiochus died, Lysias made Antiochus V Eupator king (6:1-17). Judas besieged the Syrian garrison in Jerusalem (6:18-27), but Lysias attacked him from the south (6:28-31), defeated him at Bathzacharias (6:32-47), captured Bethsura (6:48-50), and forced the surrender of Zion (6:51-54). Lysias and Judas signed a peace treaty (6:55-61). Philip (cf. 6:16) was defeated by Lysias (6:62-63).

8. The wars against Demetrius I Soter (161-150) and the death of Judas in 161 (7:1-9:22). After slaying Lysias and Antiochus V (7:1-7), Demetrius I sent Bacchides against Judas (7:8-20), but Judas defeated Nicanor at Adasa (7:21-50). Judas made a treaty of friendship with Rome (8:1-32); he fell fighting against Bacchides at Eleasa (9:1-22).

9. Jonathan and Bacchides (9:23-73). Jonathan succeeded Judas (9:23-31). He was forced across the Jordan (9:32-34) where the Nabateans and the Arabs proved unfriendly (9:35-42), and Bacchides defeated him (9:43-49). After the death of Alcimus (9:50-56) he signed a peace treaty with Bacchides in 158 (9:57-73).

10. Jonathan and Alexander Balas (10:1-11:19). In 153 a pretender, Balas who called himself Alexander, arose against Demetrius I (10:1-14) and made Jonathan high priest (10:15-21). Despite the promises of Demetrius (10:22-45), Jonathan supported Balas (10:46-47). Demetrius died fighting in 150 (10:48-50). Jonathan was honored by Balas when he attended the wedding of Balas with Cleopatra (10:51-66). Jonathan defeated Apollonius, a general of Demetrius II Nicator, at Ashdod in 147 (10:67-89). Balas was doomed when his father-in-law Ptolemy VI supported Demetrius II (11:1-19).

11. Jonathan and Demetrius II (11:20–12:53). In 145 Demetrius increased the power of Jonathan (11:20-37). The Jews helped him fight Tryphon, who had crowned Antiochus VI, son of Balas, as king (11:38-51). When, however, Demetrius failed to keep his promises (11:52-53), Jonathan allied himself with Tryphon and took the field against Demetrius (11:54-74). He signed pacts with the Romans and the Spartans (12:1-23) and continued to fight with success (12:24-38). But in 143 Jonathan was treacherously taken prisoner by Tryphon (12:39-53).

12. Simon and Demetrius II (13:1–14:3). Simon sent tribute and hostages to Tryphon for the deliverance of Jonathan, but the latter was killed (13:1-30). Tryphon made himself king

(13:31-32). In 142 Demetrius II granted independence to the Jews (13:33-42), and Simon occupied Gezer (13:43-48) and the Syrian citadel in Jerusalem (13:49-53). Thus "the yoke of the heathen was taken away from Israel" (13:41).

13. Simon's rule (14:1-49). Demetrius II was captured by the Parthians (14:1-3). In prose (14:4-5) and verse (14:6-15) Simon's deeds were extolled. The treaties with Rome and Sparta were renewed (14:16-24). His nation appointed him and his descendants as rulers in perpetuity (14:25-49).

14. Simon and Antiochus VII Sidetes (15:1-16:24). Antiochus VII, brother of Demetrius II, confirmed Simon's autonomy (15:1-9) and besieged Tryphon in Dor (15:10-14) in 138. The Romans reasserted their friendship for the Jews (15:15-24). Simon rejected an ultimatum of Antiochus VII; his sons defeated Cendebeus sent to enforce it (15:25-16:10). In 135 Simon and two of his sons were killed by his son-in-law Ptolemy (16:11-18). His son, John Hyrcanus (135-104), whose deeds were recorded in a (lost) book, became high priest and ruler (16:19-24).

The First Book of Maccabees was manifestly written in Hebrew, as Jerome recognized, for the extant Greek version often reproduces literally Hebrew idioms. The date must be later than the death of Simon in 135 B.C. (16:14), for modern research has conclusively refuted the theory that I Macc. 14:16-16:24 is spurious (Josephus used only the earlier part of the book). If the reference to the chronicles of John Hyrcanus in 16:23-24 is genuine, the author must have written after the death of Hyrcanus in 104. It seems likely that the book was written about 100 B.C. The author drew inspiration from the great historical books of the Old Testament (Judges, Samuel, Kings), although, like Chronicles-Ezra-Nehemiah, to a really accurate historical narrative he added speeches, poems, and official documents. He himself may have composed these, with the exception of some diplomatic documents (opinions differ about the authenticity of these state papers), but he was nevertheless a notable historian, whom neither faith nor patriotism induced to tamper with the truth.

The Second Book of the Maccabees

This book begins with *two letters* written by the Palestinian Jews to the Jews in Egypt. The first (1:1-10a), dated in 123 B.C., reports that after the persecutions of Antiochus IV Epiphanes (168-165) the Temple in Jerusalem had been rededicated (165) and the annual festival (*Hanukka*, Rededication;

cf. Ps. 30, superscription; John 10:22) should be celebrated on the 25th of Chisleu (December) in commemoration of that event. The second letter (1:10b–2:18) was written just before the rededication of the Temple. It reports the death of Antiochus Epiphanes; the discovery of naphtha when Nehemiah searched for the sacred fire before he rededicated the Temple; Jeremiah's hiding of the Tabernacle, and of the sacred fire which had fallen from heaven in Solomon's time; Nehemiah's founding of a library of biblical books. It also, like the first, exhorts the Egyptian Jews to celebrate the Feast of Rededication.

In his *preface* (2:19-32) the author states that he has summarized for the general reader the five volumes of Simon of Cyrene on the Maccabean wars.

The events which precipitated the Maccabean rebellion (176-168) are reported in chs. 3–7: angelic beings prevented Heliodorus from plundering the Temple (3:1–4:6); Jason supplanted Onias as high priest and proceeded to hellenize the Jews in Jerusalem (4:7-22); Menelaus was appointed high priest (4:23-50); Antiochus Epiphanes profaned the Temple (5) and forbade the practice of Judaism (6:1-17), torturing Eleazar, as well as seven brothers and their mother (6:18–7:42).

The Maccabean rebellion (168-165 B.C.) is the subject of 8:1–10:9. Judas Maccabeus defeated Nicanor (8:1-29) and Timotheus (8:30-36). Antiochus Epiphanes died (9) and the Temple was rededicated (10:1-9). The subsequent campaigns of Judas (165-161) are described in 10:10–15:36. Judas defeated Lysias, the prime minister of Antiochus V Eupator, and forced him to make peace (10:10–11:38). Judas punished his enemies at Joppa and Jamnia (12:1-9), defeated some Arabs (12:10-12), and campaigned successfully in Transjordania (12:13-31). He routed Gorgias (12:32-37), but to his horror discovered that some of his dead soldiers were wearing heathen amulets (12:38-45). After a second victory over Lysias (13), Judas defeated and slew in battle Nicanor (14:1–15:36). Taking leave of the reader, the author in 15:37-39 explains that he has striven to combine true history with romantic style.

The differences between I and II Maccabees are more conspicuous than their similarities. The two works were written independently. While I Maccabees describes the history of forty years (175-135 B.C.), II Maccabees begins earlier but confines itself to fifteen years (176-161); the two books have in common only the period from the accession of Antiochus Epiphanes (175) to the death of Nicanor (161), described in

the Apocrypha

I Macc. I:10–7:50 and II Macc. 4:7–15:36. Although II Maccabees abounds in legends, tales, and moralizing reflections, it
occasionally adds some historical details to the reliable information in I Maccabees; see, for instance, II Macc. 4; 6:2;
13:3-8; 14:1. II Maccabees deliberately and erroneously places
the death of Antiochus Epiphanes (of which three irreconcil-
able accounts are given in I Macc. 6:1-16; II Macc. I:12-16;
ch. 9) before the rededication of the Temple, and takes other
liberties with the order of the events. The basic difference
between the two books is that I Maccabees was written to
glorify Israel and its heroic Maccabean leaders, while II Maccabees is chiefly concerned with God's protection of his Temple in
Jerusalem and with the immeasurable superiority of Judaism
over heathenism. Consequently religion, both as ritual practice
and as theology, is much more prominent in II Maccabees,
where divine interventions in behalf of the Temple and of Israel,
divine punishment of the enemies of the Jews, miracles, and
sacred legends—all absent in I Maccabees—are abundantly conspicuous. Beginning with the third century, the book furnished
proof texts for Christian, and particularly for Roman Catholic
doctrines—for instance: the creation of the world out of nothing (7:28); the intercession of the saints (15:14); the eternal
death of the wicked (7:9; 14); the resurrection of the flesh
(7:11; 14:46); the deliverance of souls from Purgatory through
the intercession of the living (12:43-45); the doctrine of angels
(3:24-28; 10:29-30; 11:8). This is why Protestants, beginning
with Luther, were so hostile to this book. But whatever may be
our opinion about the religious ideas in II Maccabees, and
about its rhetorical style and dramatized history, we should be
grateful to the Epitomist who has preserved for us a summary
of the work which Jason of Cyrene wrote in Greek a few years
after 100 B.C.

The Apocrypha

According to the Authorized Version

Her Majesty's Printers

LONDON: EYRE AND SPOTTISWOODE LIMITED
NEW YORK: HARPER & BROTHERS PUBLISHERS

TABLE OF SIGNS USED IN THIS BOOK

THE words of which the pronunciation is marked are divided into syllables by short hyphens (-). The syllable on which most stress is to be laid in reading is marked ('). In compound names two accents are often introduced. The longer hyphen (–) indicates the division into parts of compound names so far as it is noted in the Authorized Version.

ä	*as in*	ah, arm, father.
ă	"	abet, hat, dilemma.
ā	"	tame.
â	"	fare.
ȧ	"	chaotic.
ĕ	"	met, her, second.
ē	"	mete.
ê	"	maker.
ĕ	"	event.
ë	=	a *of* tame.
ī	*as in*	fine.
ĭ	"	him, fir, plentiful.
î	"	machine.
i̧	"	peculiar.
î	"	idea.
ō	"	alone.
ŏ	"	on, protect.
ô	"	nor.
ǫ	"	son.
ð	"	obey.
ọ	"	seldom.
ū	"	tune.
û	"	rude.

ŭ	*as in*	us.
ū	"	unite.
ù	"	turner.
ȳ	"	lyre.
y̆	"	typical, fully.
ẏ	"	cyclorama.
āā	=	a *of* am.
āē	*as in*	mediæval.
âı	"	aisle.
ai	"	hail.
ay	"	delay.
āō	=	o *of* alone.
âū	*as in*	maul.
ēē	"	seem.
êı	=	i *of* fine.
êū	*as in*	neuter.
īē	"	belief.
ðı	"	oil.
ç	"	celestial.
ch	"	character.
ġ	"	giant.
ġ	"	Iraq.
ś	"	his.

I ESDRAS

CHAPTER I

AND Josias held the feast of the passover in Jerusalem unto his Lord, and offered the passover the fourteenth day of the first month;

2 Having set the priests according to their daily courses, being arrayed in long garments, in the temple of the Lord.

3 And he spake unto the Levites, the holy ministers of Israel, that they should hallow themselves unto the Lord, to set the holy ark of the Lord in the house that king Solomon the son of David had built:

4 *And said*, Ye shall no more bear the ark upon your shoulders: now therefore serve the Lord your God, and minister unto his people Israel, and prepare you after your families and kindreds,

5 According as David the king of Israel prescribed, and according to the magnificence of Solomon his son: and standing in the temple according to the several dignity of the families of you the Levites, who minister in the presence of your brethren the children of Israel,

6 Offer the passover in order, and make ready the sacrifices for your brethren, and keep the passover according to the commandment of the Lord, which was given unto Moses.

7 And unto the people that was found there Josias gave thirty thousand lambs and kids, and three thousand calves: these things were given of the king's allowance, according as he promised, to the people, to the priests, and to the Levites.

8 And Hĕl-kī′-ăs, Zăch-ă-rī′-ăs, and Sÿ-ē′-lŭs, the governors of the temple, gave to the priests for the passover two thousand and six hundred sheep, and three hundred calves.

9 And Jĕc-ŏ-nī′-ăs, and Să-maī′-ăs, and Nă-thăn′-ă-ĕl his brother, and Ăs-să-bī′-ăs, and Ō′-chĭ-ĕl, and Jō′-răm, captains over thousands, gave to the Levites for the passover five thousand sheep, and seven hundred calves.

10 And when these things were done, the priests and Levites, having the unleavened bread, stood in very comely order according to the kindreds,

11 And according to the several dignities of the fathers, before the people, to offer to the Lord, as it is written in the book of Moses: and thus did they in the morning.

12 And they roasted the passover with fire, as appertaineth: as for the sacrifices, they sod them in brass pots and pans with a good savour,

13 And set them before all the people: and afterward

3

they prepared for themselves, and for the priests their brethren, the sons of Aaron.

14 For the priests offered the fat until night: and the Levites prepared for themselves, and the priests their brethren, the sons of Aaron.

15 The holy singers also, the sons of Ā'-săph, were in their order, according to the appointment of David, to wit, Asaph, Zăch-ă-rī'-ăs, and Jĕd-ū'-thŭn, who was of the king's retinue.

16 Moreover the porters were at every gate; it was not lawful for any to go from his ordinary service: for their brethren the Levites prepared for them.

17 Thus were the things that belonged to the sacrifices of the Lord accomplished in that day, that they might hold the passover,

18 And offer sacrifices upon the altar of the Lord, according to the commandment of king Josias.

19 So the children of Israel which were present held the passover at that time, and the feast of sweet bread seven days.

20 And such a passover was not kept in Israel since the time of the prophet Samuel.

21 Yea, all the kings of Israel held not such a passover as Josias, and the priests, and the Levites, and the Jews, held with all Israel that were found dwelling at Jerusalem.

22 In the eighteenth year of the reign of Josias was this passover kept.

23 And the works of Josias were upright before his Lord with an heart full of godliness.

24 As for the things that came to pass in his time, they were written in former times, concerning those that sinned, and did wickedly against the Lord above all people and kingdoms, and how they grieved him exceedingly, so that the words of the Lord rose up against Israel.

25 Now after all these acts of Josias it came to pass, that Phă'-raōh the king of Egypt came to raise war at Cär'-chă-mĭs upon Eu-phră'-tēs: and Josias went out against him.

26 But the king of Egypt sent to him, saying, What have I to do with thee, O king of Judea?

27 I am not sent out from the Lord God against thee; for my war is upon Eu-phră'-tēs: and now the Lord is with me, yea, the Lord is with me hasting me forward: depart from me, and be not against the Lord.

28 Howbeit Josias did not turn back his chariot from him, but undertook to fight with him, not regarding the words of the prophet Jeremy spoken by the mouth of the Lord:

29 But joined battle with him in the plain of Mă-gĭd'-dō, and the princes came against king Josias.

30 Then said the king unto his servants, Carry me away out of the battle; for I am very weak. And immediately his servants took him away out of the battle.

31 Then gat he up upon his second chariot; and being brought back to Jerusalem died, and was buried in his father's sepulchre.

32 And in all Jewry they

mourned for Josias, yea, Jeremy the prophet amented for Josias, and the chief men with the women made lamentation for him unto this day: and this was given out for an ordinance to be done continually in all the nation of Israel.

33 These things are written in the book of the stories of the kings of Judah, and every one of the acts that Josias did, and his glory, and his understanding in the law of the Lord, and the things that he had done before, and the things now recited, are reported in the book of the kings of Israel and Judea.

34 And the people took Jō′-ă-chăz the son of Josias, and made him king instead of Josias his father, when he was twenty and three years old.

35 And he reigned in Judea and in Jerusalem three months: and then the king of Egypt deposed him from reigning in Jerusalem.

36 And he set a tax upon the land of an hundred talents of silver and one talent of gold.

37 The king of Egypt also made king Jō′-ă-cĭm his brother king of Judea and Jerusalem.

38 And he bound Jō′-ă-cĭm and the nobles: but Zăr′-ă-çēs his brother he apprehended, and brought him out of Egypt.

39 Five and twenty years old was Jō′-ă-cĭm when he was made king in the land of Judea and Jerusalem; and he did evil before the Lord.

40 Wherefore against him Năb′-ŭ-chŏ-dŏn′-ŏ-sôr the king of Babylon came up, and bound him with a chain of brass, and carried him into Babylon.

41 Năb′-ŭ-chŏ-dŏn-ŏ-sor also took of the holy vessels of the Lord, and carried them away, and set them in his own temple at Babylon.

42 But those things that are recorded of him, and of his uncleanness and impiety, are written in the chronicles of the kings.

43 And Jō′-ă-cĭm his son reigned in his stead: he was made king being eighteen years old;

44 And reigned but three months and ten days in Jerusalem; and did evil before the Lord.

45 So after a year Năb′-ŭ-chŏ-dŏn′-ŏ-sôr sent and caused him to be brought into Babylon with the holy vessels of the Lord;

46 And made Zĕd-ĕ-chī′-ăs king of Judea and Jerusalem, when he was one and twenty years old; and he reigned eleven years:

47 And he did evil also in the sight of the Lord, and cared not for the words that were spoken unto him by the prophet Jeremy from the mouth of the Lord.

48 And after that king Năb′-ŭ-chŏ-dŏn′-ŏ-sôr had made him to swear by the name of the Lord, he forswore himself, and rebelled; and hardening his neck, and his heart, he transgressed the laws of the Lord God of Israel.

49 The governors also of the people and of the priests did many things against the laws, and passed all the pollutions of all nations, and defiled the temple of the Lord, which was sanctified in Jerusalem.

50 Nevertheless the God of their fathers sent by his messenger to call them back, because he spared them and his tabernacle also.

51 But they had his messengers in derision; and, look, when the Lord spake unto them, they made a sport of his prophets:

52 So far forth, that he, being wroth with his people for their great ungodliness, commanded the kings of the Chăl-dēes' to come up against them;

53 Who slew their young men with the sword, yea, even within the compass of their holy temple, and spared neither young man nor maid, old man nor child, among them; for he delivered all into their hands.

54 And they took all the holy vessels of the Lord, both great and small, with the vessels of the ark of God, and the king's treasures, and carried them away into Babylon.

55 As for the house of the Lord, they burnt it, and brake down the walls of Jerusalem, and set fire upon her towers:

56 And as for her glorious things, they never ceased till they had consumed and brought them all to nought: and the people that were not slain with the sword he carried unto Babylon:

57 Who became servants to him and his children, till the Persians reigned; to fulfil the word of the Lord spoken by the mouth of Jeremy:

58 Until the land had enjoyed her sabbaths, the whole time of her desolation shall she rest, until the full term of seventy years.

CHAPTER II

IN the first year of Cyrus king of the Persians, that the word of the Lord might be accomplished, that he had promised by the mouth of Jeremy;

2 The Lord raised up the spirit of Cyrus the king of the Persians, and he made proclamation through all his kingdom, and also by writing,

3 Saying, Thus saith Cyrus king of the Persians; The Lord of Israel, the most high Lord, hath made me king of the whole world,

4 And commanded me to build him an house at Jerusalem in Jewry.

5 If therefore there be any of you that are of his people, let the Lord, even his Lord, be with him, and let him go up to Jerusalem that is in Judea, and build the house of the Lord of Israel: for he is the Lord that dwelleth in Jerusalem.

6 Whosoever then dwell in the places about, let them help him, those, I say, that are his neighbours, with gold, and with silver,

7 With gifts, with horses, and with cattle, and other things, which have been set forth by vow, for the temple of the Lord at Jerusalem.

8 ¶ Then the chief of the families of Judea and of the tribe of Benjamin stood up; the priests also, and the Levites, and all they whose mind the Lord had moved to go up, and to build an house for the Lord at Jerusalem,

9 And they that dwelt round about them, and helped them in all things with silver and

6

gold, with horses and cattle, and with very many free gifts of a great number whose minds were stirred up thereto.

10 King Cyrus also brought forth the holy vessels, which Năb′-ŭ-chŏ-dŏn′-ŏ-sôr had carried away from Jerusalem, and had set up in his temple of idols.

11 Now when Cyrus king of the Persians had brought them forth, he delivered them to Mĭth-rĭ-dā′-tēs his treasurer:

12 And by him they were delivered to Săn-ă-băs′-săr the governor of Judea.

13 And this was the number of them; A thousand golden cups, and a thousand of silver, censers of silver twenty nine, vials of gold thirty, and of silver two thousand four hundred and ten, and a thousand other vessels.

14 So all the vessels of gold and of silver, which were carried away, were five thousand four hundred threescore and nine.

15 These were brought back by Săn-ă-băs′-săr, together with them of the captivity, from Babylon to Jerusalem.

16 But in the time of Är-tăx-ērx′-ēs king of the Persians Bĕl-ē′-mŭs, and Mĭth-rĭ-dā′-tēs, and Tă-bĕl′-lĭ-ŭs, and Răth′-û-mŭs, and Bĕ-ĕl-tĕth′-mŭs, and Sĕ-mĕl′-lĭ-ŭs the secretary, with others that were in commission with them, dwelling in Samaria and other places, wrote unto him against them that dwelt in Judea and Jerusalem these letters following;

17 To king Är-tăx-ērx′-ēs our lord, Thy servants, Răth′-û-mŭs the storywriter, and Sĕ-mĕl′-lĭ-ŭs the scribe, and the rest of their council, and the judges that are in Çē′-lŏ-sŷr′-ĭ-ă and Phĕ-nī′-çĕ.

18 Be it now known to the lord the king, that the Jews that are come up from you to us, being come into Jerusalem, that rebellious and wicked city, do build the market-places, and repair the walls of it, and do lay the foundation of the temple.

19 Now if this city and the walls thereof be made up again, they will not only refuse to give tribute, but also rebel against kings.

20 And forasmuch as the things pertaining to the temple are now in hand, we think it meet not to neglect such a matter,

21 But to speak unto our lord the king, to the intent that, if it be thy pleasure, it may be sought out in the books of thy fathers:

22 And thou shalt find in the chronicles what is written concerning these things, and shalt understand that that city was rebellious, troubling both kings and cities:

23 And that the Jews were rebellious, and raised always wars therein; for the which cause even this city was made desolate.

24 Wherefore now we do declare unto thee, O lord the king, that if this city be built again, and the walls thereof set up anew, thou shalt from henceforth have no passage into Çē′-lŏ-sŷr′-ĭ-ă and Phĕ-nī′-çĕ.

25 Then the king wrote back again to Răth′-û-mŭs the story-writer, to Bĕ-ĕl-tĕth′-mŭs, to Sĕ-mĕl′-lĭ-ŭs the scribe, and to the rest that were in

commission, and dwellers in Samaria and Syria and Phĕ-nĭ'-çĕ, after this manner;

26 I have read the epistle which ye have sent unto me: therefore I commanded to make diligent search, and it hath been found that that city was from the beginning practising against kings;

27 And the men therein were given to rebellion and war: and that mighty kings and fierce were in Jerusalem, who reigned and exacted tributes in Çē'-lŏ-sȳr'-ĭ-ă and Phĕ-nĭ'-çĕ.

28 Now therefore I have commanded to hinder those men from building the city, and heed to be taken that there be no more done in it;

29 And that those wicked workers proceed no further to the annoyance of kings.

30 Then king Är-tăx-ērx'-ēs his letters being read, Răth'-û-mŭs, and Sĕ-mĕl'-lĭ-ŭs the scribe, and the rest that were in commission with them, removing in haste toward Jerusalem with a troop of horsemen and a multitude of people in battle array, began to hinder the builders; and the building of the temple in Jerusalem ceased until the second year of the reign of Dă-rī'-ŭs king of the Persians.

CHAPTER III

NOW when Dă-rī'-ŭs reigned, he made a great feast unto all his subjects, and unto all his household, and unto all the princes of Mē'-dĭ-ă and Persia,

2 And to all the governors and captains and lieutenants that were under him, from India unto E-thĭ-ŏ'-pĭ-ă, of an hundred twenty and seven provinces.

3 And when they had eaten and drunken, and being satisfied were gone home, then Dă-rī'-ŭs the king went into his bedchamber, and slept, and soon after awaked.

4 Then three young men, that were of the guard that kept the king's body, spake one to another;

5 Let every one of us speak a sentence: he that shall overcome, and whose sentence shall seem wiser than the others, unto him shall the king Dă-rī'-ŭs give great gifts, and great things in token of victory:

6 As, to be clothed in purple, to drink in gold, and to sleep upon gold, and a chariot with bridles of gold, and an head-tire of fine linen, and a chain about his neck:

7 And he shall sit next to Dă-rī'-ŭs because of his wisdom, and shall be called Darius his cousin.

8 And then every one wrote his sentence, sealed it, and laid it under king Dă-rī'-ŭs his pillow;

9 And said that, when the king is risen, some will give him the writings; and of whose side the king and the three princes of Persia shall judge that his sentence is the wisest, to him shall the victory be given, as was appointed.

10 The first wrote, Wine is the strongest.

11 The second wrote, The king is strongest.

12 The third wrote, Women are strongest: but above all things Truth beareth away the victory.

13 ¶ Now when the king was risen up, they took their writings, and delivered them

unto him, and so he read them:

14 And sending forth he called all the princes of Persia and Mē'-di-ă, and the governors, and the captains, and the lieutenants, and the chief officers;

15 And sat him down in the royal seat of judgment; and the writings were read before them.

16 And he said, Call the young men, and they shall declare their own sentences. So they were called, and came in.

17 And he said unto them, Declare unto us your mind concerning the writings. Then began the first, who had spoken of the strength of wine;

18 And he said thus, O ye men, how exceeding strong is wine! it causeth all men to err that drink it:

19 It maketh the mind of the king and of the fatherless child to be all one; of the bondman and of the freeman, of the poor man and of the rich:

20 It turneth also every thought into jollity and mirth, so that a man remembereth neither sorrow nor debt:

21 And it maketh every heart rich, so that a man remembereth neither king nor governor; and it maketh to speak all things by talents:

22 And when they are in their cups, they forget their love both to friends and brethren, and a little after draw out swords:

23 But when they are from the wine, they remember not what they have done.

24 O ye men, is not wine the strongest, that enforceth to do thus? And when he had so spoken, he held his peace.

CHAPTER IV

THEN the second, that had spoken of the strength of the king, began to say,

2 O ye men, do not men excel in strength, that bear rule over sea and land, and all things in them?

3 But yet the king is more mighty: for he is lord of all these things, and hath dominion over them; and whatsoever he commandeth them they do.

4 If he bid them make war the one against the other, they do it: if he send them out against the enemies, they go, and break down mountains, walls, and towers.

5 They slay and are slain, and transgress not the king's commandment: if they get the victory, they bring all to the king, as well the spoil, as all things else.

6 Likewise for those that are no soldiers, and have not to do with wars, but use husbandry, when they have reaped again that which they had sown, they bring it to the king, and compel one another to pay tribute unto the king.

7 And yet he is but one man: if he command to kill, they kill; if he command to spare, they spare;

8 If he command to smite, they smite; if he command to make desolate, they make desolate; if he command to build, they build;

9 If he command to cut down, they cut down; if he command to plant, they plant.

10 So all his people and his armies obey him: furthermore he lieth down, he eateth and drinketh, and taketh his rest:

11 And these keep watch

round about him, neither may any one depart, and do his own business, neither disobey they him in any thing.

12 O ye men, how should not the king be mightiest, when in such sort he is obeyed? And he held his tongue.

13 ¶ Then the third, who had spoken of women, and of the truth, (this was Zō-rō'-bă-bĕl) began to speak.

14 O ye men, it is not the great king, nor the multitude of men, neither is it wine, that excelleth; who is it then that ruleth them, or hath the lordship over them? are they not women?

15 Women have borne the king and all the people that bear rule by sea and land.

16 Even of them came they: and they nourished them up that planted the vineyards, from whence the wine cometh.

17 These also make garments for men; these bring glory unto men; and without women cannot men be.

18 Yea, and if men have gathered together gold and silver, or any other goodly thing, do they not love a woman which is comely in favour and beauty?

19 And letting all those things go, do they not gape, and even with open mouth fix their eyes fast on her; and have not all men more desire unto her than unto silver or gold, or any goodly thing whatsoever?

20 A man leaveth his own father that brought him up, and his own country, and cleaveth unto his wife.

21 He sticketh not to spend his life with his wife, and remembereth neither father, nor mother, nor country.

22 By this also ye must know that women have dominion over you: do ye not labour and toil, and give and bring all to the woman?

23 Yea, a man taketh his sword, and goeth his way to rob and to steal, to sail upon the sea and upon rivers;

24 And looketh upon a lion, and goeth in the darkness; and when he hath stolen, spoiled, and robbed, he bringeth it to his love.

25 Wherefore a man loveth his wife better than father or mother.

26 Yea, many there be that have run out of their wits for women, and become servants for their sakes.

27 Many also have perished, have erred, and sinned, for women.

28 And now do ye not believe me? is not the king great in his power? do not all regions fear to touch him?

29 Yet did I see him and Ā-pā'-mĕ the king's concubine, the daughter of the admirable Bär'-tă-cŭs, sitting at the right hand of the king,

30 And taking the crown from the king's head, and setting it upon her own head; she also struck the king with her left hand.

31 And yet for all this the king gaped and gazed upon her with open mouth: if she laughed upon him, he laughed also: but if she took any displeasure at him, the king was fain to flatter, that she might be reconciled to him again.

32 O ye men, how can it be but women should be strong, seeing they do thus?

33 Then the king and the princes looked one upon

another: so he began to speak of the truth.

34 O ye men, are not women strong? great is the earth, high is the heaven, swift is the sun in his course, for he compasseth the heavens round about, and fetcheth his course again to his own place in one day.

35 Is he not great that maketh these things? therefore great is the truth, and stronger than all things.

36 All the earth calleth upon the truth, and the heaven blesseth it: all works shake and tremble at it, and with it is no unrighteous thing.

37 Wine is wicked, the king is wicked, women are wicked, all the children of men are wicked, and such are all their wicked works; and there is no truth in them; in their unrighteousness also they shall perish.

38 As for the truth, it endureth, and is always strong; it liveth and conquereth for evermore.

39 With her there is no accepting of persons or rewards; but she doeth the things that are just, and refraineth from all unjust and wicked things; and all men do well like of her works.

40 Neither in her judgment is any unrighteousness; and she is the strength, kingdom, power, and majesty, of all ages. Blessed be the God of truth.

41 And with that he held his peace. And all the people then shouted, and said, Great is Truth, and mighty above all things.

42 Then said the king unto him, Ask what thou wilt more than is appointed in the writing, and we will give it thee,

because thou art found wisest; and thou shalt sit next me, and shalt be called my cousin.

43 Then said he unto the king, Remember thy vow, which thou hast vowed to build Jerusalem, in the day when thou camest to thy kingdom,

44 And to send away all the vessels that were taken away out of Jerusalem, which Cyrus set apart, when he vowed to destroy Babylon, and to send them again thither.

45 Thou also hast vowed to build up the temple, which the E'-dom-ites burned when Judea was made desolate by the Chăl-dēēs'.

46 And now, O lord the king, this is that which I require, and which I desire of thee, and this is the princely liberality proceeding from thyself: I desire therefore that thou make good the vow, the performance whereof with thine own mouth thou hast vowed to the King of heaven.

47 Then Dă-rī'-ŭs the king stood up, and kissed him, and wrote letters for him unto all the treasurers and lieutenants and captains and governors, that they should safely convey on their way both him, and all those that go up with him to build Jerusalem.

48 He wrote letters also unto the lieutenants that were in Çē'-lŏ-sўr'-ĭ-ä and Phĕ-nī'-çĕ, and unto them in Lĭb'-ă-nŭs, that they should bring cedar wood from Libanus unto Jerusalem, and that they should build the city with him.

49 Moreover he wrote for all the Jews that went out of his realm up into Jewry, concerning their freedom, that no officer, no ruler, no lieutenant,

nor treasurer, should forcibly enter into their doors;

50 And that all the country which they hold should be free without tribute; and that the E'-dom-ites should give over the villages of the Jews which then they held:

51 Yea, that there should be yearly given twenty talents to the building of the temple, until the time that it were built;

52 And other ten talents yearly, to maintain the burnt offerings upon the altar every day, as they had a commandment to offer seventeen:

53 And that all they that went from Babylon to build the city should have free liberty, as well they as their posterity, and all the priests that went away.

54 He wrote also concerning the charges, and the priests' vestments wherein they minister;

55 And likewise for the charges of the Levites, to be given them until the day that the house were finished, and Jerusalem builded up.

56 And he commanded to give to all that kept the city pensions and wages.

57 He sent away also all the vessels from Babylon, that Cyrus had set apart; and all that Cyrus had given in commandment, the same charged he also to be done. and sent unto Jerusalem.

58 Now when this young man was gone forth, he lifted up his face to heaven toward Jerusalem, and praised the King of heaven,

59 And said, From thee cometh victory, from thee cometh wisdom, and thine is the glory, and I am thy servant.

60 Blessed art thou, who hast given me wisdom: for to thee I give thanks, O Lord of our fathers.

61 And so he took the letters, and went out, and came unto Babylon, and told it all his brethren.

62 And they praised the God of their fathers, because he had given them freedom and liberty

63 To go up, and to build Jerusalem, and the temple which is called by his name: and they feasted with instruments of musick and gladness seven days.

CHAPTER V

AFTER this were the principal men of the families chosen according to their tribes, to go up with their wives and sons and daughters, with their menservants and maidservants, and their cattle.

2 And Dă-rī'-ŭs sent with them a thousand horsemen, till they had brought them back to Jerusalem safely, and with musical [instruments], tabrets and flutes.

3 And all their brethren played, and he made them go up together with them.

4 And these are the names of the men which went up, according to their families among their tribes, after their several heads.

5 The priests, the sons of Phin'-ĕ-ĕs the son of Aaron: Jesus the son of Jŏs'-ĕ-dĕc, the son of Să-rai'-ăs, and Jō'-ă-cĭm the son of Zŏ-rō'-bă-bĕl, the son of Să-lā'-thĭ-ĕl, of the house of David, out of the kindred of

Phăr'-ēs, of the tribe of Judah;

6 Who spake wise sentences before Dā-rī'-ŭs the king of Persia in the second year of his reign, in the month Nī'-săn, which is the first month.

7 And these are they of Jewry that came up from the captivity, where they dwelt as strangers, whom Năb'-ŭ-<u>ch</u>ŏ-dŏn'-ŏ-sôr the king of Babylon had carried away unto Babylon.

8 And they returned unto Jerusalem, and to the other parts of Jewry, every man to his own city, who came with Zŏ-rō'-bă-bĕl, with Jesus, Nĕ-hĕ-mī'-ăs, and Zăch-ă-rī'-ăs, and Rē-ĕ-săI'-ăs, Ĕn-ē'-nĭ-ŭs, Măr-dŏ-<u>ch</u>ē'-ŭs, Bĕ-ĕl-să'-rŭs, Ăs-phăr'-ă-sŭs, Rĕ-ĕl'-ĭ-ŭs, Rŏ-ī'-mŭs, and Bā-ä'-nă, their guides.

9 The number of them of the nation, and their governors, sons of Phŏ'-rŏs, two thousand an hundred seventy and two; the sons of Sā'-phăt, four hundred seventy and two:

10 The sons of Ā'-rēs, seven hundred fifty and six:

11 The sons of Phă'-ăth Mŏ'-ăb, two thousand eight hundred and twelve:

12 The sons of Ē'-lăm, a thousand two hundred fifty and four: the sons of Ză'-thŭ-ĭ, nine hundred forty and five: the sons of Cŏr'-bĕ, seven hundred and five: the sons of Bä'-nĭ, six hundred forty and eight:

13 The sons of Bē'-bă-ī, six hundred twenty and three: the sons of Sā'-dăs, three thousand two hundred twenty and two:

14 The sons of Ăd-ŏ-nī'-kăm, six hundred sixty and seven: the sons of Bă-gŏ'-ĭ, two thousand sixty and six: the

sons of Ā'-dĭn, four hundred nĭfty and four:

15 The sons of A'-tēr-ĕ-zī'-ăs, ninety and two: the sons of Çē'-ĭ-län and Ā-zē'-tăs, threescore and seven: the sons of Ā-zū'-răn, four hundred thirty and two:

16 The sons of Ăn-ă-nī'-ăs, an hundred and one: the sons of Ā'-rŏm, thirty two: and the sons of Băs'-să, three hundred twenty and three: the sons of Ăz-ē-phū'-rĭth, an hundred and two:

17 The sons of Mĕ-tē'-rŭs, three thousand and five: the sons of Bĕth-lŏ'-mŏn, an hundred twenty and three:

18 They of Nĕ-tō'-phăh, fifty and five: they of Ăn'-ă-thŏth, an hundred fifty and eight: they of Bĕth-săm'-ŏs, forty and two:

19 They of Kĭr'-ĭ-ăth'-ĭ-ā-rī-ŭs, twenty and five: they of Că-phī'-ră and Bē'-rôth, seven hundred forty and three: they of Pī'-ră, seven hundred:

20 They of <u>Ch</u>ă'-dĭ-ăs and Ăm'-mĭ-dŏ-ĭ, four hundred twenty and two: they of Çĭ-ră'-mă and Găb'-dēs, six hundred twenty and one:

21 They of Măc'-ă-lŏn, an hundred twenty and two: they of Bĕ-tō'-lĭ-ŭs, fifty and two: the sons of Nĕ'-phĭs, an hundred fifty and six:

22 The sons of Căl'-ă-mŏl'-ă-lŭs and Ō'-nŭs, seven hundred twenty and five: the sons of Jĕr'-ē-<u>ch</u>ŭs, two hundred forty and five:

23 The sons of Ăn-nā'-ăs, three thousand three hundred and thirty.

24 The priests: the sons of Jĕd'-dū, the son of Jesus, among the sons of Săn'-ă-sĭb, nine hundred seventy and two:

the sons of Mĕr'-ŭth, a thousand fifty and two:

25 The sons of Phăs'-să-ron, a thousand forty and seven: the sons of Cär'-mĕ, a thousand and seventeen.

26 The Levites: the sons of Jĕs'-sû-ĕ, and Căd'-mĭ-ĕl, and Bă-nū'-ăs, and Sū'-dĭ-ăs, seventy and four.

27 The holy singers: the sons of Ā'-săph, an hundred twenty and eight.

28 The porters: the sons of Sā'-lŭm, the sons of Jā'-tăl, the sons of Tăl'-mon, the sons of Dā'-cŏ-bī, the sons of Tē'-tă, the sons of Sā'-mī, in all an hundred thirty and nine.

29 The servants of the temple: the sons of Esau, the sons of Ăs'-ĭ-phă, the sons of Tă-bă'-ŏth, the sons of Çē'-răs, the sons of Sŭd, the sons of Phăl'-ĕ-ăs, the sons of Lă-bă'-nă, the sons of Grä'-bă,

30 The sons of Ā'-cŭ-ă, the sons of Ū'-tă, the sons of Çē'-tăb, the sons of Ā-gă'-bă, the sons of Sū'-bă-ī, the sons of Ā'-năn, the sons of Că-thū'-ă, the sons of Gĕd'-dûr,

31 The sons of Ă-ī'-rŭs, the sons of Dai'-săn, the sons of Nō-ē'-bă, the sons of Chă-sē'-bă, the sons of Gă-zē'-ră, the sons of Ā-zī'-ă, the sons of Phĭn'-ĕ-ĕs, the sons of Ā'-ză-ră, the sons of Băs'-tă-ī, the sons of Ā-să'-nă, the sons of Mĕ-ă'-nī, the sons of Nă-phī'-sī, the sons of Ā'-cŭb, the sons of Ă-çī'-phă, the sons of Ăs'-sûr, the sons of Phăr'-ă-çĭm, the sons of Bă-să'-lŏth,

32 The sons of Mĕ-ē'-dă, the sons of Cŏ-ū'-thă, the sons of Chă-rē'-ă, the sons of Charcus, the sons of Ā-sē'-rēr, the sons of Thŏ-mŏ'-ī, the sons of Nā'-sĭth, the sons of Ă-tī'-phă.

33 The sons of the servants of

Solomon: the sons of Ăz-ă-phī'-on, the sons of Phă-rī'-ră, the sons of Jĕ-ē'-lī, the sons of Lŏ'-zon, the sons of Ĭs-dā'-ĕl, the sons of Sā'-phĕth.

34 The sons of Hă-gī'-ă, the sons of Phă-cā'-rĕth, the sons of Sā'-bī, the sons of Să-rŏ-thī'-ĕ, the sons of Mă-sī'-ăs, the sons of Gär, the sons of Ăd'-dŭs, the sons of Sū'-bă, the sons of Ă-phĕr'-ră, the sons of Bă-rŏ'-dĭs, the sons of Săb'-ăt, the sons of Ăl'-lom.

35 All the ministers of the temple, and the sons of the servants of Solomon, were three hundred seventy and two.

36 These came up from Thĕr'-mĕ-lĕth and Thĕ-lĕr'-săs, Chăr'-ă-ăth'-ă-lär leading them, and Ā'-ă-lär;

37 Neither could they shew their families, nor their stock, how they were of Israel: the sons of Lā'-dăn, the son of Băn, the sons of Nĕ'-cŏ-dăn, six hundred fifty and two.

38 And of the priests that usurped the office of the priesthood, and were not found: the sons of Ōb-dī'-ă, the sons of Ăc'-coz, the sons of Ăd'-dŭs, who married Ău'-gĭ-ă one of the daughters of Bĕr-zē'-lŭs, and was named after his name.

39 And when the description of the kindred of these men was sought in the register, and was not found, they were removed from executing the office of the priesthood:

40 For unto them said Nĕ-hĕ-mī'-ăs and Ăth-ă-rī'-ăs, that they should not be partakers of the holy things, till there arose up an high priest clothed with doctrine and truth.

41 So of Israel, from them of twelve years old and upward,

14

they were all in number forty thousand, beside menservants and womenservants two thousand three hundred and sixty.

42 Their menservants and handmaids were seven thousand three hundred forty and seven: the singing men and singing women, two hundred forty and five:

43 Four hundred thirty and five camels, seven thousand thirty and six horses, two hundred forty and five mules, five thousand five hundred twenty and five beasts used to the yoke.

44 And certain of the chief of their families, when they came to the temple of God that is in Jerusalem, vowed to set up the house again in his own place according to their ability,

45 And to give into the holy treasury of the works a thousand pounds of gold, five thousand of silver, and an hundred priestly vestments.

46 And so dwelt the priests and the Levites and the people in Jerusalem, and in the country, the singers also and the porters; and all Israel in their villages.

47 But when the seventh month was at hand, and when the children of Israel were every man in his own place, they came all together with one consent into the open place of the first gate which is toward the east.

48 Then stood up Jesus the son of Jŏs'-ĕ-dĕc, and his brethren the priests, and Zŏ-rŏ'-bă-bĕl the son of Să-lā'-thĭ-ĕl, and his brethren, and made ready the altar of the God of Israel,

49 To offer burnt sacrifices upon it, according as it is expressly commanded in the book of Moses the man of God.

50 And there were gathered unto them out of the other nations of the land, and they erected the altar upon his own place, because all the nations of the land were at enmity with them, and oppressed them; and they offered sacrifices according to the time, and burnt offerings to the Lord both morning and evening.

51 Also they held the feast of tabernacles, as it is commanded in the law, and *offered* sacrifices daily, as was meet:

52 And after that, the continual oblations, and the sacrifice of the sabbaths, and of the new moons, and of all holy feasts.

53 And all they that had made any vow to God began to offer sacrifices to God from the first day of the seventh month, although the temple of the Lord was not yet built.

54 And they gave unto the masons and carpenters money, meat, and drink, with cheerfulness.

55 Unto them of Zī'-don also and Tyre they gave carrs, that they should bring cedar trees from Lĭb'-ă-nŭs, which should be brought by floats to the haven of Jŏp'-pĕ, according as it was commanded them by Cyrus king of the Persians.

56 And in the second year and second month after his coming to the temple of God at Jerusalem began Zŏ-rŏ'-bă-bĕl the son of Să-lā'-thĭ-ĕl, and Jesus the son of Jŏs'-ĕ-dĕc, and their brethren, and the priests, and the Levites, and all they that were come unto Jerusalem out of the captivity:

57 And they laid the foundation of the house of God in the

first day of the second month, in the second year after they were come to Jewry and Jerusalem.

58 And they appointed the Levites from twenty years old over the works of the Lord. Then stood up Jesus, and his sons and brethren, and Căd'-mi-ĕl his brother, and the sons of Mă-dī'-ă-bŭn, with the sons of Joda the son of Ĕlī'-ă-dŭn, with their sons and brethren, all Levites, with one accord setters forward of the business, labouring to advance the works in the house of God. So the workmen built the temple of the Lord.

59 And the priests stood arrayed in their vestments with musical instruments and trumpets; and the Levites the sons of Ā'-săph had cymbals,

60 Singing songs of thanksgiving, and praising the Lord, according as David the king of Israel had ordained.

61 And they sung *with* loud voices songs to the praise of the Lord, because his mercy and glory is for ever in all Israel.

62 And all the people sounded trumpets, and shouted with a loud voice, singing songs of thanksgiving unto the Lord for the rearing up of the house of the Lord.

63 Also of the priests and Levites, and of the chief of their families, the ancients who had seen the former house came to the building of this with weeping and great crying.

64 But many with trumpets and joy shouted with loud voice,

65 Insomuch that the trumpets might not be heard for the weeping of the people: yet the multitude sounded marvellously, so that it was heard afar off.

66 Wherefore when the enemies of the tribe of Judah and Benjamin heard it, they came to know what that noise of trumpets should mean.

67 And they perceived that they that were of the captivity did build the temple unto the Lord God of Israel.

68 So they went to Zŏ-rō'-bă-bĕl and Jesus, and to the chief of the families, and said unto them, We will build together with you.

69 For we likewise, as ye, do obey your Lord, and do sacrifice unto him from the days of Ăz-băz'-ă-rĕth the king of the Ăs-sўr'-ĭ-ăns, who brought us hither.

70 Then Zŏ-rō'-bă-bĕl and Jesus and the chief of the families of Israel said unto them, It is not for us and you to build together an house unto the Lord our God.

71 We ourselves alone will build unto the Lord of Israel, according as Cyrus the king of the Persians hath commanded us.

72 But the heathen of the land lying heavy upon the inhabitants of Judea, and holding them strait, hindered their building;

73 And by their secret plots, and popular persuasions and commotions, they hindered the finishing of the building all the time that king Cyrus lived: so they were hindered from building for the space of two years, until the reign of Dă-rī'-ŭs.

CHAPTER VI

NOW in the second year of the reign of Dă-rī'-ŭs Ăg'-

gĕ-ŭs and Zăch-ă-rī'-ăs the son of Addo, the prophets, prophesied unto the Jews in Jewry and Jerusalem in the name of the Lord God of Israel, which was upon them.

2 Then stood up Zŏ-rŏ'-bă-bĕl the son of Săl-ā'-thĭ-ĕl, and Jesus the son of Jŏs'-ĕ-dĕc, and began to build the house of the Lord at Jerusalem, the prophets of the Lord being with them, *and* helping them.

3 At the same time came unto them Sī'-sĭn-nĕs the governor of Syria and Phĕ-nī'-çĕ, with Săth'-ră-bū'-ză-nĕs and his companions, and said unto them,

4 By whose appointment do ye build this house and this roof, and perform all the other things? and who are the workmen that perform these things?

5 Nevertheless the elders of the Jews obtained favour, because the Lord had visited the captivity;

6 And they were not hindered from building, until such time as signification was given unto Dă-rī'-ŭs concerning them, and an answer received.

7 The copy of the letters which Sī'-sĭn-nĕs, governor of Syria and Phĕ-nī'-çĕ, and Săth'-ră-bū'-ză-nĕs, with their companions, rulers in Syria and Phenice, wrote and sent unto Dă-rī'-ŭs; To king Darius, greeting:

8 Let all things be known unto our lord the king, that being come into the country of Judea, and entered into the city of Jerusalem, we found in the city of Jerusalem the ancients of the Jews that were of the captivity,

9 Building an house unto the Lord, great *and* new, of hewn and costly stones, and the timber already laid upon the walls.

10 And those works are done with great speed, and the work goeth on prosperously in their hands, and with all glory and diligence is it made.

11 Then asked we these elders, saying, By whose commandment build ye this house, and lay the foundations of these works?

12 Therefore to the intent that we might give knowledge unto thee by writing, we demanded of them who were the chief doers, and we required of them the names in writing of their principal men.

13 So they gave us this answer, We are the servants of the Lord which made heaven and earth.

14 And as for this house, it was builded many years ago by a king of Israel great and strong, and was finished.

15 But when our fathers provoked God unto wrath, and sinned against the Lord of Israel which is in heaven, he gave them over into the power of Năb'-ŭ-chŏ-dŏn'-ŏ-sôr king of Babylon, of the Chăl-dĕes';

16 Who pulled down the house, and burned it, and carried away the people captives unto Babylon.

17 But in the first year that king Cyrus reigned over the country of Babylon Cyrus the king wrote to build up this house.

18 And the holy vessels of gold and of silver, that Năb'-ŭ-chŏ-dŏn'-ŏ-sôr had carried away out of the house at Jerusalem, and had set them in his own temple, those Cyrus the king brought forth again out of the temple at Babylon,

17

and they were delivered to Zŏ-rŏ'-bă-bĕl and to Săn'-ă-băs'-să-rŭs the ruler,

19 With commandment that he should carry away the same vessels and put them in the temple at Jerusalem; and that the temple of the Lord should be built in his place.

20 Then the same Săn'-ă-băs'-să-rŭs, being come hither, laid the foundations of the house of the Lord at Jerusalem; and from that time to this being still a building, it is not yet fully ended.

21 Now therefore, if it seem good unto the king, let search be made among the records of king Cyrus:

22 And if it be found that the building of the house of the Lord at Jerusalem hath been done with the consent of king Cyrus, and if our lord the king be so minded, let him signify unto us thereof.

23 Then commanded king Dă-rī'-ŭs to seek among the records at Babylon: and so at Ĕc-băt'-ă-nă the palace, which is in the country of Mē'-dĭ-ă, there was found a roll wherein these things were recorded.

24 In the first year of the reign of Cyrus king Cyrus commanded that the house of the Lord at Jerusalem should be built again, where they do sacrifice with continual fire:

25 Whose height shall be sixty cubits, and the breadth sixty cubits, with three rows of hewn stones, and one row of new wood of that country; and the expences thereof to be given out of the house of king Cyrus:

26 And that the holy vessels of the house of the Lord, both of gold and silver, that Năb'-

ŭ-chŏ-dŏn'-ŏ-sôr took out of the house at Jerusalem, and brought to Babylon, should be restored to the house at Jerusalem, and be set in the place where they were before.

27 And also he commanded that Sĭ'-sĭn-nēs the governor of Syria and Phē-nī'-çĕ, and Săth'-ră-bū'-ză-nēs, and their companions, and those which were appointed rulers in Syria and Phenice, should be careful not to meddle with the place, but suffer Zŏ-rŏ'-bă-bĕl, the servant of the Lord, and governor of Judea, and the elders of the Jews, to build the house of the Lord in that place.

28 I have commanded also to have it built up whole again; and that they look diligently to help those that be of the captivity of the Jews, till the house of the Lord be finished:

29 And out of the tribute of Çē'-lŏ-sȳr'-ĭ-ă and Phē-nī'-çĕ a portion carefully to be given these men for the sacrifices of the Lord, *that is*, to Zŏ-rŏ'-bă-bĕl the governor, for bullocks, and rams, and lambs;

30 And also corn, salt, wine, and oil, and that continually every year without further question, according as the priests that be in Jerusalem shall signify to be daily spent:

31 That offerings may be made to the most high God for the king and for his children, and that they may pray for their lives.

32 And he commanded that whosoever should transgress, yea, or make light of any thing afore spoken or written, out of his own house should a tree be taken, and he thereon be hanged, and all his goods seized for the king.

33 The Lord therefore, whose name is there called upon, utterly destroy every king and nation, that stretcheth out his hand to hinder or endamage that house of the Lord in Jerusalem.

34 I Dă-rī′-ŭs the king have ordained that according unto these things it be done with diligence.

CHAPTER VII

THEN Sĭ′-sĭn-nēs the governor of Çē′-lŏ-sÿr′-ĭ-ă and Phē-nī′-çĕ, and Săth′-ră-bū′-ză-nēs, with their companions, following the commandments of king Dă-rī′-ŭs,

2 Did very carefully oversee the holy works, assisting the ancients of the Jews and governors of the temple.

3 And so the holy works prospered, when Ăg′-gĕ-ŭs and Zăch-ă-rī′-ăs the prophets prophesied.

4 And they finished these things by the commandment of the Lord God of Israel, and with the consent of Cyrus, Dă-rī′-ŭs, and Är-tăx-ĕrx′-ēs, kings of Persia.

5 And thus was the holy house finished in the three and twentieth day of the month Ă-där′, in the sixth year of Dă-rī′-ŭs king of the Persians.

6 And the children of Israel, the priests, and the Levites, and others that were of the captivity, that were added unto them, did according to the things written in the book of Moses.

7 And to the dedication of the temple of the Lord they offered an hundred bullocks, two hundred rams, four hundred lambs;

8 And twelve goats for the sin of all Israel, according to the number of the chief of the tribes of Israel.

9 The priests also and the Levites stood arrayed in their vestments, according to their kindreds, in the service of the Lord God of Israel, according to the book of Moses: and the porters at every gate.

10 And the children of Israel that were of the captivity held the passover the fourteenth day of the first month, after that the priests and the Levites were sanctified.

11 They that were of the captivity were not all sanctified together: but the Levites were all sanctified together.

12 And so they offered the passover for all them of the captivity, and for their brethren the priests, and for themselves.

13 And the children of Israel that came out of the captivity did eat, even all they that had separated themselves from the abominations of the people of the land, and sought the Lord.

14 And they kept the feast of unleavened bread seven days, making merry before the Lord,

15 For that he had turned the counsel of the king of Assyria toward them, to strengthen their hands in the works of the Lord God of Israel.

CHAPTER VIII

AND after these things, when Är-tăx-ĕrx′-ēs the king of the Persians reigned, came Esdras the son of Să-raī′-ăs, the son of Ė-zē′-rĭ-ăs, the son of Hĕl-chī′-ăh, the son of Să′-lŭm,

2 The son of Săd′-dŭc, the son

of Ā'-chi-tŏb, the son of Ăm-
a-rī'-ăs, the son of Ē-zī'-ăs, the
son of Mĕ-rē'-mŏth, the son of
Zá-raī'-ăs, the son of Sá-vī'-ăs,
the son of Bŏc'-căs, the son of
Ă-bī'-sŭm, the son of Phin'-ĕ-ĕs,
the son of Ēl-ĕ-ā'-zär, the son of
Aaron the chief priest.

3 This Esdras went up from
Babylon, as a scribe, being
very ready in the law of Moses,
that was given by the God of
Israel.

4 And the king did him
honour: for he found grace in
his sight in all his requests.

5 There went up with him also
certain of the children of
Israel, of the priests, of the
Levites, of the holy singers,
porters, and ministers of the
temple, unto Jerusalem,

6 In the seventh year of the
reign of Är-tăx-ērx'-ēs, in the
fifth month, this was the king's
seventh year; for they went
from Babylon in the first day
of the first month, and came to
Jerusalem, according to the
prosperous journey which the
Lord gave them.

7 For Esdras had very great
skill, so that he omitted nothing of the law and commandments of the Lord, but taught
all Israel the ordinances and
judgments.

8 Now the copy of the commission, which was written
from Är-tăx-ērx'-ēs the king,
and came to Esdras the priest
and reader of the law of the
Lord, is this that followeth;

9 King Är-tăx-ērx'-ēs unto
Esdras the priest and reader
of the law of the Lord sendeth
greeting:

10 Having determined to deal
graciously, I have given order,
that such of the nation of the
Jews, and of the priests and

Levites, being within our
realm, as are willing and desirous, should go with thee unto
Jerusalem.

11 As many therefore as have
a mind thereunto, let them
depart with thee, as it hath
seemed good both to me and
my seven friends the counsellors;

12 That they may look unto
the affairs of Judea and
Jerusalem, agreeably to that
which is in the law of the Lord;

13 And carry the gifts unto
the Lord of Israel to Jerusalem, which I and my friends
have vowed, and all the gold
and silver that in the country
of Babylon can be found, to
the Lord in Jerusalem,

14 With that also which is
given of the people for the
temple of the Lord their God
at Jerusalem: and that silver
and gold may be collected for
bullocks, rams, and lambs, and
things thereunto appertaining;

15 To the end that they may
offer sacrifices unto the Lord
upon the altar of the Lord their
God, which is in Jerusalem.

16 And whatsoever thou and
thy brethren will do with the
silver and gold, that do,
according to the will of thy
God.

17 And the holy vessels of the
Lord, which are given thee for
the use of the temple of thy
God, which is in Jerusalem,
thou shalt set before thy God
in Jerusalem.

18 And whatsoever thing else
thou shalt remember for the
use of the temple of thy God,
thou shalt give it out of the
king's treasury.

19 And I king Är-tăx-ērx'-ēs
have also commanded the

keepers of the treasures in Syria and Phē-nī'-cĕ, that whatsoever Esdras the priest and the reader of the law of the most high God shall send for, they should give it him with speed,

20 To the sum of an hundred talents of silver, likewise also of wheat even to an hundred cors, and an hundred pieces of wine, and other things in abundance.

21 Let all things be performed after the law of God diligently unto the most high God, that wrath come not upon the kingdom of the king and his sons.

22 I command you also, that ye require no tax, nor any other imposition, of any of the priests, or Levites, or holy singers, or porters, or ministers of the temple, or of any that have doings in this temple, and that no man have authority to impose any thing upon them.

23 And thou, Esdras, according to the wisdom of God ordain judges and justices, that they may judge in all Syria and Phē-nī'-cĕ all those that know the law of thy God; and those that know it not thou shalt teach.

24 And whosoever shall transgress the law of thy God, and of the king, shall be punished diligently, whether it be by death, or other punishment, by penalty of money, or by imprisonment.

25 ¶ Then said Esdras the scribe, Blessed be the only Lord God of my fathers, who hath put these things into the heart of the king, to glorify his house that is in Jerusalem:

26 And hath honoured me in the sight of the king, and his counsellors, and all his friends and nobles.

27 Therefore was I encouraged by the help of the Lord my God, and gathered together men of Israel to go up with me.

28 And these are the chief according to their families and several dignities, that went up with me from Babylon in the reign of king Är-tăx-ẽrx'-ēs:

29 Of the sons of Phin'-ĕ-es, Gēr'-son: of the sons of Ith'-ā-mär, Gä-mä'-ĕl: of the sons of David, Lĕt'-tŭs the son of Sĕch-ĕ-nī'-ăs:

30 Of the sons of Phā'-rĕz, Zăch-ă-rī'-ăs; and with him were counted an hundred and fifty men:

31 Of the sons of Pā'-hăth Mō'-ăb, Ĕ-lī'-ă-ŏ-nī'-ăs, the son of Ză-rai'-ăs, and with him two hundred men:

32 Of the sons of Ză-thō'-ĕ, Sĕch-ĕ-nī'-ăs the son of Jĕ-zē'-lŭs, and with him three hundred men: of the sons of Ā'-dĭn, Ō'-bĕth the son of Jonathan, and with him two hundred and fifty men:

33 Of the sons of Elam, Josias son of Gŏth-ŏ-lī'-ăs, and with him seventy men:

34 Of the sons of Săph-ă-tī'-ăs, Ză-raī'-ăs son of Michael, and with him threescore and ten men:

35 Of the sons of Jŏ'-ăb, Ăb-ă-dī'-ăs son of Jĕ-zē'-lŭs, and with him two hundred and twelve men:

36 Of the sons of Bā'-nĭd, Ăs-săl'-i-mŏth son of Jŏs-ă-phī'-ăs, and with him an hundred and threescore men:

37 Of the sons of Bā'-bĭ, Zăch-ă-rī'-ăs son of Bē'-bă-ī, and with him twenty and eight men:

21

38 Of the sons of Ā'-stǎth, Jŏ-hǎn'-nēs *son of* Ăc-ǎ-tǎn', and with him an hundred and ten men:

39 Of the sons of Ăd-ŏ-nī'-kǎm the last, and these are the names of them, Ē-lǐph'-ǎ-lĕt, Jĕ-ū'-ĕl, and Sǎ-maī'-ǎs, and with them seventy men:

40 Of the sons of Bā'-gō, Ū'-thī the son of Ĭs-tǎl-cū'-rǔs, and with him seventy men.

41 And these I gathered together to the river called Thĕ'-rǎs, where we pitched our tents three days: and then I surveyed them.

42 But when I had found there none of the priests and Levites,

43 Then sent I unto Ĕl-ĕ-ā'-zär, and Ĭd'-ū-ĕl, and Mǎs'-mǎn,

44 And Ăl-nā'-thǎn, and Mǎ-maī'-ǎs, and Jŏ-rī'-bǎs, and Nathan, and Ēu-nā'-tǎn, Zǎch-ǎ-rī'-ǎs, and Mŏ-sŏl'-lǎ-mon, principal men and learned.

45 And I bade them that they should go unto Sǎd'-dě-ǔs the captain, who was in the place of the treasury:

46 And commanded them that they should speak unto Dǎd'-dě-ǔs, and to his brethren, and to the treasurers in that place, to send us such men as might execute the priests' office in the house of the Lord.

47 And by the mighty hand of our Lord they brought unto us skilful men of the sons of Mō'-li the son of Levi, the son of Israel, Ă-sĕb'-ĕ-bī'-ǎ, and his sons, and his brethren, who were eighteen.

48 And Ā-sĕ'-bǐ-ǎ, and Ăn'-nǔ-ǔs, and Ŏ-sai'-ǎs his brother, of the sons of Chǎn-nǔ-nē'-ǔs, and their sons, were twenty men.

49 And of the servants of the temple whom David had ordained, and the principal men for the service of the Levites, to wit, the servants of the temple, two hundred and twenty, the catalogue of whose names were shewed.

50 And there I vowed a fast unto the young men before our Lord, to desire of him a prosperous journey both for us and them that were with us, for our children, and for the cattle:

51 For I was ashamed to ask the king footmen, and horsemen, and conduct for safeguard against our adversaries.

52 For we had said unto the king, that the power of the Lord our God should be with them that seek him, to support them in all ways.

53 And again we besought our Lord as touching these things, and found him favourable unto us.

54 Then I separated twelve of the chief of the priests, Ē-sē'-brĭ-ǎs, and Ăs-sǎ-nī'-ǎs, and ten men of their brethren with them:

55 And I weighed them the gold, and the silver, and the holy vessels of the house of our Lord, which the king, and his council, and the princes, and all Israel, had given.

56 And when I had weighed it, I delivered unto them six hundred and fifty talents of silver, and silver vessels of an hundred talents, and an hundred talents of gold,

57 And twenty golden vessels, and twelve vessels of brass, even of fine brass, glittering like gold.

58 And I said unto them, Both ye are holy unto the Lord, and the vessels are holy,

and the gold and the silver is a vow unto the Lord, the Lord of our fathers.

59 Watch ye, and keep them till ye deliver them to the chief of the priests and Levites, and to the principal men of the families of Israel, in Jerusalem, into the chambers of the house of our God.

60 So the priests and the Levites, who had received the silver and the gold and the vessels, brought them unto Jerusalem, into the temple of the Lord.

61 And from the river Thē´-răs we departed the twelfth day of the first month, and came to Jerusalem by the mighty hand of our Lord, which was with us: and from the beginning of our journey the Lord delivered us from every enemy, and *so* we came to Jerusalem.

62 And when we had been there three days, the gold and silver that was weighed was delivered in the house of our Lord on the fourth day unto Mär´-mŏth the priest the son of Ī´-rī.

63 And with him was Ĕl-ĕ-ā´-zär the son of Phĭn´-ĕ-ĕs, and with them were Jŏs´-ă-băd the son of Jē´-sū and Mō´-ĕth the son of Săb´-băn, Levites: all was *delivered them* by number and weight.

64 And all the weight of them was written up the same hour.

65 Moreover they that were come out of the captivity offered sacrifice unto the Lord God of Israel, even twelve bullocks for all Israel, fourscore and sixteen rams,

66 Threescore and twelve lambs, goats for a peace offering, twelve; all of them a sacrifice to the Lord.

67 And they delivered the king's commandments unto the king's stewards, and to the governors of Çē´-lŏ-sўr´-ĭ-ă and Phē-nī´-çē; and they honoured the people and the temple of God.

68 Now when these things were done, the rulers came unto me, and said,

69 The nation of Israel, the princes, the priests and Levites, have not put away from them the strange people of the land, nor the pollutions of the Gentiles, *to wit,* of the Canaanites, Hittites, Phĕr´-ĕ-sītes, Jĕb´-ŭ-sītes, and the Mō´-ă-bītes, Egyptians, and E´-dom-ītes.

70 For both they and their sons have married with their daughters, and the holy seed is mixed with the strange people of the land; and from the beginning of this matter the rulers and the great men have been partakers of this iniquity.

71 And as soon as I had heard these things, I rent my clothes, and the holy garment, and pulled off the hair from off my head and beard, and sat me down sad and very heavy.

72 So all they that were then moved at the word of the Lord God of Israel assembled unto me, whilst I mourned for the iniquity: but I sat still full of heaviness until the evening sacrifice.

73 Then rising up from the fast with my clothes and the holy garment rent, and bowing my knees, and stretching forth my hands unto the Lord,

74 I said, O Lord, I am confounded and ashamed before thy face;

75 For our sins are multiplied above our heads, and our

23

ignorances have reached up unto heaven.

76 For ever since the time of our fathers we *have been* and are in great sin, even unto this day.

77 And for our sins and our fathers' we with our brethren and our kings and our priests were given up unto the kings of the earth, to the sword, and to captivity, and for a prey with shame, unto this day.

78 And now in some measure hath mercy been shewed unto us from thee, O Lord, that there should be left us a root and a name in the place of thy sanctuary;

79 And to discover unto us a light in the house of the Lord our God, and to give us food in the time of our servitude.

80 Yea, when we were in bondage, we were not forsaken of our Lord; but he made us gracious before the kings of Persia, so that they gave us food;

81 Yea, and honoured the temple of our Lord, and raised up the desolate Sion, that they have given us a sure abiding in Jewry and Jerusalem.

82 And now, O Lord, what shall we say, having these things? for we have transgressed thy commandments, which thou gavest by the hand of thy servants the prophets, saying,

83 That the land, which ye enter into to possess as an heritage, is a land polluted with the pollutions of the strangers of the land, and they have filled it with their uncleanness.

84 Therefore now shall ye not join your daughters unto their sons, neither shall ye take their daughters unto your sons.

85 Moreover ye shall never seek to have peace with them, that ye may be strong, and eat the good things of the land, and that ye may leave the inheritance of the land unto your children for evermore.

86 And all that is befallen is done unto us for our wicked works and great sins: for thou, O Lord, didst make our sins light,

87 And didst give unto us such a root: but we have turned back again to transgress thy law, and to mingle ourselves with the uncleanness of the nations of the land.

88 Mightest not thou be angry with us to destroy us, till thou hadst left us neither root, seed, nor name?

89 O Lord of Israel, thou art true: for we are left a root this day.

90 Behold, now are we before thee in our iniquities, for we cannot stand any longer by reason of these things before thee.

91 And as Esdras in his prayer made his confession, weeping, and lying flat upon the ground before the temple, there gathered unto him from Jerusalem a very great multitude of men and women and children: for there was great weeping among the multitude.

92 Then Jĕch-ŏ-nī'-ăs the son of Jĕ-ē'-lŭs, one of the sons of Israel, called out, and said, O Esdras, we have sinned against the Lord God, we have married strange women of the nations of the land, and now is all Israel aloft.

93 Let us make an oath to the Lord, that we will put away all our wives, which we have taken of the heathen, with their children,

94 Like as thou hast decreed, and as many as do obey the law of the Lord.

95 Arise, and put in execution: for to thee doth this matter appertain, and we will be with thee: do valiantly.

96 So Esdras arose, and took an oath of the chief of the priests and Levites of all Israel to do after these things; and so they sware.

CHAPTER IX

THEN Esdras rising from the court of the temple went to the chamber of Jŏ-ā'-năn the son of Ē-lī'-ă-sïb,

2 And remained there, and did eat no meat nor drink water, mourning for the great iniquities of the multitude.

3 And there was a proclamation in all Jewry and Jerusalem to all them that were of the captivity, that they should be gathered together at Jerusalem:

4 And that whosoever met not there within two or three days, according as the elders that bare rule appointed, their cattle should be seized to the use of the temple, and himself cast out from them that were of the captivity.

5 And in three days were all they of the tribe of Judah and Benjamin gathered together at Jerusalem the twentieth day of the ninth month.

6 And all the multitude sat trembling in the broad court of the temple because of the present foul weather.

7 So Esdras arose up, and said unto them, Ye have transgressed the law in marrying strange wives, thereby to increase the sins of Israel.

8 And now by confessing give glory unto the Lord God of our fathers,

9 And do his will, and separate yourselves from the heathen of the land, and from the strange women.

10 Then cried the whole multitude, and said with a loud voice, Like as thou hast spoken, so will we do.

11 But forasmuch as the people are many, and it is foul weather, so that we cannot stand without, and this is not a work of a day or two, seeing our sin in these things is spread far:

12 Therefore let the rulers of the multitude stay, and let all them of our habitations that have strange wives come at the time appointed,

13 And with them the rulers and judges of every place, till we turn away the wrath of the Lord from us for this matter.

14 Then Jonathan the son of Ăz'-ă-ĕl and Ĕz-ĕ-kī'-ăs the son of Thĕ-ŏc'-ă-nŭs accordingly took this matter upon them: and Mŏ-sŏl'-lăm and Lē'-vĭs and Săb-bă-thē'-ŭs helped them.

15 And they that were of the captivity did according to all these things.

16 And Esdras the priest chose unto him the principal men of their families, all by name: and in the first day of the tenth month they sat together to examine the matter.

17 So their cause that held strange wives was brought to an end in the first day of the first month.

18 And of the priests that were come together, and had strange wives, there were found;

19 Of the sons of Jesus the son

25

of Jŏs'-ĕ-dĕc, and his brethren; Măt'-thē-lăs, and Ĕl-ĕ-ā'-zăr, and Jôr'-ĭ-bŭs, and Jŏ-ăd'-ă-nŭs.

20 And they gave their hands to put away their wives, and to offer rams to make reconcilement for their errors.

21 And of the sons of Ĕm'-mēr; Ăn-ă-nī'-ăs, and Zăb'-dĕ-ŭs, and Ē'-ă-nēs, and Să-mē'-ĭ-ŭs, and Hī-ĕ-rē'-ĕl, and Ăz-ă-rī'-ăs.

22 And of the sons of Phai'-sûr; Ē-lī'-ŏ-năs, Măs-sī'-ăs, Ĭs'-mă-ĕl, and Nathanael, and Ō-çĭ-dē'-lŭs, and Tăl'-săs.

23 And of the Levites; Jŏz'-ă-băd, and Sē'-mĭs, and Cŏ-lī'-ŭs, who was called Că-lī'-tăs, and Pă-thē'-ŭs, and Judas, and Jonas.

24 Of the holy singers; Ĕl'-ĕ-ă-zū'-rŭs, Băc-chū'-rŭs.

25 Of the porters; Săl-lū'-mŭs, and Tŏl-bā'-nēs.

26 Of them of Israel, of the sons of Phŏ'-rŏs; Hī-ĕr'-măs, and Ĕd-dī'-ăs, and Mĕl-chī'-ăs, and Mă-ē'-lŭs, and Ĕl-ĕ-ā'-zăr, and Ăs-ĭ-bī'-ăs, and Bā-ă-nī'-ăs.

27 Of the sons of Ela; Măt-thă-nī'-ăs, Zăch-ă-rī'-ăs, and Hī-ĕr'-ĭ-ē'-lŭs, and Hī-ĕr-ē'-mŏth, and Ā-ē'-dī-ăs.

28 And of the sons of Zā'-mŏth; Ē-lī'-ă-dăs, Ē-lī'-sī-mŭs, Ŏ-thŏ-nī'-ăs, Jă-rī'-mŏth, and Să-bă'-tŭs, and Sär-dē'-ŭs.

29 Of the sons of Bē'-bă-ī; Jŏ-hän-nēs, and Ăn-ă-nī'-ăs, and Jŏs'-ă-băd, and Ăm-ă-thē'-ĭs.

30 Of the sons of Mā'-nī; Ŏ-lā'-mŭs, Mă-mū'-chŭs, Jĕ-dē'-ŭs, Jā'-sŭ-bŭs, Jā'-să-ĕl, and Hī-ĕr-ē'-mŏth.

31 And of the sons of Ăd'-dī; Nā'-ă-thŭs, and Mō-ŏ-sī'-ăs, Lă-cū'-nŭs, and Nă-ī'-dŭs, and Mă-thă-nī'-ăs, and Sĕs'-thĕl, Băl-nū'-ŭs, and Mă-năs'-sĕ-ăs.

32 And of the sons of Annas; Ē-lī'-ŏ-năs, and Ă-sē'-ăs, and Mĕl-chī'-ăs, and Săb-bē'-ŭs, and Simon Chŏ-sā'-mē-ŭs.

33 And of the sons of Ā'-sŏm; Ăl-tă-nē'-ŭs, and Măt-thī'-ăs, and Băn-nai'-ă, Ē-līph'-ă-lăt, and Mă-năs'-sēs, and Sē'-mē-ī.

34 And of the sons of Mā'-ă-nī; Jeremias, Mŏm'-dīs, Ŏ-mă-ē'-rŭs, Jū'-ĕl, Măb'-dă-ī, and Pĕ-lī'-ăs, and Ā'-nŏs, Căr'-ă-bā'-sĭ-on, and Ĕn-ă-sī'-bŭs, and Măm'-nĭ-tă-naī'-mŭs, Ē-lī'-ă-sĭs, Băn'-nŭs, Ē-lī'-ă-lī, Sē'-măs, Sē-lē-mī'-ăs, Nă-thăn'-ĭ-ăs: and of the sons of Ŏ-zō'-ră; Sē'-sĭs, Ĕs'-rĭl, Ā-zā'-ē-lŭs, Să-mā'-tŭs, Zăm'-bĭs, Jŏ-sē'-phŭs.

35 And of the sons of Ĕth'-mă; Măz-ĭ-tī'-ăs, Zăb-ă-daī'-ăs, Ē'-dēs, Jū'-ĕl, Băn-ă-ī'-ăs.

36 All these had taken strange wives, and they put them away with their children.

37 And the priests and Levites, and they that were of Israel, dwelt in Jerusalem, and in the country, in the first day of the seventh month: so the children of Israel were in their habitations.

38 And the whole multitude came together with one accord into the broad place of the holy porch toward the east:

39 And they spake unto Esdras the priest and reader, that he would bring the law of Moses, that was given of the Lord God of Israel.

40 So Esdras the chief priest brought the law unto the whole multitude from man to woman, and to all the priests, to hear the law in the first day of the seventh month.

41 And he read in the broad court before the holy porch from morning unto midday, before both men and women;

and all the multitude gave heed unto the law.

42 And Esdras the priest and reader of the law stood up upon a pulpit of wood, which was made *for that purpose.*

43 And there stood up by him Măt-tă-thī'-ăs, Săm'-mŭs, Ăn-ă-nī'-ăs, Ăz-ă-rī'-ăs, Ū-rī'-ăs, Ĕz-ĕ-cī'-ăs, Băl-ă-sā'-mŭs, upon the right hand;

44 And upon his left hand stood Phăl-dai'-ŭs, Mī'-să-ĕl, Mĕl-chī'-ăs, Lŏth-ă-sū'-bŭs, and Năb-ă-rī'-ăs.

45 Then took Esdras the book of the law before the multitude: for he sat honourably in the first place in the sight of them all.

46 And when he opened the law, they stood all straight up. So Esdras blessed the Lord God most High, the God of hosts, Almighty.

47 And all the people answered, Amen; and lifting up their hands they fell to the ground, and worshipped the Lord.

48 Also Jesus, Ā'-nŭs, Săr-ă-bī'-ăs, Ă-dī'-nŭs, Jă-cū'-bŭs, Săb-ă-tē'-ăs, Āu-tē'-ăs, Măi-ăn'-ĕ-ăs, and Că-lī'-tăs, Ăz-ă-rī'-ăs, and Jŏ-ă-zăb'-dŭs, and Ăn-ă-nī'-ăs, Bī-ăt'-ăs, the Levites, taught the law of the Lord, making them withal to understand it.

49 Then spake Ăt-thă-rā'-tēs unto Esdras the chief priest and reader, and to the Levites that taught the multitude, even to all, saying,

50 This day is holy unto the Lord; (for they all wept when they heard the law:)

51 Go then, and eat the fat, and drink the sweet, and send part to them that have nothing;

52 For this day is holy unto the Lord: and be not sorrowful; for the Lord will bring you to honour.

53 So the Levites published all things to the people, saying, This day is holy to the Lord; be not sorrowful.

54 Then went they their way, every one to eat and drink, and make merry, and to give part to them that had nothing, and to make great cheer;

55 Because they understood the words wherein they were instructed, and for the which they had been assembled.

II ESDRAS

CHAPTER I

THE second book of the prophet Esdras, the son of Să-răi'-ăs, the son of Ăz-ă-rī'-ăs, the son of Hĕl-chī'-ăs, the son of Săd-ă-mī'-ăs, the son of Sā'-dŏc, the son of Ăch'-ĭ-tŏb,

2 The son of Ă-chī'-ăs, the son of Phīn'-ĕ-ĕs, the son of Hē'-lī, the son of Ăm-ă-rī'-ăs, the son of Ă-zī'-ĕ-ī, the son of Mā'-rī-mŏth, the son of Ăr'-nă, the son of Ŏ-zī'-ăs, the son of Bō'-rĭth, the son of Ăb-ĭ-sē'-ī, the son of Phīn'-ĕ-ĕs, the son of Ĕl-ĕ-ă'-zăr,

3 The son of Aaron, of the tribe of Levi; which was captive in the land of the Medes, in the reign of Ăr-tăx-ērx'-ĕs king of the Persians.

4 And the word of the Lord came unto me, saying,

5 Go thy way, and shew my people their sinful deeds, and their children their wickedness which they have done against me; that they may tell their children's children:

6 Because the sins of their fathers are increased in them: for they have forgotten me, and have offered unto strange gods.

7 Am not I even he that brought them out of the land of Egypt, from the house of bondage? but they have provoked me unto wrath, and despised my counsels.

8 Pull thou off then the hair of thy head, and cast all evil upon them, for they have not been obedient unto my law, but it is a rebellious people.

9 How long shall I forbear them, unto whom I have done so much good?

10 Many kings have I destroyed for their sakes; Phā'-rāōh with his servants and all his power have I smitten down.

11 All the nations have I destroyed before them, and in the east I have scattered the people of two provinces, even of Tyrus and Sidon, and have slain all their enemies.

12 Speak thou therefore unto them, saying, Thus saith the Lord,

13 I led you through the sea, and in the beginning gave you a large and safe passage; I gave you Moses for a leader, and Aaron for a priest.

14 I gave you light in a pillar of fire, and great wonders have I done among you; yet have ye forgotten me, saith the Lord.

15 Thus saith the Almighty Lord, The quails were as a token to you; I gave you tents for your safeguard: nevertheless ye murmured there,

16 And triumphed not in my name for the destruction of your enemies, but ever to this day do ye yet murmur.

17 Where are the benefits that I have done for you? when ye were hungry and thirsty in the wilderness, did ye not cry unto me,

18 Saying, Why hast thou brought us into this wilderness to kill us? it had been better for us to have served the Egyptians, than to die in this wilderness.

19 Then had I pity upon your mournings, and gave you manna to eat; so ye did eat angels' bread.

20 When ye were thirsty, did I not cleave the rock, and waters flowed out to your fill? for the heat I covered you with the leaves of the trees.

21 I divided among you a fruitful land, I cast out the Canaanites, the Phĕr'-ĕ-zītes, and the Phī-lĭs'-tīnes, before you: what shall I yet do more for you? saith the Lord.

22 Thus saith the Almighty Lord, When ye were in the wilderness, in the river of the Ām'-ō-rītes, being athirst, and blaspheming my name,

23 I gave you not fire for your blasphemies, but cast a tree in the water, and made the river sweet.

24 What shall I do unto thee, O Jacob? thou, Juda, wouldest not obey me: I will turn me to other nations, and unto those will I give my name, that they may keep my statutes.

25 Seeing ye have forsaken me, I will forsake you also;

when ye desire me to be gracious unto you, I shall have no mercy upon you.

26 Whensoever ye shall call upon me, I will not hear you: for ye have defiled your hands with blood, and your feet are swift to commit manslaughter.

27 Ye have not as it were forsaken me, but your own selves, saith the Lord.

28 Thus saith the Almighty Lord, Have I not prayed you as a father his sons, as a mother her daughters, and a nurse her young babes,

29 That ye would be my people, and I should be your God; that ye would be my children, and I should be your father?

30 I gathered you together, as a hen gathereth her chickens under her wings: but now, what shall I do unto you? I will cast you out from my face.

31 When ye offer unto me, I will turn my face from you: for your solemn feast days, your new moons, and your circumcisions, have I forsaken.

32 I sent unto you my servants the prophets, whom ye have taken and slain, and torn their bodies in pieces, whose blood I will require of your hands, saith the Lord.

33 Thus saith the Almighty Lord, Your house is desolate, I will cast you out as the wind doth stubble.

34 And your children shall not be fruitful; for they have despised my commandment, and done the thing that is evil before me.

35 Your houses will I give to a people that shall come; which not having heard of me yet shall believe me: to whom I have shewed no signs, yet they shall do that I have commanded them.

36 They have seen no prophets, yet they shall call their sins to remembrance, and acknowledge them.

37 I take to witness the grace of the people to come, whose little ones rejoice in gladness: and though they have not seen me with bodily eyes, yet in spirit they believe the thing that I say.

38 And now, brother, behold what glory; and see the people that come from the east:

39 Unto whom I will give for leaders, Abraham, Isaac, and Jacob, Ŏ-sē'-ăs, Amos, and Mĭ'-chē-ăs, Joel, Ăb-dī'-ăs, and Jonas,

40 Nahum, and Ă-băc'-ŭc, Sŏ-phŏ-nī'-ăs, Ăg-gē'-ŭs, Zachary, and Măl'-ă-chȳ, which is called also an angel of the Lord.

CHAPTER II

THUS saith the Lord, I brought this people out of bondage, and I gave them my commandments by my servants the prophets; whom they would not hear, but despised my counsels.

2 The mother that bare them saith unto them, Go your way, ye children; for I am a widow and forsaken.

3 I brought you up with gladness; but with sorrow and heaviness have I lost you: for ye have sinned before the Lord your God, and done that thing that is evil before him.

4 But what shall I now do unto you? I am a widow and forsaken: go your way, O my children, and ask mercy of the Lord.

5 As for me, O father, I call

29

upon thee for a witness over the mother of these children, which would not keep my covenant,

6 That thou bring them to confusion, and their mother to a spoil, that there may be no offspring of them.

7 Let them be scattered abroad among the heathen, let their names be put out of the earth: for they have despised my covenant.

8 Woe be unto thee, Ăs'-sûr, thou that hidest the unrighteous in thee! O thou wicked people, remember what I did unto Sodom and Gŏ-môr'-rhä;

9 Whose land lieth in clods of pitch and heaps of ashes: even so also will I do unto them that hear me not, saith the Almighty Lord.

10 Thus saith the Lord unto Esdras, Tell my people that I will give them the kingdom of Jerusalem, which I would have given unto Israel.

11 Their glory also will I take unto me, and give these the everlasting tabernacles, which I had prepared for them.

12 They shall have the tree of life for an ointment of sweet savour; they shall neither labour, nor be weary.

13 Go, and ye shall receive: pray for few days unto you, that they may be shortened: the kingdom is already prepared for you: watch.

14 Take heaven and earth to witness; for I have broken the evil in pieces, and created the good: for I live, saith the Lord.

15 Mother, embrace thy children, and bring them up with gladness, make their feet as fast as a pillar: for I have chosen thee, saith the Lord.

16 And those that be dead

will I raise up again from their places, and bring them out of the graves: for I have known my name in Israel.

17 Fear not, thou mother of the children: for I have chosen thee, saith the Lord.

18 For thy help will I send my servants Ē'-say and Jeremy, after whose counsel I have sanctified and prepared for thee twelve trees laden with divers fruits,

19 And as many fountains flowing with milk and honey, and seven mighty mountains, whereupon there grow roses and lilies, whereby I will fill thy children with joy.

20 Do right to the widow, judge for the fatherless, give to the poor, defend the orphan, clothe the naked,

21 Heal the broken and the weak, laugh not a lame man to scorn, defend the maimed, and let the blind man come into the sight of my clearness.

22 Keep the old and young within thy walls.

23 Wheresoever thou findest the dead, take them and bury them, and I will give thee the first place in my resurrection.

24 Abide still, O my people, and take thy rest, for thy quietness shall come.

25 Nourish thy children, O thou good nurse; stablish their feet.

26 As for the servants whom I have given thee, there shall not one of them perish; for I will require them from among thy number.

27 Be not weary: for when the day of trouble and heaviness cometh, others shall weep and be sorrowful, but thou shalt be merry and have abundance.

28 The heathen shall envy

thee, but they shall be able to do nothing against thee, saith the Lord.

29 My hands shall cover thee, so that thy children shall not see hell.

30 Be joyful, O thou mother, with thy children; for I will deliver thee, saith the Lord.

31 Remember thy children that sleep, for I shall bring them out of the sides of the earth, and shew mercy unto them: for I am merciful, saith the Lord Almighty.

32 Embrace thy children until I come and shew mercy unto them: for my wells run over, and my grace shall not fail.

33 I Esdras received a charge of the Lord upon the mount Ō'-rĕb, that I should go unto Israel; but when I came unto them, they set me at nought, and despised the commandment of the Lord.

34 And therefore I say unto you, O ye heathen, that hear and understand, look for your Shepherd, he shall give you everlasting rest; for he is nigh at hand, that shall come in the end of the world.

35 Be ready to the reward of the kingdom, for the everlasting light shall shine upon you for evermore.

36 Flee the shadow of this world, receive the joyfulness of your glory: I testify my Saviour openly.

37 O receive the gift that is given you, and be glad, giving thanks unto him that hath called you to the heavenly kingdom.

38 Arise up and stand, behold the number of those that be sealed in the feast of the Lord;

39 Which are departed from the shadow of the world, and have received glorious garments of the Lord.

40 Take thy number, O Sion, and shut up those of thine that are clothed in white, which have fulfilled the law of the Lord.

41 The number of thy children, whom thou longedst for, is fulfilled: beseech the power of the Lord, that thy people, which have been called from the beginning, may be hallowed.

42 I Esdras saw upon the mount Sion a great people, whom I could not number, and they all praised the Lord with songs.

43 And in the midst of them there was a young man of a high stature, taller than all the rest, and upon every one of their heads he set crowns, and was more exalted; which I marvelled at greatly.

44 So I asked the angel, and said, Sir, what are these?

45 He answered and said unto me, These be they that have put off the mortal clothing, and put on the immortal, and have confessed the name of God: now are they crowned, and receive palms.

46 Then said I unto the angel, What young person is it that crowneth them, and giveth them palms in their hands?

47 So he answered and said unto me, It is the Son of God, whom they have confessed in the world. Then began I greatly to commend them that stood so stiffly for the name of the Lord.

48 Then the angel said unto me, Go thy way, and tell my people what manner of things, and how great wonders of the Lord thy God, thou hast seen.

CHAPTER III

IN the thirtieth year after the ruin of the city I was in Babylon, and lay troubled upon my bed, and my thoughts came up over my heart:

2 For I saw the desolation of Sion, and the wealth of them that dwelt at Babylon.

3 And my spirit was sore moved, so that I began to speak words full of fear to the most High, and said,

4 O Lord, who bearest rule, thou spakest at the beginning, when thou didst plant the earth, and that thyself alone, and commandedst the people,

5 And gavest a body unto Adam without soul, which was the workmanship of thine hands, and didst breathe into him the breath of life, and he was made living before thee.

6 And thou leddest him into paradise, which thy right hand had planted, before ever the earth came forward.

7 And unto him thou gavest commandment to love thy way: which he transgressed, and immediately thou appointedst death in him and in his generations, of whom came nations, tribes, people, and kindreds, out of number.

8 And every people walked after their own will, and did wonderful things before thee, and despised thy commandments.

9 And again in process of time thou broughtest the flood upon those that dwelt in the world, and destroyedst them.

10 And it came to pass in every of them, that as death was to Adam, so was the flood to these.

11 Nevertheless one of them thou leftest, namely, Noah with his household, of whom came all righteous men.

12 And it happened, that when they that dwelt upon the earth began to multiply, and had gotten them many children, and were a great people, they began again to be more ungodly than the first.

13 Now when they lived so wickedly before thee, thou didst choose thee a man from among them, whose name was Abraham.

14 Him thou lovedst, and unto him only thou shewedst thy will:

15 And madest an everlasting covenant with him, promising him that thou wouldest never forsake his seed.

16 And unto him thou gavest Isaac, and unto Isaac also thou gavest Jacob and Esau. As for Jacob, thou didst choose him to thee, and put by Esau: and so Jacob became a great multitude.

17 And it came to pass, that when thou leddest his seed out of Egypt, thou broughtest them up to the mount Sī-nāi.

18 And bowing the heavens, thou didst set fast the earth, movedst the whole world, and madest the depths to tremble, and troubledst the men of that age.

19 And thy glory went through four gates, of fire, and of earthquake, and of wind, and of cold, that thou mightest give the law unto the seed of Jacob, and diligence unto the generation of Israel.

20 And yet tookest thou not away from them a wicked heart, that thy law might bring forth fruit in them.

21 For the first Adam bearing

a wicked heart transgressed, and was overcome; and so be all they that are born of him.

22 Thus infirmity was made permanent; and the law (also) in the heart of the people with the malignity of the root; so that the good departed away, and the evil abode still.

23 So the times passed away, and the years were brought to an end: then didst thou raise thee up a servant, called David:

24 Whom thou commandedst to build a city unto thy name, and to offer incense and oblations unto thee therein.

25 When this was done many years, then they that inhabited the city forsook thee,

26 And in all things did even as Adam and all his generations had done: for they also had a wicked heart:

27 And so thou gavest thy city over into the hands of thine enemies.

28 Are their deeds then any better that inhabit Babylon, that they should therefore have the dominion over Sion?

29 For when I came thither, and had seen impieties without number, then my soul saw many evildoers in this thirtieth year, so that my heart failed me.

30 For I have seen how thou sufferest them sinning, and hast spared wicked doers: and hast destroyed thy people, and hast preserved thine enemies, and hast not signified it.

31 I do not remember how this way may be left: Are they then of Babylon better than they of Sion?

32 Or is there any other people that knoweth thee be-side Israel? or what generation hath so believed thy covenants as Jacob?

33 And yet their reward appeareth not, and their labour hath no fruit: for I have gone here and there through the heathen, and I see that they flow in wealth, and think not upon thy commandments.

34 Weigh thou therefore our wickedness now in the balance, and theirs also that dwell in the world; and so shall thy name nowhere be found but in Israel.

35 Or when was it that they which dwell upon the earth have not sinned in thy sight? or what people have so kept thy commandments?

36 Thou shalt find that Israel by name hath kept thy precepts; but not the heathen.

CHAPTER IV

AND the angel that was sent unto me, whose name was Ū'-rĭ-ĕl, gave me an answer,

2 And said, Thy heart hath gone too far in this world, and thinkest thou to comprehend the way of the most High?

3 Then said I, Yea, my lord. And he answered me, and said, I am sent to shew thee three ways, and to set forth three similitudes before thee:

4 Whereof if thou canst declare me one, I will shew thee also the way that thou desirest to see, and I shall shew thee from whence the wicked heart cometh.

5 And I said, Tell on, my lord. Then said he unto me, Go thy way, weigh me the weight of the fire, or measure me the blast of the wind, or call me again the day that is past.

6 Then answered I and said,

B

33

What man is able to do that, that thou shouldest ask such things of me?

7 And he said unto me, If I should ask thee how great dwellings are in the midst of the sea, or how many springs are in the beginning of the deep, or how many springs are above the firmament, or which are the outgoings of paradise:

8 Peradventure thou wouldest say unto me, I never went down into the deep, nor as yet into hell, neither did I ever climb up into heaven.

9 Nevertheless now have I asked thee but only of the fire and wind, and of the day wherethrough thou hast passed, and of things from which thou canst not be separated, and yet canst thou give me no answer of them.

10 He said moreover unto me, Thine own things, and such as are grown up with thee, canst thou not know;

11 How should thy vessel then be able to comprehend the way of the Highest, and, the world being now outwardly corrupted, to understand the corruption that is evident in my sight?

12 Then said I unto him, It were better that we were not at all, than that we should live still in wickedness, and to suffer, and not to know wherefore.

13 He answered me, and said, I went into a forest into a plain, and the trees took counsel,

14 And said, Come, let us go and make war against the sea, that it may depart away before us, and that we may make us more woods.

15 The floods of the sea also in like manner took counsel, and said, Come, let us go up and subdue the woods of the plain, that there also we may make us another country.

16 The thought of the wood was in vain, for the fire came and consumed it.

17 The thought of the floods of the sea came likewise to nought, for the sand stood up and stopped them.

18 If thou wert judge now betwixt these two, whom wouldest thou begin to justify? or whom wouldest thou condemn?

19 I answered and said, Verily it is a foolish thought that they both have devised, for the ground is given unto the wood, and the sea also hath his place to bear his floods.

20 Then answered he me, and said, Thou hast given a right judgment, but why judgest thou not thyself also?

21 For like as the ground is given unto the wood, and the sea to his floods: even so they that dwell upon the earth may understand nothing but that which is upon the earth: and he that dwelleth above the heavens may only understand the things that are above the height of the heavens.

22 Then answered I and said, I beseech thee, O Lord, let me have understanding:

23 For it was not my mind to be curious of the high things, but of such as pass by us daily, namely, wherefore Israel is given up as a reproach to the heathen, and for what cause the people whom thou hast loved is given over unto ungodly nations, and why the law of our forefathers is brought to nought, and the written covenants come to none effect,

34

24 And we pass away out of the world as grasshoppers, and our life is astonishment and fear, and we are not worthy to obtain mercy.

25 What will he then do unto his name whereby we are called? of these things have I asked.

26 Then answered he me, and said, The more thou searchest, the more thou shalt marvel; for the world hasteth fast to pass away,

27 And cannot comprehend the things that are promised to the righteous in time to come: for this world is full of unrighteousness and infirmities.

28 But as concerning the things whereof thou askest me, I will tell thee; for the evil is sown, but the destruction thereof is not yet come.

29 If therefore that which is sown be not turned upside down, and if the place where the evil is sown pass not away, then cannot it come that is sown with good.

30 For the grain of evil seed hath been sown in the heart of Adam from the beginning, and how much ungodliness hath it brought up unto this time? and how much shall it yet bring forth until the time of threshing come?

31 Ponder now by thyself, how great fruit of wickedness the grain of evil seed hath brought forth.

32 And when the ears shall be cut down, which are without number, how great a floor shall they fill?

33 Then I answered and said, How, and when shall these things come to pass? wherefore are our years few and evil?

34 And he answered me, saying, Do not thou hasten above the most Highest: for thy haste is in vain to be above him, for thou hast much exceeded.

35 Did not the souls also of the righteous ask question of these things in their chambers, saying, How long shall I hope on this fashion? when cometh the fruit of the floor of our reward?

36 And unto these things U-ri-el the archangel gave them answer, and said, Even when the number of seeds is filled in you: for he hath weighed the world in the balance.

37 By measure hath he measured the times, and by number hath he numbered the times; and he doth not move nor stir them, until the said measure be fulfilled.

38 Then answered I and said, O Lord that bearest rule, even we all are full of impiety.

39 And for our sakes peradventure it is that the floors of the righteous are not filled, because of the sins of them that dwell upon the earth.

40 So he answered me, and said, Go thy way to a woman with child, and ask of her when she hath fulfilled her nine months, if her womb may keep the birth any longer within her.

41 Then said I, No, Lord, that can she not. And he said unto me, In the grave the chambers of souls are like the womb of a woman:

42 For like as a woman that travaileth maketh haste to escape the necessity of the travail: even so do these places haste to deliver those things that are committed unto them.

43 From the beginning, look,

35

what thou desirest to see, it shall be shewed thee.

44 Then answered I and said, If I have found favour in thy sight, and if it be possible, and if I be meet therefore,

45 Shew me then whether there be more to come than is past, or more past than is to come.

46 What is past I know, but what is for to come I know not.

47 And he said unto me, Stand up upon the right side, and I shall expound the similitude unto thee.

48 So I stood, and saw, and, behold, an hot burning oven passed by before me: and it happened, that when the flame was gone by I looked, and, behold, the smoke remained still.

49 After this there passed by before me a watery cloud, and sent down much rain with a storm; and when the stormy rain was past, the drops remained still.

50 Then said he unto me, Consider with thyself; as the rain is more than the drops, and as the fire is greater than the smoke; but the drops and the smoke remain behind: so the quantity which is past did more exceed.

51 Then I prayed, and said, May I live, thinkest thou, until that time? or what shall happen in those days?

52 He answered me, and said, As for the tokens whereof thou askest me, I may tell thee of them in part: but as touching thy life, I am not sent to shew thee; for I do not know it.

CHAPTER V

NEVERTHELESS as concerning the tokens, behold,

the days shall come, that they which dwell upon earth shall be taken in a great number, and the way of truth shall be hidden, and the land shall be barren of faith.

2 But iniquity shall be increased above that which now thou seest, or that thou hast heard long ago.

3 And the land, that thou seest now to have root, shalt thou see wasted suddenly.

4 But if the most High grant thee to live, thou shalt see after the third trumpet that the sun shall suddenly shine again in the night, and the moon thrice in the day:

5 And blood shall drop out of wood, and the stone shall give his voice, and the people shall be troubled:

6 And even he shall rule, whom they look not for that dwell upon the earth, and the fowls shall take their flight away together:

7 And the Sodomitish sea shall cast out fish, and make a noise in the night, which many have not known: but they shall all hear the voice thereof.

8 There shall be a confusion also in many places, and the fire shall be oft sent out again, and the wild beasts shall change their places, and menstruous women shall bring forth monsters:

9 And salt waters shall be found in the sweet, and all friends shall destroy one another; then shall wit hide itself, and understanding withdraw itself into his secret chamber,

10 And shall be sought of many, and yet not be found: then shall unrighteousness and incontinency be multiplied upon earth.

11 One land also shall ask another, and say, Is righteousness that maketh a man righteous gone through thee? And it shall say, No.

12 At the same time shall men hope, but nothing obtain: they shall labour, but their ways shall not prosper.

13 To shew thee such tokens I have leave; and if thou wilt pray again, and weep as now, and fast seven days, thou shalt hear yet greater things.

14 Then I awaked, and an extreme fearfulness went through all my body, and my mind was troubled, so that it fainted.

15 So the angel that was come to talk with me held me, comforted me, and set me up upon my feet.

16 And in the second night it came to pass, that Să-lā'-thĭ-ĕl the captain of the people came unto me, saying, Where hast thou been? and why is thy countenance so heavy?

17 Knowest thou not that Israel is committed unto thee in the land of their captivity?

18 Up then, and eat bread, and forsake us not, as the shepherd that leaveth his flock in the hands of cruel wolves.

19 Then said I unto him, Go thy ways from me, and come not nigh me. And he heard what I said, and went from me.

20 And so I fasted seven days, mourning and weeping, like as Ū'-rĭ-ĕl the angel commanded me.

21 And after seven days so it was, that the thoughts of my heart were very grievous unto me again,

22 And my soul recovered the spirit of understanding, and I began to talk with the most High again,

23 And said, O Lord that bearest rule, of every wood of the earth, and of all the trees thereof, thou hast chosen thee one only vine:

24 And of all lands of the whole world thou hast chosen thee one pit: and of all the flowers thereof one lily:

25 And of all the depths of the sea thou hast filled thee one river: and of all builded cities thou hast hallowed Sion unto thyself:

26 And of all the fowls that are created thou hast named thee one dove: and of all the cattle that are made thou hast provided thee one sheep:

27 And among all the multitudes of people thou hast gotten thee one people: and unto this people, whom thou lovedst, thou gavest a law that is approved of all.

28 And now, O Lord, why hast thou given this one people over unto many? and upon the one root hast thou prepared others, and why hast thou scattered thy only one people among many?

29 And they which did gainsay thy promises, and believed not thy covenants, have trodden them down.

30 If thou didst so much hate thy people, yet shouldest thou punish them with thine own hands.

31 Now when I had spoken these words, the angel that came to me the night afore was sent unto me,

32 And said unto me, Hear me, and I will instruct thee; hearken to the thing that I say, and I shall tell thee more.

33 And I said, Speak on, my Lord. Then said he unto me, Thou art sore troubled in mind

for Israel's sake: lovest thou that people better than he that made them?

34 And I said, No, Lord: but of very grief have I spoken: for my reins pain me every hour, while I labour to comprehend the way of the most High, and to seek out part of his judgment.

35 And he said unto me, Thou canst not. And I said, Wherefore, Lord? whereunto was I born then? or why was not my mother's womb then my grave, that I might not have seen the travail of Jacob, and the wearisome toil of the stock of Israel?

36 And he said unto me, Number me the things that are not yet come, gather me together the drops that are scattered abroad, make me the flowers green again that are withered,

37 Open me the places that are closed, and bring me forth the winds that in them are shut up, shew me the image of a voice: and then I will declare to thee the thing that thou labourest to know.

38 And I said, O Lord that bearest rule, who may know these things, but he that hath not his dwelling with men?

39 As for me, I am unwise: how may I then speak of these things whereof thou askest me?

40 Then said he unto me, Like as thou canst do none of these things that I have spoken of, even so canst thou not find out my judgment, or in the end the love that I have promised unto my people.

41 And I said, Behold, O Lord, yet art thou nigh unto them that be reserved till the end: and what shall they do

38

that have been before me, or we that be now, or they that shall come after us?

42 And he said unto me, I will liken my judgment unto a ring; like as there is no slackness of the last, even so there is no swiftness of the first.

43 So I answered and said, Couldest thou not make those that have been made, and be now, and that are for to come, at once; that thou mightest shew thy judgment the sooner?

44 Then answered he me, and said, The creature may not haste above the maker; neither may the world hold them at once that shall be created therein.

45 And I said, As thou hast said unto thy servant, that thou, which givest life to all, hast given life at once to the creature that thou hast created, and the creature bare it: even so it might now also bear them that now be present at once.

46 And he said unto me, Ask the womb of a woman, and say unto her, If thou bringest forth children, why dost thou it not together, but one after another? pray her therefore to bring forth ten children at once.

47 And I said, She cannot: but must do it by distance of time.

48 Then said he unto me, Even so have I given the womb of the earth to those that be sown in it in their times.

49 For like as a young child may not bring forth the things that belong to the aged, even so have I disposed the world which I created.

50 And I asked, and said, Seeing thou hast now given me the way, I will *proceed to* speak

before thee: for our mother, of whom thou hast told me that she is young, draweth now nigh unto age.

51 He answered me, and said, Ask a woman that beareth children, and she shall tell thee.

52 Say unto her, Wherefore are not they whom thou hast now brought forth like those that were before, but less of stature?

53 And she shall answer thee, They that be born in the strength of youth are of one fashion, and they that are born in the time of age, when the womb faileth, are otherwise.

54 Consider thou therefore also, how that ye are less of stature than those that were before you.

55 And so are they that come after you less than ye, as the creatures which now begin to be old, and have passed over the strength of youth.

56 Then said I, Lord, I beseech thee, if I have found favour in thy sight, shew thy servant by whom thou visitest thy creature.

CHAPTER VI

AND he said unto me, In the beginning, when the earth was made, before the borders of the world stood, or ever the winds blew,

2 Before it thundered and lightened, or ever the foundations of paradise were laid,

3 Before the fair flowers were seen, or ever the moveable powers were established, before the innumerable multitude of angels were gathered together,

4 Or ever the heights of the air were lifted up, before the measures of the firmament were named, or ever the chimneys in Sion were hot,

5 And ere the present years were sought out, and or ever the inventions of them that now sin were turned, before they were sealed that have gathered faith for a treasure:

6 Then did I consider these things, and they all were made through me alone, and through none other: by me also they shall be ended, and by none other.

7 Then answered I and said, What shall be the parting asunder of the times? or when shall be the end of the first, and the beginning of it that followeth?

8 And he said unto me, From Abraham unto Isaac, when Jacob and Esau were born of him, Jacob's hand held first the heel of Esau.

9 For Esau is the end of the world, and Jacob is the beginning of it that followeth.

10 The hand of man is betwixt the heel and the hand: other question, Esdras, ask thou not.

11 I answered then and said, O Lord that bearest rule, if I have found favour in thy sight,

12 I beseech thee, shew thy servant the end of thy tokens, whereof thou shewedst me part the last night.

13 So he answered and said unto me, Stand up upon thy feet, and hear a mighty sounding voice.

14 And it shall be as it were a great motion; but the place where thou standest shall not be moved.

15 And therefore when it speaketh be not afraid: for the word is of the end, and the

foundation of the earth is understood.

16 And why? because the speech of these things trembleth and is moved: for it knoweth that the end of these things must be changed.

17 And it happened, that when I had heard it I stood up upon my feet, and hearkened, and, behold, there was a voice that spake, and the sound of it was like the sound of many waters.

18 And it said, Behold, the days come, that I will begin to draw nigh, and to visit them that dwell upon the earth,

19 And will begin to make inquisition of them, what they be that have hurt unjustly with their unrighteousness, and when the affliction of Sion shall be fulfilled;

20 And when the world, that shall begin to vanish away, shall be finished, then will I shew these tokens: the books shall be opened before the firmament, and they shall see all together:

21 And the children of a year old shall speak with their voices, the women with child shall bring forth untimely children of three or four months old, and they shall live, and be raised up.

22 And suddenly shall the sown places appear unsown, the full storehouses shall suddenly be found empty:

23 And the trumpet shall give a sound, which when every man heareth, they shall be suddenly afraid.

24 At that time shall friends fight one against another like enemies, and the earth shall stand in fear with those that dwell therein, the springs of the fountains shall stand still, and in three hours they shall not run.

25 Whosoever remaineth from all these that I have told thee shall escape, and see my salvation, and the end of your world.

26 And the men that are received shall see it, who have not tasted death from their birth: and the heart of the inhabitants shall be changed, and turned into another meaning.

27 For evil shall be put out, and deceit shall be quenched.

28 As for faith, it shall flourish, corruption shall be overcome, and the truth, which hath been so long without fruit, shall be declared.

29 And when he talked with me, behold, I looked by little and little upon him before whom I stood.

30 And these words said he unto me; I am come to shew thee the time of the night to come.

31 If thou wilt pray yet more, and fast seven days again, I shall tell thee greater things by day than I have heard.

32 For thy voice is heard before the most High: for the Mighty hath seen thy righteous dealing, he hath seen also thy chastity, which thou hast had ever since thy youth.

33 And therefore hath he sent me to shew thee all these things, and to say unto thee, Be of good comfort, and fear not.

34 And hasten not with the times that are past, to think vain things, that thou mayest not hasten from the latter times.

35 And it came to pass after this, that I wept again, and fasted seven days in like manner, that I might fulfil the three weeks which he told me.

36 And in the eighth night was my heart vexed within me again, and I began to speak before the most High.

37 For my spirit was greatly set on fire, and my soul was in distress.

38 And I said, O Lord, thou spakest from the beginning of the creation, even the first day, and saidst thus; Let heaven and earth be made; and thy word was a perfect work.

39 And then was the spirit, and darkness and silence were on every side; the sound of man's voice was not yet formed.

40 Then commandedst thou a fair light to come forth of thy treasures, that thy work might appear.

41 Upon the second day thou madest the spirit of the firmament, and commandedst it to part asunder, and to make a division betwixt the waters, that the one part might go up, and the other remain beneath.

42 Upon the third day thou didst command that the waters should be gathered in the seventh part of the earth: six parts hast thou dried up, and kept them, to the intent that of these some being planted of God and tilled might serve thee.

43 For as soon as thy word went forth the work was made.

44 For immediately there was great and innumerable fruit, and many and divers pleasures for the taste, and flowers of unchangeable colour, and odours of wonderful smell: and this was done the third day.

45 Upon the fourth day thou commandedst that the sun should shine, and the moon give her light, and the stars should be in order:

46 And gavest them a charge to do service unto man, that was to be made.

47 Upon the fifth day thou saidst unto the seventh part, where the waters were gathered, that it should bring forth living creatures, fowls and fishes: and so it came to pass.

48 For the dumb water and without life brought forth living things at the commandment of God, that all people might praise thy wondrous works.

49 Then didst thou ordain two living creatures, the one thou calledst Enoch, and the other Lĕ-vī'-ă-thăn;

50 And didst separate the one from the other: for the seventh part, namely, where the water was gathered together, might not hold them both.

51 Unto Enoch thou gavest one part, which was dried up the third day, that he should dwell in the same part, wherein are a thousand hills:

52 But unto Lĕ-vī'-ă-thăn thou gavest the seventh part, namely, the moist; and hast kept him to be devoured of whom thou wilt, and when.

53 Upon the sixth day thou gavest commandment unto the earth, that before thee it should bring forth beasts, cattle, and creeping things:

54 And after these, Adam also, whom thou madest lord of all thy creatures: of him come we all, and the people also whom thou hast chosen.

41

55 All this have I spoken before thee, O Lord, because thou madest the world for our sakes.

56 As for the other people, which also come of Adam, thou hast said that they are nothing, but be like unto spittle: and hast likened the abundance of them unto a drop that falleth from a vessel.

57 And now, O Lord, behold, these heathen, which have ever been reputed as nothing, have begun to be lords over us, and to devour us.

58 But we thy people, whom thou hast called thy firstborn, thy only begotten, and thy fervent lover, are given into their hands.

59 If the world now be made for our sakes, why do we not possess an inheritance with the world? how long shall this endure?

CHAPTER VII

AND when I had made an end of speaking these words, there was sent unto me the angel which had been sent unto me the nights afore:

2 And he said unto me, Up, Esdras, and hear the words that I am come to tell thee.

3 And I said, Speak on, my God. Then said he unto me, The sea is set in a wide place, that it might be deep and great.

4 But put the case the entrance were narrow, and like a river;

5 Who then could go into the sea to look upon it, and to rule it? if he went not through the narrow, how could he come into the broad?

6 There is also another thing; A city is builded, and set upon a broad field, and is full of all good things:

7 The entrance thereof is narrow, and is set in a dangerous place to fall, like as if there were a fire on the right hand, and on the left a deep water:

8 And one only path between them both, even between the fire and the water, *so small* that there could but one man go there at once.

9 If this city now were given unto a man for an inheritance, if he never shall pass the danger set before it, how shall he receive this inheritance?

10 And I said, It is so, Lord. Then said he unto me, Even so also is Israel's portion.

11 Because for their sakes I made the world: and when Adam transgressed my statutes, then was decreed that now is done.

12 Then were the entrances of this world made narrow, full of sorrow and travail: they are but few and evil, full of perils, and very painful.

13 For the entrances of the elder world were wide and sure, and brought immortal fruit.

14 If then they that live labour not to enter these strait and vain things, they can never receive those that are laid up for them.

15 Now therefore why disquietest thou thyself, seeing thou art but a corruptible man? and why art thou moved, whereas thou art but mortal?

16 Why hast thou not considered in thy mind this thing that is to come, rather than that which is present?

17 Then answered I and said, O Lord that bearest rule, thou hast ordained in thy law, that the righteous should inherit

42

these things, but that the ungodly should perish.

18 Nevertheless the righteous shall suffer strait things, and hope for wide: for they that have done wickedly have suffered the strait things, and yet shall not see the wide.

19 And he said unto me, There is no judge above God, and none that hath understanding above the Highest.

20 For there be many that perish in this life, because they despise the law of God that is set before them.

21 For God hath given strait commandment to such as came, what they should do to live, even as they came, and what they should observe to avoid punishment.

22 Nevertheless they were not obedient unto him; but spake against him, and imagined vain things;

23 And deceived themselves by their wicked deeds; and said of the most High, that he is not; and knew not his ways:

24 But his law have they despised, and denied his covenants: in his statutes have they not been faithful, and have not performed his works.

25 And therefore, Esdras, for the empty are empty things, and for the full are the full things.

26 Behold, the time shall come, that these tokens which I have told thee shall come to pass, and the bride shall appear, and she coming forth shall be seen, that now is withdrawn from the earth.

27 And whosoever is delivered from the foresaid evils shall see my wonders.

28 For my son Jesus shall be revealed with those that be

with him, and they that remain shall rejoice within four hundred years.

29 After these years shall my son Christ die, and all men that have life.

30 And the world shall be turned into the old silence seven days, like as in the former judgments: so that no man shall remain.

31 And after seven days the world, that yet awaketh not, shall be raised up, and that shall die that is corrupt.

32 And the earth shall restore those that are asleep in her, and so shall the dust those that dwell in silence, and the secret places shall deliver those souls that were committed unto them.

33 And the most High shall appear upon the seat of judgment, and misery shall pass away, and the long suffering shall have an end:

34 But judgment only shall remain, truth shall stand, and faith shall wax strong:

35 And the work shall follow, and the reward shall be shewed, and the good deeds shall be of force, and wicked deeds shall bear no rule:

36 Then said I, Abraham prayed first for the Sodomites, and Moses for the fathers that sinned in the wilderness:

37 And Jesus after him for Israel in the time of Ā'-chăn:

38 And Samuel and David for the destruction: and Solomon for them that should come to the sanctuary:

39 And Hĕ-lī'-ăs for those that received rain; and for the dead, that he might live:

40 And Ĕz-ĕ-chī'-ăs for the people in the time of Sĕn-năch'-ĕr-ĭb: and many for many.

41 Even so now, seeing corruption is grown up, and wickedness increased, and the righteous have prayed for the ungodly: wherefore shall it not be so now also?

42 He answered me, and said, This present life is not the end where much glory doth abide; therefore have they prayed for the weak.

43 But the day of doom shall be the end of this time, and the beginning of the immortality for to come, wherein corruption is past,

44 Intemperance is at an end, infidelity is cut off, righteousness is grown, and truth is sprung up.

45 Then shall no man be able to save him that is destroyed, nor to oppress him that hath gotten the victory.

46 I answered then and said, This is my first and last saying, that it had been better not to have given the earth unto Adam: or else, when it was given him, to have restrained him from sinning.

47 For what profit is it for men now in this present time to live in heaviness, and after death to look for punishment?

48 O thou Adam, what hast thou done? for though it was thou that sinned, thou art not fallen alone, but we all that come of thee.

49 For what profit is it unto us, if there be promised us an immortal time, whereas we have done the works that bring death?

50 And that there is promised us an everlasting hope, whereas ourselves being most wicked are made vain?

51 And that there are laid up for us dwellings of health and safety, whereas we have lived wickedly?

52 And that the glory of the most High is kept to defend them which have led a wary life, whereas we have walked in the most wicked ways of all?

53 And that there should be shewed a paradise, whose fruit endureth for ever, wherein is security and medicine, since we shall not enter into it?

54 (For we have walked in unpleasant places.)

55 And that the faces of them which have used abstinence shall shine above the stars, whereas our faces shall be blacker than darkness?

56 For while we lived and committed iniquity, we considered not that we should begin to suffer for it after death.

57 Then answered he me, and said, This is the condition of the battle, which man that is born upon the earth shall fight;

58 That, if he be overcome, he shall suffer as thou hast said: but if he get the victory, he shall receive the thing that I say.

59 For this is the life whereof Moses spake unto the people while he lived, saying, Choose thee life, that thou mayest live.

60 Nevertheless they believed not him, nor yet the prophets after him, no nor me which have spoken unto them,

61 That there should not be such heaviness in their destruction, as shall be joy over them that are persuaded to salvation.

62 I answered then, and said, I know, Lord, that the most High is called merciful, in that he hath mercy upon them which are not yet come into the world,

63 And upon those also that turn to his law;

64 And that he is patient, and long suffereth those that have sinned, as his creatures;

65 And that he is bountiful, for he is ready to give where it needeth;

66 And that he is of great mercy, for he multiplieth more and more mercies to them that are present, and that are past, and also to them which are to come.

67 For if he shall not multiply his mercies, the world would not continue with them that inherit therein.

68 And he pardoneth; for if he did not so of his goodness, that they which have committed iniquities might be eased of them, the ten thousandth part of men should not remain living.

69 And being judge, if he should not forgive them that are cured with his word, and put out the multitude of contentions,

70 There should be very few left peradventure in an innumerable multitude.

CHAPTER VIII

AND he answered me, saying, The most High hath made this world for many, but the world to come for few.

2 I will tell thee a similitude, Esdras; As when thou askest the earth, it shall say unto thee, that it giveth much mould whereof earthen vessels are made, but little dust that gold cometh of: even so is the course of this present world.

3 There be many created, but few shall be saved.

4 So answered I and said,

Swallow then down, O my soul, understanding, and devour wisdom.

5 For thou hast agreed to give ear, and art willing to prophesy: for thou hast no longer space than only to live.

6 O Lord, if thou suffer not thy servant, that we may pray before thee, and thou give us seed unto our heart, and culture to our understanding, that there may come fruit of it; how shall each man live that is corrupt, who beareth the place of a man?

7 For thou art alone, and we all one workmanship of thine hands, like as thou hast said.

8 For when the body is fashioned now in the mother's womb, and thou givest it members, thy creature is preserved in fire and water, and nine months doth thy workmanship endure thy creature which is created in her.

9 But that which keepeth and is kept shall both be preserved: and when the time cometh, the womb preserved delivereth up the things that grew in it.

10 For thou hast commanded out of the parts of the body, that is to say, out of the breasts, milk to be given, which is the fruit of the breasts,

11 That the thing which is fashioned may be nourished for a time, till thou disposest it to thy mercy.

12 Thou broughtest it up with thy righteousness, and nurturedst it in thy law, and reformedst it with thy judgment.

13 And thou shalt mortify it as thy creature, and quicken it as thy work.

14 If therefore thou shalt destroy him which with so great labour was fashioned, it is an

45

easy thing to be ordained by thy commandment, that the thing which was made might be preserved.

15 Now therefore, Lord, I will speak; touching man in general, thou knowest best; but touching thy people, for whose sake I am sorry;

16 And for thine inheritance, for whose cause I mourn; and for Israel, for whom I am heavy; and for Jacob, for whose sake I am troubled;

17 Therefore will I begin to pray before thee for myself and for them: for I see the falls of us that dwell in the land.

18 But I have heard the swiftness of the judge which is to come.

19 Therefore hear my voice, and understand my words, and I shall speak before thee. This is the beginning of the words of Esdras, before he was taken up: and I said,

20 O Lord, thou that dwellest in everlastingness, which beholdest from above things in the heaven and in the air;

21 Whose throne is inestimable; whose glory may not be comprehended; before whom the hosts of angels stand with trembling,

22 Whose service is conversant in wind and fire; whose word is true, and sayings constant; whose commandment is strong, and ordinance fearful;

23 Whose look drieth up the depths, and indignation maketh the mountains to melt away; which the truth witnesseth:

24 O hear the prayer of thy servant, and give ear to the petition of thy creature.

25 For while I live I will speak, and so long as I have understanding I will answer

26 O look not upon the sins of thy people; but on them which serve thee in truth.

27 Regard not the wicked inventions of the heathen, but the desire of those that keep thy testimonies in afflictions.

28 Think not upon those that have walked feignedly before thee: but remember them, which according to thy will have known thy fear.

29 Let it not be thy will to destroy them which have lived like beasts; but to look upon them that have clearly taught thy law.

30 Take thou no indignation at them which are deemed worse than beasts; but love them that alway put their trust in thy righteousness and glory.

31 For we and our fathers do languish of such diseases: but because of us sinners thou shalt be called merciful.

32 For if thou hast a desire to have mercy upon us, thou shalt be called merciful, to us namely, that have no works of righteousness.

33 For the just, which have many good works laid up with thee, shall out of their own deeds receive reward.

34 For what is man, that thou shouldest take displeasure at him? or what is a corruptible generation, that thou shouldest be so bitter toward it?

35 For in truth there is no man among them that be born, but he hath dealt wickedly; and among the faithful there is none which hath not done amiss.

36 For in this, O Lord, thy righteousness and thy goodness shall be declared, if thou

be merciful unto them which have not the confidence of good works.

37 Then answered he me, and said, Some things hast thou spoken aright, and according unto thy words it shall be.

38 For indeed I will not think on the disposition of them which have sinned before death, before judgment, before destruction:

39 But I will rejoice over the disposition of the righteous, and I will remember also their pilgrimage, and the salvation, and the reward, that they shall have.

40 Like as I have spoken now, so shall it come to pass.

41 For as the husbandman soweth much seed upon the ground, and planteth many trees, and yet the thing that is sown good in his season cometh not up, neither doth all that is planted take root: even so is it of them that are sown in the world; they shall not all be saved.

42 I answered then and said, If I have found grace, let me speak.

43 Like as the husbandman's seed perisheth, if it come not up, and receive not thy rain in due season; or if there come too much rain, and corrupt it:

44 Even so perisheth man also, which is formed with thy hands, and is called thine own image, because thou art like unto him, for whose sake thou hast made all things, and likened him unto the husbandman's seed.

45 Be not wroth with us, but spare thy people, and have mercy upon thine own inheritance: for thou art merciful unto thy creature.

46 Then answered he me, and said, Things present are for the present, and things to come for such as be to come.

47 For thou comest far short that thou shouldest be able to love my creature more than I: but I have ofttimes drawn nigh unto thee, and unto it, but never to the unrighteous.

48 In this also thou art marvellous before the most High:

49 In that thou hast humbled thyself, as it becometh thee, and hast not judged thyself worthy to be much glorified among the righteous.

50 For many great miseries shall be done to them that in the latter time shall dwell in the world, because they have walked in great pride.

51 But understand thou for thyself, and seek out the glory for such as be like thee.

52 For unto you is paradise opened, the tree of life is planted, the time to come is prepared, plenteousness is made ready, a city is builded, and rest is allowed, yea, perfect goodness and wisdom.

53 The root of evil is sealed up from you, weakness and the moth is hid from you, and corruption is fled into hell to be forgotten:

54 Sorrows are passed, and in the end is shewed the treasure of immortality.

55 And therefore ask thou no more questions concerning the multitude of them that perish.

56 For when they had taken liberty, they despised the most High, thought scorn of his law, and forsook his ways.

57 Moreover they have trodden down his righteous,

58 And said in their heart, that there is no God; yea, and

47

that knowing they must die.

59 For as the things aforesaid shall receive you, so thirst and pain are prepared for them: for it was not his will that men should come to nought:

60 But they which be created have defiled the name of him that made them, and were unthankful unto him which prepared life for them.

61 And therefore is my judgment now at hand.

62 These things have I not shewed unto all men, but unto thee, and a few like thee. Then answered I and said,

63 Behold, O Lord, now hast thou shewed me the multitude of the wonders, which thou wilt begin to do in the last times: but at what time, thou hast not shewed me.

CHAPTER IX

HE answered me then, and said, Measure thou the time diligently in itself: and when thou seest part of the signs past, which I have told thee before,

2 Then shalt thou understand, that it is the very same time, wherein the Highest will begin to visit the world which he made.

3 Therefore when there shall be seen earthquakes and uproars of the people in the world:

4 Then shalt thou well understand, that the most High spake of those things from the days that were before thee, even from the beginning.

5 For like as all that is made in the world hath a beginning and an end, and the end is manifest:

6 Even so the times also of the Highest have plain beginnings

in wonders and powerful works, and endings in effects and signs.

7 And every one that shall be saved, and shall be able to escape by his works, and by faith, whereby ye have believed,

8 Shall be preserved from the said perils, and shall see my salvation in my land, and within my borders: for I have sanctified them for me from the beginning.

9 Then shall they be in pitiful case, which now have abused my ways: and they that have cast them away despitefully shall dwell in torments.

10 For such as in their life have received benefits, and have not known me;

11 And they that have lothed my law, while they had yet liberty, and, when as yet place of repentance was open unto them, understood not, but despised it;

12 The same must know it after death by pain.

13 And therefore be thou not curious how the ungodly shall be punished, and when: but enquire how the righteous shall be saved, whose the world is, and for whom the world is created.

14 Then answered I and said,

15 I have said before, and now do speak, and will speak it also hereafter, that there be many more of them which perish, than of them which shall be saved:

16 Like as a wave is greater than a drop.

17 And he answered me, saying, Like as the field is, so is also the seed; as the flowers be, such are the colours also; such as the workman is, such also is

the work; and as the husbandman is himself, so is his husbandry also: for it was the time of the world.

18 And now when I prepared the world, which was not yet made, even for them to dwell in that now live, no man spake against me.

19 For then every one obeyed: but now the manners of them which are created in this world that is made are corrupted by a perpetual seed, and by a law which is unsearchable rid themselves.

20 So I considered the world, and, behold, there was peril because of the devices that were come into it.

21 And I saw, and spared it greatly, and have kept me a grape of the cluster, and a plant of a great people.

22 Let the multitude perish then, which was born in vain; and let my grape be kept, and my plant; for with great labour have I made it perfect.

23 Nevertheless, if thou wilt cease yet seven days more, (but thou shalt not fast in them,

24 But go into a field of flowers, where no house is builded, and eat only the flowers of the field; taste no flesh, drink no wine, but eat flowers only;)

25 And pray unto the Highest continually, then will I come and talk with thee.

26 So I went my way into the field which is called Ardath, like as he commanded me; and there I sat among the flowers, and did eat of the herbs of the field, and the meat of the same satisfied me.

27 After seven days I sat upon the grass, and my heart was vexed within me, like as before.

28 And I opened my mouth, and began to talk before the most High, and said,

29 O Lord, thou that shewest thyself unto us, thou wast shewed unto our fathers in the wilderness, in a place where no man treadeth, in a barren place, when they came out of Egypt.

30 And thou spakest, saying, Hear me, O Israel; and mark my words, thou seed of Jacob.

31 For, behold, I sow my law in you, and it shall bring fruit in you, and ye shall be honoured in it for ever.

32 But our fathers, which received the law, kept it not, and observed not thy ordinances: and though the fruit of thy law did not perish, neither could it, for it was thine;

33 Yet they that received it perished, because they kept not the thing that was sown in them.

34 And, lo, it is a custom, when the ground hath received seed, or the sea a ship, or any vessel meat or drink, that, that being perished wherein it was sown or cast into,

35 That thing also which was sown, or cast therein, or received, doth perish, and remaineth not with us: but with us it hath not happened so.

36 For we that have received the law perish by sin, and our heart also which received it.

37 Notwithstanding the law perisheth not, but remaineth in his force.

38 And when I spake these things in my heart, I looked back with mine eyes, and upon the right side I saw a woman, and, behold, she mourned and wept with a loud voice, and was much grieved in heart, and

her clothes were rent, and she had ashes upon her head.

39 Then let I my thoughts go that I was in, and turned me unto her,

40 And said unto her, Wherefore weepest thou? why art thou so grieved in thy mind?

41 And she said unto me, Sir, let me alone, that I may bewail myself, and add unto my sorrow, for I am sore vexed in my mind, and brought very low.

42 And I said unto her, What aileth thee? tell me.

43 She said unto me, I thy servant have been barren, and had no child, though I had an husband thirty years.

44 And those thirty years I did nothing else day and night, and every hour, but make my prayer to the Highest.

45 After thirty years God heard me thine handmaid, looked upon my misery, considered my trouble, and gave me a son: and I was very glad of him, so was my husband also, and all my neighbours: and we gave great honour unto the Almighty.

46 And I nourished him with great travail.

47 So when he grew up, and came to the time that he should have a wife, I made a feast.

CHAPTER X

AND it so came to pass, that when my son was entered into his wedding chamber, he fell down, and died.

2 Then we all overthrew the lights, and all my neighbours rose up to comfort me: so I took my rest unto the second day at night.

3 And it came to pass, when

they had all left off to comfort me, to the end I might be quiet; then rose I up by night, and fled, and came hither into this field, as thou seest.

4 And I do now purpose not to return into the city, but here to stay, and neither to eat nor drink, but continually to mourn and to fast until I die.

5 Then left I the meditations wherein I was, and spake to her in anger, saying,

6 Thou foolish woman above all other, seest thou not our mourning, and what happeneth unto us?

7 How that Sion our mother is full of all heaviness, and much humbled, mourning very sore?

8 And now, seeing we all mourn and are sad, for we are all in heaviness, art thou grieved for one son?

9 For ask the earth, and she shall tell thee, that it is she which ought to mourn for the fall of so many that grow upon her.

10 For out of her came all at the first, and out of her shall all others come, and, behold, they walk almost all into destruction, and a multitude of them is utterly rooted out.

11 Who then should make more mourning than she, that hath lost so great a multitude; and not thou, which art sorry but for one?

12 But if thou sayest unto me, My lamentation is not like the earth's, because I have lost the fruit of my womb, which I brought forth with pains, and bare with sorrows;

13 But the earth *not so*: for the multitude present in it according to the course of the earth is gone, as it came:

14 Then say I unto thee, Like as thou hast brought forth with labour; even so the earth also hath given her fruit, namely, man, ever since the beginning unto him that made her.

15 Now therefore keep thy sorrow to thyself, and bear with a good courage that which hath befallen thee.

16 For if thou shalt acknowledge the determination of God to be just, thou shalt both receive thy son in time, and shalt be commended among women.

17 Go thy way then into the city to thine husband.

18 And she said unto me, That will I not do: I will not go into the city, but here will I die.

19 So I proceeded to speak further unto her, and said,

20 Do not so, but be counselled by me: for how many are the adversities of Sion? be comforted in regard of the sorrow of Jerusalem.

21 For thou seest that our sanctuary is laid waste, our altar broken down, our temple destroyed;

22 Our psaltery is laid on the ground, our song is put to silence, our rejoicing is at an end, the light of our candlestick is put out, the ark of our covenant is spoiled, our holy things are defiled, and the name that is called upon us is almost profaned; our children are put to shame, our priests are burnt, our Levites are gone into captivity, our virgins are defiled, and our wives ravished; our righteous men carried away, our little ones destroyed, our young men are brought in bondage, and our strong men are become weak;

23 And, which is the greatest of all, the seal of Sion hath now lost her honour; for she is delivered into the hands of them that hate us.

24 And therefore shake off thy great heaviness, and put away the multitude of sorrows, that the Mighty may be merciful unto thee again, and the Highest shall give thee rest and ease from thy labour.

25 And it came to pass, while I was talking with her, behold, her face upon a sudden shined exceedingly, and her countenance glistered, so that I was afraid of her, and mused what it might be.

26 And, behold, suddenly she made a great cry very fearful: so that the earth shook at the noise of the woman.

27 And I looked, and, behold, the woman appeared unto me no more, but there was a city builded, and a large place shewed itself from the foundations: then was I afraid, and cried with a loud voice, and said,

28 Where is Ū'-rĭ-ĕl the angel, who came unto me at the first? for he hath caused me to fall into many trances, and mine end is turned into corruption, and my prayer to rebuke.

29 And as I was speaking these words, behold, he came unto me, and looked upon me.

30 And, lo, I lay as one that had been dead, and mine understanding was taken from me: and he took me by the right hand, and comforted me, and set me upon my feet, and said unto me,

31 What aileth thee? and why art thou so disquieted? and why is thine understanding

51

troubled, and the thoughts of thine heart?

32 And I said, Because thou hast forsaken me, and yet I did according to thy words, and I went into the field, and, lo, I have seen, and yet see, that I am not able to express.

33 And he said unto me, Stand up manfully, and I will advise thee.

34 Then said I, Speak on, my lord, in me; only forsake me not, lest I die frustrate of my hope.

35 For I have seen that I knew not, and hear that I do not know.

36 Or is my sense deceived, or my soul in a dream?

37 Now therefore I beseech thee that thou wilt shew thy servant of this vision.

38 He answered me then, and said, Hear me, and I shall inform thee, and tell thee wherefore thou art afraid: for the Highest will reveal many secret things unto thee.

39 He hath seen that thy way is right: for that thou sorrowest continually for thy people, and makest great lamentation for Sion.

40 This therefore is the meaning of the vision which thou lately sawest:

41 Thou sawest a woman mourning, and thou begannest to comfort her:

42 But now seest thou the likeness of the woman no more, but there appeared unto thee a city builded.

43 And whereas she told thee of the death of her son, this is the solution:

44 This woman, whom thou sawest, is Sion: and whereas she said unto thee, even she whom thou seest as a city builded,

45 Whereas, I say, she said unto thee, that she hath been thirty years barren: those are the thirty years wherein there was no offering made in her.

46 But after thirty years Solomon builded the city, and offered offerings: and then bare the barren a son.

47 And whereas she told thee that she nourished him with labour: that was the dwelling in Jerusalem.

48 But whereas she said unto thee, That my son coming into his marriage chamber happened to have a fall, and died: this was the destruction that came to Jerusalem.

49 And behold, thou sawest her likeness, and because she mourned for her son, thou begannest to comfort her: and of these things which have chanced, these are to be opened unto thee.

50 For now the most High seeth that thou art grieved unfeignedly, and sufferest from thy whole heart for her, so hath he shewed thee the brightness of her glory, and the comeliness of her beauty:

51 And therefore I bade thee remain in the field where no house was builded:

52 For I knew that the Highest would shew this unto thee.

53 Therefore I commanded thee to go into the field, where no foundation of any building was.

54 For in the place wherein the Highest beginneth to shew his city, there can no man's building be able to stand.

55 And therefore fear not, let not thine heart be affrighted, but go thy way in, and see the beauty and greatness of the

building, as much as thine eyes be able to see:

56 And then shalt thou hear as much as thine ears may comprehend.

57 For thou art blessed above many other, and art called with the Highest; and so are but few.

58 But to morrow at night thou shalt remain here;

59 And so shall the Highest shew thee visions of the high things, which the most High will do unto them that dwell upon earth in the last days. So I slept that night and another, like as he commanded me.

CHAPTER XI

THEN saw I a dream, and, behold, there came up from the sea an eagle, which had twelve feathered wings, and three heads.

2 And I saw, and, behold, she spread her wings over all the earth, and all the winds of the air blew on her, and were gathered together.

3 And I beheld, and out of her feathers there grew other contrary feathers; and they became little feathers and small.

4 But her heads were at rest: the head in the midst was greater than the other, yet rested it with the residue.

5 Moreover I beheld, and, lo, the eagle flew with her feathers, and reigned upon earth, and over them that dwelt therein.

6 And I saw that all things under heaven were subject unto her, and no man spake against her, no, not one creature upon earth.

7 And I beheld, and, lo, the eagle rose upon her talons, and spake to her feathers, saying,

8 Watch not all at once: sleep every one in his own place, and watch by course:

9 But let the heads be preserved for the last.

10 And I beheld, and, lo, the voice went not out of her heads, but from the midst of her body.

11 And I numbered her contrary feathers, and, behold, there were eight of them.

12 And I looked, and, behold, on the right side there arose one feather, and reigned over all the earth;

13 And so it was, that when it reigned, the end of it came, and the place thereof appeared no more: so the next following stood up, and reigned, and had a great time;

14 And it happened, that when it reigned, the end of it came also, like as the first, so that it appeared no more.

15 Then came there a voice unto it, and said,

16 Hear thou that hast borne rule over the earth so long: this I say unto thee, before thou beginnest to appear no more,

17 There shall none after thee attain unto thy time, neither unto the half thereof.

18 Then arose the third, and reigned as the other before, and appeared no more also.

19 So went it with all the residue one after another, as that every one reigned, and then appeared no more.

20 Then I beheld, and, lo, in process of time the feathers that followed stood up upon the right side, that they might rule also; and some of them ruled, but within a while they appeared no more:

21 For some of them were set up, but ruled not.

22 After this I looked, and, behold, the twelve feathers appeared no more, nor the two little feathers:

23 And there was no more upon the eagle's body, but three heads that rested, and six little wings.

24 Then saw I also that two little feathers divided themselves from the six, and remained under the head that was upon the right side: for the four continued in their place.

25 And I beheld, and, lo, the feathers that were under the wing thought to set up themselves, and to have the rule.

26 And I beheld, and, lo, there was one set up, but shortly it appeared no more.

27 And the second was sooner away than the first.

28 And I beheld, and, lo, the two that remained thought also in themselves to reign:

29 And when they so thought, behold, there awaked one of the heads that were at rest, namely, it that was in the midst; for that was greater than the two other heads.

30 And then I saw that the two other heads were joined with it.

31 And, behold, the head was turned with them that were with it, and did eat up the two feathers under the wing that would have reigned.

32 But this head put the whole earth in fear, and bare rule in it over all those that dwelt upon the earth with much oppression; and it had the governance of the world more than all the wings that had been.

33 And after this I beheld, and, lo, the head that was in the midst suddenly appeared no more, like as the wings.

34 But there remained the two heads, which also in like sort ruled upon the earth, and over those that dwelt therein.

35 And I beheld, and, lo, the head upon the right side devoured it that was upon the left side.

36 Then I heard a voice, which said unto me, Look before thee, and consider the thing that thou seest.

37 And I beheld, and lo as it were a roaring lion chased out of the wood: and I saw that he sent out a man's voice unto the eagle, and said,

38 Hear thou, I will talk with thee, and the Highest shall say unto thee,

39 Art not thou it that remainest of the four beasts, whom I made to reign in my world, that the end of their times might come through them?

40 And the fourth came, and overcame all the beasts that were past, and had power over the world with great fearfulness, and over the whole compass of the earth with much wicked oppression; and so long time dwelt he upon the earth with deceit.

41 For the earth hast thou not judged with truth.

42 For thou hast afflicted the meek, thou hast hurt the peaceable, thou hast loved liars, and destroyed the dwellings of them that brought forth fruit, and hast cast down the walls of such as did thee no harm.

43 Therefore is thy wrongful dealing come up unto the Highest, and thy pride unto the Mighty.

44 The Highest also hath looked upon the proud times, and, behold, they are ended, and his abominations are fulfilled.

45 And therefore appear no more, thou eagle, nor thy horrible wings, nor thy wicked feathers, nor thy malicious heads, nor thy hurtful claws, nor all thy vain body:

46 That all the earth may be refreshed, and may return, being delivered from thy violence, and that she may hope for the judgment and mercy of him that made her.

CHAPTER XII

AND it came to pass, whiles the lion spake these words unto the eagle, I saw,

2 And, behold, the head that remained and the four wings appeared no more, and the two went unto it, and set themselves up to reign, and their kingdom was small, and full of uproar.

3 And I saw, and, behold, they appeared no more, and the whole body of the eagle was burnt, so that the earth was in great fear: then awaked I out of the trouble and trance of my mind, and from great fear, and said unto my spirit,

4 Lo, this hast thou done unto me, in that thou searchest out the ways of the Highest.

5 Lo, yet am I weary in my mind, and very weak in my spirit; and little strength is there in me, for the great fear wherewith I was affrighted this night.

6 Therefore will I now beseech the Highest, that he will comfort me unto the end.

7 And I said, Lord that bearest rule, if I have found grace before thy sight, and if I am justified with thee before many others, and if my prayer indeed be come up before thy face;

8 Comfort me then, and shew me thy servant the interpretation and plain difference of this fearful vision, that thou mayest perfectly comfort my soul.

9 For thou hast judged me worthy to shew me the last times.

10 And he said unto me, This is the interpretation of the vision:

11 The eagle, whom thou sawest come up from the sea, is the kingdom which was seen in the vision of thy brother Daniel.

12 But it was not expounded unto him, therefore now I declare it unto thee.

13 Behold, the days will come, that there shall rise up a kingdom upon earth, and it shall be feared above all the kingdoms that were before it.

14 In the same shall twelve kings reign, one after another:

15 Whereof the second shall begin to reign, and shall have more time than any of the twelve.

16 And this do the twelve wings signify, which thou sawest.

17 As for the voice which thou heardest speak, and that thou sawest not to go out from the heads, but from the midst of the body thereof, this is the interpretation:

18 That after the time of that kingdom there shall arise great strivings, and it shall stand in peril of falling: nevertheless it shall not then fall, but shall be restored again to his beginning.

19 And whereas thou sawest

the eight small under feathers sticking to her wings, this is the interpretation:

20 That in him there shall arise eight kings, whose times shall be but small, and their years swift.

21 And two of them shall perish, the middle time approaching: four shall be kept until their end begin to approach: but two shall be kept unto the end.

22 And whereas thou sawest three heads resting, this is the interpretation:

23 In his last days shall the most High raise up three kingdoms, and renew many things therein, and they shall have the dominion of the earth,

24 And of those that dwell therein, with much oppression, above all those that were before them: therefore are they called the heads of the eagle.

25 For these are they that shall accomplish his wickedness, and that shall finish his last end.

26 And whereas thou sawest that the great head appeared no more, it signifieth that one of them shall die upon his bed, and yet with pain.

27 For the two that remain shall be slain with the sword.

28 For the sword of the one shall devour the other: but at the last shall he fall through the sword himself.

29 And whereas thou sawest two feathers under the wings passing over the head that is on the right side;

30 It signifieth that these are they, whom the Highest hath kept unto their end: this is the small kingdom and full of trouble, as thou sawest.

31 And the lion, whom thou sawest rising up out of the wood, and roaring, and speaking to the eagle, and rebuking her for her unrighteousness with all the words which thou hast heard;

32 This is the anointed, which the Highest hath kept for them and for their wickedness unto the end: he shall reprove them, and shall upbraid them with their cruelty.

33 For he shall set them before him alive in judgment, and shall rebuke them, and correct them.

34 For the rest of my people shall he deliver with mercy, those that have been preserved upon my borders, and he shall make them joyful until the coming of the day of judgment, whereof I have spoken unto thee from the beginning.

35 This is the dream that thou sawest, and these are the interpretations.

36 Thou only hast been meet to know this secret of the Highest.

37 Therefore write all these things that thou hast seen in a book, and hide them:

38 And teach them to the wise of the people, whose hearts thou knowest may comprehend and keep these secrets.

39 But wait thou here thyself yet seven days more, that it may be shewed thee, whatsoever it pleaseth the Highest to declare unto thee. And with that he went his way.

40 And it came to pass, when all the people saw that the seven days were past, and I not come again into the city, they gathered them all together, from the least unto the greatest, and came unto me, and said,

41 What have we offended thee? and what evil have we done against thee, that thou forsakest us, and sittest here in this place?

42 For of all the prophets thou only art left us, as a cluster of the vintage, and as a candle in a dark place, and as a haven or ship preserved from the tempest.

43 Are not the evils which are come to us sufficient?

44 If thou shalt forsake us, how much better had it been for us, if we also had been burned in the midst of Sion?

45 For we are not better than they that died there. And they wept with a loud voice. Then answered I them, and said,

46 Be of good comfort, O Israel; and be not heavy, thou house of Jacob:

47 For the Highest hath you in remembrance, and the Mighty hath not forgotten you in temptation.

48 As for me, I have not forsaken you, neither am I departed from you: but am come into this place, to pray for the desolation of Sion, and that I might seek mercy for the low estate of your sanctuary.

49 And now go your way home every man, and after these days will I come unto you.

50 So the people went their way into the city, like as I commanded them:

51 But I remained still in the field seven days, as the angel commanded me; and did eat only in those days of the flowers of the field, and had my meat of the herbs.

CHAPTER XIII

AND it came to pass after seven days, I dreamed a dream by night:

2 And, lo, there arose a wind from the sea, that it moved all the waves thereof.

3 And I beheld, and, lo, that man waxed strong with the thousands of heaven: and when he turned his countenance to look, all the things trembled that were seen under him.

4 And whensoever the voice went out of his mouth, all they burned that heard his voice, like as the earth faileth when it feeleth the fire.

5 And after this I beheld, and, lo, there was gathered together a multitude of men, out of number, from the four winds of the heaven, to subdue the man that came out of the sea.

6 But I beheld, and, lo, he had graved himself a great mountain, and flew up upon it.

7 But I would have seen the region or place whereout the hill was graven, and I could not.

8 And after this I beheld, and, lo, all they which were gathered together to subdue him were sore afraid, and yet durst fight.

9 And, lo, as he saw the violence of the multitude that came, he neither lifted up his hand, nor held sword, nor any instrument of war:

10 But only I saw that he sent out of his mouth as it had been a blast of fire, and out of his lips a flaming breath, and out of his tongue he cast out sparks and tempests.

11 And they were all mixed together; the blast of fire, the flaming breath, and the great

tempest; and fell with violence upon the multitude which was prepared to fight, and burned them up every one, so that upon a sudden of an innumerable multitude nothing was to be perceived, but only dust and smell of smoke: when I saw this I was afraid.

12 Afterward saw I the same man come down from the mountain, and call unto him another peaceable multitude.

13 And there came much people unto him, whereof some were glad, some were sorry, some of them were bound, and other some brought of them that were offered: then was I sick through great fear, and I awaked, and said,

14 Thou hast shewed thy servant these wonders from the beginning, and hast counted me worthy that thou shouldest receive my prayer:

15 Shew me now yet the interpretation of this dream.

16 For as I conceive in mine understanding, woe unto them that shall be left in those days! and much more woe unto them that are not left behind!

17 For they that were not left were in heaviness.

18 Now understand I the things that are laid up in the latter days, which shall happen unto them, and to those that are left behind.

19 Therefore are they come into great perils and many necessities, like as these dreams declare.

20 Yet is it easier for him that is in danger to come into these things, than to pass away as a cloud out of the world, and not to see the things that happen in the last days. And he answered unto me, and said,

21 The interpretation of the vision shall I shew thee, and I will open unto thee the thing that thou hast required.

22 Whereas thou hast spoken of them that are left behind, this is the interpretation:

23 He that shall endure the peril in that time hath kept himself: they that be fallen into danger are such as have works, and faith toward the Almighty.

24 Know this therefore, that they which be left behind are more blessed than they that be dead.

25 This is the meaning of the vision: Whereas thou sawest a man coming up from the midst of the sea:

26 The same is he whom God the Highest hath kept a great season, which by his own self shall deliver his creature: and he shall order them that are left behind.

27 And whereas thou sawest, that out of his mouth there came as a blast of wind, and fire, and storm;

28 And that he held neither sword, nor any instrument of war, but that the rushing in of him destroyed the whole multitude that came to subdue him; this is the interpretation:

29 Behold, the days come, when the most High will begin to deliver them that are upon the earth.

30 And he shall come to the astonishment of them that dwell on the earth.

31 And one shall undertake to fight against another, one city against another, one place against another, one people against another, and one realm against another.

32 And the time shall be when

these things shall come to pass, and the signs shall happen which I shewed thee before, and then shall my Son be declared, whom thou sawest as a man ascending.

33 And when all the people hear his voice, every man shall in their own land leave the battle they have one against another.

34 And an innumerable multitude shall be gathered together, as thou sawest them, willing to come, and to overcome him by fighting.

35 But he shall stand upon the top of the mount Sion.

36 And Sion shall come, and shall be shewed to all men, being prepared and builded, like as thou sawest the hill graven without hands.

37 And this my Son shall rebuke the wicked inventions of those nations, which for their wicked life are fallen into the tempest;

38 And shall lay before them their evil thoughts, and the torments wherewith they shall begin to be tormented, which are like unto a flame: and he shall destroy them without labour by the law which is like unto fire.

39 And whereas thou sawest that he gathered another peaceable multitude unto him;

40 Those are the ten tribes, which were carried away prisoners out of their own land in the time of Ŏ-sē′-ă the king, whom Săl-măn-ā′-sär the king of Assyria led away captive, and he carried them over the waters, and so came they into another land.

41 But they took this counsel among themselves, that they would leave the multitude of the heathen, and go forth into a further country, where never mankind dwelt,

42 That they might there keep their statutes, which they never kept in their own land.

43 And they entered into Eū-phrā′-tēs by the narrow passages of the river.

44 For the most High then shewed signs for them, and held still the flood, till they were passed over.

45 For through that country there was a great way to go, namely, of a year and a half: and the same region is called Är′-să-rĕth.

46 Then dwelt they there until the latter time; and now when they shall begin to come,

47 The Highest shall stay the springs of the stream again, that they may go through: therefore sawest thou the multitude with peace.

48 But those that be left behind of thy people are they that are found within my borders.

49 Now when he destroyeth the multitude of the nations that are gathered together, he shall defend his people that remain.

50 And then shall he shew them great wonders.

51 Then said I, O Lord that bearest rule, shew me this: Wherefore have I seen the man coming up from the midst of the sea?

52 And he said unto me, Like as thou canst neither seek out nor know the things that are in the deep of the sea: even so can no man upon earth see my Son, or those that be with him, but in the day time.

53 This is the interpretation

59

of the dream which thou sawest, and whereby thou only art here lightened.

54 For thou hast forsaken thine own way, and applied thy diligence unto my law, and sought it.

55 Thy life hast thou ordered in wisdom, and hast called understanding thy mother.

56 And therefore have I shewed thee the treasures of the Highest: after other three days I will speak other things unto thee, and declare unto thee mighty and wondrous things.

57 Then went I forth into the field, giving praise and thanks greatly unto the most High because of his wonders, which he did in time;

58 And because he governeth the same, and such things as fall in their seasons: and there I sat three days.

CHAPTER XIV

AND it came to pass upon the third day, I sat under an oak, and, behold, there came a voice out of a bush over against me, and said, Esdras, Esdras.

2 And I said, Here am I, Lord. And I stood up upon my feet.

3 Then said he unto me, In the bush I did manifestly reveal myself unto Moses, and talked with him, when my people served in Egypt:

4 And I sent him, and led my people out of Egypt, and brought him up to the mount of Sī-nâi, where I held him by me a long season,

5 And told him many wondrous things, and shewed him the secrets of the times, and

the end; and commanded him, saying,

6 These words shalt thou declare, and these shalt thou hide.

7 And now I say unto thee,

8 That thou lay up in thy heart the signs that I have shewed, and the dreams that thou hast seen, and the interpretations which thou hast heard:

9 For thou shalt be taken away from all, and from henceforth thou shalt remain with my Son, and with such as be like thee, until the times be ended.

10 For the world hath lost his youth, and the times begin to wax old.

11 For the world is divided into twelve parts, and the ten parts of it are gone already, and half of a tenth part:

12 And there remaineth that which is after the half of the tenth part.

13 Now therefore set thine house in order, and reprove thy people, comfort such of them as be in trouble, and now renounce corruption,

14 Let go from thee mortal thoughts, cast away the burdens of man, put off now the weak nature,

15 And set aside the thoughts that are most heavy unto thee, and haste thee to flee from these times.

16 For yet greater evils than those which thou hast seen happen shall be done hereafter.

17 For look how much the world shall be weaker through age, so much the more shall evils increase upon them that dwell therein.

18 For the truth is fled far away, and leasing is hard at

60

hand: for now hasteth the vision to come, which thou hast seen.

19 Then answered I before thee, and said,

20 Behold, Lord, I will go, as thou hast commanded me, and reprove the people which are present: but they that shall be born afterward, who shall admonish them? thus the world is set in darkness, and they that dwell therein are without light.

21 For thy law is burnt, therefore no man knoweth the things that are done of thee, or the works that shall begin.

22 But if I have found grace before thee, send the Holy Ghost into me, and I shall write all that hath been done in the world since the beginning, which were written in thy law, that men may find thy path, and that they which will live in the latter days may live.

23 And he answered me, saying, Go thy way, gather the people together, and say unto them, that they seek thee not for forty days.

24 But look thou prepare thee many box trees, and take with thee Sä-rē´-ä, Dăb´-rĭ-ä, Sĕl-ĕ-mĭ´-ä, Ē-cā´-nŭs, and Ā´-sĭ-ĕl, these five which are ready to write swiftly;

25 And come hither, and I shall light a candle of understanding in thine heart, which shall not be put out, till the things be performed which thou shalt begin to write.

26 And when thou hast done, some things shalt thou publish, and some things shalt thou shew secretly to the wise: to morrow this hour shalt thou begin to write.

27 Then went I forth, as he commanded, and gathered all the people together, and said,

28 Hear these words, O Israel.

29 Our fathers at the beginning were strangers in Egypt, from whence they were delivered:

30 And received the law of life, which they kept not, which ye also have transgressed after them.

31 Then was the land, even the land of Sion, parted among you by lot: but your fathers, and ye yourselves, have done unrighteousness, and have not kept the ways which the Highest commanded you.

32 And forasmuch as he is a righteous judge, he took from you in time the thing that he had given you.

33 And now are ye here, and your brethren among you.

34 Therefore if so be that ye will subdue your own understanding, and reform your hearts, ye shall be kept alive, and after death ye shall obtain mercy.

35 For after death shall the judgment come, when we shall live again: and then shall the names of the righteous be manifest, and the works of the ungodly shall be declared.

36 Let no man therefore come unto me now, nor seek after me these forty days.

37 So I took the five men, as he commanded me, and we went into the field, and remained there.

38 And the next day, behold, a voice called me, saying, Esdras, open thy mouth, and drink that I give thee to drink.

39 Then opened I my mouth, and, behold, he reached me a full cup, which was full as it were with water, but the colour of it was like fire.

40 And I took it, and drank: and when I had drunk of it, my heart uttered understanding, and wisdom grew in my breast, for my spirit strengthened my memory:

41 And my mouth was opened, and shut no more.

42 The Highest gave understanding unto the five men, and they wrote the wonderful visions of the night that were told, which they knew not: and they sat forty days, and they wrote in the day, and at night they ate bread.

43 As for me, I spake in the day, and I held not my tongue by night.

44 In forty days they wrote two hundred and four books.

45 And it came to pass, when the forty days were fulfilled, that the Highest spake, saying, The first that thou hast written publish openly, that the worthy and unworthy may read it:

46 But keep the seventy last, that thou mayest deliver them only to such as be wise among the people:

47 For in them is the spring of understanding, the fountain of wisdom, and the stream of knowledge.

48 And I did so.

CHAPTER XV

BEHOLD, speak thou in the ears of my people the words of prophecy, which I will put in thy mouth, saith the Lord:

2 And cause them to be written in paper: for they are faithful and true.

3 Fear not the imaginations against thee, let not the incredulity of them trouble thee, that speak against thee.

4 For all the unfaithful shall die in their unfaithfulness.

5 Behold, saith the Lord, I will bring plagues upon the world; the sword, famine, death, and destruction.

6 For wickedness hath exceedingly polluted the whole earth, and their hurtful works are fulfilled.

7 Therefore saith the Lord,

8 I will hold my tongue no more as touching their wickedness, which they profanely commit, neither will I suffer them in those things, in which they wickedly exercise themselves: behold, the innocent and righteous blood crieth unto me, and the souls of the just complain continually.

9 And therefore, saith the Lord, I will surely avenge them, and receive unto me all the innocent blood from among them.

10 Behold, my people is led as a flock to the slaughter: I will not suffer them now to dwell in the land of Egypt:

11 But I will bring them with a mighty hand and a stretched out arm, and smite Egypt with plagues, as before, and will destroy all the land thereof.

12 Egypt shall mourn, and the foundation of it shall be smitten with the plague and punishment that God shall bring upon it.

13 They that till the ground shall mourn: for their seeds shall fail through the blasting and hail, and with a fearful constellation.

14 Woe to the world and them that dwell therein!

15 For the sword and their destruction draweth nigh, and one people shall stand up to

62

fight against another, and swords in their hands.

16 For there is sedition among men, and invading one another; they shall not regard their kings nor princes, and the course of their actions shall stand in their power.

17 A man shall desire to go into a city, and shall not be able.

18 For because of their pride the cities shall be troubled, the houses shall be destroyed, and men shall be afraid.

19 A man shall have no pity upon his neighbour, but shall destroy their houses with the sword, and spoil their goods, because of the lack of bread, and for great tribulation.

20 Behold, saith God, I will call together all the kings of the earth to reverence me, which are from the rising of the sun, from the south, from the east, and Lĭb′-ă-nŭs; to turn themselves one against another, and repay the things that they have done to them.

21 Like as they do yet this day unto my chosen, so will I do also, and recompense in their bosom. Thus saith the Lord God;

22 My right hand shall not spare the sinners, and my sword shall not cease over them that shed innocent blood upon the earth.

23 The fire is gone forth from his wrath, and hath consumed the foundations of the earth, and the sinners, like the straw that is kindled.

24 Woe to them that sin, and keep not my commandments! saith the Lord.

25 I will not spare them: go your way, ye children, from the power, defile not my sanctuary.

26 For the Lord knoweth all them that sin against him, and therefore delivereth he them unto death and destruction.

27 For now are the plagues come upon the whole earth, and ye shall remain in them: for God shall not deliver you, because ye have sinned against him.

28 Behold an horrible vision, and the appearance thereof from the east:

29 Where the nations of the dragons of Arabia shall come out with many chariots, and the multitude of them shall be carried as the wind upon earth, that all they which hear them may fear and tremble.

30 Also the Carmanians raging in wrath shall go forth as the wild boars of the wood, and with great power shall they come, and join battle with them, and shall waste a portion of the land of the Assyrians.

31 And then shall the dragons have the upper hand, remembering their nature; and if they shall turn themselves, conspiring together in great power to persecute them,

32 Then these shall be troubled, and keep silence through their power, and shall flee.

33 And from the land of the Assyrians shall the enemy besiege them, and consume some of them, and in their host shall be fear and dread, and strife among their kings.

34 Behold clouds from the east and from the north unto the south, and they are very horrible to look upon, full of wrath and storm.

35 They shall smite one upon another and they shall smite

down a great multitude of stars upon the earth, even their own star; and blood shall be from the sword unto the belly,

36 And dung of men unto the camel's hough.

37 And there shall be great fearfulness and trembling upon earth: and they that see the wrath shall be afraid, and trembling shall come upon them.

38 And then shall there come great storms from the south, and from the north, and another part from the west.

39 And strong winds shall arise from the east, and shall open it; and the cloud which he raised up in wrath, and the star stirred to cause fear toward the east and west wind, shall be destroyed.

40 The great and mighty clouds shall be lifted up full of wrath, and the star, that they may make all the earth afraid, and them that dwell therein; and they shall pour out over every high and eminent place an horrible star,

41 Fire, and hail, and flying swords, and many waters, that all fields may be full, and all rivers, with the abundance of great waters.

42 And they shall break down the cities and walls, mountains and hills, trees of the wood, and grass of the meadows, and their corn.

43 And they shall go stedfastly unto Babylon, and make her afraid.

44 They shall come to her, and besiege her, the star and all wrath shall they pour out upon her: then shall the dust and smoke go up unto the heaven, and all they that be about her shall bewail her.

45 And they that remain under her shall do service unto them that have put her in fear.

46 And thou, Asia, that art partaker of the hope of Babylon, and art the glory of her person:

47 Woe be unto thee, thou wretch, because thou hast made thyself like unto her; and hast decked thy daughters in whoredom, that they might please and glory in thy lovers, which have alway desired to commit whoredom with thee!

48 Thou hast followed her that is hated in all her works and inventions: therefore saith God,

49 I will send plagues upon thee; widowhood, poverty, famine, sword, and pestilence, to waste thy houses with destruction and death.

50 And the glory of thy power shall be dried up as a flower, when the heat shall arise that is sent over thee.

51 Thou shalt be weakened as a poor woman with stripes, and as one chastised with wounds, so that the mighty and lovers shall not be able to receive thee.

52 Would I with jealousy have so proceeded against thee, saith the Lord,

53 If thou hadst not always slain my chosen, exalting the stroke of thine hands, and saying over their dead, when thou wast drunken,

54 Set forth the beauty of thy countenance?

55 The reward of thy whoredom shall be in thy bosom, therefore shalt thou receive recompence.

56 Like as thou hast done unto my chosen, saith the Lord, even so shall God do

unto thee, and shall deliver thee into mischief.

57 Thy children shall die of hunger, and thou shalt fall through the sword: thy cities shall be broken down, and all thine shall perish with the sword in the field.

58 They that be in the mountains shall die of hunger, and eat their own flesh, and drink their own blood, for very hunger of bread, and thirst of water.

59 Thou as unhappy shalt come through the sea, and receive plagues again.

60 And in the passage they shall rush on the idle city, and shall destroy some portion of thy land, and consume part of thy glory, and shall return to Babylon that was destroyed.

61 And thou shalt be cast down by them as stubble, and they shall be unto thee as fire;

62 And shall consume thee, and thy cities, thy land, and thy mountains; all thy woods and thy fruitful trees shall they burn up with fire.

63 Thy children shall they carry away captive, and, look, what thou hast, they shall spoil it, and mar the beauty of thy face.

CHAPTER XVI

WOE be unto thee, Babylon, and Asia! woe be unto thee, Egypt, and Syria!

2 Gird up yourselves with cloths of sack and hair, bewail your children, and be sorry; for your destruction is at hand.

3 A sword is sent upon you, and who may turn it back?

4 A fire is sent among you, and who may quench it?

5 Plagues are sent unto you, and what is he that may drive them away?

6 May any man drive away an hungry lion in the wood? or may any one quench the fire in stubble, when it hath begun to burn?

7 May one turn again the arrow that is shot of a strong archer?

8 The mighty Lord sendeth the plagues, and who is he that can drive them away?

9 A fire shall go forth from his wrath, and who is he that may quench it?

10 He shall cast lightnings, and who shall not fear? he shall thunder, and who shall not be afraid?

11 The Lord shall threaten, and who shall not be utterly beaten to powder at his presence?

12 The earth quaketh, and the foundations thereof; the sea ariseth up with waves from the deep, and the waves of it are troubled, and the fishes thereof also, before the Lord, and before the glory of his power:

13 For strong is his right hand that bendeth the bow, his arrows that he shooteth are sharp, and shall not miss, when they begin to be shot into the ends of the world.

14 Behold, the plagues are sent, and shall not return again, until they come upon the earth.

15 The fire is kindled, and shall not be put out, till it consume the foundation of the earth.

16 Like as an arrow which is shot of a mighty archer returneth not backward: even so the plagues that shall be sent upon earth shall not return again.

17 Woe is me! woe is me! who will deliver me in those days?

18 The beginning of sorrows and great mournings; the beginning of famine and great death; the beginning of wars, and the powers shall stand in fear; the beginning of evils! what shall I do when these evils shall come?

19 Behold, famine and plague, tribulation and anguish, are sent as scourges for amendment.

20 But for all these things they shall not turn from their wickedness, nor be alway mindful of the scourges.

21 Behold, victuals shall be so good cheap upon earth, that they shall think themselves to be in good case, and even then shall evils grow upon earth, sword, famine, and great confusion.

22 For many of them that dwell upon earth shall perish of famine; and the other, that escape the hunger, shall the sword destroy.

23 And the dead shall be cast out as dung, and there shall be no man to comfort them: for the earth shall be wasted, and the cities shall be cast down.

24 There shall be no man left to till the earth, and to sow it.

25 The trees shall give fruit, and who shall gather them?

26 The grapes shall ripen, and who shall tread them? for all places shall be desolate of men:

27 So that one man shall desire to see another, and to hear his voice.

28 For of a city there shall be ten left, and two of the field, which shall hide themselves in the thick groves, and in the clefts of the rocks.

29 As in an orchard of olives upon every tree there are left three or four olives;

30 Or as when a vineyard is gathered, there are left some clusters of them that diligently seek through the vineyard:

31 Even so in those days there shall be three or four left by them that search their houses with the sword.

32 And the earth shall be laid waste, and the fields thereof shall wax old, and her ways and all her paths shall grow full of thorns, because no man shall travel therethrough.

33 The virgins shall mourn, having no bridegrooms; the women shall mourn, having no husbands; their daughters shall mourn, having no helpers.

34 In the wars shall their bridegrooms be destroyed, and their husbands shall perish of famine.

35 Hear now these things, and understand them, ye servants of the Lord.

36 Behold the word of the Lord, receive it: believe not the gods of whom the Lord spake.

37 Behold, the plagues draw nigh, and are not slack.

38 As when a woman with child in the ninth month bringeth forth her son, within two or three hours of her birth great pains compass her womb, which pains, when the child cometh forth, they slack not a moment:

39 Even so shall not the plagues be slack to come upon the earth, and the world shall mourn, and sorrows shall come upon it on every side.

40 O my people, hear my word: make you ready to the battle, and in those evils be

even as pilgrims upon the earth.

41 He that selleth, let him be as he that fleeth away: and he that buyeth, as one that will lose:

42 He that occupieth merchandise, as he that hath no profit by it: and he that buildeth, as he that shall not dwell therein:

43 He that soweth, as if he should not reap: so also he that planteth the vineyard, as he that shall not gather the grapes:

44 They that marry, as they that shall get no children; and they that marry not, as the widowers.

45 And therefore they that labour labour in vain:

46 For strangers shall reap their fruits, and spoil their goods, overthrow their houses, and take their children captives, for in captivity and famine shall they get children.

47 And they that occupy their merchandise with robbery, the more they deck their cities, their houses, their possessions, and their own persons:

48 The more will I be angry with them for their sin, saith the Lord.

49 Like as a whore envieth a right honest and virtuous woman:

50 So shall righteousness hate iniquity, when she decketh herself, and shall accuse her to her face, when he cometh that shall defend him that diligently searcheth out every sin upon earth.

51 And therefore be ye not like thereunto, nor to the works thereof.

52 For yet a little, and iniquity shall be taken away out of the earth, and righteousness shall reign among you.

53 Let not the sinner say that he hath not sinned: for God shall burn coals of fire upon his head, which saith before the Lord God and his glory, I have not sinned.

54 Behold, the Lord knoweth all the works of men, their imaginations, their thoughts, and their hearts:

55 Which spake but the word, Let the earth be made; and it was made: Let the heaven be made; and it was created.

56 In his word were the stars made, and he knoweth the number of them.

57 He searcheth the deep, and the treasures thereof; he hath measured the sea, and what it containeth.

58 He hath shut the sea in the midst of the waters, and with his word hath he hanged the earth upon the waters.

59 He spreadeth out the heavens like a vault; upon the waters hath he founded it.

60 In the desert hath he made springs of water, and pools upon the tops of the mountains, that the floods might pour down from the high rocks to water the earth.

61 He made man, and put his heart in the midst of the body, and gave him breath, life, and understanding.

62 Yea, and the Spirit of Almighty God, which made all things, and searcheth out all hidden things in the secrets of the earth,

63 Surely he knoweth your inventions, and what ye think in your hearts, even them that sin, and would hide their sin.

64 Therefore hath the Lord exactly searched out all your

works, and he will put you all
to shame.

65 And when your sins are
brought forth, ye shall be
ashamed before men, and your
own sins shall be your accusers
in that day.

66 What will ye do? or how
will ye hide your sins before
God and his angels?

67 Behold, God himself is the
judge, fear him: leave off from
your sins, and forget your iniquities, to meddle no more
with them for ever: so shall
God lead you forth, and deliver
you from all trouble.

68 For, behold, the burning
wrath of a great multitude is
kindled over you, and they
shall take away certain of you,
and feed you, being idle, with
things offered unto idols.

69 And they that consent
unto them shall be had in derision and in reproach, and trodden under foot.

70 For there shall be in every
place, and in the next cities, a
great insurrection upon those
that fear the Lord.

71 They shall be like mad
men, sparing none, but still
spoiling and destroying those
that fear the Lord.

72 For they shall waste and
take away their goods, and
cast them out of their houses.

73 Then shall they be known,
who are my chosen; and they
shall be tried as the gold in the
fire.

74 Hear, O ye my beloved,
saith the Lord: behold, the
days of trouble are at hand,
but I will deliver you from the
same.

75 Be ye not afraid, neither
doubt; for God is your guide,

76 And the guide of them who
keep my commandments and
precepts, saith the Lord God:
let not your sins weigh you
down, and let not your iniquities lift up themselves.

77 Woe be unto them that are
bound with their sins, and
covered with their iniquities,
like as a field is covered over
with bushes, and the path
thereof covered with thorns,
that no man may travel
through!

78 It is left undressed, and is
cast into the fire to be consumed therewith.

TOBIT

CHAPTER 1

THE book of the words of
Tobit, son of Tŏ-bī'-ĕl, the
son of Ăn-ă-nī'-ĕl, the son of
Ă-dū'-ĕl, the son of Găb'-ă-ĕl,
of the seed of Ăs'-ă-ĕl, of the
tribe of Nĕph'-thă-lī;

2 Who in the time of Ĕn-ĕ-
mĕs'-sär king of the Assyrians
was led captive out of Thĭs'-bĕ,
which is at the right hand of
that city, which is called prop-
erly Nĕph'-thă-lī in Galilee
above Ā'-sĕr.

3 I Tobit have walked all the
days of my life in the way of
truth and justice, and I did
many almsdeeds to my brethren, and my nation, who came
with me to Nĭn'-ĕ-vĕ, into the
land of the Assyrians.

4 And when I was in mine own
country, in the land of Israel,

being but young, all the tribe of Něph'-thǎ-lī my father fell from the house of Jerusalem, which was chosen out of all the tribes of Israel, that all the tribes should sacrifice *there*, where the temple of the habitation of the most High was consecrated and built for all ages.

5 Now all the tribes which together revolted, and the house of my father Něph'-thǎ-lī, sacrificed unto the heifer Bā'-ǎl.

6 But I alone went often to Jerusalem at the feasts, as it was ordained unto all the people of Israel by an everlasting decree, having the first-fruits and tenths of increase, with that which was first shorn; and them gave I at the altar to the priests the children of Aaron.

7 The first tenth part of all increase I gave to the sons of Aaron, who ministered at Jerusalem: another tenth part I sold away, and went, and spent it every year at Jerusalem:

8 And the third I gave unto them to whom it was meet, as Děb'-ô-rǎ my father's mother had commanded me, because I was left an orphan by my father.

9 Furthermore, when I was come to the age of a man, I married Anna of mine own kindred, and of her I begat Tǒ-bī'-ǎs.

10 And when we were carried away captives to Nǐn'-ě-vě, all my brethren and those that were of my kindred did eat of the bread of the Gentiles.

11 But I kept myself from eating:

12 Because I remembered God with all my heart.

13 And the most High gave me grace and favour before Ěn-ě-měs'-sär, so that I was his purveyor.

14 And I went into Mē'-dī-ǎ, and left in trust with Gäb'-ǎ-ěl, the brother of Gā'-brī-ǎs, at Rā'-gēs a city of Media ten talents of silver.

15 Now when Ěn-ě-měs'-sär was dead, Sěn-nǎch'-ěr-ǐb his son reigned in his stead; whose estate was troubled, that I could not go into Mē'-dī-ǎ.

16 And in the time of Ěn-ě-měs'-sär I gave many alms to my brethren, and gave my bread to the hungry,

17 And my clothes to the naked: and if I saw any of my nation dead, or cast about the walls of Nǐn'-ě-vě, I buried him.

18 And if the king Sěn-nǎch'-ěr-ǐb had slain any, when he was come, and fled from Judea, I buried them privily; for in his wrath he killed many; but the bodies were not found, when they were sought for of the king.

19 And when one of the Ninevites went and complained of me to the king, that I buried them, and hid myself; understanding that I was sought for to be put to death, I withdrew myself for fear.

20 Then all my goods were forcibly taken away, neither was there any thing left me, beside my wife Anna and my son Tǒ-bī'-ǎs.

21 And there passed not five and fifty days, before two of his sons killed him, and they fled into the mountains of Ǎr'-ǎ-räth; and Sär-chěd'-ǒ-nǔs his son reigned in his stead; who appointed over his father's accounts, and over all his

affairs, Ā'-chī-ăch'-ă-rŭs my brother Ăn'-ă-ĕl's son.

22 And Ā'-chī-ăch'-ă-rŭs intreating for me, I returned to Nĭn'-ĕ-vĕ. Now Achiacharus was cupbearer, and keeper of the signet, and steward, and overseer of the accounts: and Sär-chĕd'-ŏ-nŭs appointed him next unto him: and he was my brother's son.

CHAPTER II

NOW when I was come home again, and my wife Anna was restored unto me, with my son Tŏ-bī'-ăs, in the feast of Pentecost, which is the holy feast of the seven weeks, there was a good dinner prepared me, in the which I sat down to eat.

2 And when I saw abundance of meat, I said to my son, Go and bring what poor man soever thou shalt find out of our brethren, who is mindful of the Lord; and, lo, I tarry for thee.

3 But he came again, and said, Father, one of our nation is strangled, and is cast out in the marketplace.

4 Then before I had tasted of any meat, I started up, and took him up into a room until the going down of the sun.

5 Then I returned, and washed myself, and ate my meat in heaviness,

6 Remembering that prophecy of Amos, as he said, Your feasts shall be turned into mourning, and all your mirth into lamentation.

7 Therefore I wept: and after the going down of the sun I went and made a grave, and buried him.

8 But my neighbours mocked me, and said, This man is not yet afraid to be put to death for this matter: who fled away; and yet, lo, he burieth the dead again.

9 The same night also I returned from the burial, and slept by the wall of my courtyard, being polluted, and my face was uncovered:

10 And I knew not that there were sparrows in the wall, and mine eyes being open, the sparrows muted warm dung into mine eyes, and a whiteness came in mine eyes; and I went to the physicians, but they helped me not: moreover Ā'-chī-ăch'-ă-rŭs did nourish me, until I went into Ĕl-ў̄-mā'-ĭs.

11 And my wife Anna did take women's works to do.

12 And when she had sent them home to the owners, they paid her wages, and gave her also besides a kid.

13 And when it was in my house, and began to cry, I said unto her, From whence is this kid? is it not stolen? render it to the owners; for it is not lawful to eat any thing that is stolen.

14 But she replied upon me, It was given for a gift more than the wages. Howbeit I did not believe her, but bade her render it to the owners: and I was abashed at her. But she replied upon me, Where are thine alms and thy righteous deeds? behold, thou and all thy works are known.

CHAPTER III

THEN I being grieved did weep, and in my sorrow prayed, saying,

2 O Lord, thou art just, and all thy works and all thy ways are mercy and truth, and thou

70

judgest truly and justly for ever.

3 Remember me, and look on me, punish me not for my sins and ignorances, and *the sins of* my fathers, who have sinned before thee:

4 For they obeyed not thy commandments: wherefore thou hast delivered us for a spoil, and unto captivity, and unto death, and for a proverb of reproach to all the nations among whom we are dispersed.

5 And now thy judgments are many and true: deal with me according to my sins and my fathers': because we have not kept thy commandments, neither have walked in truth before thee.

6 Now therefore deal with me as seemeth best unto thee, and command my spirit to be taken from me, that I may be dissolved, and become earth: for it is profitable for me to die rather than to live, because I have heard false reproaches, and have much sorrow: command therefore that I may now be delivered out of this distress, and go into the everlasting place: turn not thy face away from me.

7 It came to pass the same day, that in Ĕc-băt'-ă-nĕ a city of Mē'-dĭ-ă Sara the daughter of Rӑ-gū'-ĕl was also reproached by her father's maids;

8 Because that she had been married to seven husbands, whom Ӑs-mŏ-dē'-ŭs the evil spirit had killed, before they had lain with her. Dost thou not know, said they, that thou hast strangled thine husbands? thou hast had already seven husbands, neither wast thou named after any of them.

9 Wherefore dost thou beat us for them? if they be dead, go thy ways after them, let us never see of thee either son or daughter.

10 When she heard these things, she was very sorrowful, so that she thought to have strangled herself; and she said, I am the only daughter of my father, and if I do this, it shall be a reproach unto him, and I shall bring his old age with sorrow unto the grave.

11 Then she prayed toward the window, and said, Blessed art thou, O Lord my God, and thine holy and glorious name is blessed and honourable for ever: let all thy works praise thee for ever.

12 And now, O Lord, I set mine eyes and my face toward thee,

13 And say, Take me out of the earth, that I may hear no more the reproach.

14 Thou knowest, Lord, that I am pure from all sin with man,

15 And that I never polluted my name, nor the name of my father, in the land of my captivity: I am the only daughter of my father, neither hath he any child to be his heir, neither any near kinsman, nor any son of his alive, to whom I may keep myself for a wife: my seven husbands are already dead; and why should I live? but if it please not thee that I should die, command some regard to be had of me, and pity taken of me, that I hear no more reproach.

16 So the prayers of them both were heard before the majesty of the great God.

17 And Rӑph'-ă-ĕl was sent to heal them both, that is, to scale away the whiteness of Tobit's

71

eyes, and to give Sara the daughter of Rӑ-gū′-ĕl for a wife to Tŏ-bī′-ӑs the son of Tobit; and to bind Ӑs-mŏ-dē′-ŭs the evil spirit; because she belonged to Tobias by right of inheritance. The selfsame time came Tobit home, and entered into his house, and Sara the daughter of Raguel came down from her upper chamber.

CHAPTER IV

IN that day Tobit remembered the money which he had committed to Gӑb′-ӑ-ĕl in Rӑ′-gēs of Mē′-di-ӑ,

2 And said with himself, I have wished for death; wherefore do I not call for my son Tŏ-bī′-ӑs, that I may signify to him *of the money* before I die?

3 And when he had called him, he said, My son, when I am dead, bury me; and despise not thy mother, but honour her all the days of thy life, and do that which shall please her, and grieve her not.

4 Remember, my son, that she saw many dangers for thee, *when thou wast* in her womb; and when she is dead, bury her by me in one grave.

5 My son, be mindful of the Lord our God all thy days, and let not thy will be set to sin, or to transgress his commandments: do uprightly all thy life long, and follow not the ways of unrighteousness.

6 For if thou deal truly, thy doings shall prosperously succeed to thee, and to all them that live justly.

7 Give alms of thy substance; and when thou givest alms, let not thine eye be envious, neither turn thy face from any poor, and the face of God shall not be turned away from thee.

8 If thou hast abundance, give alms accordingly: if thou have but a little, be not afraid to give according to that little:

9 For thou layest up a good treasure for thyself against the day of necessity:

10 Because that alms do deliver from death, and suffereth not to come into darkness.

11 For alms is a good gift unto all that give it in the sight of the most High.

12 Beware of all whoredom, my son, and chiefly take a wife of the seed of thy fathers, and take not a strange woman to wife, which is not of thy father's tribe: for we are the children of the prophets, Nō′-ĕ, Abraham, Isaac, and Jacob: remember, my son, that our fathers from the beginning, even that they all married wives of their own kindred, and were blessed in their children, and their seed shall inherit the land.

13 Now therefore, my son, love thy brethren, and despise not in thy heart thy brethren, the sons and daughters of thy people, in *not* taking a wife of them: for in pride is destruction and much trouble, and in lewdness is decay and great want: for lewdness is the mother of famine.

14 Let not the wages of any man, which hath wrought for thee, tarry with thee, but give him it out of hand: for if thou serve God, he will also repay thee: be circumspect, my son, in all things thou doest, and be wise in all thy conversation.

15 Do that to no man which thou hatest: drink not wine to make thee drunken: neither

let drunkenness go with thee in thy journey.

16 Give of thy bread to the hungry, and of thy garments to them that are naked; and according to thine abundance give alms; and let not thine eye be envious, when thou givest alms.

17 Pour out thy bread on the burial of the just, but give nothing to the wicked.

18 Ask counsel of all that are wise, and despise not any counsel that is profitable.

19 Bless the Lord thy God alway, and desire of him that thy ways may be directed, and that all thy paths and counsels may prosper: for every nation hath not counsel; but the Lord himself giveth all good things, and he humbleth whom he will, as he will; now therefore, my son, remember my commandments, neither let them be put out of thy mind.

20 And now I signify this to thee, that I committed ten talents to Găb'-ă-ĕl the *son of* Gā'-brī-ăs at Rā'-gēs in Mē'-dĭ-ă.

21 And fear not, my son, that we are made poor: for thou hast much wealth, if thou fear God, and depart from all sin, and do that which is pleasing in his sight.

CHAPTER V

Tŏ-Bī'-ĂS then answered and said, Father, I will do all things which thou hast commanded me:

2 But how can I receive the money, seeing I know him not?

3 Then he gave him the handwriting, and said unto him, Seek thee a man which may go with thee, whiles I yet live, and I will give him wages: and go and receive the money.

4 Therefore when he went to seek a man, he found Răph'-ă-ĕl that was an angel.

5 But he knew not; and he said unto him, Canst thou go with me to Rā'-gēs? and knowest thou those places well?

6 To whom the angel said, I will go with thee, and I know the way well: for I have lodged with our brother Găb'-ă-ĕl.

7 Then Tŏ-bī'-ăs said unto him, Tarry for me, till I tell my father.

8 Then he said unto him, Go, and tarry not. So he went in and said to his father, Behold, I have found one which will go with me. Then he said, Call him unto me, that I may know of what tribe he is, and whether he be a trusty man to go with thee.

9 So he called him, and he came in, and they saluted one another.

10 Then Tobit said unto him, Brother, shew me of what tribe and family thou art.

11 To whom he said, Dost thou seek for a tribe or family, or an hired man to go with thy son? Then Tobit said unto him, I would know, brother, thy kindred and name.

12 Then he said, I am Ăz-ă-rī'-ăs, the son of Ăn-ă-nī'-ăs the great, and of thy brethren.

13 Then Tobit said, Thou art welcome, brother; be not now angry with me, because I have enquired to know thy tribe and thy family; for thou art my brother, of an honest and good stock: for I know Ăn-ă-nī'-ăs and Jŏn'-ă-thăs, sons of that great Să-măi'-ăs, as we went together to Jerusalem to worship, and offered the

firstborn, and the tenths of the fruits; and they were not seduced with the error of our brethren: my brother, thou art of a good stock.

14 But tell me, what wages shall I give thee? *wilt thou* a drachm a day, and things necessary, as to mine own son?

15 Yea, moreover, if ye return safe, I will add something to thy wages.

16 So they were well pleased. Then said he to Tŏ-bī′-ăs, Prepare thyself for the journey, and God send you a good journey. And when his son had prepared all things for the journey, his father said, Go thou with this man, and God, which dwelleth in heaven, prosper your journey, and the angel of God keep you company. So they went forth both, and the young man's dog with them.

17 But Anna his mother wept, and said to Tobit, Why hast thou sent away our son? is he not the staff of our hand, in going in and out before us?

18 Be not greedy to add money to money: but let it be as refuse in respect of our child.

19 For that which the Lord hath given us to live with doth suffice us.

20 Then said Tobit to her, Take no care, my sister; he shall return in safety, and thine eyes shall see him.

21 For the good angel will keep him company, and his journey shall be prosperous, and he shall return safe.

22 Then she made an end of weeping.

CHAPTER VI

AND as they went on their journey, they came in the evening to the river Tī′-grĭs, and they lodged there.

2 And when the young man went down to wash himself, a fish leaped out of the river, and would have devoured him.

3 Then the angel said unto him, Take the fish. And the young man laid hold of the fish, and drew it to land.

4 To whom the angel said, Open the fish, and take the heart and the liver and the gall, and put them up safely.

5 So the young man did as the angel commanded him; and when they had roasted the fish, they did eat it: then they both went on their way, till they drew near to Ĕc-băt′-ă-nĕ.

6 Then the young man said to the angel, Brother Ăz-ă-rī′-ăs, to what use is the heart and the liver and the gall of the fish?

7 And he said unto him, Touching the heart and the liver, if a devil or an evil spirit trouble any, we must make a smoke thereof before the man or the woman, and the party shall be no more vexed.

8 As for the gall, *it is good* to anoint a man that hath whiteness in his eyes, and he shall be healed.

9 And when they were come near to Rā′-gēs,

10 The angel said to the young man, Brother, to day we shall lodge with Ră-gū′-ĕl, who is thy cousin; he also hath one only daughter, named Sara; I will speak for her, that she may be given thee for a wife.

11 For to thee doth the right of her appertain, seeing thou only art of her kindred.

12 And the maid is fair and wise: now therefore hear me, and I will speak to her father;

74

and when we return from Rā́-gēs we will celebrate the marriage: for I know that Ră-gū́-ĕl cannot marry her to another according to the law of Moses, but he shall be guilty of death, because the right of inheritance doth rather appertain to thee than to any other.

13 Then the young man answered the angel, I have heard, brother Ăz-ă-rī́-ăs, that this maid hath been given to seven men, who all died in the marriage chamber.

14 And now I am the only son of my father, and I am afraid, lest, if I go in unto her, I die, as the other before: for a wicked spirit loveth her, which hurteth no body, but those which come unto her: wherefore I also fear lest I die, and bring my father's and my mother's life because of me to the grave with sorrow: for they have no other son to bury them.

15 Then the angel said unto him, Dost thou not remember the precepts which thy father gave thee, that thou shouldest marry a wife of thine own kindred? wherefore hear me, O my brother; for she shall be given thee to wife; and make thou no reckoning of the evil spirit; for this same night shall she be given thee in marriage.

16 And when thou shalt come into the marriage chamber, thou shalt take the ashes of perfume, and shalt lay upon them some of the heart and liver of the fish, and shalt make a smoke with it:

17 And the devil shall smell it, and flee away, and never come again any more: but when thou shalt come to her, rise up both of you, and pray to God which is merciful, who

will have pity on you, and save you: fear not, for she is appointed unto thee from the beginning; and thou shalt preserve her, and she shall go with thee. Moreover I suppose that she shall bear thee children. Now when Tŏ-bī́-ăs had heard these things, he loved her, and his heart was effectually joined to her.

CHAPTER VII

AND when they were come to Ĕc-băt́-ă-nĕ, they came to the house of Ră-gū́-ĕl, and Sara met them: and after they had saluted one another, she brought them into the house.

2 Then said Ră-gū́-ĕl to Edna his wife, How like is this young man to Tobit my cousin!

3 And Ră-gū́-ĕl asked them, From whence are ye, brethren? To whom they said, We are of the sons of Nĕph́-thă-lĭm, which are captives in Nĭń-ĕ-vĕ.

4 Then he said to them, Do ye know Tobit our kinsman? And they said, We know him. Then said he, Is he in good health?

5 And they said, He is both alive, and in good health: and Tŏ-bī́-ăs said, He is my father.

6 Then Ră-gū́-ĕl leaped up, and kissed him, and wept,

7 And blessed him, and said unto him, Thou art the son of an honest and good man. But when he had heard that Tobit was blind, he was sorrowful, and wept.

8 And likewise Edna his wife and Sara his daughter wept. Moreover they entertained them cheerfully; and after that they had killed a ram of the flock, they set store of meat on the table. Then said Tŏ-bī́-ăs to

Răph′-ă-ĕl, Brother Ăz-ă-rī′-ăs, speak of those things of which thou didst talk in the way, and let this business be dispatched.

9 So he communicated the matter with Ră-gū′-ĕl: and Raguel said to Tŏ-bī′-ăs, Eat and drink, and make merry:

10 For it is meet that thou shouldest marry my daughter: nevertheless I will declare unto thee the truth.

11 I have given my daughter in marriage to seven men, who died that night they came in unto her: nevertheless for the present be merry. But Tŏ-bī′-ăs said, I will eat nothing here, till we agree and swear one to another.

12 Ră-gū′-ĕl said, Then take her from henceforth according to the manner, for thou art her cousin, and she is thine, and the merciful God give you good success in all things.

13 Then he called his daughter Sara, and she came to her father, and he took her by the hand, and gave her to be wife to Tŏ-bī′-ăs, saying, Behold, take her after the law of Moses, and lead her away to thy father. And he blessed them;

14 And called Edna his wife, and took paper, and did write an instrument *of covenants*, and sealed it.

15 Then they began to eat.

16 After Ră-gū′-ĕl called his wife Edna, and said unto her, Sister, prepare another chamber, and bring her in thither.

17 Which when she had done as he had bidden her, she brought her thither: and she wept, and she received the tears of her daughter, and said unto her,

18 Be of good comfort, my daughter; the Lord of heaven and earth give thee joy for this thy sorrow: be of good comfort, my daughter.

CHAPTER VIII

AND when they had supped, they brought Tŏ-bī′-ăs in unto her.

2 And as he went, he remembered the words of Răph′-ă-ĕl, and took the ashes of the perfumes, and put the heart and the liver of the fish thereupon, and made a smoke *therewith*.

3 The which smell when the evil spirit had smelled, he fled into the utmost parts of Egypt, and the angel bound him.

4 And after that they were both shut in together, Tŏ-bī′-ăs rose out of the bed, and said, Sister, arise, and let us pray that God would have pity on us.

5 Then began Tŏ-bī′-ăs to say, Blessed art thou, O God of our fathers, and blessed *is* thy holy and glorious name for ever; let the heavens bless thee, and all thy creatures.

6 Thou madest Adam, and gavest him Eve his wife for an helper and stay: of them came mankind: thou hast said, It is not good that man should be alone; let us make unto him an aid like unto himself.

7 And now, O Lord, I take not this my sister for lust, but uprightly: *therefore* mercifully ordain that we may become aged together.

8 And she said with him, Amen.

9 So they slept both that night. And Ră-gū′-ĕl arose, and went and made a grave,

10 Saying, *I fear* lest he also be dead.

11 But when Ră-gū′-ĕl was come into his house,

12 He said unto his wife Edna, Send one of the maids, and let her see whether he be alive: if *he be* not, that we may bury him, and no man know it.

13 So the maid opened the door, and went in, and found them both asleep.

14 And came forth, and told them that he was alive.

15 Then Ră-gū'-ĕl praised God, and said, O God, thou art worthy to be praised with all pure and holy praise; therefore let thy saints praise thee with all thy creatures; and let all thine angels and thine elect praise thee for ever.

16 Thou art to be praised, for thou hast made me joyful; and that is not come to me which I suspected; but thou hast dealt with us according to thy great mercy.

17 Thou art to be praised, because thou hast had mercy of two that were the only begotten children of their fathers: grant them mercy, O Lord, and finish their life in health with joy and mercy.

18 Then Ră-gū'-ĕl bade his servants to fill the grave.

19 And he kept the wedding feast fourteen days.

20 For before the days of the marriage were finished, Ră-gū'-ĕl had said unto him by an oath, that he should not depart till the fourteen days of the marriage were expired;

21 And then he should take the half of his goods, and go in safety to his father; and should have the rest when I and my wife be dead.

CHAPTER IX

THEN Tŏ-bī'-ăs called Răph'-ă-ĕl, and said unto him,

2 Brother Ăz-ă-rī'-ăs, take with thee a servant, and two camels, and go to Ră'-gēs of Mē'-dĭ-ă to Găb'-ă-ĕl, and bring me the money, and bring him to the wedding.

3 For Ră-gū'-ĕl hath sworn that I shall not depart.

4 But my father counteth the days; and if I tarry long, he will be very sorry.

5 So Răph'-ă-ĕl went out, and lodged with Găb'-ă-ĕl, and gave him the handwriting: who brought forth bags which were sealed up, and gave them to him.

6 And early in the morning they went forth both together, and came to the wedding: and Tŏ-bī'-ăs blessed his wife.

CHAPTER X

NOW Tobit his father counted every day: and when the days of the journey were expired, and they came not,

2 Then Tobit said, Are they detained? or is Găb'-ă-ĕl dead, and there is no man to give him the money?

3 Therefore he was very sorry.

4 Then his wife said unto him, My son is dead, seeing he stayeth long; and she began to bewail him, and said,

5 *Now I care for nothing,* my son, *since I have let thee go,* the light of mine eyes.

6 To whom Tobit said, Hold thy peace, take no care, for he is safe.

7 But she said, Hold thy peace, and deceive me not; my son is dead. And she went out every day into the way which they went, and did eat no meat in the daytime, and ceased not whole nights to bewail her son Tŏ-bī'-ăs, until the fourteen

days of the wedding were expired, which Ră-gū'-ĕl had sworn that he should spend there. Then Tobias said to Raguel, Let me go, for my father and my mother look no more to see me.

8 But his father in law said unto him, Tarry with me, and I will send to thy father, and they shall declare unto him how things go with thee.

9 But Tŏ-bī'-ăs said, No; but let me go to my father.

10 Then Ră-gū'-ĕl arose, and gave him Sara his wife, and half his goods, servants, and cattle, and money:

11 And he blessed them, and sent them away, saying, The God of heaven give you a prosperous journey, my children.

12 And he said to his daughter, Honour thy father and thy mother in law, which are now thy parents, that I may hear good report of thee. And he kissed her. Edna also said to Tŏ-bī'-ăs, The Lord of heaven restore thee, my dear brother, and grant that I may see thy children of my daughter Sara before I die, that I may rejoice before the Lord: behold, I commit my daughter unto thee of special trust; wherefore do not entreat her evil.

CHAPTER XI

AFTER these things Tŏ-bī'-ăs went his way, praising God that he had given him a prosperous journey, and blessed Ră-gū'-ĕl and Edna his wife, and went on his way till they drew near unto Nĭn'-ĕ-vĕ.

2 Then Răph'-ă-ĕl said to Tŏ-bī'-ăs, Thou knowest, brother, how thou didst leave thy father:

3 Let us haste before thy wife, and prepare the house.

4 And take in thine hand the gall of the fish. So they went their way, and the dog went after them.

5 Now Anna sat looking about toward the way for her son.

6 And when she espied him coming, she said to his father, Behold, thy son cometh, and the man that went with him.

7 Then said Răph'-ă-ĕl, I know, Tŏ-bī'-ăs, that thy father will open his eyes.

8 Therefore anoint thou his eyes with the gall, and being pricked therewith, he shall rub, and the whiteness shall fall away, and he shall see thee.

9 Then Anna ran forth, and fell upon the neck of her son, and said unto him, Seeing I have seen thee, my son, from henceforth I am content to die. And they wept both.

10 Tobit also went forth toward the door, and stumbled: but his son ran unto him,

11 And took hold of his father: and he strake of the gall on his father's eyes, saying, Be of good hope, my father.

12 And when his eyes began to smart, he rubbed them;

13 And the whiteness pilled away from the corners of his eyes: and when he saw his son, he fell upon his neck.

14 And he wept, and said, Blessed art thou, O God, and blessed is thy name for ever; and blessed are all thine holy angels:

15 For thou hast scourged, and hast taken pity *on me:* for, behold, I see my son Tŏ-bī'-ăs. And his son went in rejoicing, and told his father the great things that had happened to him in Mē'-dĭ-ă.

16 Then Tobit went out to meet his daughter in law at the gate of Nĭn'-ĕ-vĕ, rejoicing, and praising God: and they which saw him go marvelled, because he had received his sight.

17 But Tobit gave thanks before them, because God had mercy on him. And when he came near to Sara his daughter in law, he blessed her, saying, Thou art welcome, daughter: God be blessed, which hath brought thee unto us, and *blessed be* thy father and thy mother. And there was joy among all his brethren which were at Nĭn'-ĕ-vĕ.

18 And Ā'-chi-ăch'-ă-rŭs, and Năs'-băs his brother's son, came:

19 And Tŏ-bī'-ăs' wedding was kept seven days with great joy.

CHAPTER XII

THEN Tobit called his son Tŏ-bī'-ăs, and said unto him, My son, see that the man have his wages, which went with thee, and thou must give him more.

2 And Tŏ-bī'-ăs said unto him, O father, it is no harm to me to give him half of those things which I have brought:

3 For he hath brought me again to thee in safety, and made whole my wife, and brought me the money, and likewise healed thee.

4 Then the old man said, It is due unto him.

5 So he called the angel, and he said unto him, Take half of all that ye have brought, and go away in safety.

6 Then he took them both apart, and said unto them, Bless God, praise him, and magnify him, and praise him for the things which he hath done unto you in the sight of all that live. It is good to praise God, and exalt his name, and honourably to shew forth the works of God; therefore be not slack to praise him.

7 It is good to keep close the secret of a king, but it is honourable to reveal the works of God. Do that which is good, and no evil shall touch you.

8 Prayer is good with fasting and alms and righteousness. A little with righteousness is better than much with unrighteousness. It is better to give alms than to lay up gold:

9 For alms doth deliver from death, and shall purge away all sin. Those that exercise alms and righteousness shall be filled with life:

10 But they that sin are enemies to their own life.

11 Surely I will keep close nothing from you. For I said, It was good to keep close the secret of a king, but that it was honourable to reveal the works of God.

12 Now therefore, when thou didst pray, and Sara thy daughter in law, I did bring the remembrance of your prayers before the Holy One: and when thou didst bury the dead, I was with thee likewise.

13 And when thou didst not delay to rise up, and leave thy dinner, to go and cover the dead, thy good deed was not hid from me: but I was with thee.

14 And now God hath sent me to heal thee and Sara thy daughter in law.

15 I am Răph'-ă-ĕl, one of the seven holy angels, which present the prayers of the saints, and which go in and out before the glory of the Holy One.

16 Then they were both troubled, and fell upon their faces: for they feared.

17 But he said unto them, Fear not, for it shall go well with you; praise God therefore.

18 For not of any favour of mine, but by the will of our God I came; wherefore praise him for ever.

19 All these days I did appear unto you; but I did neither eat nor drink, but ye did see a vision.

20 Now therefore give God thanks: for I go up to him that sent me; but write all things which are done in a book.

21 And when they arose, they saw him no more.

22 Then they confessed the great and wonderful works of God, and how the angel of the Lord had appeared unto them.

CHAPTER XIII

THEN Tobit wrote a prayer of rejoicing, and said, Blessed be God that liveth for ever, and blessed be his kingdom.

2 For he doth scourge, and hath mercy: he leadeth down to hell, and bringeth up again: neither is there any that can avoid his hand.

3 Confess him before the Gentiles, ye children of Israel: for he hath scattered us among them.

4 There declare his greatness, and extol him before all the living: for he is our Lord, and he is the God our Father for ever.

5 And he will scourge us for our iniquities, and will have mercy again, and will gather us out of all nations, among whom he hath scattered us.

6 If ye turn to him with your whole heart, and with your whole mind, and deal uprightly before him, then will he turn unto you, and will not hide his face from you. Therefore see what he will do with you, and confess him with your whole mouth, and praise the Lord of might, and extol the everlasting King. In the land of my captivity do I praise him, and declare his might and majesty to a sinful nation. O ye sinners, turn and do justice before him: who can tell if he will accept you, and have mercy on you?

7 I will extol my God, and my soul shall praise the King of heaven, and shall rejoice in his greatness.

8 Let all men speak, and let all praise him for *his* righteousness.

9 O Jerusalem, the holy city, he will scourge thee for thy children's works, and will have mercy again on the sons of the righteous.

10 Give praise to the Lord, *for he is* good: and praise the everlasting King, that his tabernacle may be builded in thee again with joy, and let him make joyful there in thee those that are captives, and love in thee for ever those that are miserable.

11 Many nations shall come from far to the name of the Lord God with gifts in their hands, even gifts to the King of heaven; all generations shall praise thee with great joy.

12 Cursed *are* all they which hate thee, and blessed shall all be which love thee for ever.

13 Rejoice and be glad for the children of the just: for they shall be gathered together, and

shall bless the Lord of the just.

14 O blessed *are* they which love thee, *for* they shall rejoice in thy peace: blessed *are* they which have been sorrowful for all thy scourges; for they shall rejoice for thee, when they have seen all thy glory, and shall be glad for ever.

15 Let my soul bless God the great King.

16 For Jerusalem shall be built up with sapphires, and emeralds, and precious stone: thy walls and towers and battlements with pure gold.

17 And the streets of Jerusalem shall be paved with beryl and carbuncle and stones of Ō'-phǐr.

18 And all her streets shall say, Alleluia; and they shall praise him, saying, Blessed be God, which hath extolled it for ever.

CHAPTER XIV

SO Tobit made an end of praising God.

2 And he was eight and fifty years old when he lost his sight, which was restored to him after eight years: and he gave alms, and he increased in the fear of the Lord God, and praised him.

3 And when he was very aged, he called his son, and the six sons of his son, and said to him, My son, take thy children; for, behold, I am aged, and am ready to depart out of this life.

4 Go into Mē'-dǐ-ă, my son, for I surely believe those things which Jonas the prophet spake of Nǐn'-ě-vě, that it shall be overthrown; and that for a time peace shall rather be in

Media; and that our brethren shall lie scattered in the earth from that good land: and Jerusalem shall be desolate, and the house of God in it shall be burned, and shall be desolate for a time;

5 And that again God will have mercy on them, and bring them again into the land, where they shall build a temple, but not like to the first, until the time of that age be fulfilled; and afterward they shall return from *all* places of their captivity, and build up Jerusalem gloriously, and the house of God shall be built in it for ever with a glorious building, as the prophets have spoken thereof.

6 And all nations shall turn, and fear the Lord God truly, and shall bury their idols.

7 So shall all nations praise the Lord, and his people shall confess God, and the Lord shall exalt his people; and all those which love the Lord God in truth and justice shall rejoice, shewing mercy to our brethren.

8 And now, my son, depart out of Nǐn'-ě-vě, because that those things which the prophet Jonas spake shall surely come to pass.

9 But keep thou the law and the commandments, and shew thyself merciful and just, that it may go well with thee.

10 And bury me decently, and thy mother with me; but tarry no longer at Nǐn'-ě-vě. Remember, my son, how Ā'-măn handled Ā'-chǐ-ăch'-ă-rŭs that brought him up, how out of light he brought him into darkness, and how he rewarded him again: yet Achiacharus was saved, but the other had

his reward: for he went down into darkness. Mă-năs´-sēs gave alms, and escaped the snares of death which they had set for him: but Aman fell into the snare, and perished.

11 Wherefore now, my son, consider what alms doeth, and how righteousness doth deliver. When he had said these things, he gave up the ghost in the bed, being an hundred and eight and fifty years old; and he buried him honourably.

12 And when Anna his mother was dead, he buried her with his father. But Tŏ-bī´-ăs departed with his wife and child-

ren to Ĕc-băt´-ă-nĕ to Ră-gū´-ĕl his father in law,

13 Where he became old with honour, and he buried his father and mother in law honourably, and he inherited their substance, and his father Tobit's.

14 And he died at Ĕc-băt´-ă-nĕ in Mē´-dĭ-ă, being an hundred and seven and twenty years old.

15 But before he died he heard of the destruction of Nĭn´-ĕ-vĕ, which was taken by Năb´-ŭ-chŏ-dŏn´-ŏ-sŏr and Ăs´-sŭ-ē´-rŭs: and before his death he rejoiced over Nineve.

JUDITH

CHAPTER I

IN the twelfth year of the reign of Năb´-ŭ-chŏ-dŏn´-ŏ-sŏr, who reigned in Nĭn´-ĕ-vĕ, the great city; in the days of Ăr-phăx´-ăd, which reigned over the Medes in Ĕc-băt´-ă-nĕ,

2 And built in Ĕc-băt´-ă-nĕ walls round about of stones hewn three cubits broad and six cubits long, and made the height of the wall seventy cubits, and the breadth thereof fifty cubits:

3 And set the towers thereof upon the gates of it, an hundred cubits *high*, and the breadth thereof in the foundation threescore cubits:

4 And he made the gates thereof, even gates that were raised to the height of seventy cubits, and the breadth of them was forty cubits, for the going forth of his mighty

armies, and for the setting in array of his footmen:

5 Even in those days king Năb´-ŭ-chŏ-dŏn´-ŏ-sŏr made war with king Ăr-phăx´-ăd in the great plain, which is the plain in the borders of Ră´-gau.

6 And there came unto him all they that dwelt in the hill country, and all that dwelt by Eu-phrā´-tēs, and Tī´-grĭs, and Hȳ-dăs´-pēs, and the plain of Ăr´-ĭ-ŏch the king of the Ĕl-ў-mē´-ăns, and very many nations of the sons of Chē´-lod, assembled themselves to the battle.

7 Then Năb´-ŭ-chŏ-dŏn´-ŏ-sŏr king of the Assyrians sent unto all that dwelt in Persia, and to all that dwelt westward, and to those that dwelt in Çĭ-lĭ´-çĭ-ă, and Damascus, and Lĭb´-ă-nŭs, and Ăn´-tī-lĭb´-ă-nŭs, and to all that dwelt upon the sea coast,

8 And to those among the nations that were of Carmel,

and Găl'-ă-ăd, and the higher Galilee, and the great plain of Ĕs-drē'-lom,

9 And to all that were in Samaria and the cities thereof, and beyond Jordan unto Jerusalem, and Bĕt'-ă-nĕ, and Chĕl'-lŭs, and Kā'-dēs, and the river of Egypt, and Tăph'-nēs, and Răm'-ĕs-sĕ, and all the land of Gĕ'-sĕm,

10 Until ye come beyond Tā'-nĭs and Memphis, and to all the inhabitants of Egypt, until ye come to the borders of Ĕ-thĭ-ō'-pĭ-ă.

11 But all the inhabitants of the land made light of the commandment of Năb'-ŭ-cho-dŏn'-ŏ-sôr king of the Assyrians, neither went they with him to the battle; for they were not afraid of him: yea, he was before them as one man, and they sent away his ambassadors from them without effect, and with disgrace.

12 Therefore Năb'-ŭ-cho-dŏn'-ŏ-sôr was very angry with all this country, and sware by his throne and kingdom, that he would surely be avenged upon all those coasts of Çĭ-lĭ'-çĭ-ă, and Damascus, and Syria, and that he would slay with the sword all the inhabitants of the land of Mō'-ăb, and the children of Ammon, and all Judea, and all that were in Egypt, till ye come to the borders of the two seas.

13 Then he marched in battle array with his power against king Är-phăx'-ăd in the seventeenth year, and he prevailed in his battle: for he overthrew all the power of Arphaxad, and all his horsemen, and all his chariots,

14 And became lord of his cities, and came unto Ĕc-băt'-

ă-nĕ, and took the towers, and spoiled the streets thereof, and turned the beauty thereof into shame.

15 He took also Är-phăx'-ăd in the mountains of Rā'-gău, and smote him through with his darts, and destroyed him utterly that day.

16 So he returned afterward to Nĭn'-ĕ-vĕ, both he and all his company of sundry nations, being a very great multitude of men of war, and there he took his ease, and banqueted, both he and his army, an hundred and twenty days.

CHAPTER II

AND in the eighteenth year, the two and twentieth day of the first month, there was talk in the house of Năb'-ŭ-cho-dŏn'-ŏ-sôr king of the Assyrians, that he should, as he said, avenge himself on all the earth.

2 So he called unto him all his officers, and all his nobles, and communicated with them his secret counsel, and concluded the afflicting of the whole earth out of his own mouth.

3 Then they decreed to destroy all flesh, that did not obey the commandment of his mouth.

4 And when he had ended his counsel, Năb'-ŭ-cho-dŏn'-ŏ-sôr king of the Assyrians called Hŏl-ŏ-fêr'-nēs the chief captain of his army, which was next unto him, and said unto him,

5 Thus saith the great king, the lord of the whole earth, Behold, thou shalt go forth from my presence, and take with thee men that trust in their own strength, of footmen an hundred and twenty thousand; and the number of horses

with their riders twelve thousand.

6 And thou shalt go against all the west country, because they disobeyed my commandment.

7 And thou shalt declare unto them, that they prepare for me earth and water: for I will go forth in my wrath against them, and will cover the whole face of the earth with the feet of mine army, and I will give them for a spoil unto them:

8 So that their slain shall fill their valleys and brooks, and the river shall be filled with their dead, till it overflow:

9 And I will lead them captives to the utmost parts of all the earth.

10 Thou therefore shalt go forth, and take beforehand for me all their coasts: and if they will yield themselves unto thee, thou shalt reserve them for me till the day of their punishment.

11 But concerning them that rebel, let not thine eye spare them; but put them to the slaughter, and spoil them wheresoever thou goest.

12 For as I live, and by the power of my kingdom, whatsoever I have spoken, that will I do by mine hand.

13 And take thou heed that thou transgress none of the commandments of thy lord, but accomplish them fully, as I have commanded thee, and defer not to do them.

14 Then Hŏl-ŏ-fēr'-nēs went forth from the presence of his lord, and called all the governors and captains, and the officers of the army of Ăs'-sŭr;

15 And he mustered the chosen men for the battle, as his lord had commanded him,

unto an hundred and twenty thousand, and twelve thousand archers on horseback;

16 And he ranged them, as a great army is ordered for the war.

17 And he took camels and asses for their carriages, a very great number; and sheep and oxen and goats without number for their provision:

18 And plenty of victual for every man of the army, and very much gold and silver out of the king's house.

19 Then he went forth and all his power to go before king Năb'-ŭ-chŏ-dŏn'-ŏ-sôr in the voyage, and to cover all the face of the earth westward with their chariots, and horsemen, and their chosen footmen.

20 A great number also of sundry countries came with them like locusts, and like the sand of the earth: for the multitude was without number.

21 And they went forth of Nĭn'-ĕ-vĕ three days' journey toward the plain of Bĕc'-tĭ-lĕth, and pitched from Bectileth near the mountain which is at the left hand of the upper Çĭ-lĭ'-çĭ-ă.

22 Then he took all his army, his footmen, and horsemen, and chariots, and went from thence into the hill country;

23 And destroyed Phŭd and Lŭd, and spoiled all the children of Răs'-sēs, and the children of Ĭs'-mă-ël, which were toward the wilderness at the south of the land of the Chĕl'-lĭ-äns.

24 Then he went over Ēŭ-phrā'-tēs, and went through Mĕs'-ŏ-pŏ-tā'-mĭ-ă, and destroyed all the high cities that were upon the river Är-bŏ-nā'-ī, till ye come to the sea.

25 And he took the borders of Çĭ-lĭ´-çĭ-ă, and killed all that resisted him, and came to the borders of Jā´-phĕth, which were toward the south, over against Arabia.

26 He compassed also all the children of Mă-dĭ-ăn, and burned up their tabernacles, and spoiled their sheepcotes.

27 Then he went down into the plain of Damascus in the time of wheat harvest, and burnt up all their fields, and destroyed their flocks and herds, also he spoiled their cities, and utterly wasted their countries, and smote all their young men with the edge of the sword.

28 Therefore the fear and dread of him fell upon all the inhabitants of the sea coasts, which were in Sidon and Tyrus, and them that dwelt in Sûr and Ŏ-çĭ´-nă, and all that dwelt in Jĕm-nā´-ăn; and they that dwelt in Ă-zō´-tŭs and Ăs´-că-lon feared him greatly.

CHAPTER III

SO they sent ambassadors unto him to treat of peace, saying,

2 Behold, we the servants of Năb´-ŭ-chŏ-dŏn´-ŏ-sôr the great king lie before thee; use us as shall be good in thy sight.

3 Behold, our houses, and all our places, and all our fields of wheat, and flocks, and herds, and all the lodges of our tents, lie before thy face; use them as it pleaseth thee.

4 Behold, even our cities and the inhabitants thereof are thy servants; come and deal with them as seemeth good unto thee.

5 So the men came to Hŏl-ŏ-

fēr´-nēs, and declared unto him after this manner.

6 Then came he down toward the sea coast, both he and his army, and set garrisons in the high cities, and took out of them chosen men for aid.

7 So they and all the country round about received them with garlands, with dances, and with timbrels.

8 Yet he did cast down their frontiers, and cut down their groves: for he had decreed to destroy all the gods of the land, that all nations should worship Năb´-ŭ-chŏ-dŏn´-ŏ-sôr only, and that all tongues and tribes should call upon him as god.

9 Also he came over against Ĕs-drā-ē´-lon, near unto Judea, over against the great strait of Judea.

10 And he pitched between Gē´-bă and Scȳth-ŏp´-ŏ-lĭs, and there he tarried a whole month, that he might gather together all the carriages of his army.

CHAPTER IV

NOW the children of Israel, that dwelt in Judea, heard all that Hŏl-ŏ-fēr´-nēs the chief captain of Năb´-ŭ-chŏ-dŏn´-ŏ-sôr king of the Assyrians had done to the nations, and after what manner he had spoiled all their temples, and brought them to nought.

2 Therefore they were exceedingly afraid of him, and were troubled for Jerusalem, and for the temple of the Lord their God:

3 For they were newly returned from the captivity, and all the people of Judea were lately gathered together: and the vessels, and the altar, and

the house, were sanctified after the profanation.

4 Therefore they sent into all the coasts of Samaria, and the villages, and to Bĕth-ŏ'-rŏn, and Belmen, and Jericho, and to Choba, and Ĕs-ŏ-rä, and to the valley of Salem:

5 And possessed themselves beforehand of all the tops of the high mountains, and fortified the villages that were in them, and laid up victuals for the provision of war: for their fields were of late reaped.

6 Also Jō'-ă-cĭm the high priest, which was in those days in Jerusalem, wrote to them that dwelt in Bĕ-thū'-lĭ-ă, and Bĕt-ŏ-mĕs'-thäm, which is over against Ĕs-drā-ē'-lŏn toward the open country, near to Dō'-thä-ĭm,

7 Charging them to keep the passages of the hill country: for by them there was an entrance into Judea, and it was easy to stop them that would come up, because the passage was strait, for two men at the most.

8 And the children of Israel did as Jō'-ă-cĭm the high priest had commanded them, with the ancients of all the people of Israel, which dwelt at Jerusalem.

9 Then every man of Israel cried to God with great fervency, and with great vehemency did they humble their souls:

10 Both they, and their wives, and their children, and their cattle, and every stranger and hireling, and their servants bought with money, put sackcloth upon their loins.

11 Thus every man and woman, and the little children, and the inhabitants of Jeru-

salem, fell before the temple, and cast ashes upon their heads, and spread out their sackcloth before the face of the Lord: also they put sackcloth about the altar,

12 And cried to the God of Israel all with one consent earnestly, that he would not give their children for a prey, and their wives for a spoil, and the cities of their inheritance to destruction, and the sanctuary to profanation and reproach, and for the nations to rejoice at.

13 So God heard their prayers, and looked upon their afflictions: for the people fasted many days in all Judea and Jerusalem before the sanctuary of the Lord Almighty.

14 And Jō'-ă-cĭm the high priest, and all the priests that stood before the Lord, and they which ministered unto the Lord, had their loins girt with sackcloth, and offered the daily burnt offerings, with the vows and free gifts of the people,

15 And had ashes on their mitres, and cried unto the Lord with all their power, that he would look upon all the house of Israel graciously.

CHAPTER V

THEN was it declared to Hŏl-ŏ-fĕr'-nēs, the chief captain of the army of Ăs'-sûr, that the children of Israel had prepared for war, and had shut up the passages of the hill country, and had fortified all the tops of the high hills, and had laid impediments in the champaign countries:

2 Wherewith he was very angry, and called all the

princes of Mō´-ăb, and the captains of Ammon, and all the governors of the sea coast,

3 And he said unto them, Tell me now, ye sons of Chā´-nā̄an, who this people is, that dwelleth in the hill country, and what are the cities that they inhabit, and what is the multitude of their army, and wherein is their power and strength, and what king is set over them, or captain of their army;

4 And why have they determined not to come and meet me, more than all the inhabitants of the west.

5 Then said Ā´-chi-ôr, the captain of all the sons of Ammon, Let my lord now hear a word from the mouth of thy servant, and I will declare unto thee the truth concerning this people, which dwelleth near thee, and inhabiteth the hill countries: and there shall no lie come out of the mouth of thy servant.

6 This people are descended of the Chăl-dē´-ăns:

7 And they sojourned heretofore in Mĕs´-ŏ-pŏ-tā´-mǐ-ă, because they would not follow the gods of their fathers, which were in the land of Chăl-dē´-ă.

8 For they left the way of their ancestors, and worshipped the God of heaven, the God whom they knew: so they cast them out from the face of their gods, and they fled into Mĕs´-ŏ-pŏ-tā´-mǐ-ă, and sojourned there many days.

9 Then their God commanded them to depart from the place where they sojourned, and to go into the land of Chā´-nā̄an: where they dwelt, and were increased with gold and silver, and with very much cattle.

10 But when a famine covered all the land of Chā´-nā̄an, they went down into Egypt, and sojourned there, while they were nourished, and became there a great multitude, so that one could not number their nation.

11 Therefore the king of Egypt rose up against them, and dealt subtilly with them, and brought them low with labouring in brick, and made them slaves.

12 Then they cried unto their God, and he smote all the land of Egypt with incurable plagues: so the Egyptians cast them out of their sight.

13 And God dried the Red sea before them,

14 And brought them to mount Sī´-nă, and Cā´-dĕs–Bär-nē´, and cast forth all that dwelt in the wilderness.

15 So they dwelt in the land of the Ăm´-ŏ-rītes, and they destroyed by their strength all them of Ĕs´-ĕ-bŏn, and passing over Jordan they possessed all the hill country.

16 And they cast forth before them the Chā´-nā̄an-īte, the Phĕr´-ĕ-zīte, the Jĕb´-ū-sīte, and the Sȳ´-chĕm-īte, and all the Gĕr´-gĕ-sītes, and they dwelt in that country many days.

17 And whilst they sinned not before their God, they prospered, because the God that hateth iniquity was with them.

18 But when they departed from the way which he appointed them, they were destroyed in many battles very sore, and were led captives into a land that was not theirs, and the temple of their God was cast to the ground, and their cities were taken by the enemies.

19 But now are they returned to their God, and are

come up from the places where they were scattered, and have possessed Jerusalem, where their sanctuary is, and are seated in the hill country; for it was desolate.

20 Now therefore, my lord and governor, if there be any error in this people, and they sin against their God, let us consider that this shall be their ruin, and let us go up, and we shall overcome them.

21 But if there be no iniquity in their nation, let my lord now pass by, lest their Lord defend them, and their God be for them, and we become a reproach before all the world.

22 And when Ā'-chi-ôr had finished these sayings, all the people standing round about the tent murmured, and the chief men of Hŏl-ŏ-fēr'-nēs, and all that dwelt by the sea side, and in Mō'-ăb, spake that he should kill him.

23 For, *say they*, we will not be afraid of the face of the children of Israel: for, lo, it is a people that have no strength nor power for a strong battle.

24 Now therefore, lord Hŏl-ŏ-fēr'-nēs, we will go up, and they shall be a prey to be devoured of all thine army.

CHAPTER VI

AND when the tumult of men that were about the council was ceased, Hŏl-ŏ-fēr'-nēs the chief captain of the army of Ăs'-sûr said unto Ā'-chi-ôr and all the Mō'-ă-bītes before all the company of other nations,

2 And who art thou, Ā'-chi-ôr, and the hirelings of Ephraim, that thou hast prophesied 88

among us as to day, and hast said, that we should not make war with the people of Israel, because their God will defend them? and who is God but Nāb'-ŭ-chŏ-dŏn'-ŏ-sôr?

3 He will send his power, and will destroy them from the face of the earth, and their God shall not deliver them: but we his servants will destroy them as one man; for they are not able to sustain the power of our horses.

4 For with them we will tread them under foot, and their mountains shall be drunken with their blood, and their fields shall be filled with their dead bodies, and their footsteps shall not be able to stand before us, for they shall utterly perish, saith king Nāb'-ŭ-chŏ-dŏn'-ŏ-sôr, lord of all the earth: for he said, None of my words shall be in vain.

5 And thou, Ā'-chi-ôr, an hireling of Ammon, which hast spoken these words in the day of thine iniquity, shalt see my face no more from this day, until I take vengeance of this nation that came out of Egypt.

6 And then shall the sword of mine army, and the multitude of them that serve me, pass through thy sides, and thou shalt fall among their slain, when I return.

7 Now therefore my servants shall bring thee back into the hill country, and shall set thee in one of the cities of the passages:

8 And thou shalt not perish, till thou be destroyed with them.

9 And if thou persuade thyself in thy mind that they shall not be taken, let not thy countenance fall: I have spoken it,

and none of my words shall be in vain.

10 Then Hŏl-ŏ-fẽr´-nēs commanded his servants, that waited in his tent, to take Ā´-chi-ôr, and bring him to Bĕ-thū´-li-ă, and deliver him into the hands of the children of Israel.

11 So his servants took him, and brought him out of the camp into the plain, and they went from the midst of the plain into the hill country, and came unto the fountains that were under Bĕ-thū´-li-ă.

12 And when the men of the city saw them, they took up their weapons, and went out of the city to the top of the hill: and every man that used a sling kept them from coming up by casting of stones against them.

13 Nevertheless having gotten privily under the hill, they bound Ā´-chi-ôr, and cast him down, and left him at the foot of the hill, and returned to their lord.

14 But the Israelites descended from their city, and came unto him, and loosed him, and brought him into Bĕ-thū´-li-ă, and presented him to the governors of the city:

15 Which were in those days Ŏ-zī´-ăs the son of Micha, of the tribe of Simeon, and Chăb´-rĭs the son of Gŏth-ŏ-nī´-ĕl, and Chăr´-mĭs the son of Mĕl-chi´-ĕl.

16 And they called together all the ancients of the city, and all their youth ran together, and their women, to the assembly, and they set Ā´-chi-ôr in the midst of all their people. Then Ŏ-zī´-ăs asked him of that which was done.

17 And he answered and declared unto them the words of the council of Hŏl-ŏ-fẽr´-nēs, and all the words that he had spoken in the midst of the princes of Ăs´-sûr, and whatsoever Holofernes had spoken proudly against the house of Israel.

18 Then the people fell down and worshipped God, and cried unto God, saying,

19 O Lord God of heaven, behold their pride, and pity the low estate of our nation, and look upon the face of those that are sanctified unto thee this day.

20 Then they comforted Ā´-chi-ôr, and praised him greatly.

21 And Ŏ-zī´-ăs took him out of the assembly unto his house, and made a feast to the elders; and they called on the God of Israel all that night for help.

CHAPTER VII

THE next day Hŏl-ŏ-fẽr´-nēs commanded all his army, and all his people which were come to take his part, that they should remove their camp against Bĕ-thū´-li-ă, to take aforehand the ascents of the hill country, and to make war against the children of Israel.

2 Then their strong men removed their camps in that day, and the army of the men of war was an hundred and seventy thousand footmen, and twelve thousand horsemen, beside the baggage, and other men that were afoot among them, a very great multitude.

3 And they camped in the valley near unto Bĕ-thū´-li-ă, by the fountain, and they spread themselves in breadth

89

over Dō'-thā-ĭm even to Bĕl'-mā-ĭm, and in length from Bethulia unto Çy'-ă-mon, which is over against Ĕs-drā-ē'-lon.

4 Now the children of Israel, when they saw the multitude of them, were greatly troubled, and said every one to his neighbour, Now will these men lick up the face of the earth; for neither the high mountains, nor the valleys, nor the hills, are able to bear their weight.

5 Then every man took up his weapons of war, and when they had kindled fires upon their towers, they remained and watched all that night.

6 But in the second day Hŏl-ŏ-fĕr'-nēs brought forth all his horsemen in the sight of the children of Israel which were in Bĕ-thū'-lĭ-ă,

7 And viewed the passages up to the city, and came to the fountains of their waters, and took them, and set garrisons of men of war over them, and he himself removed toward his people.

8 Then came unto him all the chief of the children of Esau, and all the governors of the people of Mō'-ăb, and the captains of the sea coast, and said,

9 Let our lord now hear a word, that there be not an overthrow in thine army.

10 For this people of the children of Israel do not trust in their spears, but in the height of the mountains wherein they dwell, because it is not easy to come up to the tops of their mountains.

11 Now therefore, my lord, fight not against them in battle array, and there shall not so much as one man of thy people perish.

12 Remain in thy camp, and keep all the men of thine army, and let thy servants get into their hands the fountain of water, which issueth forth of the foot of the mountain:

13 For all the inhabitants of Bĕ-thū'-lĭ-ă have their water thence; so shall thirst kill them, and they shall give up their city, and we and our people shall go up to the tops of the mountains that are near, and will camp upon them, to watch that none go out of the city.

14 So they and their wives and their children shall be consumed with famine, and before the sword come against them, they shall be overthrown in the streets where they dwell.

15 Thus shalt thou render them an evil reward; because they rebelled, and met not thy person peaceably.

16 And these words pleased Hŏl-ŏ-fĕr'-nēs and all his servants, and he appointed to do as they had spoken.

17 So the camp of the children of Ammon departed, and with them five thousand of the Assyrians, and they pitched in the valley, and took the waters, and the fountains of the waters of the children of Israel.

18 Then the children of Esau went up with the children of Ammon, and camped in the hill country over against Dō'-thā-ĭm: and they sent some of them toward the south, and toward the east, over against Ĕk-rē'-bĕl, which is near unto Chū'-sī, that is upon the brook Mŏch'-mûr; and the rest of the army of the Assyrians camped in the plain, and covered the face of the whole land; and their tents and carriages were

pitched to a very great multitude.

19 Then the children of Israel cried unto the Lord their God, because their heart failed, for all their enemies had compassed them round about, and there was no way to escape out from among them.

20 Thus all the company of Ăs'-sûr remained about them, both their footmen, chariots, and horsemen, four and thirty days, so that all their vessels of water failed all the inhabitants of Bĕ-thū'-lĭ-ă.

21 And the cisterns were emptied, and they had not water to drink their fill for one day; for they gave them drink by measure.

22 Therefore their young children were out of heart, and their women and young men fainted for thirst, and fell down in the streets of the city, and by the passages of the gates, and there was no longer any strength in them.

23 Then all the people assembled to Ŏ-zī'-ăs, and to the chief of the city, both young men, and women, and children, and cried with a loud voice, and said before all the elders,

24 God be judge between us and you: for ye have done us great injury, in that ye have not required peace of the children of Ăs'-sûr.

25 For now we have no helper: but God hath sold us into their hands, that we should be thrown down before them with thirst and great destruction.

26 Now therefore call them unto you, and deliver the whole city for a spoil to the people of Hŏl-ŏ-fēr'-nēs, and to all his army.

27 For it is better for us to be made a spoil unto them, than to die for thirst: for we will be his servants, that our souls may live, and not see the death of our infants before our eyes, nor our wives nor our children to die.

28 We take to witness against you the heaven and the earth, and our God and Lord of our fathers, which punisheth us according to our sins and the sins of our fathers, that he do not according as we have said this day.

29 Then there was great weeping with one consent in the midst of the assembly; and they cried unto the Lord God with a loud voice.

30 Then said Ŏ-zī'-ăs to them, Brethren, be of good courage, let us yet endure five days, in the which space the Lord our God may turn his mercy toward us; for he will not forsake us utterly.

31 And if these days pass, and there come no help unto us, I will do according to your word.

32 And he dispersed the people, every one to their own charge; and they went unto the walls and towers of their city, and sent the women and children into their houses: and they were very low brought in the city.

CHAPTER VIII

NOW at that time Judith heard thereof, which was the daughter of Mĕ-rā'-rī, the son of Ox, the son of Joseph, the son of Ŏ-zī'-ĕl, the son of Ĕl-çī'-ă, the son of Ăn-ă-nī'-ăs, the son of Gĕd'-ĕ-on, the son of Rā'-phă-ĭm, the son of Ā'-çĭ-thō, the son of Ĕl'-ĭ-ū, the son

91

of Ĕ-lī'-ăb, the son of Nă-thăn'-ă-ĕl, the son of Săm'-ă-ĕl, the son of Săl'-ă-săd'-ă-ī, the son of Israel.

2 And Mă-năs'-sēs was her husband, of her tribe and kindred, who died in the barley harvest.

3 For as he stood overseeing them that bound sheaves in the field, the heat came upon his head, and he fell on his bed, and died in the city of Bĕ-thū'-lị-ă: and they buried him with his fathers in the field between Dō'-thă-ĭm and Băl'-ă-mō.

4 So Judith was a widow in her house three years and four months.

5 And she made her a tent upon the top of her house, and put on sackcloth upon her loins, and ware her widow's apparel.

6 And she fasted all the days of her widowhood, save the eves of the sabbaths, and the sabbaths, and the eves of the new moons, and the new moons, and the feasts and solemn days of the house of Israel.

7 She was also of a goodly countenance, and very beautiful to behold: and her husband Mă-năs'-sēs had left her gold, and silver, and menservants, and maidservants, and cattle, and lands; and she remained upon them.

8 And there was none that gave her an ill word; for she feared God greatly.

9 Now when she heard the evil words of the people against the governor, that they fainted for lack of water; for Judith had heard all the words that Ŏ-zī'-ăs had spoken unto them, and that he had sworn to deliver the city unto the Assyrians after five days;

10 Then she sent her waiting-woman, that had the government of all things that she had, to call Ŏ-zī'-ăs and Chăb'-rĭs and Chăr'-mĭs, the ancients of the city.

11 And they came unto her, and she said unto them, Hear me now, O ye governors of the inhabitants of Bĕ-thū'-lị-ă: for your words that ye have spoken before the people this day are not right, touching this oath which ye made and pronounced between God and you, and have promised to deliver the city to our enemies, unless within these days the Lord turn to help you.

12 And now who are ye that have tempted God this day, and stand instead of God among the children of men?

13 And now try the Lord Almighty, but ye shall never know any thing.

14 For ye cannot find the depth of the heart of man, neither can ye perceive the things that he thinketh: then how can ye search out God, that hath made all these things, and know his mind, or comprehend his purpose? Nay, my brethren, provoke not the Lord our God to anger.

15 For if he will not help us within these five days, he hath power to defend us when he will, even every day, or to destroy us before our enemies.

16 Do not bind the counsels of the Lord our God: for God is not as man, that he may be threatened; neither is he as the son of man, that he should be wavering.

17 Therefore let us wait for salvation of him, and call upon him to help us, and he will hear our voice, if it please him.

18 For there arose none in our age, neither is there any now in these days, neither tribe, nor family, nor people, nor city, among us, which worship gods made with hands, as hath been aforetime.

19 For the which cause our fathers were given to the sword, and for a spoil, and had a great fall before our enemies.

20 But we know none other god, therefore we trust that he will not despise us, nor any of our nation.

21 For if we be taken so, all Judea shall lie waste, and our sanctuary shall be spoiled; and he will require the profanation thereof at our mouth.

22 And the slaughter of our brethren, and the captivity of the country, and the desolation of our inheritance, will he turn upon our heads among the Gentiles, wheresoever we shall be in bondage; and we shall be an offence and a reproach to all them that possess us.

23 For our servitude shall not be directed to favour; but the Lord our God shall turn it to dishonour.

24 Now therefore, O brethren, let us shew an example to our brethren, because their hearts depend upon us, and the sanctuary, and the house, and the altar, rest upon us.

25 Moreover let us give thanks to the Lord our God, which trieth us, even as he did our fathers.

26 Remember what things he did to Abraham, and how he tried Isaac, and what happened to Jacob in Mĕs′-ŏ-pŏ-tā′-mĭ-ă of Syria, when he kept the sheep of Laban his mother's brother.

27 For he hath not tried us in the fire, as he did them, for the examination of their hearts, neither hath he taken vengeance on us: but the Lord doth scourge them that come near unto him, to admonish them.

28 Then said Ŏ-zī′-ăs to her, All that thou hast spoken hast thou spoken with a good heart, and there is none that may gainsay thy words.

29 For this is not the first day wherein thy wisdom is manifested; but from the beginning of thy days all the people have known thy understanding, because the disposition of thine heart is good.

30 But the people were very thirsty, and compelled us to do unto them as we have spoken, and to bring an oath upon ourselves, which we will not break.

31 Therefore now pray thou for us, because thou art a godly woman, and the Lord will send us rain to fill our cisterns, and we shall faint no more.

32 Then said Judith unto them, Hear me, and I will do a thing, which shall go throughout all generations to the children of our nation.

33 Ye shall stand this night in the gate, and I will go forth with my waitingwoman: and within the days that ye have promised to deliver the city to our enemies the Lord will visit Israel by mine hand.

34 But enquire not ye of mine act: for I will not declare it unto you, till the things be finished that I do.

35 Then said Ŏ-zī′-ăs and the princes unto her, Go in peace, and the Lord God be before thee, to take vengeance on our enemies.

36 So they returned from the tent, and went to their wards.

93

CHAPTER IX

THEN Judith fell upon her face, and put ashes upon her head, and uncovered the sackcloth wherewith she was clothed; and about the time that the incense of that evening was offered in Jerusalem in the house of the Lord Judith cried with a loud voice, and said,

2 O Lord God of my father Simeon, to whom thou gavest a sword to take vengeance of the strangers, who loosened the girdle of a maid to defile her, and discovered the thigh to her shame, and polluted her virginity to her reproach; for thou saidst, It shall not be so; and yet they did so:

3 Wherefore thou gavest their rulers to be slain, so that they dyed their bed in blood, being deceived, and smotest the servants with their lords, and the lords upon their thrones;

4 And hast given their wives for a prey, and their daughters to be captives, and all their spoils to be divided among thy dear children; which were moved with thy zeal, and abhorred the pollution of their blood, and called upon thee for aid: O God, O my God, hear me also a widow.

5 For thou hast wrought not only those things, but also the things which fell out before, and which ensued after; thou hast thought upon the things which are now, and which are to come.

6 Yea, what things thou didst determine were ready at hand, and said, Lo, we are here: for all thy ways are prepared, and thy judgments are in thy foreknowledge.

7 For, behold, the Assyrians are multiplied in their powers; they are exalted with horse and man; they glory in the strength of their footmen; they trust in shield, and spear, and bow, and sling; and know not that thou art the Lord that breakest the battles: the Lord is thy name.

8 Throw down their strength in thy power, and bring down their force in thy wrath: for they have purposed to defile thy sanctuary, and to pollute the tabernacle where thy glorious name resteth, and to cast down with sword the horn of thy altar.

9 Behold their pride, and send thy wrath upon their heads: give into mine hand, which am a widow, the power that I have conceived.

10 Smite by the deceit of my lips the servant with the prince, and the prince with the servant: break down their stateliness by the hand of a woman.

11 For thy power standeth not in multitude, nor thy might in strong men: for thou art a God of the afflicted, an helper of the oppressed, an upholder of the weak, a protector of the forlorn, a saviour of them that are without hope.

12 I pray thee, I pray thee, O God of my father, and God of the inheritance of Israel, Lord of the heavens and earth, Creator of the waters, King of every creature, hear thou my prayer:

13 And make my speech and deceit to be their wound and stripe, who have purposed cruel things against thy covenant, and thy hallowed house, and against the top of Sion,

94

and against the house of the possession of thy children.

14 And make every nation and tribe to acknowledge that thou art the God of all power and might, and that there is none other that protecteth the people of Israel but thou.

CHAPTER X

NOW after that she had ceased to cry unto the God of Israel, and had made an end of all these words,

2 She rose where she had fallen down, and called her maid, and went down into the house, in the which she abode in the sabbath days, and in her feast days,

3 And pulled off the sackcloth which she had on, and put off the garments of her widowhood, and washed her body all over with water, and anointed herself with precious ointment, and braided the hair of her head, and put on a tire upon it, and put on her garments of gladness, wherewith she was clad during the life of Mă-năs'-sēs her husband.

4 And she took sandals upon her feet, and put about her her bracelets, and her chains, and her rings, and her earrings, and all her ornaments, and decked herself bravely, to allure the eyes of all men that should see her.

5 Then she gave her maid a bottle of wine, and a cruse of oil, and filled a bag with parched corn, and lumps of figs, and with fine bread; so she folded all these things together, and laid them upon her.

6 Thus they went forth to the gate of the city of Bĕ-thū'-lĭ-ă, and found standing there Ō-zī'-ăs, and the ancients of the city, Chăb'-rĭs and Chär'-mĭs.

7 And when they saw her, that her countenance was altered, and her apparel was changed, they wondered at her beauty very greatly, and said unto her,

8 The God, the God of our fathers, give these favour, and accomplish thine enterprizes to the glory of the children of Israel, and to the exaltation of Jerusalem. Then they worshipped God.

9 And she said unto them, Command the gates of the city to be opened unto me, that I may go forth to accomplish the things whereof ye have spoken with me. So they commanded the young men to open unto her, as she had spoken.

10 And when they had done so, Judith went out, she, and her maid with her; and the men of the city looked after her, until she was gone down the mountain, and till she had passed the valley, and could see her no more.

11 Thus they went straight forth in the valley: and the first watch of the Assyrians met her,

12 And took her, and asked her, Of what people art thou? and whence comest thou? and whither goest thou? And she said, I am a woman of the Hebrews, and am fled from them: for they shall be given you to be consumed:

13 And I am coming before Hŏl-ŏ-fĕr'-nēs the chief captain of your army, to declare words of truth; and I will shew him a way, whereby he shall go, and win all the hill country, without losing the body or life of any one of his men.

14 Now when the men heard her words, and beheld her countenance, they wondered greatly at her beauty, and said unto her,

15 Thou hast saved thy life, in that thou hast hasted to come down to the presence of our lord: now therefore come to his tent, and some of us shall conduct thee, until they have delivered thee to his hands.

16 And when thou standest before him, be not afraid in thine heart, but shew unto him according to thy word; and he will entreat thee well.

17 Then they chose out of them an hundred men to accompany her and her maid; and they brought her to the tent of Hŏl-ŏ-fēr'-nēs.

18 Then was there a concourse throughout all the camp: for her coming was noised among the tents, and they came about her, as she stood without the tent of Hŏl-ŏ-fēr'-nēs, till they told him of her.

19 And they wondered at her beauty, and admired the children of Israel because of her, and every one said to his neighbour, Who would despise this people, that have among them such women? surely it is not good that one man of them be left, who being let go might deceive the whole earth.

20 And they that lay near Hŏl-ŏ-fēr'-nēs went out, and all his servants, and they brought her into the tent.

21 Now Hŏl-ŏ-fēr'-nēs rested upon his bed under a canopy, which was woven with purple, and gold, and emeralds, and precious stones.

22 So they shewed him of her; and he came out before his tent with silver lamps going before him.

23 And when Judith was come before him and his servants, they all marvelled at the beauty of her countenance: and she fell down upon her face, and did reverence unto him: and his servants took her up.

CHAPTER XI

THEN said Hŏl-ŏ-fēr'-nēs unto her, Woman, be of good comfort, fear not in thine heart: for I never hurt any that was willing to serve Năb'-ŭ-chŏ-dŏn'-ŏ-sŏr, the king of all the earth.

2 Now therefore, if thy people that dwelleth in the mountains had not set light by me, I would not have lifted up my spear against them: but they have done these things to themselves.

3 But now tell me wherefore thou art fled from them, and art come unto us: for thou art come for safeguard; be of good comfort, thou shalt live this night, and hereafter:

4 For none shall hurt thee, but entreat thee well, as they do the servants of king Năb'-ŭ-chŏ-dŏn'-ŏ-sŏr my lord.

5 Then Judith said unto him, Receive the words of thy servant, and suffer thine handmaid to speak in thy presence, and I will declare no lie to my lord this night.

6 And if thou wilt follow the words of thine handmaid, God will bring the thing perfectly to pass by thee; and my lord shall not fail of his purposes.

7 As Năb'-ŭ-chŏ-dŏn'-ŏ-sŏr king of all the earth liveth, and as his power liveth, who hath

sent thee for the upholding of every living thing: for not only men shall serve him by thee, but also the beasts of the field, and the cattle, and the fowls of the air, shall live by thy power under Nabuchodonosor and all his house.

8 For we have heard of thy wisdom and thy policies, and it is reported in all the earth, that thou only art excellent in all the kingdom, and mighty in knowledge, and wonderful in feats of war.

9 Now as concerning the matter, which Ā'-chí-òr did speak in thy council, we have heard his words; for the men of Bĕ-thū'-lĭ-ă saved him, and he declared unto them all that he had spoken unto thee.

10 Therefore, O lord and governor, reject not his word; but lay it up in thine heart, for it is true: for our nation shall not be punished, neither can the sword prevail against them, except they sin against their God.

11 And now, that my lord be not defeated and frustrate of his purpose, even death is now fallen upon them, and their sin hath overtaken them, wherewith they will provoke their God to anger, whensoever they shall do that which is not fit to be done:

12 For their victuals fail them, and all their water is scant, and they have determined to lay hands upon their cattle, and purposed to consume all those things, that God hath forbidden them to eat by his laws:

13 And are resolved to spend the firstfruits of the corn, and the tenths of wine and oil, which they had sanctified, and

reserved for the priests that serve in Jerusalem before the face of our God; the which things it is not lawful for any of the people so much as to touch with their hands.

14 For they have sent some to Jerusalem, because they also that dwell there have done the like, to bring them a licence from the senate.

15 Now when they shall bring them word, they will forthwith do it, and they shall be given thee to be destroyed the same day.

16 Wherefore I thine handmaid, knowing all this, am fled from their presence; and God hath sent me to work things with thee, whereat all the earth shall be astonished, and whosoever shall hear it.

17 For thy servant is religious, and serveth the God of heaven day and night: now therefore, my lord, I will remain with thee, and thy servant will go out by night into the valley, and I will pray unto God, and he will tell me when they have committed their sins:

18 And I will come and shew it unto thee: then thou shalt go forth with all thine army, and there shall be none of them that shall resist thee.

19 And I will lead thee through the midst of Judea, until thou come before Jerusalem; and I will set thy throne in the midst thereof; and thou shalt drive them as sheep that have no shepherd, and a dog shall not so much as open his mouth at thee: for these things were told me according to my foreknowledge, and they were declared unto me, and I am sent to tell thee.

D

20 Then her words pleased Hŏl-ŏ-fēr'-nēs and all his servants; and they marvelled at her wisdom, and said,

21 There is not such a woman from one end of the earth to the other, both for beauty of face, and wisdom of words.

22 Likewise Hŏl-ŏ-fēr'-nēs said unto her, God hath done well to send thee before the people, that strength might be in our hands, and destruction upon them that lightly regard my lord.

23 And now thou art both beautiful in thy countenance, and witty in thy words: surely if thou do as thou hast spoken, thy God shall be my God, and thou shalt dwell in the house of king Năb'-ŭ-chŏ-dŏn'-ŏ-sŏr, and shalt be renowned through the whole earth.

CHAPTER XII

THEN he commanded to bring her in where his plate was set; and bade that they should prepare for her of his own meats, and that she drink of his own wine.

2 And Judith said, I will not eat thereof, lest there be an offence: but provision shall be made for me of the things that I have brought.

3 Then Hŏl-ŏ-fēr'-nēs said unto her, If thy provision should fail, how should we give thee the like? for there be none with us of thy nation.

4 Then said Judith unto him, As thy soul liveth, my lord, thine handmaid shall not spend those things that I have, before the Lord work by mine hand the things that he hath determined.

5 Then the servants of Hŏl-ŏ-fēr'-nēs brought her into the tent, and she slept till midnight, and she arose when it was toward the morning watch,

6 And sent to Hŏl-ŏ-fēr'-nēs, saying, Let my lord now command that thine handmaid may go forth unto prayer.

7 Then Hŏl-ŏ-fēr'-nēs commanded his guard that they should not stay her: thus she abode in the camp three days, and went out in the night into the valley of Bĕ-thū'-lĭ-ă, and washed herself in a fountain of water by the camp.

8 And when she came out, she besought the Lord God of Israel to direct her way to the raising up of the children of her people.

9 So she came in clean, and remained in the tent, until she did eat her meat at evening.

10 And in the fourth day Hŏl-ŏ-fēr'-nēs made a feast to his own servants only, and called none of the officers to the banquet.

11 Then said he to Bă-gō'-ăs the eunuch, who had charge over all that he had, Go now, and persuade this Hebrew woman which is with thee, that she come unto us, and eat and drink with us.

12 For, lo, it will be a shame for our person, if we shall let such a woman go, not having had her company; for if we draw her not unto us, she will laugh us to scorn.

13 Then went Bă-gō'-ăs from the presence of Hŏl-ŏ-fēr'-nēs, and came to her, and he said, Let not this fair damsel fear to come to my lord, and to be honoured in his presence, and drink wine, and be merry with us, and be made this day as

one of the daughters of the Assyrians, which serve in the house of Năb'-ŭ-chŏ-dŏn'-ŏ-sôr.

14 Then said Judith unto him, Who am I now, that I should gainsay my lord? surely whatsoever pleaseth him I will do speedily, and it shall be my joy unto the day of my death.

15 So she arose, and decked herself with her apparel and all her woman's attire, and her maid went and laid soft skins on the ground for her over against Hŏl-ŏ-fĕr'-nēs, which she had received of Bă-gō'-ăs for her daily use, that she might sit and eat upon them.

16 Now when Judith came in and sat down, Hŏl-ŏ-fĕr'-nēs his heart was ravished with her, and his mind was moved, and he desired greatly her company; for he waited a time to deceive her, from the day that he had seen her.

17 Then said Hŏl-ŏ-fĕr'-nēs unto her, Drink now, and be merry with us.

18 So Judith said, I will drink now, my lord, because my life is magnified in me this day more than all the days since I was born.

19 Then she took and ate and drank before him what her maid had prepared.

20 And Hŏl-ŏ-fĕr'-nēs took great delight in her, and drank much more wine than he had drunk at any time in one day since he was born.

CHAPTER XIII

NOW when the evening was come, his servants made haste to depart, and Bă-gō'-ăs shut his tent without, and dismissed the waiters from the presence of his lord; and they went to their beds: for they were all weary, because the feast had been long.

2 And Judith was left alone in the tent, and Hŏl-ŏ-fĕr'-nēs lying along upon his bed: for he was filled with wine.

3 Now Judith had commanded her maid to stand without her bedchamber, and to wait for her coming forth, as she did daily: for she said she would go forth to her prayers, and she spake to Bă-gō'-ăs according to the same purpose.

4 So all went forth, and none was left in the bedchamber, neither little nor great. Then Judith, standing by his bed, said in her heart, O Lord God of all power, look at this present upon the works of mine hands for the exaltation of Jerusalem.

5 For now is the time to help thine inheritance, and to execute mine enterprizes to the destruction of the enemies which are risen against us.

6 Then she came to the pillar of the bed, which was at Hŏl-ŏ-fĕr'-nēs' head, and took down his fauchion from thence,

7 And approached to his bed, and took hold of the hair of his head, and said, Strengthen me, O Lord God of Israel, this day.

8 And she smote twice upon his neck with all her might, and she took away his head from him,

9 And tumbled his body down from the bed, and pulled down the canopy from the pillars; and anon after she went forth, and gave Hŏl-ŏ-fĕr'-nēs his head to her maid;

10 And she put it in her bag of meat: so they twain went together according to their custom unto prayer: and when

they passed the camp, they compassed the valley, and went up the mountain of Bĕthū'-li-ă, and came to the gates thereof.

11 Then said Judith afar off to the watchmen at the gate, Open, open now the gate: God, even our God, is with us, to shew his power yet in Jerusalem, and his forces against the enemy, as he hath even done this day.

12 Now when the men of her city heard her voice, they made haste to go down to the gate of their city, and they called the elders of the city.

13 And then they ran all together, both small and great, for it was strange unto them that she was come: so they opened the gate, and received them, and made a fire for a light, and stood round about them.

14 Then she said to them with a loud voice, Praise, praise God, praise God, I say, for he hath not taken away his mercy from the house of Israel, but hath destroyed our enemies by mine hands this night.

15 So she took the head out of the bag, and shewed it, and said unto them, Behold the head of Hŏl-ŏ-fĕr'-nēs, the chief captain of the army of Ăs'-sûr, and behold the canopy, wherein he did lie in his drunkenness; and the Lord hath smitten him by the hand of a woman.

16 As the Lord liveth, who hath kept me in my way that I went, my countenance hath deceived him to his destruction, and yet hath he not committed sin with me, to defile and shame me.

17 Then all the people were wonderfully astonished, and bowed themselves, and worshipped God, and said with one accord, Blessed be thou, O our God, which hast this day brought to nought the enemies of thy people.

18 Then said Ŏ-zī'-ăs unto her, O daughter, blessed art thou of the most high God above all the women upon the earth; and blessed be the Lord God, which hath created the heavens and the earth, which hath directed thee to the cutting off of the head of the chief of our enemies.

19 For this thy confidence shall not depart from the heart of men, which remember the power of God for ever.

20 And God turn these things to thee for a perpetual praise, to visit thee in good things, because thou hast not spared thy life for the affliction of our nation, but hast revenged our ruin, walking a straight way before our God. And all the people said, So be it, so be it.

CHAPTER XIV

THEN said Judith unto them, Hear me now, my brethren, and take this head, and hang it upon the highest place of your walls.

2 And so soon as the morning shall appear, and the sun shall come forth upon the earth, take ye every one his weapons, and go forth every valiant man out of the city, and set ye a captain over them, as though ye would go down into the field toward the watch of the Assyrians; but go not down.

3 Then they shall take their armour, and shall go into their camp, and raise up the captains

of the army of Ăs´-sûr, and they shall run to the tent of Hŏl-ŏ-fēr´-nēs, but shall not find him: then fear shall fall upon them, and they shall flee before your face.

4 So ye, and all that inhabit the coast of Israel, shall pursue them, and overthrow them as they go.

5 But before ye do these things, call me Ā´-chi-ôr the Ammonite, that he may see and know him that despised the house of Israel, and that sent him to us, as it were to his death.

6 Then they called Ā´-chi-ôr out of the house of Ŏ-zī´-äs; and when he was come, and saw the head of Hŏl-ŏ-fēr´-nēs in a man's hand in the assembly of the people, he fell down on his face, and his spirit failed.

7 But when they had recovered him, he fell at Judith's feet, and reverenced her, and said, Blessed art thou in all the tabernacle of Juda, and in all nations, which hearing thy name shall be astonished.

8 Now therefore tell me all the things that thou hast done in these days. Then Judith declared unto him in the midst of the people all that she had done, from the day that she went forth until that hour she spake unto them.

9 And when she had left off speaking, the people shouted with a loud voice, and made a joyful noise in their city.

10 And when Ā´-chi-ôr had seen all that the God of Israel had done, he believed in God greatly, and circumcised the flesh of his foreskin, and was joined unto the house of Israel unto this day.

11 And as soon as the morning arose, they hanged the head of Hŏl-ŏ-fēr´-nēs upon the wall, and every man took his weapons, and they went forth by bands unto the straits of the mountain.

12 But when the Assyrians saw them, they sent to their leaders, which came to their captains and tribunes, and to every one of their rulers.

13 So they came to Hŏl-ŏ-fēr´-nēs' tent, and said to him that had the charge of all his things, Waken now our lord: for the slaves have been bold to come down against us to battle, that they may be utterly destroyed.

14 Then went in Bă-gō´-äs, and knocked at the door of the tent; for he thought that he had slept with Judith.

15 But because none answered, he opened it, and went into the bedchamber, and found him cast upon the floor dead, and his head was taken from him.

16 Therefore he cried with a loud voice, with weeping, and sighing, and a mighty cry, and rent his garments.

17 After he went into the tent where Judith lodged: and when he found her not, he leaped out to the people, and cried,

18 These slaves have dealt treacherously; one woman of the Hebrews hath brought shame upon the house of king Năb´-ŭ-chŏ-dŏn´-ŏ-sôr: for, behold, Hŏl-ŏ-fēr´-nēs *lieth* upon the ground without a head.

19 When the captains of the Assyrians' army heard these words, they rent their coats, and their minds were wonderfully troubled, and there was a cry and a very great noise throughout the camp.

CHAPTER XV

AND when they that were in the tents heard, they were astonished at the thing that was done.

2 And fear and trembling fell upon them, so that there was no man that durst abide in the sight of his neighbour, but rushing out all together, they fled into every way of the plain, and of the hill country.

3 They also that had camped in the mountains round about Bĕ-thū'-lĭ-ă fled away. Then the children of Israel, every one that was a warrior among them, rushed out upon them.

4 Then sent Ŏ-zī'-ăs to Bĕt-ŏ-măs'-thĕm, and to Bē'-bă-ī, and Chō'-bă-ī, and Cola, and to all the coasts of Israel, such as should tell the things that were done, and that all should rush forth upon their enemies to destroy them.

5 Now when the children of Israel heard it, they all fell upon them with one consent, and slew them unto Chō'-bă-ī: likewise also they that came from Jerusalem, and from all the hill country, (for men had told them what things were done in the camp of their enemies,) and they that were in Găl'-ă-ăd, and in Galilee, chased them with a great slaughter, until they were past Damascus and the borders thereof.

6 And the residue, that dwelt at Bĕ-thū'-lĭ-ă, fell upon the camp of Ăs'-sûr, and spoiled them, and were greatly enriched.

7 And the children of Israel that returned from the slaughter had that which remained; and the villages and the cities, that were in the mountains and in the plain, gat many spoils: for the multitude was very great.

8 Then Jō'-ă-cĭm the high priest, and the ancients of the children of Israel that dwelt in Jerusalem, came to behold the good things that God had shewed to Israel, and to see Judith, and to salute her.

9 And when they came unto her, they blessed her with one accord, and said unto her, Thou art the exaltation of Jerusalem, thou art the great glory of Israel, thou art the great rejoicing of our nation:

10 Thou hast done all these things by thine hand: thou hast done much good to Israel, and God is pleased therewith: blessed be thou of the Almighty Lord for evermore. And all the people said, So be it.

11 And the people spoiled the camp the space of thirty days: and they gave unto Judith Hŏl-ŏ-fēr'-nēs his tent, and all his plate, and beds, and vessels, and all his stuff: and she took it, and laid it on her mule; and made ready her carts, and laid them thereon.

12 Then all the women of Israel ran together to see her, and blessed her, and made a dance among them for her: and she took branches in her hand, and gave also to the women that were with her.

13 And they put a garland of olive upon her and her maid that was with her, and she went before all the people in the dance, leading all the women: and all the men of Israel followed in their armour with garlands, and with songs in their mouths.

CHAPTER XVI

THEN Judith began to sing this thanksgiving in all Israel, and all the people sang after her this song of praise.

2 And Judith said, Begin unto my God with timbrels, sing unto my Lord with cymbals: tune unto him a new psalm: exalt him, and call upon his name.

3 For God breaketh the battles: for among the camps in the midst of the people he hath delivered me out of the hands of them that persecuted me.

4 Ăs'-sûr came out of the mountains from the north, he came with ten thousands of his army, the multitude whereof stopped the torrents, and their horsemen have covered the hills.

5 He bragged that he would burn up my borders, and kill my young men with the sword, and dash the sucking children against the ground, and make mine infants as a prey, and my virgins as a spoil.

6 But the Almighty Lord hath disappointed them by the hand of a woman.

7 For the mighty one did not fall by the young men, neither did the sons of the Titans smite him, nor high giants set upon him: but Judith the daughter of Mĕ-rā'-rī weakened him with the beauty of her countenance.

8 For she put off the garment of her widowhood for the exaltation of those that were oppressed in Israel, and anointed her face with ointment, and bound her hair in a tire, and took a linen garment to deceive him.

9 Her sandals ravished his eyes, her beauty took his mind prisoner, and the fauchion passed through his neck.

10 The Persians quaked at her boldness, and the Medes were daunted at her hardiness.

11 Then my afflicted shouted for joy, and my weak ones cried aloud; but they were astonished: these lifted up their voices, but they were overthrown.

12 The sons of the damsels have pierced them through, and wounded them as fugitives' children: they perished by the battle of the Lord.

13 I will sing unto the Lord a new song: O Lord, thou art great and glorious, wonderful in strength, and invincible.

14 Let all creatures serve thee: for thou spakest, and they were made, thou didst send forth thy spirit, and it created them, and there is none that can resist thy voice.

15 For the mountains shall be moved from their foundations with the waters, the rocks shall melt as wax at thy presence: yet thou art merciful to them that fear thee.

16 For all sacrifice is too little for a sweet savour unto thee, and all the fat is not sufficient for thy burnt offering: but he that feareth the Lord is great at all times.

17 Woe to the nations that rise up against my kindred! the Lord Almighty will take vengeance of them in the day of judgment, in putting fire and worms in their flesh; and they shall feel them, and weep for ever.

18 Now as soon as they entered into Jerusalem, they worshipped the Lord; and as soon

as the people were purified, they offered their burnt offerings, and their free offerings, and their gifts.

19 Judith also dedicated all the stuff of Hŏl-ŏ-fẽr'-nēs, which the people had given her, and gave the canopy, which she had taken out of his bedchamber, for a gift unto the Lord.

20 So the people continued feasting in Jerusalem before the sanctuary for the space of three months, and Judith remained with them.

21 After this time every one returned to his own inheritance, and Judith went to Bē-thū'-lĭ-ă, and remained in her own possession, and was in her time honourable in all the country.

22 And many desired her, but none knew her all the days of her life, after that Mă-năs'-sēs her husband was dead, and was gathered to his people.

23 But she increased more and more in honour, and waxed old in her husband's house, being an hundred and five years old, and made her maid free; so she died in Bē-thū'-lĭ-ă: and they buried her in the cave of her husband Mă-năs'-sēs.

24 And the house of Israel lamented her seven days: and before she died, she did distribute her goods to all them that were nearest of kindred to Mă-năs'-sēs her husband, and to them that were the nearest of her kindred.

25 And there was none that made the children of Israel any more afraid in the days of Judith, nor a long time after her death.

THE REST OF THE CHAPTERS OF

THE BOOK OF ESTHER,

WHICH ARE FOUND NEITHER IN THE HEBREW NOR IN THE CHALDEE

Part of the Tenth Chapter after the Greek

THEN Mär-dŏ-chē'-ŭs said, God hath done these things.

5 For I remember a dream which I saw concerning these matters, and nothing thereof hath failed.

6 A little fountain became a river, and there was light, and the sun, and much water: this river is Esther, whom the king married, and made queen:

7 And the two dragons are I and Ā'-măn.

8 And the nations were those that were assembled to destroy the name of the Jews:

9 And my nation is this Israel, which cried to God, and were saved: for the Lord hath saved his people, and the Lord hath delivered us from all those evils, and God hath wrought signs and great wonders, which have not been done among the Gentiles.

10 Therefore hath he made two lots, one for the people of God, and another for all the Gentiles.

11 And these two lots came at the hour, and time, and day of judgment, before God among all nations.

12 So God remembered his people, and justified his inheritance.

13 Therefore those days shall be unto them in the month Ă-där′, the fourteenth and fifteenth day of the same month, with an assembly, and joy, and with gladness before God, according to the generations for ever among his people.

CHAPTER XI

IN the fourth year of the reign of Ptŏl-ĕ-mē′-ŭs and Cleopatra, Dŏ-sĭth′-ĕ-ŭs, who said he was a priest and Levite, and Ptolemeus his son, brought this epistle of Phū′-rĭm, which they said was the same, and that Lў-sĭm′-ă-chŭs the son of Ptolemeus, that was in Jerusalem, had interpreted it.

2 In the second year of the reign of Är-tăx-ĕrx′-ēs the great, in the first day of the month Nĭ′-săn, Mär-dŏ-chē′-ŭs the son of Jā′-ĭ-rŭs, the son of Sĕm′-ĕ-ī, the son of Cĭ′-sā-ī, of the tribe of Benjamin, had a dream;

3 Who was a Jew, and dwelt in the city of Susa, a great man, being a servitor in the king's court.

4 He was also one of the captives, which Năb′-ŭ-chŏ-dŏn′-ŏ-sôr the king of Babylon carried from Jerusalem with Jĕch-ŏ-nī′-ăs king of Judea; and this was his dream:

5 Behold a noise of a tumult, with thunder, and earthquakes, and uproar in the land:

6 And, behold, two great dragons came forth ready to fight, and their cry was great.

7 And at their cry all nations were prepared to battle, that they might fight against the righteous people.

8 And lo a day of darkness and obscurity, tribulation and anguish, affliction and great uproar, upon earth.

9 And the whole righteous nation was troubled, fearing their own evils, and were ready to perish.

10 Then they cried unto God, and upon their cry, as it were from a little fountain, was made a great flood, even much water.

11 The light and the sun rose up, and the lowly were exalted, and devoured the glorious.

12 Now when Mär-dŏ-chē′-ŭs, who had seen this dream, and what God had determined to do, was awake, he bare this dream in mind, and until night by all means was desirous to know it.

CHAPTER XII

AND Mär-dŏ-chē′-ŭs took his rest in the court with Găb′-ă-thă and Tharra, the two eunuchs of the king, and keepers of the palace.

2 And he heard their devices, and searched out their purposes, and learned that they were about to lay hands upon Är-tăx-ĕrx′-ēs the king; and so he certified the king of them.

3 Then the king examined the two eunuchs, and after that they had confessed it, they were strangled.

4 And the king made a record of these things, and Mär-dŏ-chē′-ŭs also wrote thereof.

5 So the king commanded

Mär-dŏ-chē'-ŭs to serve in the court, and for this he rewarded him.

6 Howbeit Ā'-măn the son of Ă-măd'-ă-thŭs the Ā'-găg-īte, who was in great honour with the king, sought to molest Mär-dŏ-chē'-ŭs and his people because of the two eunuchs of the king.

CHAPTER XIII

THE copy of the letters was this: The great king Är-tăx-ērx'-ēs writeth these things to the princes and governors that are under him from India unto E-thĭ-ō'-pĭ-ă, in an hundred and seven and twenty provinces.

2 After that I became lord over many nations, and had dominion over the whole world, not lifted up with presumption of my authority, but carrying myself alway with equity and mildness, I purposed to settle my subjects continually in a quiet life, and making my kingdom peaceable, and open for passage to the utmost coasts, to renew peace, which is desired of all men.

3 Now when I asked my counsellors how this might be brought to pass, Ā'-măn, that excelled in wisdom among us, and was approved for his constant good will and stedfast fidelity, and had the honour of the second place in the kingdom,

4 Declared unto us, that in all nations throughout the world there was scattered a certain malicious people, that had laws contrary to all nations, and continually despised the commandments of kings, so as the uniting of our kingdoms,

honourably intended by us, cannot go forward.

5 Seeing then we understand that this people alone is continually in opposition unto all men, differing in the strange manner of their laws, and evil affected to our state, working all the mischief they can, that our kingdom may not be firmly established:

6 Therefore have we commanded, that all they that are signified in writing unto you by Ā'-măn, who is ordained over the affairs, and is next unto us, shall all, with their wives and children, be utterly destroyed by the sword of their enemies, without all mercy and pity, the fourteenth day of the twelfth month Ă-där' of this present year:

7 That they, who of old and now also are malicious, may in one day with violence go into the grave, and so ever hereafter cause our affairs to be well settled, and without trouble.

8 Then Mär-dŏ-chē'-ŭs thought upon all the works of the Lord, and made his prayer unto him,

9 Saying, O Lord, Lord, the King Almighty: for the whole world is in thy power, and if thou hast appointed to save Israel, there is no man that can gainsay thee:

10 For thou hast made heaven and earth, and all the wondrous things under the heaven.

11 Thou art Lord of all things, and there is no man that can resist thee, which art the Lord.

12 Thou knowest all things, and thou knowest, Lord, that it was neither in contempt nor pride, nor for any desire of glory, that I did not bow down to proud Ā'-măn.

13 For I could have been content with good will for the salvation of Israel to kiss the soles of his feet.

14 But I did this, that I might not prefer the glory of man above the glory of God: neither will I worship any but thee, O God, neither will I do it in pride.

15 And now, O Lord God and King, spare thy people: for their eyes are upon us to bring us to nought; yea, they desire to destroy the inheritance, that hath been thine from the beginning.

16 Despise not the portion, which thou hast delivered out of Egypt for thine own self.

17 Hear my prayer, and be merciful unto thine inheritance: turn our sorrow into joy, that we may live, O Lord, and praise thy name: and destroy not the mouths of them that praise thee, O Lord.

18 All Israel in like manner cried most earnestly unto the Lord, because their death was before their eyes.

CHAPTER XIV

QUEEN Esther also, being in fear of death, resorted unto the Lord:

2 And laid away her glorious apparel, and put on the garments of anguish and mourning: and instead of precious ointments, she covered her head with ashes and dung, and she humbled her body greatly, and all the places of her joy she filled with her torn hair.

3 And she prayed unto the Lord God of Israel, saying, O my Lord, thou only art our King: help me, desolate woman, which have no helper but thee:

4 For my danger is in mine hand.

5 From my youth up I have heard in the tribe of my family, that thou, O Lord, tookest Israel from among all people, and our fathers from all their predecessors, for a perpetual inheritance, and thou hast performed whatsoever thou didst promise them.

6 And now we have sinned before thee: therefore hast thou given us into the hands of our enemies,

7 Because we worshipped their gods: O Lord, thou art righteous.

8 Nevertheless it satisfieth them not, that we are in bitter captivity: but they have stricken hands with their idols,

9 That they will abolish the thing that thou with thy mouth hast ordained, and destroy thine inheritance, and stop the mouth of them that praise thee, and quench the glory of thy house, and of thine altar,

10 And open the mouths of the heathen to set forth the praises of the idols, and to magnify a fleshly king for ever.

11 O Lord, give not thy sceptre unto them that be nothing, and let them not laugh at our fall; but turn their device upon themselves, and make him an example, that hath begun this against us.

12 Remember, O Lord, make thyself known in time of our affliction, and give me boldness, O King of the nations, and Lord of all power.

13 Give me eloquent speech in my mouth before the lion: turn his heart to hate him that fighteth against us, that there may be an end of him, and of

all that are likeminded to him:

14 But deliver us with thine hand, and help me that am desolate, and which have no other help but thee.

15 Thou knowest all things, O Lord; thou knowest that I hate the glory of the unrighteous, and abhor the bed of the uncircumcised, and of all the heathen.

16 Thou knowest my necessity: for I abhor the sign of my high estate, which is upon mine head in the days wherein I shew myself, and that I abhor it as a menstruous rag, and that I wear it not when I am private by myself,

17 And that thine handmaid hath not eaten at Ā'-măn's table, and that I have not greatly esteemed the king's feast, nor drunk the wine of the drink offerings.

18 Neither had thine handmaid any joy since the day that I was brought hither to this present, but in thee, O Lord God of Abraham.

19 O thou mighty God above all, hear the voice of the forlorn, and deliver us out of the hands of the mischievous, and deliver me out of my fear.

CHAPTER XV

AND upon the third day, when she had ended her prayer, she laid away her mourning garments, and put on her glorious apparel.

2 And being gloriously adorned, after she had called upon God, who is the beholder and saviour of all things, she took two maids with her:

3 And upon the one she leaned, as carrying herself daintily;

4 And the other followed, bearing up her train.

5 And she was ruddy through the perfection of her beauty, and her countenance was cheerful and very amiable: but her heart was in anguish for fear.

6 Then having passed through all the doors, she stood before the king, who sat upon his royal throne, and was clothed with all his robes of majesty, all glittering with gold and precious stones; and he was very dreadful.

7 Then lifting up his countenance that shone with majesty, he looked very fiercely upon her: and the queen fell down, and was pale, and fainted, and bowed herself upon the head of the maid that went before her.

8 Then God changed the spirit of the king into mildness, who in a fear leaped from his throne, and took her in his arms, till she came to herself again, and comforted her with loving words, and said unto her,

9 Esther, what is the matter? I am thy brother, be of good cheer:

10 Thou shalt not die, though our commandment be general: come near.

11 And so he held up his golden sceptre, and laid it upon her neck,

12 And embraced her, and said, Speak unto me.

13 Then said she unto him, I saw thee, my lord, as an angel of God, and my heart was troubled for fear of thy majesty.

14 For wonderful art thou, lord, and thy countenance is full of grace.

15 And as she was speaking, she fell down for faintness.

16 Then the king was troubled, and all his servants comforted her.

CHAPTER XVI

THE great king Är-tăx-ẽrx'-ĕs unto the princes and governors of an hundred and seven and twenty provinces from India unto E-thi-ō'-pi-ă and unto all our faithful subjects, greeting.

2 Many, the more often they are honoured with the great bounty of their gracious princes, the more proud they are waxen,

3 And endeavour to hurt not our subjects only, but not being able to bear abundance, do take in hand to practise also against those that do them good:

4 And take not only thankfulness away from among men, but also lifted up with the glorious words of lewd persons, that were never good, they think to escape the justice of God, that seeth all things, and hateth evil.

5 Oftentimes also fair speech of those, that are put in trust to manage their friends' affairs, hath caused many that are in authority to be partakers of innocent blood, and hath enwrapped them in remediless calamities:

6 Beguiling with the falsehood and deceit of their lewd disposition the innocency and goodness of princes.

7 Now ye may see this, as we have declared, not so much by ancient histories, as ye may, if ye search what hath been wickedly done of late through the pestilent behaviour of them that are unworthily placed in authority.

8 And we must take care for the time to come, that our kingdom may be quiet and peaceable for all men,

9 Both by changing our purposes, and always judging things that are evident with more equal proceeding.

10 For Ā'-măn, a Macedonian, the son of Ă-măd'-ă-thă, being indeed a stranger from the Persian blood, and far distant from our goodness, and as a stranger received of us,

11 Had so far forth obtained the favour that we shew toward every nation, as that he was called our father, and was continually honoured of all men, as the next person unto the king.

12 But he, not bearing his great dignity, went about to deprive us of our kingdom and life:

13 Having by manifold and cunning deceits sought of us the destruction, as well of Mär-dŏ-<u>che</u>'-ŭs, who saved our life, and continually procured our good, as also of blameless Esther, partaker of our kingdom, with their whole nation.

14 For by these means he thought, finding us destitute of friends, to have translated the kingdom of the Persians to the Macedonians.

15 But we find that the Jews, whom this wicked wretch hath delivered to utter destruction, are no evildoers, but live by most just laws:

16 And that they be children of the most high and most mighty living God, who hath ordered the kingdom both unto us and to our progenitors in the most excellent manner.

17 Wherefore ye shall do well not to put in execution the letters sent unto you by Ā'-măn the son of Ā-măd'-ă-thã.

18 For he, that was the worker of these things, is hanged at the gates of Susa with all his family: God, who ruleth all things, speedily rendering vengeance to him according to his deserts.

19 Therefore ye shall publish the copy of this letter in all places, that the Jews may freely live after their own laws.

20 And ye shall aid them, that even the same day, being the thirteenth day of the twelfth month Ā-där', they may be avenged on them, who in the time of their affliction shall set upon them.

21 For Almighty God hath turned to joy unto them the day, wherein the chosen people should have perished.

22 Ye shall therefore among your solemn feasts keep it an high day with all feasting:

23 That both now and hereafter there may be safety to us, and the well affected Persians; but to those which do conspire against us a memorial of destruction.

24 Therefore every city and country whatsoever, which shall not do according to these things, shall be destroyed without mercy with fire and sword, and shall be made not only unpassable for men, but also most hateful to wild beasts and fowls for ever.

THE
WISDOM OF SOLOMON

CHAPTER I

LOVE righteousness, ye that be judges of the earth: think of the Lord with a good (heart,) and in simplicity of heart seek him.

2 For he will be found of them that tempt him not; and sheweth himself unto such as do not distrust him.

3 For froward thoughts separate from God: and his power, when it is tried, reproveth the unwise.

4 For into a malicious soul wisdom shall not enter; nor dwell in the body that is subject unto sin.

5 For the holy spirit of discipline will flee deceit, and re-

move from thoughts that are without understanding, and will not abide when unrighteousness cometh in.

6 For wisdom is a loving spirit; and will not acquit a blasphemer of his words: for God is witness of his reins, and a true beholder of his heart, and a hearer of his tongue.

7 For the Spirit of the Lord filleth the world: and that which containeth all things hath knowledge of the voice.

8 Therefore he that speaketh unrighteous things cannot be hid: neither shall vengeance, when it punisheth, pass by him.

9 For inquisition shall be made into the counsels of the ungodly: and the sound of his

words shall come unto the Lord for the manifestation of his wicked deeds.

10 For the ear of jealousy heareth all things: and the noise of murmurings is not hid.

11 Therefore beware of murmuring, which is unprofitable; and refrain your tongue from backbiting: for there is no word so secret, that shall go for nought: and the mouth that belieth slayeth the soul.

12 Seek not death in the error of your life: and pull not upon yourselves destruction with the works of your hands.

13 For God made not death: neither hath he pleasure in the destruction of the living.

14 For he created all things, that they might have their being: and the generations of the world were healthful; and there is no poison of destruction in them, nor the kingdom of death upon the earth:

15 (For righteousness is immortal:)

16 But ungodly men with their works and words called *it* to them: for when they thought to have it their friend, they consumed to nought, and made a covenant with it, because they are worthy to take part with it.

CHAPTER II

FOR the *ungodly* said, reasoning with themselves, but not aright, Our life is short and tedious, and in the death of a man there is no remedy: neither was there any man known to have returned from the grave.

2 For we are born at all adventure: and we shall be hereafter as though we had never been: for the breath in our nostrils is as smoke, and a little spark in the moving of our heart:

3 Which being extinguished, our body shall be turned into ashes, and our spirit shall vanish as the soft air,

4 And our name shall be forgotten in time, and no man shall have our works in remembrance, and our life shall pass away as the trace of a cloud, and shall be dispersed as a mist, that is driven away with the beams of the sun, and overcome with the heat thereof.

5 For our time is a very shadow that passeth away; and after our end there is no returning: for it is fast sealed, so that no man cometh again.

6 Come on therefore, let us enjoy the good things that are present: and let us speedily use the creatures like as in youth.

7 Let us fill ourselves with costly wine and ointments: and let no flower of the spring pass by us:

8 Let us crown ourselves with rosebuds, before they be withered:

9 Let none of us go without his part of our voluptuousness: let us leave tokens of our joyfulness in every place: for this is our portion, and our lot is this.

10 Let us oppress the poor righteous man, let us not spare the widow, nor reverence the ancient gray hairs of the aged.

11 Let our strength be the law of justice: for that which is feeble is found to be nothing worth.

12 Therefore let us lie in wait

for the righteous; because he is not for our turn, and he is clean contrary to our doings: he upbraideth us with our offending the law, and objecteth to our infamy the transgressings of our education.

13 He professeth to have the knowledge of God: and he calleth himself the child of the Lord.

14 He was made to reprove our thoughts.

15 He is grievous unto us even to behold: for his life is not like other men's, his ways are of another fashion.

16 We are esteemed of him as counterfeits: he abstaineth from our ways as from filthiness: he pronounceth the end of the just to be blessed, and maketh his boast that God is his father.

17 Let us see if his words be true: and let us prove what shall happen in the end of him.

18 For if the just man be the son of God, he will help him, and deliver him from the hand of his enemies.

19 Let us examine him with despitefulness and torture, that we may know his meekness, and prove his patience.

20 Let us condemn him with a shameful death: for by his own saying he shall be respected.

21 Such things they did imagine, and were deceived: for their own wickedness hath blinded them.

22 As for the mysteries of God, they knew them not: neither hoped they for the wages of righteousness, nor discerned a reward for blameless souls.

23 For God created man to be immortal, and made him to be an image of his own eternity.

24 Nevertheless through envy of the devil came death into the world: and they that do hold of his side do find it.

CHAPTER III

BUT the souls of the righteous are in the hand of God, and there shall no torment touch them.

2 In the sight of the unwise they seemed to die: and their departure is taken for misery,

3 And their going from us to be utter destruction: but they are in peace.

4 For though they be punished in the sight of men, yet is their hope full of immortality.

5 And having been a little chastised, they shall be greatly rewarded: for God proved them, and found them worthy for himself.

6 As gold in the furnace hath he tried them, and received them as a burnt offering.

7 And in the time of their visitation they shall shine, and run to and fro like sparks among the stubble.

8 They shall judge the nations, and have dominion over the people, and their Lord shall reign for ever.

9 They that put their trust in him shall understand the truth: and such as be faithful in love shall abide with him: for grace and mercy is to his saints, and he hath care for his elect.

10 But the ungodly shall be punished according to their own imaginations, which have neglected the righteous, and forsaken the Lord.

11 For whoso despiseth wisdom and nurture, he is miserable, and their hope is vain,

their labours unfruitful, and their works unprofitable:

12 Their wives are foolish, and their children wicked:

13 Their offspring is cursed. Wherefore blessed is the barren that is undefiled, which hath not known the sinful bed: she shall have fruit in the visitation of souls.

14 And *blessed is* the eunuch, which with his hands hath wrought no iniquity, nor imagined wicked things against God: for unto him shall be given the special gift of faith, and an inheritance in the temple of the Lord more acceptable to his mind.

15 For glorious is the fruit of good labours: and the root of wisdom shall never fall away.

16 As for the children of adulterers, they shall not come to their perfection, and the seed of an unrighteous bed shall be rooted out.

17 For though they live long, yet shall they be nothing regarded: and their last age shall be without honour.

18 Or, if they die quickly, they have no hope, neither comfort in the day of trial.

19 For horrible is the end of the unrighteous generation.

CHAPTER IV

BETTER it is to have no children, and to have virtue: for the memorial thereof is immortal: because it is known with God, and with men.

2 When it is present, men take example at it; and when it is gone, they desire it: it weareth a crown, and triumpheth for ever, having gotten the victory, striving for undefiled rewards.

3 But the multiplying brood of the ungodly shall not thrive, nor take deep rooting from bastard slips, nor lay any fast foundation.

4 For though they flourish in branches for a time; yet standing not fast, they shall be shaken with the wind, and through the force of winds they shall be rooted out.

5 The imperfect branches shall be broken off, their fruit unprofitable, not ripe to eat, yea, meet for nothing.

6 For children begotten of unlawful beds are witnesses of wickedness against their parents in their trial.

7 But though the righteous be prevented with death, yet shall he be in rest.

8 For honourable age is not that which standeth in length of time, nor that is measured by number of years.

9 But wisdom is the gray hair unto men, and an unspotted life is old age.

10 He pleased God, and was beloved of him: so that living among sinners he was translated.

11 Yea, speedily was he taken away, lest that wickedness should alter his understanding, or deceit beguile his soul.

12 For the bewitching of naughtiness doth obscure things that are honest; and the wandering of concupiscence doth undermine the simple mind.

13 He, being made perfect in a short time, fulfilled a long time:

14 For his soul pleased the Lord: therefore hasted he *to take him away* from among the wicked.

15 This the people saw, and

understood it not, neither laid they up this in their minds, That his grace and mercy is with his saints, and that he hath respect unto his chosen.

16 Thus the righteous that is dead shall condemn the ungodly which are living; and youth that is soon perfected the many years and old age of the unrighteous.

17 For they shall see the end of the wise, and shall not understand what God in his counsel hath decreed of him, and to what end the Lord hath set him in safety.

18 They shall see him, and despise him; but God shall laugh them to scorn: and they shall hereafter be a vile carcase, and a reproach among the dead for evermore.

19 For he shall rend them, and cast them down headlong, that they shall be speechless; and he shall shake them from the foundation; and they shall be utterly laid waste, and be in sorrow; and their memorial shall perish.

20 And when they cast up the accounts of their sins, they shall come with fear: and their own iniquities shall convince them to their face.

CHAPTER V

THEN shall the righteous man stand in great boldness before the face of such as have afflicted him, and made no account of his labours.

2 When they see it, they shall be troubled with terrible fear, and shall be amazed at the strangeness of his salvation, so far beyond all that they looked for.

3 And they repenting and

groaning for anguish of spirit shall say within themselves, This was he, whom we had sometimes in derision, and a proverb of reproach:

4 We fools accounted his life madness, and his end to be without honour:

5 How is he numbered among the children of God, and his lot is among the saints!

6 Therefore have we erred from the way of truth, and the light of righteousness hath not shined unto us, and the sun of righteousness rose not upon us.

7 We wearied ourselves in the way of wickedness and destruction: yea, we have gone through deserts, where there lay no way: but as for the way of the Lord, we have not known it.

8 What hath pride profited us? or what good hath riches with *our* vaunting brought us?

9 All those things are passed away like a shadow, and as a post that hasted by;

10 And as a ship that passeth over the waves of the water, which when it is gone by, the trace thereof cannot be found, neither the pathway of the keel in the waves;

11 Or as when a bird hath flown through the air, there is no token of her way to be found, but the light air being beaten with the stroke of her wings, and parted with the violent noise and motion of them, is passed through, and therein afterwards no sign where she went is to be found;

12 Or like as when an arrow is shot at a mark, it parteth the air, which immediately cometh together again, so that a man cannot know where it went through:

13 Even so we in like manner, as soon as we were born, began to draw to our end, and had no sign of virtue to shew; but were consumed in our own wickedness.

14 For the hope of the ungodly is like dust that is blown away with the wind; like a thin froth that is driven away with the storm; like as the smoke which is dispersed here and there with a tempest, and passeth away as the remembrance of a guest that tarrieth but a day.

15 But the righteous live for evermore; their reward also is with the Lord, and the care of them is with the most High.

16 Therefore shall they receive a glorious kingdom, and a beautiful crown from the Lord's hand: for with his right hand shall he cover them, and with his arm shall he protect them.

17 He shall take to him his jealousy for complete armour, and make the creature his weapon for the revenge of *his* enemies.

18 He shall put on righteousness as a breastplate, and true judgment instead of an helmet.

19 He shall take holiness for an invincible shield.

20 His severe wrath shall he sharpen for a sword, and the world shall fight with him against the unwise.

21 Then shall the right aiming thunderbolts go abroad; and from the clouds, as from a well drawn bow, shall they fly to the mark.

22 And hailstones full of wrath shall be cast *as* out of a stone bow, and the water of the sea shall rage against them, and the floods shall cruelly drown them.

23 Yea, a mighty wind shall stand up against them, and like a storm shall blow them away: thus iniquity shall lay waste the whole earth, and ill dealing shall overthrow the thrones of the mighty.

CHAPTER VI

HEAR therefore, O ye kings, and understand; learn, ye that be judges of the ends of the earth.

2 Give ear, ye that rule the people, and glory in the multitude of nations.

3 For power is given you of the Lord, and sovereignty from the Highest, who shall try your works, and search out your counsels.

4 Because, being ministers of his kingdom, ye have not judged aright, nor kept the law, nor walked after the counsel of God;

5 Horribly and speedily shall he come upon you: for a sharp judgment shall be to them that be in high places.

6 For mercy will soon pardon the meanest: but mighty men shall be mightily tormented.

7 For he which is Lord over all shall fear no man's person, neither shall he stand in awe of any man's greatness: for he hath made the small and great, and careth for all alike.

8 But a sore trial shall come upon the mighty.

9 Unto you therefore, O kings, do I speak, that ye may learn wisdom, and not fall away.

10 For they that keep holiness holily shall be judged holy: and they that have

learned such things shall find what to answer.

11 Wherefore set your affection upon my words; desire them, and ye shall be instructed.

12 Wisdom is glorious, and never fadeth away: yea, she is easily seen of them that love her, and found of such as seek her.

13 She preventeth them that desire her, in making herself first known unto them.

14 Whoso seeketh her early shall have no great travail: for he shall find her sitting at his doors.

15 To think therefore upon her is perfection of wisdom: and whoso watcheth for her shall quickly be without care.

16 For she goeth about seeking such as are worthy of her, sheweth herself favourably unto them in the ways, and meeteth them in every thought.

17 For the very true beginning of her is the desire of discipline; and the care of discipline is love;

18 And love is the keeping of her laws; and the giving heed unto her laws is the assurance of incorruption;

19 And incorruption maketh us near unto God:

20 Therefore the desire of wisdom bringeth to a kingdom.

21 If your delight be then in thrones and sceptres, O ye kings of the people, honour wisdom, that ye may reign for evermore.

22 As for wisdom, what she is, and how she came up, I will tell you, and will not hide mysteries from you: but will seek her out from the beginning of her nativity, and bring the knowledge of her into

116

light, and will not pass over the truth.

23 Neither will I go with consuming envy; for such a man shall have no fellowship with wisdom.

24 But the multitude of the wise is the welfare of the world: and a wise king is the upholding of the people.

25 Receive therefore instruction through my words, and it shall do you good.

CHAPTER VII

I MYSELF also am a mortal man, like to all, and the offspring of him that was first made of the earth,

2 And in my mother's womb was fashioned to be flesh in the time of ten months, being compacted in blood, of the seed of man, and the pleasure that came with sleep.

3 And when I was born, I drew in the common air, and fell upon the earth, which is of like nature, and the first voice which I uttered was crying, as all others do.

4 I was nursed in swaddling clothes, and that with cares.

5 For there is no king that had any other beginning of birth.

6 For all men have one entrance into life, and the like going out.

7 Wherefore I prayed, and understanding was given me: I called *upon* God, and the spirit of wisdom came to me.

8 I preferred her before sceptres and thrones, and esteemed riches nothing in comparison of her.

9 Neither compared I unto her any precious stone, because all gold in respect of her is as a little sand, and silver

shall be counted as clay before her.

10 I loved her above health and beauty, and chose to have her instead of light: for the light that cometh from her never goeth out.

11 All good things together came to me with her, and innumerable riches in her hands.

12 And I rejoiced in *them* all, because wisdom goeth before them: and I knew not that she was the mother of them.

13 I learned diligently, and do communicate *her* liberally: I do not hide her riches.

14 For she is a treasure unto men that never faileth: which they that use become the friends of God, being commended for the gifts that come from learning.

15 God hath granted me to speak as I would, and to conceive as is meet for the things that are given me: because it is he that leadeth unto wisdom, and directeth the wise.

16 For in his hand are both we and our words; all wisdom also, and knowledge of workmanship.

17 For he hath given me certain knowledge of the things that are, namely, to know how the world was made, and the operation of the elements:

18 The beginning, ending, and midst of the times: the alterations of the turning *of the sun*, and the change of seasons:

19 The circuits of years, and the positions of stars:

20 The natures of living creatures, and the furies of wild beasts: the violence of winds, and the reasonings of men: the diversities of plants, and the virtues of roots:

21 And all such things as are either secret or manifest, them I know.

22 For wisdom, which is the worker of all things, taught me: for in her is an understanding spirit, holy, one only, manifold, subtil, lively, clear, undefiled, plain, not subject to hurt, loving the thing that is good, quick, which cannot be letted, ready to do good,

23 Kind to man, stedfast, sure, free from care, having all power, overseeing all things, and going through all understanding, pure, and most subtil, spirits.

24 For wisdom is more moving than any motion: she passeth and goeth through all things by reason of her pureness.

25 For she is the breath of the power of God, and a pure influence flowing from the glory of the Almighty: therefore can no defiled thing fall into her.

26 For she is the brightness of the everlasting light, the unspotted mirror of the power of God, and the image of his goodness.

27 And being but one, she can do all things: and remaining in herself, she maketh all things new: and in all ages entering into holy souls, she maketh them friends of God, and prophets.

28 For God loveth none but him that dwelleth with wisdom.

29 For she is more beautiful than the sun, and above all the order of stars: being compared with the light, she is found before it.

30 For after this cometh night: but vice shall not prevail against wisdom.

CHAPTER VIII

*W*ISDOM reacheth from one end to another mightily: and sweetly doth she order all things.

2 I loved her, and sought *her* out from my youth, I desired to make *her* my spouse, and I was a lover of her beauty.

3 In that she is conversant with God, she magnifieth her nobility: yea, the Lord of all things himself loved her.

4 For she is privy to the mysteries of the knowledge of God, and a lover of his works.

5 If riches be a possession to be desired in this life; what is richer than wisdom, that worketh all things?

6 And if prudence work; who of all that are is a more cunning workman than she?

7 And if a man love righteousness, her labours are virtues: for she teacheth temperance and prudence, justice and fortitude: which are such things, as men can have nothing more profitable in their life.

8 If a man desire much experience, she knoweth things of old, and conjectureth *aright* what is to come: she knoweth the subtilties of speeches, and can expound dark sentences: she foreseeth signs and wonders, and the events of seasons and times.

9 Therefore I purposed to take her to me to live with me, knowing that she would be a counsellor of good things, and a comfort in cares and grief.

10 For her sake I shall have estimation among the multitude, and honour with the elders, though I be young.

11 I shall be found of a quick conceit in judgment, and shall be admired in the sight of great men.

12 When I hold my tongue, they shall bide my leisure, and when I speak, they shall give good ear unto me: if I talk much, they shall lay their hands upon their mouth.

13 Moreover by the means of her I shall obtain immortality, and leave behind me an everlasting memorial to them that come after me.

14 I shall set the people in order, and the nations shall be subject unto me.

15 Horrible tyrants shall be afraid, when they do but hear of me; I shall be found good among the multitude, and valiant in war.

16 After I am come into mine house, I will repose myself with her: for her conversation hath no bitterness; and to live with her hath no sorrow, but mirth and joy.

17 Now when I considered these things in myself, and pondered them in my heart, how that to be allied unto wisdom is immortality;

18 And great pleasure it is to have her friendship; and in the works of her hands are infinite riches; and in the exercise of conference with her, prudence; and in talking with her, a good report; I went about seeking how to take her to me.

19 For I was a witty child, and had a good spirit.

20 Yea rather, being good, I came into a body undefiled.

21 Nevertheless, when I perceived that I could not otherwise obtain her, except God gave her me; and that was a point of wisdom also to know whose gift she was; I prayed

unto the Lord, and besought him, and with my whole heart I said,

CHAPTER IX

O GOD of my fathers, and Lord of mercy, who hast made all things with thy word,

2 And ordained man through thy wisdom, that he should have dominion over the creatures which thou hast made,

3 And order the world according to equity and righteousness, and execute judgment with an upright heart:

4 Give me wisdom, that sitteth by thy throne; and reject me not from among thy children:

5 For I thy servant and son of thine handmaid am a feeble person, and of a short time, and too young for the understanding of judgment and laws.

6 For though a man be never so perfect among the children of men, yet if thy wisdom be not with him, he shall be nothing regarded.

7 Thou hast chosen me to be a king of thy people, and a judge of thy sons and daughters:

8 Thou hast commanded me to build a temple upon thy holy mount, and an altar in the city wherein thou dwellest, a resemblance of the holy tabernacle, which thou hast prepared from the beginning.

9 And wisdom was with thee: which knoweth thy works, and was present when thou madest the world, and knew what was acceptable in thy sight, and right in thy commandments.

10 O send her out of thy holy heavens, and from the throne of thy glory, that being present she may labour with me, that I may know what is pleasing unto thee.

11 For she knoweth and understandeth all things, and she shall lead me soberly in my doings, and preserve me in her power.

12 So shall my works be acceptable, and then shall I judge thy people righteously, and be worthy to sit in my father's seat.

13 For what man is he that can know the counsel of God? or who can think what the will of the Lord is?

14 For the thoughts of mortal men are miserable, and our devices are but uncertain.

15 For the corruptible body presseth down the soul, and the earthy tabernacle weigheth down the mind that museth upon many things.

16 And hardly do we guess aright at things that are upon earth, and with labour do we find the things that are before us: but the things that are in heaven who hath searched out?

17 And thy counsel who hath known, except thou give wisdom, and send thy Holy Spirit from above?

18 For so the ways of them which lived on the earth were reformed, and men were taught the things that are pleasing unto thee, and were saved through wisdom.

CHAPTER X

SHE preserved the first formed father of the world, that was created alone, and brought him out of his fall,

2 And gave him power to rule all things.

3 But when the unrighteous went away from her in his

anger, he perished also in the fury wherewith he murdered his brother.

4 For whose cause the earth being drowned with the flood, wisdom again preserved it, and directed the course of the righteous in a piece of wood of small value.

5 Moreover, the nations in their wicked conspiracy being confounded, she found out the righteous, and preserved him blameless unto God, and kept him strong against his tender compassion toward his son.

6 When the ungodly perished, she delivered the righteous man, who fled from the fire which fell down upon the five cities.

7 Of whose wickedness even to this day the waste land that smoketh is a testimony, and plants bearing fruit that never come to ripeness: and a standing pillar of salt is a monument of an unbelieving soul.

8 For regarding not wisdom, they gat not only this hurt, that they knew not the things which were good; but also left behind them to the world a memorial of their foolishness: so that in the things wherein they offended they could not so much as be hid.

9 But wisdom delivered from pain those that attended upon her.

10 When the righteous fled from his brother's wrath, she guided him in right paths, shewed him the kingdom of God, and gave him knowledge of holy things, made him rich in his travels, and multiplied *the fruit of* his labours.

11 In the covetousness of such as oppressed him she stood

by him, and made him rich.

12 She defended him from his enemies, and kept him safe from those that lay in wait, and in a sore conflict she gave him the victory; that he might know that godliness is stronger than all.

13 When the righteous was sold, she forsook him not, but delivered him from sin: she went down with him into the pit,

14 And left him not in bonds, till she brought him the sceptre of the kingdom, and power against those that oppressed him: as for them that had accused him, she shewed them to be liars, and gave him perpetual glory.

15 She delivered the righteous people and blameless seed from the nation that oppressed them.

16 She entered into the soul of the servant of the Lord, and withstood dreadful kings in wonders and signs;

17 Rendered to the righteous a reward of their labours, guided them in a marvellous way, and was unto them for a cover by day, and a light of stars in the night season;

18 Brought them through the Red sea, and led them through much water:

19 But she drowned their enemies, and cast them up out of the bottom of the deep.

20 Therefore the righteous spoiled the ungodly, and praised thy holy name, O Lord, and magnified with one accord thine hand, that fought for them.

21 For wisdom opened the mouth of the dumb, and made the tongues of them that cannot speak eloquent.

CHAPTER XI

SHE prospered their works in the hand of the holy prophet.

2 They went through the wilderness that was not inhabited, and pitched tents in places where there lay no way.

3 They stood against their enemies, and were avenged of their adversaries.

4 When they were thirsty, they called upon thee, and water was given them out of the flinty rock, and their thirst was quenched out of the hard stone.

5 For by what things their enemies were punished, by the same they in their need were benefited.

6 For instead of a fountain of a perpetual running river troubled with foul blood,

7 For a manifest reproof of that commandment, whereby the infants were slain, thou gavest unto them abundance of water by a means which they hoped not for:

8 Declaring by that thirst then how thou hadst punished their adversaries.

9 For when they were tried, albeit but in mercy chastised, they knew how the ungodly were judged in wrath and tormented, thirsting in another manner than the just.

10 For these thou didst admonish and try, as a father: but the other, as a severe king, thou didst condemn and punish.

11 Whether they were absent or present, they were vexed alike.

12 For a double grief came upon them, and a groaning for the remembrance of things past.

13 For when they heard by their own punishments the other to be benefited, they had some feeling of the Lord.

14 For whom they rejected with scorn, when he was long before thrown out at the casting forth *of the infants*, him in the end, when they saw what came to pass, they admired.

15 But for the foolish devices of their wickedness, wherewith being deceived they worshipped serpents void of reason, and vile beasts, thou didst send a multitude of unreasonable beasts upon them for vengeance;

16 That they might know, that wherewithal a man sinneth, by the same also shall he be punished.

17 For thy Almighty hand, that made the world of matter without form, wanted not means to send among them a multitude of bears, or fierce lions,

18 Or unknown wild beasts, full of rage, newly created, breathing out either a fiery vapour, or filthy scents of scattered smoke, or shooting horrible sparkles out of their eyes:

19 Whereof not only the harm might dispatch them at once, but also the terrible sight utterly destroy them.

20 Yea, and without these might they have fallen down with one blast, being persecuted of vengeance, and scattered abroad through the breath of thy power: but thou hast ordered all things in measure and number and weight.

21 For thou canst shew thy great strength at all times

when thou wilt; and who may withstand the power of thine arm?

22 For the whole world before thee is as a little grain of the balance, yea, as a drop of the morning dew that falleth down upon the earth.

23 But thou hast mercy upon all; for thou canst do all things, and winkest at the sins of men, because they should amend.

24 For thou lovest all the things that are, and abhorrest nothing which thou hast made: for never wouldest thou have made any thing, if thou hadst hated it.

25 And how could any thing have endured, if it had not been thy will? or been preserved, if not called by thee?

26 But thou sparest all: for they are thine, O Lord, thou lover of souls.

CHAPTER XII

FOR thine incorruptible Spirit is in all things.

2 Therefore chastenest thou them by little and little that offend, and warnest them by putting them in remembrance wherein they have offended, that leaving their wickedness they may believe on thee, O Lord.

3 For it was thy will to destroy by the hands of our fathers both those old inhabitants of thy holy land,

4 Whom thou hatedst for doing most odious works of witchcrafts, and wicked sacrifices;

5 And also those merciless murderers of children, and devourers of man's flesh, and the feasts of blood,

6 With their priests out of the midst of their idolatrous crew, and the parents, that killed with their own hands souls destitute of help:

7 That the land, which thou esteemedst above all other, might receive a worthy colony of God's children.

8 Nevertheless even those thou sparedst as men, and didst send wasps, forerunners of thine host, to destroy them by little and little.

9 Not that thou wast unable to bring the ungodly under the hand of the righteous in battle, or to destroy them at once with cruel beasts, or with one rough word:

10 But executing thy judgments upon them by little and little, thou gavest them place of repentance, not being ignorant that they were a naughty generation, and that their malice was bred in them, and that their cogitation would never be changed.

11 For it was a cursed seed from the beginning; neither didst thou for fear of any man give them pardon for those things wherein they sinned.

12 For who shall say, What hast thou done? or who shall withstand thy judgment? or who shall accuse thee for the nations that perish, whom thou hast made? or who shall come to stand against thee, to be revenged for the unrighteous men?

13 For neither is there any God but thou that careth for all, to whom thou mightest shew that thy judgment is not unright.

14 Neither shall king or tyrant be able to set his face against thee for any whom thou hast punished.

15 Forsomuch then as thou art righteous thyself, thou orderest all things righteously: thinking it not agreeable with thy power to condemn him that hath not deserved to be punished.

16 For thy power is the beginning of righteousness, and because thou art the Lord of all, it maketh thee to be gracious unto all.

17 For when men will not believe that thou art of a full power, thou shewest thy strength, and among them that know it thou makest their boldness manifest.

18 But thou, mastering thy power, judgest with equity, and orderest us with great favour: for thou mayest use power when thou wilt.

19 But by such works hast thou taught thy people that the just man should be merciful, and hast made thy children to be of a good hope that thou givest repentance for sins.

20 For if thou didst punish the enemies of thy children, and the condemned to death, with such deliberation, giving them time and place, whereby they might be delivered from their malice:

21 With how great circumspection didst thou judge thine own sons, unto whose fathers thou hast sworn, and made covenants of good promises?

22 Therefore, whereas thou dost chasten us, thou scourgest our enemies a thousand times more, to the intent that, when we judge, we should carefully think of thy goodness, and when we ourselves are judged, we should look for mercy.

23 Wherefore, whereas men have lived dissolutely and unrighteously, thou hast tormented them with their own abominations.

24 For they went astray very far in the ways of error, and held them for gods, which even among the beasts of their enemies were despised, being deceived, as children of no understanding.

25 Therefore unto them, as to children without the use of reason, thou didst send a judgment to mock them.

26 But they that would not be reformed by that correction, wherein he dallied with them, shall feel a judgment worthy of God.

27 For, look, for what things they grudged, when they were punished, that is, for them whom they thought to be gods; [now] being punished in them, when they saw it, they acknowledged him to be the true God, whom before they denied to know; and therefore came extreme damnation upon them.

CHAPTER XIII

SURELY vain are all men by nature, who are ignorant of God, and could not out of the good things that are seen know him that is: neither by considering the works did they acknowledge the workmaster;

2 But deemed either fire, or wind, or the swift air, or the circle of the stars, or the violent water, or the lights of heaven, to be the gods which govern the world.

3 With whose beauty if they being delighted took them to be gods; let them know how much better the Lord of them

is: for the first author of beauty hath created them.

4 But if they were astonished at their power and virtue, let them understand by them, how much mightier he is that made them.

5 For by the greatness and beauty of the creatures proportionably the maker of them is seen.

6 But yet for this they are the less to be blamed: for they peradventure err, seeking God, and desirous to find him.

7 For being conversant in his works they search *him* diligently, and believe their sight: because the things are beautiful that are seen.

8 Howbeit neither are they to be pardoned.

9 For if they were able to know so much, that they could aim at the world; how did they not sooner find out the Lord thereof?

10 But miserable are they, and in dead things is their hope, who called them gods, which are the works of men's hands, gold and silver, to shew art in, and resemblances of beasts, or a stone good for nothing, the work of an ancient hand.

11 Now a carpenter that felleth timber, after he hath sawn down a tree meet for the purpose, and taken off all the bark skilfully round about, and hath wrought it handsomely, and made a vessel thereof fit for the service of man's life;

12 And after spending the refuse of his work to dress his meat, hath filled himself;

13 And taking the very refuse among those which served to no use, being a crooked piece

of wood, and full of knots, hath carved it diligently, when he had nothing else to do, and formed it by the skill of his understanding, and fashioned it to the image of a man;

14 Or made it like some vile beast, laying it over with vermilion, and with paint colouring it red, and covering every spot therein;

15 And when he had made a convenient room for it, set it in a wall, and made it fast with iron:

16 For he provided for it that it might not fall, knowing that it was unable to help itself; for it is an image, and hath need of help:

17 Then maketh he prayer for his goods, for his wife and children, and is not ashamed to speak to that which hath no life.

18 For health he calleth upon that which is weak: for life prayeth to that which is dead: for aid humbly beseecheth that which hath least means to help: and for a good journey he asketh of that which cannot set a foot forward:

19 And for gaining and getting, and for good success of his hands, asketh ability to do of him, that is most unable to do any thing.

CHAPTER XIV

AGAIN, one preparing himself to sail, and about to pass through the raging waves, calleth upon a piece of wood more rotten than the vessel that carrieth him.

2 For verily desire of gain devised that, and the workman built it by his skill.

3 But thy providence, O

Father, governeth it: for thou hast made a way in the sea, and a safe path in the waves;

4 Shewing that thou canst save from all danger: yea, though a man went to sea without art.

5 Nevertheless thou wouldest not that the works of thy wisdom should be idle, and therefore do men commit their lives to a small piece of wood, and passing the rough sea in a weak vessel are saved.

6 For in the old time also, when the proud giants perished, the hope of the world governed by thy hand escaped in a weak vessel, and left to all ages a seed of generation.

7 For blessed is the wood whereby righteousness cometh.

8 But that which is made with hands is cursed, as well it, as he that made it: he, because he made it; and it, because, being corruptible, it was called god.

9 For the ungodly and his ungodliness are both alike hateful unto God.

10 For that which is made shall be punished together with him that made it.

11 Therefore even upon the idols of the Gentiles shall there be a visitation: because in the creature of God they are become an abomination, and stumblingblocks to the souls of men, and a snare to the feet of the unwise.

12 For the devising of idols was the beginning of *spiritual* fornication, and the invention of them the corruption of life.

13 For neither were they from the beginning, neither shall they be for ever.

14 For by the vain glory of men they entered into the world, and therefore shall they come shortly to an end.

15 For a father afflicted with untimely mourning, when he hath made an image of his child soon taken away, now honoured him as a god, which was then a dead man, and delivered to those that were under him ceremonies and sacrifices.

16 Thus in process of time an ungodly custom grown strong was kept as a law, and graven images were worshipped by the commandments of kings.

17 Whom men could not honour in presence, because they dwelt far off, they took the counterfeit of his visage from far, and made an express image of a king whom they honoured, to the end that by this their forwardness they might flatter him that was absent, as if he were present.

18 Also the singular diligence of the artificer did help to set forward the ignorant to more superstition.

19 For he, peradventure willing to please one in authority, forced all his skill to make the resemblance of the best fashion.

20 And so the multitude, allured by the grace of the work, took him now for a god, which a little before was but honoured as a man.

21 And this was an occasion to deceive the world: for men, serving either calamity or tyranny, did ascribe unto stones and stocks the incommunicable name.

22 Moreover this was not enough for them, that they erred in the knowledge of God; but whereas they lived in the great war of ignorance, those

so great plagues called they peace.

23 For whilst they slew their children in sacrifices, or used secret ceremonies, or made revellings of strange rites;

24 They kept neither lives nor marriages any longer undefiled: but either one slew another traitorously, or grieved him by adultery.

25 So that there reigned in all men without exception blood, manslaughter, theft, and dissimulation, corruption, unfaithfulness, tumults, perjury,

26 Disquieting of good men, forgetfulness of good turns, defiling of souls, changing of kind, disorder in marriages, adultery, and shameless uncleanness.

27 For the worshipping of idols not to be named is the beginning, the cause, and the end, of all evil.

28 For either they are mad when they be merry, or prophesy lies, or live unjustly, or else lightly forswear themselves.

29 For insomuch as their trust is in idols, which have no life; though they swear falsely, yet they look not to be hurt.

30 Howbeit for both causes shall they be justly punished: both because they thought not well of God, giving heed unto idols, and also unjustly swore in deceit, despising holiness.

31 For it is not the power of them by whom they swear: but it is the just vengeance of sinners, that punisheth always the offence of the ungodly.

CHAPTER XV

BUT thou, O God, art gracious and true, longsuffering, and in mercy ordering all things.

2 For if we sin, we are thine, knowing thy power: but we will not sin, knowing that we are counted thine.

3 For to know thee is perfect righteousness: yea, to know thy power is the root of immortality.

4 For neither did the mischievous invention of men deceive us, nor an image spotted with divers colours, the painter's fruitless labour;

5 The sight whereof enticeth fools to lust after it, and so they desire the form of a dead image, that hath no breath.

6 Both they that make them, they that desire them, and they that worship them, are lovers of evil things, and are worthy to have such things to trust upon.

7 For the potter, tempering soft earth, fashioneth every vessel with much labour for our service: yea, of the same clay he maketh both the vessels that serve for clean uses, and likewise also all such as serve to the contrary: but what is the use of either sort, the potter himself is the judge.

8 And employing his labours lewdly, he maketh a vain god of the same clay, even he which a little before was made of earth himself, and within a little while after returneth to the same, out of the which he was taken, when his life which was lent him shall be demanded.

9 Notwithstanding his care is, not that he shall have much labour, nor that his life is short: but striveth to excel goldsmiths and silversmiths, and endeavoureth to do like

the workers in brass, and counteth it his glory to make counterfeit things.

10 His heart is ashes, his hope is more vile than earth, and his life of less value than clay:

11 Forasmuch as he knew not his Maker, and him that inspired into him an active soul, and breathed in a living spirit.

12 But they counted our life a pastime, and our time here a market for gain: for, say they, we must be getting every way, though it be by evil means.

13 For this man, that of earthly matter maketh brittle vessels and graven images, knoweth himself to offend above all others.

14 And all the enemies of thy people, that hold them in subjection, are most foolish, and are more miserable than very babes.

15 For they counted all the idols of the heathen to be gods: which neither have the use of eyes to see, nor noses to draw breath, nor ears to hear, nor fingers of hands to handle; and as for their feet, they are slow to go.

16 For man made them, and he that borrowed his own spirit fashioned them: but no man can make a god like unto himself.

17 For being mortal, he worketh a dead thing with wicked hands: for he himself is better than the things which he worshippeth: whereas he lived *once*, but they never.

18 Yea, they worshipped those beasts also that are most hateful: for being compared together, some are worse than others.

19 Neither are they beautiful, so much as to be desired in re-

spect of beasts: but they went without the praise of God and his blessing.

CHAPTER XVI

THEREFORE by the like were they punished worthily, and by the multitude of beasts tormented.

2 Instead of which punishment, dealing graciously with thine own people, thou preparedst for them meat of a strange taste, even quails to stir up their appetite:

3 To the end that they, desiring food, might for the ugly sight of the beasts sent among them lothe even that, which they must needs desire; but these, suffering penury for a short space, might be made partakers of a strange taste.

4 For it was requisite, that upon them exercising tyranny should come penury, which they could not avoid: but to these it should only be shewed how their enemies were tormented.

5 For when the horrible fierceness of beasts came upon these, and they perished with the stings of crooked serpents, thy wrath endured not for ever:

6 But they were troubled for a small season, that they might be admonished, having a sign of salvation, to put them in remembrance of the commandment of thy law.

7 For he that turned himself toward it was not saved by the thing that he saw, but by thee, that art the Saviour of all.

8 And in this thou madest thine enemies confess, that it is thou who deliverest from all evil:

9 For them the bitings of grasshoppers and flies killed, neither was there found any remedy for their life: for they were worthy to be punished by such.

10 But thy sons not the very teeth of venomous dragons overcame: for thy mercy was *ever* by them, and healed them.

11 For they were pricked, that they should remember thy words; and were quickly saved, that not falling into deep forgetfulness, they might be continually mindful of thy goodness.

12 For it was neither herb, nor mollifying plaister, that restored them to health: but thy word, O Lord, which healeth all things.

13 For thou hast power of life and death: thou leadest to the gates of hell, and bringest up again.

14 A man indeed killeth through his malice: and the spirit, when it is gone forth, returneth not; neither the soul received up cometh again.

15 But it is not possible to escape thine hand.

16 For the ungodly, that denied to know thee, were scourged by the strength of thine arm: with strange rains, hails, and showers, were they persecuted, that they could not avoid, and through fire were they consumed.

17 For, which is most to be wondered at, the fire had more force in the water, that quencheth all things: for the world fighteth for the righteous.

18 For sometime the flame was mitigated, that it might not burn up the beasts that were sent against the ungodly; but themselves might see and perceive that they were persecuted with the judgment of God.

19 And at another time it burneth even in the midst of water above the power of fire, that it might destroy the fruits of an unjust land.

20 Instead whereof thou feddest thine own people with angels' food, and didst send them from heaven bread prepared without their labour, able to content every man's delight, and agreeing to every taste.

21 For thy sustenance declared thy sweetness unto thy children, and serving to the appetite of the eater, tempered itself to every man's liking.

22 But snow and ice endured the fire, and melted not, that they might know that fire burning in the hail, and sparkling in the rain, did destroy the fruits of the enemies.

23 But this again did even forget his own strength, that the righteous might be nourished.

24 For the creature that serveth thee, who art the Maker, increaseth his strength against the unrighteous for their punishment, and abateth his strength for the benefit of such as put their trust in thee.

25 Therefore even then was it altered into all fashions, and was obedient to thy grace, that nourisheth all things, according to the desire of them that had need:

26 That thy children, O Lord, whom thou lovest, might know, that it is not the growing of fruits that nourisheth man: but that it is thy word, which

preserveth them that put their trust in thee.

27 For that which was not destroyed of the fire, being warmed with a little sunbeam, soon melted away:

28 That it might be known, that we must prevent the sun to give thee thanks, and at the dayspring pray unto thee.

29 For the hope of the unthankful shall melt away as the winter's hoar frost, and shall run away as unprofitable water.

CHAPTER XVII

FOR great are thy judgments, and cannot be expressed: therefore unnurtured souls have erred.

2 For when unrighteous men thought to oppress the holy nation; they being shut up in their houses, the prisoners of darkness, and fettered with the bonds of a long night, lay [there] exiled from the eternal providence.

3 For while they supposed to lie hid in their secret sins, they were scattered under a dark veil of forgetfulness, being horribly astonished, and troubled with [strange] apparitions.

4 For neither might the corner that held them keep them from fear: but noises [as of waters] falling down sounded about them, and sad visions appeared unto them with heavy countenances.

5 No power of the fire might give them light: neither could the bright flames of the stars endure to lighten that horrible night.

6 Only there appeared unto them a fire kindled of itself, very dreadful: for being much

terrified, they thought the things which they saw to be worse than the sight they saw not.

7 As for the illusions of art magick, they were put down, and their vaunting in wisdom was reproved with disgrace.

8 For they, that promised to drive away terrors and troubles from a sick soul, were sick themselves of fear, worthy to be laughed at.

9 For though no terrible thing did fear them; yet being scared with beasts that passed by, and hissing of serpents,

10 They died for fear, denying that they saw the air, which could of no side be avoided.

11 For wickedness, condemned by her own witness, is very timorous, and being pressed with conscience, always forecasteth grievous things.

12 For fear is nothing else but a betraying of the succours which reason offereth.

13 And the expectation from within, being less, counteth the ignorance more than the cause which bringeth the torment.

14 But they sleeping the same sleep that night, which was indeed intolerable, and which came upon them out of the bottoms of inevitable hell,

15 Were partly vexed with monstrous apparitions, and partly fainted, their heart failing them: for a sudden fear, and not looked for, came upon them.

16 So then whosoever there fell down was straitly kept, shut up in a prison without iron bars.

17 For whether he were husbandman, or shepherd, or a

E

labourer in the field, he was overtaken, and endured that necessity, which could not be avoided: for they were all bound with one chain of darkness.

18 Whether it were a whistling wind, or a melodious noise of birds among the spreading branches, or a pleasing fall of water running violently,

19 Or a terrible sound of stones cast down, or a running that could not be seen of skipping beasts, or a roaring voice of most savage wild beasts, or a rebounding echo from the hollow mountains; these things made them to swoon for fear.

20 For the whole world shined with clear light, and none were hindered in their labour:

21 Over them only was spread an heavy night, an image of that darkness which should afterward receive them: but yet were they unto themselves more grievous than the darkness.

CHAPTER XVIII

NEVERTHELESS thy saints had a very great light, whose voice they hearing, and not seeing their shape, because they also had not suffered the same things, they counted them happy.

2 But for that they did not hurt them *now*, of whom they had been wronged before, they thanked them, and besought them pardon for that they had been enemies.

3 Instead whereof thou gavest them a burning pillar of fire, both to be a guide of the unknown journey, and an harmless sun to entertain them honourably.

130

4 For they were worthy to be deprived of light, and imprisoned in darkness, who had kept thy sons shut up, by whom the uncorrupt light of the law was to be given unto the world.

5 And when they had determined to slay the babes of the saints, one child being cast forth, and saved, to reprove them, thou tookest away the multitude of their children, and destroyedst them altogether in a mighty water.

6 Of that night were our fathers certified afore, that assuredly knowing unto what oaths they had given credence, they might afterwards be of good cheer.

7 So of thy people was accepted both the salvation of the righteous, and destruction of the enemies.

8 For wherewith thou didst punish our adversaries, by the same thou didst glorify us, whom thou hadst called.

9 For the righteous children of good men did sacrifice secretly, and with one consent made a holy law, that the saints should be like partakers of the same good and evil, the fathers now singing out the songs of praise.

10 But on the other side there sounded an ill according cry of the enemies, and a lamentable noise was carried abroad for children that were bewailed.

11 The master and the servant were punished after one manner; and like as the king, so suffered the common person.

12 So they all together had innumerable dead with one kind of death; neither were the living sufficient to bury them:

for in one moment the noblest offspring of them was destroyed.

13 For whereas they would not believe any thing by reason of the enchantments; upon the destruction of the firstborn, they acknowledged this people to be the sons of God.

14 For while all things were in quiet silence, and that night was in the midst of her swift course,

15 Thine Almighty word leaped down from heaven out of thy royal throne, as a fierce man of war into the midst of a land of destruction,

16 And brought thine unfeigned commandment as a sharp sword, and standing up filled all things with death; and it touched the heaven, but it stood upon the earth.

17 Then suddenly visions of horrible dreams troubled them sore, and terrors came upon them unlooked for.

18 And one thrown here, and another there, half dead, shewed the cause of his death.

19 For the dreams that troubled them did foreshew this, lest they should perish, and not know why they were afflicted.

20 Yea, the tasting of death touched the righteous also, and there was a destruction of the multitude in the wilderness: but the wrath endured not long.

21 For then the blameless man made haste, and stood forth to defend them; and bringing the shield of his proper ministry, even prayer, and the propitiation of incense, set himself against the wrath, and so brought the calamity to an end, declaring that he was thy servant.

22 So he overcame the destroyer, not with strength of body, nor force of arms, but with a word subdued he him that punished, alleging the oaths and covenants made with the fathers.

23 For when the dead were now fallen down by heaps one upon another, standing between, he stayed the wrath, and parted the way to the living.

24 For in the long garment was the whole world, and in the four rows of the stones was the glory of the fathers graven, and thy Majesty upon the diadem of his head.

25 Unto these the destroyer gave place, and was afraid of them: for it was enough that they only tasted of the wrath.

CHAPTER XIX

AS for the ungodly, wrath came upon them without mercy unto the end: for he knew before what they would do;

2 How that having given them leave to depart, and sent them hastily away, they would repent and pursue them.

3 For whilst they were yet mourning and making lamentation at the graves of the dead, they added another foolish device, and pursued them as fugitives, whom they had intreated to be gone.

4 For the destiny, whereof they were worthy, drew them unto this end, and made them forget the things that had already happened, that they might fulfil the punishment which was wanting to their torments:

5 And that thy people might

pass a wonderful way: but they might find a strange death.

6 For the whole creature in his proper kind was fashioned again anew, serving the peculiar commandments that were given unto them, that thy children might be kept without hurt:

7 As *namely*, a cloud shadowing the camp; and where water stood before, dry land appeared; and out of the Red sea a way without impediment; and out of the violent stream a green field:

8 Wherethrough all the people went that were defended with thy hand, seeing thy marvellous strange wonders.

9 For they went at large like horses, and leaped like lambs, praising thee, O Lord, who hadst delivered them.

10 For they were yet mindful of the things that were done while they sojourned in the strange land, how the ground brought forth flies instead of cattle, and how the river cast up a multitude of frogs instead of fishes.

11 But afterwards they saw a new generation of fowls, when, being led with their appetite, they asked delicate meats.

12 For quails came up unto them from the sea for their contentment.

13 And punishments came upon the sinners not without former signs by the force of thunders: for they suffered justly according to their own wickedness, insomuch as they used a more hard and hateful behaviour toward strangers.

14 For the *Sodomites* did not receive those, whom they knew not when they came: but

these brought friends into bondage, that had well deserved of them.

15 And not only so, but peradventure some respect shall be had of those, because they used strangers not friendly:

16 But these very grievously afflicted them, whom they had received with feastings, and were already made partakers of the same laws with them.

17 Therefore even with blindness were these stricken, as those were at the doors of the righteous man: when, being compassed about with horrible great darkness, every one sought the passage of his own doors.

18 For the elements were changed in themselves by a kind of harmony, like as in a psaltery notes change the name of the tune, and yet are always sounds; which may well be perceived by the sight of the things that have been done.

19 For earthly things were turned into watery, and the things, that before swam in the water, now went upon the ground.

20 The fire had power in the water, forgetting his own virtue: and the water forgat his own quenching nature.

21 On the other side, the flames wasted not the flesh of the corruptible living things, though they walked therein; neither melted they the icy kind of heavenly meat, that was of nature apt to melt.

22 For in all things, O Lord, thou didst magnify thy people, and glorify them, neither didst thou lightly regard them: but didst assist them in every time and place.

ECCLESIASTICUS

A Prologue made by an uncertain Author.

THIS Jesus was the son of Sĭ'-răch, and grandchild to Jesus of the same name with him: this man therefore lived in the latter times, after the people had been led away captive, and called home again, and almost after all the prophets. Now his grandfather Jesus, as he himself witnesseth, was a man of great diligence and wisdom among the Hebrews, who did not only gather the grave and short sentences of wise men, that had been before him, but himself also uttered some of his own, full of much understanding and wisdom. When as therefore the first Jesus died, leaving this book almost perfected, Sirach his son receiving it after him left it to his own son Jesus, who, having gotten it into his hands, compiled it all orderly into one volume, and called it Wisdom, intituling it both by his own name, his father's name, and his grandfather's; alluring the hearer by the very name of Wisdom to have a greater love to the study of this book. It containeth therefore wise sayings, dark sentences, and parables, and certain particular ancient godly stories of men that pleased God; also his prayer and song; moreover, what benefits God had vouchsafed his people, and what plagues he had heaped upon their enemies. This Jesus did imitate Solomon, and was no less famous for wisdom and learning, both being indeed a man of great learning, and so reputed also.

The Prologue of the Wisdom of Jesus the Son of Sirach.

WHEREAS many and great things have been delivered unto us by the law and the prophets, and by others that have followed their steps, for the which things Israel ought to be commended for learning and wisdom; and whereof not only the readers must needs become skilful themselves, but also they that desire to learn be able to profit them which are without, both by speaking and writing: my grandfather Jesus, when he had much given himself to the reading of the law, and the prophets, and other books of our fathers, and had gotten therein good judgment, was drawn on also himself to write something pertaining to learning and wisdom; to the intent that those which are desirous to learn, and are addicted to these things, might profit much more in living according to the law. Wherefore let me intreat you to read it with favour and attention, and to pardon us, wherein we may seem to come short of some words, which we have laboured to interpret. For the same things uttered in Hebrew, and translated into another tongue, have not the same force in them: and not only these things, but the law itself, and the prophets, and the rest of the books, have no small difference, when they are spoken in their own language. For in the eight and thirtieth year coming into Egypt, when Eu-ĕr-gĕ-tēs was king, and continuing there some time, I found a book of no small learning: therefore I thought it most necessary for me to bestow some diligence and travail to interpret it; using great watchfulness and skill in that space to bring the book to an end, and set it forth for them also, which in a strange country are willing to learn, being prepared before in manners to live after the law.

CHAPTER 1

A LL wisdom *cometh* from the Lord, and is with him for ever.

2 Who can number the sand of the sea, and the drops of rain, and the days of eternity?

3 Who can find out the height of heaven, and the breadth of the earth, and the deep, and wisdom?

4 Wisdom hath been created before all things, and the understanding of prudence from everlasting.

5 The word of God most high is the fountain of wisdom; and her ways are everlasting commandments.

6 To whom hath the root of wisdom been revealed? or who hath known her wise counsels?

7 [Unto whom hath the knowledge of wisdom been made manifest? and who hath understood her great experience?]

8 There is one wise and greatly to be feared, the Lord sitting upon his throne.

9 He created her, and saw her, and numbered her, and poured her out upon all his works.

10 She *is* with all flesh according to his gift, and he hath given her to them that love him.

11 The fear of the Lord is honour, and glory, and gladness, and a crown of rejoicing.

12 The fear of the Lord maketh a merry heart, and giveth joy, and gladness, and a long life.

13 Whoso feareth the Lord, it shall go well with him at the last, and he shall find favour in the day of his death.

14 To fear the Lord is the beginning of wisdom: and it was created with the faithful in the womb.

15 She hath built an everlasting foundation with men, and she shall continue with their seed.

16 To fear the Lord is fulness of wisdom, and filleth men with her fruits.

17 She filleth all their house with things desirable, and the garners with her increase.

18 The fear of the Lord is a crown of wisdom, making peace and perfect health to flourish; both which are the gifts of God: and it enlargeth their rejoicing that love him.

19 Wisdom raineth down skill and knowledge of understanding, and exalteth them to honour that hold her fast.

20 The root of wisdom is to fear the Lord, and the branches thereof are long life.

21 The fear of the Lord driveth away sins: and where it is present, it turneth away wrath.

22 A furious man cannot be justified; for the sway of his fury shall be his destruction.

23 A patient man will bear for a time, and afterward joy shall spring up unto him.

24 He will hide his words for a time, and the lips of many shall declare his wisdom.

25 The parables of knowledge are in the treasures of wisdom: but godliness is an abomination to a sinner.

26 If thou desire wisdom, keep the commandments, and the Lord shall give her unto thee.

27 For the fear of the Lord is wisdom and instruction: and faith and meekness are his delight.

28 Distrust not the fear of the Lord when thou art poor: and come not unto him with a double heart.

29 Be not an hypocrite in the sight of men, and take good heed what thou speakest.

30 Exalt not thyself, lest thou fall, and bring dishonour upon thy soul, and so God discover thy secrets, and cast thee down in the midst of the congregation, because thou camest not in truth to the fear of the Lord, but thy heart is full of deceit.

CHAPTER II

MY son, if thou come to serve the Lord, prepare thy soul for temptation.

2 Set thy heart aright, and constantly endure, and make not haste in time of trouble.

3 Cleave unto him, and depart not away, that thou mayest be increased at thy last end.

4 Whatsoever is brought upon thee take cheerfully, and be patient when thou art changed to a low estate.

5 For gold is tried in the fire, and acceptable men in the furnace of adversity.

6 Believe in him, and he will help thee; order thy way aright, and trust in him.

7 Ye that fear the Lord, wait for his mercy; and go not aside, lest ye fall.

8 Ye that fear the Lord, believe him; and your reward shall not fail.

9 Ye that fear the Lord, hope for good, and for everlasting joy and mercy.

10 Look at the generations of old, and see; did ever any trust in the Lord, and was confounded? or did any abide in his fear, and was forsaken? or whom did he ever despise, that called upon him?

11 For the Lord is full of compassion and mercy, longsuffering, and very pitiful, and forgiveth sins, and saveth in time of affliction.

12 Woe be to fearful hearts, and faint hands, and the sinner that goeth two ways!

13 Woe unto him that is fainthearted! for he believeth not; therefore shall he not be defended.

14 Woe unto you that have lost patience! and what will ye do when the Lord shall visit you?

15 They that fear the Lord will not disobey his word; and they that love him will keep his ways.

16 They that fear the Lord will seek that which is wellpleasing unto him; and they that love him shall be filled with the law.

17 They that fear the Lord will prepare their hearts, and

humble their souls in his sight,

18 *Saying*, We will fall into the hands of the Lord, and not into the hands of men: for as his majesty is, so is his mercy.

CHAPTER III

HEAR me your father, O children, and do thereafter, that ye may be safe.

2 For the Lord hath given the father honour over the children, and hath confirmed the authority of the mother over the sons.

3 Whoso honoureth his father maketh an atonement for his sins:

4 And he that honoureth his mother is as one that layeth up treasure.

5 Whoso honoureth his father shall have joy of *his own* children; and when he maketh his prayer, he shall be heard.

6 He that honoureth his father shall have a long life; and he that is obedient unto the Lord shall be a comfort to his mother.

7 He that feareth the Lord will honour his father, and will do service unto his parents, as to his masters.

8 Honour thy father and mother both in word and deed, that a blessing may come upon thee from them.

9 For the blessing of the father establisheth the houses of children; but the curse of the mother rooteth out foundations.

10 Glory not in the dishonour of thy father; for thy father's dishonour is no glory unto thee.

11 For the glory of a man is from the honour of his father;

and a mother in dishonour is a reproach to the children.

12 My son, help thy father in his age, and grieve him not as long as he liveth.

13 And if his understanding fail, have patience with him; and despise him not when thou art in thy full strength.

14 For the relieving of thy father shall not be forgotten: and instead of sins it shall be added to build thee up.

15 In the day of thine affliction it shall be remembered; thy sins also shall melt away, as the ice in the fair warm weather.

16 He that forsaketh his father is as a blasphemer; and he that angereth his mother is cursed of God.

17 My son, go on with thy business in meekness; so shalt thou be beloved of him that is approved.

18 The greater thou art, the more humble thyself, and thou shalt find favour before the Lord.

19 Many are in high place, and of renown: but mysteries are revealed unto the meek.

20 For the power of the Lord is great, and he is honoured of the lowly.

21 Seek not out the things that are too hard for thee, neither search the things that are above thy strength.

22 But what is commanded thee, think thereupon *with reverence*; for it is not needful for thee *to see with thine eyes* the things that are in secret.

23 Be not curious in unnecessary matters: for more things are shewed unto thee than men understand.

24 For many are deceived by their own vain opinion; and an

evil suspicion hath overthrown their judgment.

25 Without eyes thou shalt want light: profess not the knowledge therefore that thou hast not.

26 A stubborn heart shall fare evil at the last; and he that loveth danger shall perish therein.

27 An obstinate heart shall be laden with sorrows; and the wicked man shall heap sin upon sin.

28 In the punishment of the proud there is no remedy; for the plant of wickedness hath taken root in him.

29 The heart of the prudent will understand a parable; and an attentive ear is the desire of a wise man.

30 Water will quench a flaming fire; and alms maketh an atonement for sins.

31 And he that requiteth good turns is mindful of that which may come hereafter; and when he falleth, he shall find a stay.

CHAPTER IV

MY son, defraud not the poor of his living, and make not the needy eyes to wait long.

2 Make not an hungry soul sorrowful; neither provoke a man in his distress.

3 Add not more trouble to an heart that is vexed; and defer not to give to him that is in need.

4 Reject not the supplication of the afflicted; neither turn away thy face from a poor man.

5 Turn not away thine eye from the needy, and give him none occasion to curse thee:

6 For if he curse thee in the bitterness of his soul, his prayer shall be heard of him that made him.

7 Get thyself the love of the congregation, and bow thy head to a great man.

8 Let it not grieve thee to bow down thine ear to the poor, and give him a friendly answer with meekness.

9 Deliver him that suffereth wrong from the hand of the oppressor; and be not faint-hearted when thou sittest in judgment.

10 Be as a father unto the fatherless, and instead of an husband unto their mother: so shalt thou be as the son of the most High, and he shall love thee more than thy mother doth.

11 Wisdom exalteth her children, and layeth hold of them that seek her.

12 He that loveth her loveth life; and they that seek to her early shall be filled with joy.

13 He that holdeth her fast shall inherit glory; and wheresoever she entereth, the Lord will bless.

14 They that serve her shall minister to the Holy One: and them that love her the Lord doth love.

15 Whoso giveth ear unto her shall judge the nations: and he that attendeth unto her shall dwell securely.

16 If a man commit himself unto her, he shall inherit her; and his generation shall hold her in possession.

17 For at the first she will walk with him by crooked ways, and bring fear and dread upon him, and torment him with her discipline, until she

may trust his soul, and try him by her laws.

18 Then will she return the straight way unto him, and comfort him, and shew him her secrets.

19 But if he go wrong, she will forsake him, and give him over to his own ruin.

20 Observe the opportunity, and beware of evil; and be not ashamed when it concerneth thy soul.

21 For there is a shame that bringeth sin; and there is a shame which is glory and grace.

22 Accept no person against thy soul, and let not the reverence of any man cause thee to fall.

23 And refrain not to speak, when there is occasion to do good, and hide not thy wisdom in her beauty.

24 For by speech wisdom shall be known: and learning by the word of the tongue.

25 In no wise speak against the truth; but be abashed of the error of thine ignorance.

26 Be not ashamed to confess thy sins; and force not the course of the river.

27 Make not thyself an underling to a foolish man; neither accept the person of the mighty.

28 Strive for the truth unto death, and the Lord shall fight for thee.

29 Be not hasty in thy tongue, and in thy deeds slack and remiss.

30 Be not as a lion in thy house, nor frantick among thy servants.

31 Let not thine hand be stretched out to receive, and shut when thou shouldest repay.

138

CHAPTER V

SET not thy heart upon thy goods; and say not, I have enough for my life.

2 Follow not thine own mind and thy strength, to walk in the ways of thy heart:

3 And say not, Who shall controul me for my works? for the Lord will surely revenge thy pride.

4 Say not, I have sinned, and what harm hath happened unto me? for the Lord is longsuffering, he will in no wise let thee go.

5 Concerning propitiation, be not without fear to add sin unto sin:

6 And say not, His mercy is great; he will be pacified for the multitude of my sins: for mercy and wrath come from him, and his indignation resteth upon sinners.

7 Make no tarrying to turn to the Lord, and put not off from day to day: for suddenly shall the wrath of the Lord come forth, and in thy security thou shalt be destroyed, and perish in the day of vengeance.

8 Set not thine heart upon goods unjustly gotten; for they shall not profit thee in the day of calamity.

9 Winnow not with every wind, and go not into every way: for so doth the sinner that hath a double tongue.

10 Be stedfast in thy understanding; and let thy word be the same.

11 Be swift to hear; and let thy life be sincere; and with patience give answer.

12 If thou hast understanding, answer thy neighbour; if not, lay thy hand upon thy mouth.

13 Honour and shame is in talk: and the tongue of man is his fall.

14 Be not called a whisperer, and lie not in wait with thy tongue: for a foul shame is upon the thief, and an evil condemnation upon the double tongue.

15 Be not ignorant of any thing in a great matter or a small.

CHAPTER VI

INSTEAD of a friend become not an enemy; for [thereby] thou shalt inherit an ill name, shame, and reproach: even so shall a sinner that hath a double tongue.

2 Extol not thyself in the counsel of thine own heart; that thy soul be not torn in pieces as a bull [straying alone.]

3 Thou shalt eat up thy leaves, and lose thy fruit, and leave thyself as a dry tree.

4 A wicked soul shall destroy him that hath it, and shall make him to be laughed to scorn of his enemies.

5 Sweet language will multiply friends: and a fairspeaking tongue will increase kind greetings.

6 Be in peace with many: nevertheless have but one counsellor of a thousand.

7 If thou wouldest get a friend, prove him first, and be not hasty to credit him.

8 For some man is a friend for his own occasion, and will not abide in the day of thy trouble.

9 And there is a friend, who being turned to enmity and strife will discover thy reproach.

10 Again, some friend is a companion at the table, and will not continue in the day of thy affliction.

11 But in thy prosperity he will be as thyself, and will be bold over thy servants.

12 If thou be brought low, he will be against thee, and will hide himself from thy face.

13 Separate thyself from thine enemies, and take heed of thy friends.

14 A faithful friend is a strong defence: and he that hath found such an one hath found a treasure.

15 Nothing doth countervail a faithful friend, and his excellency is invaluable.

16 A faithful friend is the medicine of life; and they that fear the Lord shall find him.

17 Whoso feareth the Lord shall direct his friendship aright: for as he is, so shall his neighbour be also.

18 My son, gather instruction from thy youth up: so shalt thou find wisdom till thine old age.

19 Come unto her as one that ploweth and soweth, and wait for her good fruits: for thou shalt not toil much in labouring about her, but thou shalt eat of her fruits right soon.

20 She is very unpleasant to the unlearned: he that is without understanding will not remain with her.

21 She will lie upon him as a mighty stone of trial; and he will cast her from him ere it be long.

22 For wisdom is according to her name, and she is not manifest unto many.

23 Give ear, my son, receive my advice, and refuse not my counsel,

24 And put thy feet into her

fetters, and thy neck into her chain.

25 Bow down thy shoulder, and bear her, and be not grieved with her bonds.

26 Come unto her with thy whole heart, and keep her ways with all thy power.

27 Search, and seek, and she shall be made known unto thee: and when thou hast got hold of her, let her not go.

28 For at the last thou shalt find her rest, and that shall be turned to thy joy.

29 Then shall her fetters be a strong defence for thee, and her chains a robe of glory.

30 For there is a golden ornament upon her, and her bands are purple lace.

31 Thou shalt put her on as a robe of honour, and shalt put her about thee as a crown of joy.

32 My son, if thou wilt, thou shalt be taught: and if thou wilt apply thy mind, thou shalt be prudent.

33 If thou love to hear, thou shalt receive understanding: and if thou bow thine ear, thou shalt be wise.

34 Stand in the multitude of the elders; and cleave unto him that is wise.

35 Be willing to hear every godly discourse; and let not the parables of understanding escape thee.

36 And if thou seest a man of understanding, get thee betimes unto him, and let thy foot wear the steps of his door.

37 Let thy mind be upon the ordinances of the Lord, and meditate continually in his commandments: he shall establish thine heart, and give thee wisdom at thine own desire.

140

CHAPTER VII

DO no evil, so shall no harm come unto thee.

2 Depart from the unjust, and iniquity shall turn away from thee.

3 My son, sow not upon the furrows of unrighteousness, and thou shalt not reap them sevenfold.

4 Seek not of the Lord preeminence, neither of the king the seat of honour.

5 Justify not thyself before the Lord; and boast not of thy wisdom before the king.

6 Seek not to be judge, being not able to take away iniquity; lest at any time thou fear the person of the mighty, and lay a stumblingblock in the way of thy uprightness.

7 Offend not against the multitude of a city, and then thou shalt not cast thyself down among the people.

8 Bind not one sin upon another; for in one thou shalt not be unpunished.

9 Say not, God will look upon the multitude of my oblations, and when I offer to the most high God, he will accept it.

10 Be not fainthearted when thou makest thy prayer, and neglect not to give alms.

11 Laugh no man to scorn in the bitterness of his soul: for there is one which humbleth and exalteth.

12 Devise not a lie against thy brother; neither do the like to thy friend.

13 Use not to make any manner of lie: for the custom thereof is not good.

14 Use not many words in a multitude of elders, and make not much babbling when thou prayest.

15 Hate not laborious work, neither husbandry, which the most High hath ordained.

16 Number not thyself among the multitude of sinners, but remember that wrath will not tarry long.

17 Humble thy soul greatly: for the vengeance of the ungodly is fire and worms.

18 Change not a friend for any good by no means; neither a faithful brother for the gold of Ō'-phĭr.

19 Forego not a wise and good woman: for her grace is above gold.

20 Whereas thy servant worketh truly, entreat him not evil, nor the hireling that bestoweth himself wholly for thee.

21 Let thy soul love a good servant, and defraud him not of liberty.

22 Hast thou cattle? have an eye to them: and if they be for thy profit, keep them with thee.

23 Hast thou children? instruct them, and bow down their neck from their youth.

24 Hast thou daughters? have a care of their body, and shew not thyself cheerful toward them.

25 Marry thy daughter, and so shalt thou have performed a weighty matter: but give her to a man of understanding.

26 Hast thou a wife after thy mind? forsake her not: but give not thyself over to a light woman.

27 Honour thy father with thy whole heart, and forget not the sorrows of thy mother.

28 Remember that thou wast begotten of them; and how canst thou recompense them the things that they have done for thee?

29 Fear the Lord with all thy soul, and reverence his priests.

30 Love him that made thee with all thy strength, and forsake not his ministers.

31 Fear the Lord, and honour the priest; and give him his portion, as it is commanded thee; the firstfruits, and the trespass offering, and the gift of the shoulders, and the sacrifice of sanctification, and the firstfruits of the holy things.

32 And stretch thine hand unto the poor, that thy blessing may be perfected.

33 A gift hath grace in the sight of every man living; and for the dead detain it not.

34 Fail not to be with them that weep, and mourn with them that mourn.

35 Be not slow to visit the sick: for that shall make thee to be beloved.

36 Whatsoever thou takest in hand, remember the end, and thou shalt never do amiss.

CHAPTER VIII

STRIVE not with a mighty man, lest thou fall into his hands.

2 Be not at variance with a rich man, lest he overweigh thee: for gold hath destroyed many, and perverted the hearts of kings.

3 Strive not with a man that is full of tongue, and heap not wood upon his fire.

4 Jest not with a rude man, lest thy ancestors be disgraced.

5 Reproach not a man that turneth from sin, but remember that we are all worthy of punishment.

6 Dishonour not a man in his old age: for even some of us wax old.

7 Rejoice not over thy

greatest enemy being dead, but remember that we die all.

8 Despise not the discourse of the wise, but acquaint thyself with their proverbs: for of them thou shalt learn instruction, and how to serve great men with ease.

9 Miss not the discourse of the elders: for they also learned of their fathers, and of them thou shalt learn understanding, and to give answer as need requireth.

10 Kindle not the coals of a sinner, lest thou be burnt with the flame of his fire.

11 Rise not up [in anger] at the presence of an injurious person, lest he lie in wait to entrap thee in thy words.

12 Lend not unto him that is mightier than thyself; for if thou lendest him, count it but lost.

13 Be not surety above thy power: for if thou be surety, take care to pay it.

14 Go not to law with a judge; for they will judge for him according to his honour.

15 Travel not by the way with a bold fellow, lest he become grievous unto thee: for he will do according to his own will, and thou shalt perish with him through his folly.

16 Strive not with an angry man, and go not with him into a solitary place: for blood is as nothing in his sight; and where there is no help, he will overthrow thee.

17 Consult not with a fool; for he cannot keep counsel.

18 Do no secret thing before a stranger; for thou knowest not what he will bring forth.

19 Open not thine heart to every man, lest he requite thee with a shrewd turn.

CHAPTER IX

BE not jealous over the wife of thy bosom, and teach her not an evil lesson against thyself.

2 Give not thy soul unto a woman to set her foot upon thy substance.

3 Meet not with an harlot, lest thou fall into her snares.

4 Use not much the company of a woman that is a singer, lest thou be taken with her attempts.

5 Gaze not on a maid, that thou fall not by those things that are precious in her.

6 Give not thy soul unto harlots, that thou lose not thine inheritance.

7 Look not round about thee in the streets of the city, neither wander thou in the solitary places thereof.

8 Turn away thine eye from a beautiful woman, and look not upon another's beauty; for many have been deceived by the beauty of a woman; for herewith love is kindled as a fire.

9 Sit not at all with another man's wife, nor sit down with her in thine arms, and spend not thy money with her at the wine; lest thine heart incline unto her, and so through thy desire thou fall into destruction.

10 Forsake not an old friend; for the new is not comparable to him: a new friend is as new wine; when it is old, thou shalt drink it with pleasure.

11 Envy not the glory of a sinner: for thou knowest not what shall be his end.

12 Delight not in the thing that the ungodly have pleasure in; but remember they shall not

go unpunished unto their grave.

13 Keep thee far from the man that hath power to kill; so shalt thou not doubt the fear of death: and if thou come unto him, make no fault, lest he take away thy life presently: remember that thou goest in the midst of snares, and that thou walkest upon the battlements of the city.

14 As near as thou canst, guess at thy neighbour, and consult with the wise.

15 Let thy talk be with the wise, and all thy communication in the law of the most High.

16 And let just men eat and drink with thee; and let thy glorying be in the fear of the Lord.

17 For the hand of the artificer the work shall be commended: and the wise ruler of the people for his speech.

18 A man of an ill tongue is dangerous in his city; and he that is rash in his talk shall be hated.

CHAPTER X

A WISE judge will instruct his people; and the government of a prudent man is well ordered.

2 As the judge of the people is himself, so are his officers; and what manner of man the ruler of the city is, such are all they that dwell therein.

3 An unwise king destroyeth his people; but through the prudence of them which are in authority the city shall be inhabited.

4 The power of the earth is in the hand of the Lord, and in due time he will set over it one that is profitable.

5 In the hand of God is the prosperity of man: and upon the person of the scribe shall he lay his honour.

6 Bear not hatred to thy neighbour for every wrong; and do nothing at all by injurious practices.

7 Pride is hateful before God and man: and by both doth one commit iniquity.

8 Because of unrighteous dealings, injuries, and riches got by deceit, the kingdom is translated from one people to another.

9 Why is earth and ashes proud? There is not a more wicked thing than a covetous man: for such an one setteth his own soul to sale; because while he liveth he casteth away his bowels.

10 The physician cutteth off a long disease; and he that is to day a king to morrow shall die.

11 For when a man is dead, he shall inherit creeping things, beasts, and worms.

12 The beginning of pride is when one departeth from God, and his heart is turned away from his Maker.

13 For pride is the beginning of sin, and he that hath it shall pour out abomination: and therefore the Lord brought upon them strange calamities, and overthrew them utterly.

14 The Lord hath cast down the thrones of proud princes, and set up the meek in their stead.

15 The Lord hath plucked up the roots of the proud nations, and planted the lowly in their place.

16 The Lord overthrew countries of the heathen, and destroyed them to the foundations of the earth.

17 He took some of them away, and destroyed them, and hath made their memorial to cease from the earth.

18 Pride was not made for men, nor furious anger for them that are born of a woman.

19 They that fear the Lord are a sure seed, and they that love him an honourable plant: they that regard not the law are a dishonourable seed; they that transgress the commandments are a deceivable seed.

20 Among brethren he that is chief is honourable; so are they that fear the Lord in his eyes.

21 The fear of the Lord goeth before the obtaining of authority: but roughness and pride is the losing thereof.

22 Whether he be rich, noble, or poor, their glory is the fear of the Lord.

23 It is not meet to despise the poor man that hath understanding; neither is it convenient to magnify a sinful man.

24 Great men, and judges, and potentates, shall be honoured; yet is there none of them greater than he that feareth the Lord.

25 Unto the servant that is wise shall they that are free do service: and he that hath knowledge will not grudge when he is reformed.

26 Be not overwise in doing thy business; and boast not thyself in the time of thy distress.

27 Better is he that laboureth, and aboundeth in all things, than he that boasteth himself, and wanteth bread.

28 My son, glorify thy soul in meekness, and give it honour according to the dignity thereof.

144

29 Who will justify him that sinneth against his own soul? and who will honour him that dishonoureth his own life?

30 The poor man is honoured for his skill, and the rich man is honoured for his riches.

31 He that is honoured in poverty, how much more in riches? and he that is dishonourable in riches, how much more in poverty?

CHAPTER XI

WISDOM lifteth up the head of him that is of low degree, and maketh him to sit among great men.

2 Commend not a man for his beauty; neither abhor a man for his outward appearance.

3 The bee is little among such as fly; but her fruit is the chief of sweet things.

4 Boast not of thy clothing and raiment, and exalt not thyself in the day of honour: for the works of the Lord are wonderful, and his works among men are hidden.

5 Many kings have sat down upon the ground; and one that was never thought of hath worn the crown.

6 Many mighty men have been greatly disgraced; and the honourable delivered into other men's hands.

7 Blame not before thou hast examined the truth: understand first, and then rebuke.

8 Answer not before thou hast heard the cause: neither interrupt men in the midst of their talk.

9 Strive not in a matter that concerneth thee not; and sit not in judgment with sinners.

10 My son, meddle not with many matters: for if thou

meddle much, thou shalt not be innocent; and if thou follow after, thou shalt not obtain, neither shalt thou escape by fleeing.

11 There is one that laboureth, and taketh pains, and maketh haste, and is so much the more behind.

12 Again, there is another that is slow, and hath need of help, wanting ability, and full of poverty; yet the eye of the Lord looked upon him for good, and set him up from his low estate,

13 And lifted up his head from misery; so that many that saw it marvelled at him.

14 Prosperity and adversity, life and death, poverty and riches, come of the Lord.

15 Wisdom, knowledge, and understanding of the law, are of the Lord: love, and the way of good works, are from him.

16 Error and darkness had their beginning together with sinners: and evil shall wax old with them that glory therein.

17 The gift of the Lord remaineth with the godly, and his favour bringeth prosperity for ever.

18 There is that waxeth rich by his wariness and pinching, and this is the portion of his reward:

19 Whereas he saith, I have found rest, and now will eat continually of my goods; and *yet* he knoweth not what time shall come upon him, and that he must leave those things to others, and die.

20 Be stedfast in thy covenant, and be conversant therein, and wax old in thy work.

21 Marvel not at the works of sinners; but trust in the Lord,

and abide in thy labour: for it is an easy thing in the sight of the Lord on the sudden to make a poor man rich.

22 The blessing of the Lord is in the reward of the godly, and suddenly he maketh his blessing to flourish.

23 Say not, What profit is there of my service? and what good things shall I have hereafter?

24 Again, say not, I have enough, and possess many things, and what evil can come to me hereafter?

25 In the day of prosperity there is a forgetfulness of affliction: and in the day of affliction there is no more remembrance of prosperity.

26 For it is an easy thing unto the Lord in the day of death to reward a man according to his ways.

27 The affliction of an hour maketh a man forget pleasure: and in his end his deeds shall be discovered.

28 Judge none blessed before his death: for a man shall be known in his children.

29 Bring not every man into thine house: for the deceitful man hath many trains.

30 Like as a partridge taken [and kept] in a cage, so is the heart of the proud; and like as a spy, watcheth he for thy fall:

31 For he lieth in wait, and turneth good into evil, and in things worthy praise will lay blame upon thee.

32 Of a spark of fire a heap of coals is kindled: and a sinful man layeth wait for blood.

33 Take heed of a mischievous man, for he worketh wickedness; lest he bring upon thee a perpetual blot.

34 Receive a stranger into

thine house, and he will disturb thee, and turn thee out of thine own.

CHAPTER XII

W HEN thou wilt do good, know to whom thou doest it; so shalt thou be thanked for thy benefits.

2 Do good to the godly man, and thou shalt find a recompence; and if not from him, yet from the most High.

3 There can no good come to him that is always occupied in evil, nor to him that giveth no alms.

4 Give to the godly man, and help not a sinner.

5 Do well unto him that is lowly, but give not to the ungodly: hold back thy bread, and give it not unto him, lest he overmaster thee thereby: for [else] thou shalt receive twice as much evil for all the good thou shalt have done unto him.

6 For the most High hateth sinners, and will repay vengeance unto the ungodly, and keepeth them against the mighty day of their punishment.

7 Give unto the good, and help not the sinner.

8 A friend cannot be known in prosperity: and an enemy cannot be hidden in adversity.

9 In the prosperity of a man enemies will be grieved: but in his adversity even a friend will depart.

10 Never trust thine enemy: for like as iron rusteth, so is his wickedness.

11 Though he humble himself, and go crouching, yet take good heed and beware of him, and thou shalt be unto him as if thou hadst wiped a looking-glass, and thou shalt know that his rust hath not been altogether wiped away.

12 Set him not by thee, lest, when he hath overthrown thee, he stand up in thy place; neither let him sit at thy right hand, lest he seek to take thy seat, and thou at the last remember my words, and be pricked therewith.

13 Who will pity a charmer that is bitten with a serpent, or any such as come nigh wild beasts?

14 So one that goeth to a sinner, and is defiled with him in his sins, who will pity?

15 For a while he will abide with thee, but if thou begin to fall, he will not tarry.

16 An enemy speaketh sweetly with his lips, but in his heart he imagineth how to throw thee into a pit: he will weep with his eyes, but if he find opportunity, he will not be satisfied with blood.

17 If adversity come upon thee, thou shalt find him there first; and though he pretend to help thee, yet shall he undermine thee.

18 He will shake his head, and clap his hands, and whisper much, and change his countenance.

CHAPTER XIII

H E that toucheth pitch shall be defiled therewith; and he that hath fellowship with a proud man shall be like unto him.

2 Burden not thyself above thy power while thou livest; and have no fellowship with one that is mightier and richer than thyself: for how agree the kettle and the earthen pot

together? for if the one be smitten against the other, it shall be broken.

3 The rich man hath done wrong, and yet he threateneth withal: the poor is wronged, and he must intreat also.

4 If thou be for his profit, he will use thee: but if thou have nothing, he will forsake thee.

5 If thou have any thing, he will live with thee: yea, he will make thee bare, and will not be sorry for it.

6 If he have need of thee, he will deceive thee, and smile upon thee, and put thee in hope; he will speak thee fair, and say, What wantest thou?

7 And he will shame thee by his meats, until he have drawn thee dry twice or thrice, and at the last he will laugh thee to scorn: afterward, when he seeth thee, he will forsake thee, and shake his head at thee.

8 Beware that thou be not deceived, and brought down in thy jollity.

9 If thou be invited of a mighty man, withdraw thyself, and so much the more will he invite thee.

10 Press thou not upon him, lest thou be put back; stand not far off, lest thou be forgotten.

11 Affect not to be made equal unto him in talk, and believe not his many words: for with much communication will he tempt thee, and smiling upon thee will get out thy secrets:

12 But cruelly he will lay up thy words, and will not spare to do thee hurt, and to put thee in prison.

13 Observe, and take good heed, for thou walkest in peril of thy overthrowing: when thou hearest these things, awake in thy sleep.

14 Love the Lord all thy life, and call upon him for thy salvation.

15 Every beast loveth his like, and every man loveth his neighbour.

16 All flesh consorteth according to kind, and a man will cleave to his like.

17 What fellowship hath the wolf with the lamb? so the sinner with the godly.

18 What agreement is there between the hyena and a dog? and what peace between the rich and the poor?

19 As the wild ass is the lion's prey in the wilderness: so the rich eat up the poor.

20 As the proud hate humility: so doth the rich abhor the poor.

21 A rich man beginning to fall is held up of his friends: but a poor man being down is thrust also away by his friends.

22 When a rich man is fallen, he hath many helpers: he speaketh things not to be spoken, and yet men justify him: the poor man slipped, and yet they rebuked him too; he spake wisely, and could have no place.

23 When a rich man speaketh, every man holdeth his tongue, and, look, what he saith, they extol it to the clouds: but if the poor man speak, they say, What fellow is this? and if he stumble, they will help to overthrow him.

24 Riches are good unto him that hath no sin, and poverty is evil in the mouth of the ungodly.

25 The heart of a man changeth his countenance, whether it be for good or evil:

and a merry heart maketh a cheerful countenance.

26 A cheerful countenance is a token of a heart that is in prosperity; and the finding out of parables is a wearisome labour of the mind.

CHAPTER XIV

BLESSED is the man that hath not slipped with his mouth, and is not pricked with the multitude of sins.

2 Blessed is he whose conscience hath not condemned him, and who is not fallen from his hope in the Lord.

3 Riches are not comely for a niggard: and what should an envious man do with money?

4 He that gathereth by defrauding his own soul gathereth for others, that shall spend his goods riotously.

5 He that is evil to himself, to whom will he be good? he shall not take pleasure in his goods.

6 There is none worse than he that envieth himself; and this is a recompence of his wickedness.

7 And if he doeth good, he doeth it unwillingly; and at the last he will declare his wickedness.

8 The envious man hath a wicked eye; he turneth away his face, and despiseth men.

9 A covetous man's eye is not satisfied with his portion; and the iniquity of the wicked drieth up his soul.

10 A wicked eye envieth [his] bread, and he is a niggard at his table.

11 My son, according to thy ability do good to thyself, and give the Lord his due offering.

12 Remember that death will not be long in coming, and that the covenant of the grave is not shewed unto thee.

13 Do good unto thy friend before thou die, and according to thy ability stretch out thy hand and give to him.

14 Defraud not thyself of the good day, and let not the part of a good desire overpass thee.

15 Shalt thou not leave thy travails unto another? and thy labours to be divided by lot?

16 Give, and take, and sanctify thy soul; for there is no seeking of dainties in the grave.

17 All flesh waxeth old as a garment: for the covenant from the beginning is, Thou shalt die the death.

18 As of the green leaves on a thick tree, some fall, and some grow; so is the generation of flesh and blood, one cometh to an end, and another is born.

19 Every work rotteth and consumeth away, and the worker thereof shall go withal.

20 Blessed is the man that doth meditate good things in wisdom, and that reasoneth of holy things by his understanding.

21 He that considereth her ways in his heart shall also have understanding in her secrets.

22 Go after her as one that traceth, and lie in wait in her ways.

23 He that prieth in at her windows shall also hearken at her doors.

24 He that doth lodge near her house shall also fasten a pin in her walls.

25 He shall pitch his tent nigh unto her, and shall lodge in a lodging where good things are.

26 He shall set his children under her shelter, and shall lodge under her branches.

27 By her he shall be covered from heat, and in her glory shall he dwell.

CHAPTER XV

HE that feareth the Lord will do good; and he that hath the knowledge of the law shall obtain her.

2 And as a mother shall she meet him, and receive him as a wife married of a virgin.

3 With the bread of understanding shall she feed him, and give him the water of wisdom to drink.

4 He shall be stayed upon her, and shall not be moved; and shall rely upon her, and shall not be confounded.

5 She shall exalt him above his neighbours, and in the midst of the congregation shall she open his mouth.

6 He shall find joy and a crown of gladness, and she shall cause him to inherit an everlasting name.

7 But foolish men shall not attain unto her, and sinners shall not see her.

8 For she is far from pride, and men that are liars cannot remember her.

9 Praise is not seemly in the mouth of a sinner, for it was not sent him of the Lord.

10 For praise shall be uttered in wisdom, and the Lord will prosper it.

11 Say not thou, It is through the Lord that I fell away: for thou oughtest not to do the things that he hateth.

12 Say not thou, He hath caused me to err: for he hath no need of the sinful man.

13 The Lord hateth all abomination; and they that fear God love it not.

14 He himself made man from the beginning, and left him in the hand of his counsel;

15 If thou wilt, to keep the commandments, and to perform acceptable faithfulness.

16 He hath set fire and water before thee: stretch forth thy hand unto whether thou wilt.

17 Before man is life and death; and whether him liketh shall be given him.

18 For the wisdom of the Lord is great, and he is mighty in power, and beholdeth all things:

19 And his eyes are upon them that fear him, and he knoweth every work of man.

20 He hath commanded no man to do wickedly, neither hath he given any man licence to sin.

CHAPTER XVI

DESIRE not a multitude of unprofitable children, neither delight in ungodly sons.

2 Though they multiply, rejoice not in them, except the fear of the Lord be with them.

3 Trust not thou in their life, neither respect their multitude: for one that is just is better than a thousand; and better it is to die without children, than to have them that are ungodly.

4 For by one that hath understanding shall the city be replenished: but the kindred of the wicked shall speedily become desolate.

5 Many such things have I seen with mine eyes, and mine ear hath heard greater things than these.

6 In the congregation of the ungodly shall a fire be kindled;

and in a rebellious nation wrath is set on fire.

7 He was not pacified toward the old giants, who fell away in the strength of their foolishness.

8 Neither spared he the place where Lot sojourned, but abhorred them for their pride.

9 He pitied not the people of perdition, who were taken away in their sins:

10 Nor the six hundred thousand footmen, who were gathered together in the hardness of their hearts.

11 And if there be one stiffnecked among the people, it is marvel if he escape unpunished: for mercy and wrath are with him; he is mighty to forgive, and to pour out displeasure.

12 As his mercy is great, so is his correction also: he judgeth a man according to his works.

13 The sinner shall not escape with his spoils: and the patience of the godly shall not be frustrate.

14 Make way for every work of mercy: for every man shall find according to his works.

15 The Lord hardened Phā'-rāōh, that he should not know him, that his powerful works might be known to the world.

16 His mercy is manifest to every creature; and he hath separated his light from the darkness with an adamant.

17 Say not thou, I will hide myself from the Lord: shall any remember me from above? I shall not be remembered among so many people: for what is my soul among such an infinite number of creatures?

18 Behold, the heaven, and the heaven of heavens, the deep, and the earth, and all

150

that therein is, shall be moved when he shall visit.

19 The mountains also and foundations of the earth shall be shaken with trembling, when the Lord looketh upon them.

20 No heart can think upon these things worthily: and who is able to conceive his ways?

21 It is a tempest which no man can see: for the most part of his works are hid.

22 Who can declare the works of his justice? or who can endure them? for his covenant is afar off, and the trial of all things is in the end.

23 He that wanteth understanding will think upon vain things: and a foolish man erring imagineth follies.

24 My son, hearken unto me, and learn knowledge, and mark my words with thy heart.

25 I will shew forth doctrine in weight, and declare his knowledge exactly.

26 The works of the Lord are done in judgment from the beginning: and from the time he made them he disposed the parts thereof.

27 He garnished his works for ever, and in his hand are the chief of them unto all generations: they neither labour, nor are weary, nor cease from their works.

28 None of them hindereth another, and they shall never disobey his word.

29 After this the Lord looked upon the earth, and filled it with his blessings.

30 With all manner of living things hath he covered the face thereof; and they shall return into it again.

CHAPTER XVII

THE Lord created man of the earth, and turned him into it again.

2 He gave them few days, and a short time, and power also over the things therein.

3 He endued them with strength by themselves, and made them according to his image,

4 And put the fear of man upon all flesh, and gave him dominion over beasts and fowls.

5 [They received the use of the five operations of the Lord, and in the sixth place he imparted them understanding, and in the seventh speech, an interpreter of the cogitations thereof.]

6 Counsel, and a tongue, and eyes, ears, and a heart, gave he them to understand.

7 Withal he filled them with the knowledge of understanding, and shewed them good and evil.

8 He set his eye upon their hearts, that he might shew them the greatness of his works.

9 He gave them to glory in his marvellous acts for ever, that they might declare his works with understanding.

10 And the elect shall praise his holy name.

11 Beside this he gave them knowledge, and the law of life for an heritage.

12 He made an everlasting covenant with them, and shewed them his judgments.

13 Their eyes saw the majesty of his glory, and their ears heard his glorious voice.

14 And he said unto them, Beware of all unrighteousness; and he gave every man commandment concerning his neighbour.

15 Their ways are ever before him, and shall not be hid from his eyes.

16 Every man from his youth is given to evil; neither could they make to themselves fleshy hearts for stony.

17 For in the division of the nations of the whole earth he set a ruler over every people; but Israel is the Lord's portion:

18 Whom, being his firstborn, he nourisheth with discipline, and giving him the light of his love doth not forsake him.

19 Therefore all their works are as the sun before him, and his eyes are continually upon their ways.

20 None of their unrighteous deeds are hid from him, but all their sins are before the Lord.

21 But the Lord being gracious, and knowing his workmanship, neither left nor forsook them, but spared them.

22 The alms of a man is as a signet with him, and he will keep the good deeds of man as the apple of the eye, and give repentance to his sons and daughters.

23 Afterwards he will rise up and reward them, and render their recompence upon their heads.

24 But unto them that repent, he granted them return, and comforted those that failed in patience.

25 Return unto the Lord, and forsake thy sins, make thy prayer before his face, and offend less.

26 Turn again to the most High, and turn away from iniquity: for he will lead thee out

of darkness into the light of health, and hate thou abomination vehemently.

27 Who shall praise the most High in the grave, instead of them which live and give thanks?

28 Thanksgiving perisheth from the dead, as from one that is not: the living and sound in heart shall praise the Lord.

29 How great is the lovingkindness of the Lord our God, and his compassion unto such as turn unto him in holiness!

30 For all things cannot be in men, because the son of man is not immortal.

31 What is brighter than the sun? yet the light thereof faileth: and flesh and blood will imagine evil.

32 He vieweth the power of the height of heaven; and all men are but earth and ashes.

CHAPTER XVIII

HE that liveth for ever created all things in general.

2 The Lord only is righteous, and there is none other but he,

3 Who governeth the world with the palm of his hand, and all things obey his will: for he is the King of all, by his power dividing holy things among them from profane.

4 To whom hath he given power to declare his works? and who shall find out his noble acts?

5 Who shall number the strength of his majesty? and who shall also tell out his mercies?

6 As for the wondrous works of the Lord, there may nothing be taken from them, neither

may any thing be put unto them, neither can the ground of them be found out.

7 When a man hath done, then he beginneth; and when he leaveth off, then he shall be doubtful.

8 What is man, and whereto serveth he? what is his good, and what is his evil?

9 The number of a man's days at the most are an hundred years.

10 As a drop of water unto the sea, and a gravelstone in comparison of the sand; so are a thousand years to the days of eternity.

11 Therefore is God patient with them, and poureth forth his mercy upon them.

12 He saw and perceived their end to be evil; therefore he multiplied his compassion.

13 The mercy of man is toward his neighbour; but the mercy of the Lord is upon all flesh: he reproveth, and nurtureth, and teacheth, and bringeth again, as a shepherd his flock.

14 He hath mercy on them that receive discipline, and that diligently seek after his judgments.

15 My son, blemish not thy good deeds, neither use uncomfortable words when thou givest any thing.

16 Shall not the dew asswage the heat? so is a word better than a gift?

17 Lo, is not a word better than a gift? but both are with a gracious man.

18 A fool will upbraid churlishly, and a gift of the envious consumeth the eyes.

19 Learn before thou speak, and use physick or ever thou be sick.

20 Before judgment examine thyself, and in the day of visitation thou shalt find mercy.

21 Humble thyself before thou be sick, and in the time of sins shew repentance.

22 Let nothing hinder thee to pay thy vow in due time, and defer not until death to be justified.

23 Before thou prayest, prepare thyself; and be not as one that tempteth the Lord.

24 Think upon the wrath that shall be at the end, and the time of vengeance, when he shall turn away his face.

25 When thou hast enough, remember the time of hunger: and when thou art rich, think upon poverty and need.

26 From the morning until the evening the time is changed, and all things are soon done before the Lord.

27 A wise man will fear in every thing, and in the day of sinning he will beware of offence: but a fool will not observe time.

28 Every man of understanding knoweth wisdom, and will give praise unto him that found her.

29 They that were of understanding in sayings became also wise themselves, and poured forth exquisite parables.

30 Go not after thy lusts, but refrain thyself from thine appetites.

31 If thou givest thy soul the desires that please her, she will make thee a laughingstock to thine enemies that malign thee.

32 Take not pleasure in much good cheer, neither be tied to the expence thereof.

33 Be not made a beggar by banqueting upon borrowing, when thou hast nothing in thy purse: for thou shalt lie in wait for thine own life, and be talked on.

CHAPTER XIX

A LABOURING man that is given to drunkenness shall not be rich: and he that contemneth small things shall fall by little and little.

2 Wine and women will make men of understanding to fall away: and he that cleaveth to harlots will become impudent.

3 Moths and worms shall have him to heritage, and a bold man shall be taken away.

4 He that is hasty to give credit is lightminded; and he that sinneth shall offend against his own soul.

5 Whoso taketh pleasure in wickedness shall be condemned: but he that resisteth pleasures crowneth his life.

6 He that can rule his tongue shall live without strife; and he that hateth babbling shall have less evil.

7 Rehearse not unto another that which is told unto thee, and thou shalt fare never the worse.

8 Whether it be to friend or foe, talk not of other men's lives; and if thou canst without offence, reveal them not.

9 For he heard and observed thee, and when time cometh he will hate thee.

10 If thou hast heard a word, let it die with thee; and be bold, it will not burst thee.

11 A fool travaileth with a word, as a woman in labour of a child.

12 As an arrow that sticketh

in a man's thigh, so is a word within a fool's belly.

13 Admonish a friend, it may be he hath not done it: and if he have done it, that he do it no more.

14 Admonish thy friend, it may be he hath not said it: and if he have, that he speak it not again.

15 Admonish a friend: for many times it is a slander, and believe not every tale.

16 There is one that slippeth in his speech, but not from his heart; and who is he that hath not offended with his tongue?

17 Admonish thy neighbour before thou threaten him; and not being angry, give place to the law of the most High.

18 The fear of the Lord is the first step to be accepted [of him,] and wisdom obtaineth his love.

19 The knowledge of the commandments of the Lord is the doctrine of life: and they that do things that please him shall receive the fruit of the tree of immortality.

20 The fear of the Lord is all wisdom; and in all wisdom is the performance of the law, and the knowledge of his omnipotency.

21 If a servant say to his master, I will not do as it pleaseth thee; though afterward he do it, he angereth him that nourisheth him.

22 The knowledge of wickedness is not wisdom, neither at any time the counsel of sinners prudence.

23 There is a wickedness, and the same an abomination; and there is a fool wanting in wisdom.

24 He that hath small understanding, and feareth God, is better than one that hath much wisdom, and transgresseth the law of the most High.

25 There is an exquisite subtilty, and the same is unjust; and there is one that turneth aside to make judgment appear; and there is a wise man that justifieth in judgment.

26 There is a wicked man that hangeth down his head sadly; but inwardly he is full of deceit,

27 Casting down his countenance, and making as if he heard not: where he is not known, he will do thee a mischief before thou be aware.

28 And if for want of power he be hindered from sinning, yet when he findeth opportunity he will do evil.

29 A man may be known by his look, and one that hath understanding by his countenance, when thou meetest him.

30 A man's attire, and excessive laughter, and gait, shew what he is.

CHAPTER XX

THERE is a reproof that is not comely: again, some man holdeth his tongue, and he is wise.

2 It is much better to reprove, than to be angry secretly: and he that confesseth his fault shall be preserved from hurt.

3 How good is it, when thou art reproved, to shew repentance! for so shalt thou escape wilful sin.

4 As is the lust of an eunuch to deflower a virgin; so is he that executeth judgment with violence.

5 There is one that keepeth silence, and is found wise: and

another by much babbling becometh hateful.

6 Some man holdeth his tongue, because he hath not to answer: and some keepeth silence, knowing his time.

7 A wise man will hold his tongue till he see opportunity: but a babbler and a fool will regard no time.

8 He that useth many words shall be abhorred; and he that taketh to himself authority therein shall be hated.

9 There is a sinner that hath good success in evil things; and there is a gain that turneth to loss.

10 There is a gift that shall not profit thee; and there is a gift whose recompence is double.

11 There is an abasement because of glory; and there is that lifteth up his head from a low estate.

12 There is that buyeth much for a little, and repayeth it sevenfold.

13 A wise man by his words maketh himself beloved: but the graces of fools shall be poured out.

14 The gift of a fool shall do thee no good when thou hast it; neither yet of the envious for his necessity: for he looketh to receive many things for one.

15 He giveth little, and upbraideth much; he openeth his mouth like a crier; to day he lendeth, and to morrow will he ask it again: such an one is to be hated of God and man.

16 The fool saith, I have no friends, I have no thank for all my good deeds, and they that eat my bread speak evil of me.

17 How oft, and of how many shall he be laughed to scorn! for he knoweth not aright what it is to have; and it is all one unto him as if he had it not.

18 To slip upon a pavement is better than to slip with the tongue: so the fall of the wicked shall come speedily.

19 An unseasonable tale will always be in the mouth of the unwise.

20 A wise sentence shall be rejected when it cometh out of a fool's mouth; for he will not speak it in due season.

21 There is that is hindered from sinning through want: and when he taketh rest, he shall not be troubled.

22 There is that destroyeth his own soul through bashfulness, and by accepting of persons overthroweth himself.

23 There is that for bashfulness promiseth to his friend, and maketh him his enemy for nothing.

24 A lie is a foul blot in a man, yet it is continually in the mouth of the untaught.

25 A thief is better than a man that is accustomed to lie: but they both shall have destruction to heritage.

26 The disposition of a liar is dishonourable, and his shame is ever with him.

27 A wise man shall promote himself *to honour* with his words: and he that hath understanding will please great men.

28 He that tilleth his land shall increase his heap: and he that pleaseth great men shall get pardon for iniquity.

29 Presents and gifts blind the eyes of the wise, and stop up his mouth that he cannot reprove.

30 Wisdom that is hid, and treasure that is hoarded up, what profit is in them both?

31 Better is he that hideth his

folly than a man that hideth his wisdom.

32 Necessary patience in seeking the Lord is better than he that leadeth his life without a guide.

CHAPTER XXI

MY son, hast thou sinned? do so no more, but ask pardon for thy former sins.

2 Flee from sin as from the face of a serpent: for if thou comest too near it, it will bite thee: the teeth thereof are as the teeth of a lion, slaying the souls of men.

3 All iniquity is as a two edged sword, the wounds whereof cannot be healed.

4 To terrify and do wrong will waste riches: thus the house of proud men shall be made desolate.

5 A prayer out of a poor man's mouth reacheth to the ears of God, and his judgment cometh speedily.

6 He that hateth to be reproved is in the way of sinners: but he that feareth the Lord will repent from his heart.

7 An eloquent man is known far and near; but a man of understanding knoweth when he slippeth.

8 He that buildeth his house with other men's money is like one that gathereth himself stones for the tomb of his burial.

9 The congregation of the wicked is like tow wrapped together: and the end of them is a flame of fire to destroy them.

10 The way of sinners is made plain with stones, but at the end thereof is the pit of hell.

11 He that keepeth the law of the Lord getteth the under-
156

standing thereof: and the perfection of the fear of the Lord is wisdom.

12 He that is not wise will not be taught: but there is a wisdom which multiplieth bitterness.

13 The knowledge of a wise man shall abound like a flood: and his counsel is like a pure fountain of life.

14 The inner parts of a fool are like a broken vessel, and he will hold no knowledge as long as he liveth.

15 If a skilful man hear a wise word, he will commend it, and add unto it: but as soon as one of no understanding heareth it, it displeaseth him, and he casteth it behind his back.

16 The talking of a fool is like a burden in the way: but grace shall be found in the lips of the wise.

17 They enquire at the mouth of the wise man in the congregation, and they shall ponder his words in their heart.

18 As is a house that is destroyed, so is wisdom to a fool: and the knowledge of the unwise is as talk without sense.

19 Doctrine unto fools is as fetters on the feet, and like manacles on the right hand.

20 A fool lifteth up his voice with laughter; but a wise man doth scarce smile a little.

21 Learning is unto a wise man as an ornament of gold, and like a bracelet upon his right arm.

22 A foolish man's foot is soon in his [neighbour's] house: but a man of experience is ashamed of him.

23 A fool will peep in at the door into the house: but he that is well nurtured will stand without.

24 It is the rudeness of a man to hearken at the door: but a wise man will be grieved with the disgrace.

25 The lips of talkers will be telling such things as pertain not unto them: but the words of such as have understanding are weighed in the balance.

26 The heart of fools is in their mouth: but the mouth of the wise is in their heart.

27 When the ungodly curseth Satan, he curseth his own soul.

28 A whisperer defileth his own soul, and is hated wheresoever he dwelleth.

CHAPTER XXII

A SLOTHFUL man is compared to a filthy stone, and every one will hiss him out to his disgrace.

2 A slothful man is compared to the filth of a dunghill: every man that takes it up will shake his hand.

3 An evilnurtured son is the dishonour of his father that begat him: and a [foolish] daughter is born to his loss.

4 A wise daughter shall bring an inheritance to her husband: but she that liveth dishonestly is her father's heaviness.

5 She that is bold dishonoureth both her father and her husband, but they both shall despise her.

6 A tale out of season [is as] musick in mourning: but stripes and correction of wisdom are never out of time.

7 Whoso teacheth a fool is as one that glueth a potsherd together, and as he that waketh one from a sound sleep.

8 He that telleth a tale to a fool speaketh to one in a slumber: when he hath told his tale,

he will say, What is the matter?

9 If children live honestly, and have wherewithal, they shall cover the baseness of their parents.

10 But children, being haughty, through disdain and want of nurture do stain the nobility of their kindred.

11 Weep for the dead, for he hath lost the light: and weep for the fool, for he wanteth understanding: make little weeping for the dead, for he is at rest: but the life of the fool is worse than death.

12 Seven days do men mourn for him that is dead; but for a fool and an ungodly man all the days of his life.

13 Talk not much with a fool, and go not to him that hath no understanding: beware of him, lest thou have trouble, and thou shalt never be defiled with his fooleries: depart from him, and thou shalt find rest, and never be disquieted with madness.

14 What is heavier than lead? and what is the name thereof, but a fool?

15 Sand, and salt, and a mass of iron, is easier to bear, than a man without understanding.

16 As timber girt and bound together in a building cannot be loosed with shaking: so the heart that is stablished by advised counsel shall fear at no time.

17 A heart settled upon a thought of understanding is as a fair plaistering on the wall of a gallery.

18 Pales set on an high place will never stand against the wind: so a fearful heart in the imagination of a fool cannot stand against any fear.

19 He that pricketh the eye

will make tears to fall: and he that pricketh the heart maketh it to shew her knowledge.

20 Whoso casteth a stone at the birds frayeth them away: and he that upbraideth his friend breaketh friendship.

21 Though thou drewest a sword at thy friend, yet despair not: for there may be a returning [to favour.]

22 If thou hast opened thy mouth against thy friend, fear not; for there may be a reconciliation: except for upbraiding, or pride, or disclosing of secrets, or a treacherous wound: for these things every friend will depart.

23 Be faithful to thy neighbour in his poverty, that thou mayest rejoice in his prosperity: abide stedfast unto him in the time of his trouble, that thou mayest be heir with him in his heritage: for a mean estate is not always to be contemned: nor the rich that is foolish to be had in admiration.

24 As the vapour and smoke of a furnace goeth before the fire; so reviling before blood.

25 I will not be ashamed to defend a friend; neither will I hide myself from him.

26 And if any evil happen unto me by him, every one that heareth it will beware of him.

27 Who shall set a watch before my mouth, and a seal of wisdom upon my lips, that I fall not suddenly by them, and that my tongue destroy me not?

CHAPTER XXIII

O LORD, Father and Governor of all my whole life, leave me not to their counsels, and let me not fall by them.

158

2 Who will set scourges over my thoughts, and the discipline of wisdom over mine heart? that they spare me not for mine ignorances, and it pass not by my sins:

3 Lest mine ignorances increase, and my sins abound to my destruction, and I fall before mine adversaries, and mine enemy rejoice over me, whose hope is far from thy mercy.

4 O Lord, Father and God of my life, give me not a proud look, but turn away from thy servants always a haughty mind.

5 Turn away from me vain hopes and concupiscence, and thou shalt hold him up that is desirous always to serve thee.

6 Let not the greediness of the belly nor lust of the flesh take hold of me; and give not over me thy servant into an impudent mind.

7 Hear, O ye children, the discipline of the mouth: he that keepeth it shall never be taken in his lips.

8 The sinner shall be left in his foolishness: both the evil speaker and the proud shall fall thereby.

9 Accustom not thy mouth to swearing; neither use thyself to the naming of the Holy One.

10 For as a servant that is continually beaten shall not be without a blue mark: so he that sweareth and nameth God continually shall not be faultless.

11 A man that useth much swearing shall be filled with iniquity, and the plague shall never depart from his house: if he shall offend, his sin shall be upon him: and if he acknowledge not his sin, he maketh a double offence: and if he swear

in vain, he shall not be innocent, but his house shall be full of calamities.

12 There is a word that is clothed about with death: God grant that it be not found in the heritage of Jacob; for all such things shall be far from the godly, and they shall not wallow in their sins.

13 Use not thy mouth to intemperate swearing, for therein is the word of sin.

14 Remember thy father and thy mother, when thou sittest among great men. Be not forgetful before them, and so thou by thy custom become a fool, and wish that thou hadst not been born, and curse the day of thy nativity.

15 The man that is accustomed to opprobrious words will never be reformed all the days of his life.

16 Two sorts of men multiply sin, and the third will bring wrath: a hot mind is as a burning fire, it will never be quenched till it be consumed: a fornicator in the body of his flesh will never cease till he hath kindled a fire.

17 All bread is sweet to a whoremonger, he will not leave off till he die.

18 A man that breaketh wedlock, saying thus in his heart, Who seeth me? I am compassed about with darkness, the walls cover me, and no body seeth me; what need I to fear? the most High will not remember my sins:

19 Such a man only feareth the eyes of men, and knoweth not that the eyes of the Lord are ten thousand times brighter than the sun, beholding all the ways of men, and considering the most secret parts.

20 He knew all things ere ever they were created; so also after they were perfected he looked upon them all.

21 This man shall be punished in the streets of the city, and where he suspecteth not he shall be taken.

22 Thus shall it go also with the wife that leaveth her husband, and bringeth in an heir by another.

23 For first, she hath disobeyed the law of the most High; and secondly, she hath trespassed against her own husband; and thirdly, she hath played the whore in adultery, and brought children by another man.

24 She shall be brought out into the congregation, and inquisition shall be made of her children.

25 Her children shall not take root, and her branches shall bring forth no fruit.

26 She shall leave her memory to be cursed, and her reproach shall not be blotted out.

27 And they that remain shall know that there is nothing better than the fear of the Lord, and that there is nothing sweeter than to take heed unto the commandments of the Lord.

28 It is great glory to follow the Lord, and to be received of him is long life.

CHAPTER XXIV

WISDOM shall praise herself, and shall glory in the midst of her people.

2 In the congregation of the most High shall she open her mouth, and triumph before his power.

3 I came out of the mouth of

the most High, and covered the earth as a cloud.

4 I dwelt in high places, and my throne is in a cloudy pillar.

5 I alone compassed the circuit of heaven, and walked in the bottom of the deep.

6 In the waves of the sea, and in all the earth, and in every people and nation, I got a possession.

7 With all these I sought rest: and in whose inheritance shall I abide?

8 So the Creator of all things gave me a commandment, and he that made me caused my tabernacle to rest, and said, Let thy dwelling be in Jacob, and thine inheritance in Israel.

9 He created me from the beginning before the world, and I shall never fail.

10 In the holy tabernacle I served before him; and so was I established in Sion.

11 Likewise in the beloved city he gave me rest, and in Jerusalem was my power.

12 And I took root in an honourable people, even in the portion of the Lord's inheritance.

13 I was exalted like a cedar in Līb′-ă-nŭs, and as a cypress tree upon the mountains of Hermon.

14 I was exalted like a palm tree in Ĕn-găd′-dī, and as a rose plant in Jericho, as a fair olive tree in a pleasant field, and grew up as a plane tree by the water.

15 I gave a sweet smell like cinnamon and aspalathus, and I yielded a pleasant odour like the best myrrh, as galbanum, and onyx, and sweet storax, and as the fume of frankincense in the tabernacle.

16 As the turpentine tree I stretched out my branches, and my branches are the branches of honour and grace.

17 As the vine brought I forth pleasant savour, and my flowers are the fruit of honour and riches.

18 I am the mother of fair love, and fear, and knowledge, and holy hope: I therefore, being eternal, am given to all my children which are named of him.

19 Come unto me, all ye that be desirous of me, and fill yourselves with my fruits.

20 For my memorial is sweeter than honey, and mine inheritance than the honeycomb.

21 They that eat me shall yet be hungry, and they that drink me shall yet be thirsty.

22 He that obeyeth me shall never be confounded, and they that work by me shall not do amiss.

23 All these things are the book of the covenant of the most high God, *even* the law which Moses commanded for an heritage unto the congregations of Jacob.

24 Faint not to be strong in the Lord; that he may confirm you, cleave unto him: for the Lord Almighty is God alone, and beside him there is no other Saviour.

25 He filleth all things with his wisdom, as Phison and as Tigris in the time of the new fruits.

26 He maketh the understanding to abound like Ēu-phrā′-tēs, and as Jordan in the time of the harvest.

27 He maketh the doctrine of knowledge appear as the light, and as Gē′-on in the time of vintage.

28 The first man knew her not perfectly: no more shall the last find her out.

29 For her thoughts are more than the sea, and her counsels profounder than the great deep.

30 I also came out as a brook from a river, and as a conduit into a garden.

31 I said, I will water my best garden, and will water abundantly my garden bed: and, lo, my brook became a river, and my river became a sea.

32 I will yet make doctrine to shine as the morning, and will send forth her light afar off.

33 I will yet pour out doctrine as prophecy, and leave it to all ages for ever.

34 Behold that I have not laboured for myself only, but for all them that seek wisdom.

CHAPTER XXV

IN three things I was beautified, and stood up beautiful both before God and men: the unity of brethren, the love of neighbours, a man and a wife that agree together.

2 Three sorts of men my soul hateth, and I am greatly offended at their life: a poor man that is proud, a rich man that is a liar, and an old adulterer that doateth.

3 If thou hast gathered nothing in thy youth, how canst thou find any thing in thine age?

4 O how comely a thing is judgment for gray hairs, and for ancient men to know counsel!

5 O how comely is the wisdom of old men, and understanding and counsel to men of honour!

6 Much experience is the crown of old men, and the fear of God is their glory.

7 There be nine things which I have judged in mine heart to be happy, and the tenth I will utter with my tongue: A man that hath joy of his children; and he that liveth to see the fall of his enemy:

8 Well is him that dwelleth with a wife of understanding, and that hath not slipped with his tongue, and that hath not served a man more unworthy than himself:

9 Well is him that hath found prudence, and he that speaketh in the ears of them that will hear:

10 O how great is he that findeth wisdom! yet is there none above him that feareth the Lord.

11 But the love of the Lord passeth all things for illumination: he that holdeth it, whereto shall he be likened?

12 The fear of the Lord is the beginning of his love: and faith is the beginning of cleaving unto him.

13 [Give me] any plague, but the plague of the heart: and any wickedness, but the wickedness of a woman:

14 And any affliction, but the affliction from them that hate me: and any revenge, but the revenge of enemies.

15 There is no head above the head of a serpent; and there is no wrath above the wrath of an enemy.

16 I had rather dwell with a lion and a dragon, than to keep house with a wicked woman.

17 The wickedness of a woman changeth her face, and darkeneth her countenance like sackcloth.

18 Her husband shall sit

among his neighbours; and when he heareth it shall sigh bitterly.

19 All wickedness is but little to the wickedness of a woman: let the portion of a sinner fall upon her.

20 As the climbing up a sandy way is to the feet of the aged, so is a wife full of words to a quiet man.

21 Stumble not at the beauty of a woman, and desire her not for pleasure.

22 A woman, if she maintain her husband, is full of anger, impudence, and much reproach.

23 A wicked woman abateth the courage, maketh an heavy countenance and a wounded heart: a woman that will not comfort her husband in distress maketh weak hands and feeble knees.

24 Of the woman came the beginning of sin, and through her we all die.

25 Give the water no passage; neither a wicked woman liberty to gad abroad.

26 If she go not as thou wouldest have her, cut her off from thy flesh, and give her a bill of divorce, and let her go.

CHAPTER XXVI

BLESSED is the man that hath a virtuous wife, for the number of his days shall be double.

2 A virtuous woman rejoiceth her husband, and he shall fulfil the years of his life in peace.

3 A good wife is a good portion, which shall be given in the portion of them that fear the Lord.

4 Whether a man be rich or poor, if he have a good heart

toward the Lord, he shall at all times rejoice with a cheerful countenance.

5 There be three things that mine heart feareth; and for the fourth I was sore afraid: the slander of a city, the gathering together of an unruly multitude, and a false accusation: all these are worse than death.

6 But a grief of heart and sorrow is a woman that is jealous over another woman, and a scourge of the tongue which communicateth with all.

7 An evil wife is a yoke shaken to and fro: he that hath hold of her is as though he held a scorpion.

8 A drunken woman and a gadder abroad causeth great anger, and she will not cover her own shame.

9 The whoredom of a woman may be known in her haughty looks and eyelids.

10 If thy daughter be shameless, keep her in straitly, lest she abuse herself through overmuch liberty.

11 Watch over an impudent eye: and marvel not if she trespass against thee.

12 She will open her mouth, as a thirsty traveller when he hath found a fountain, and drink of every water near her: by every hedge will she sit down, and open her quiver against every arrow.

13 The grace of a wife delighteth her husband, and her discretion will fatten his bones.

14 A silent and loving woman is a gift of the Lord; and there is nothing so much worth as a mind well instructed.

15 A shamefaced and faithful woman is a double grace, and her continent mind cannot be valued.

16 As the sun when it ariseth in the high heaven; so is the beauty of a good wife in the ordering of her house.

17 As the clear light is upon the holy candlestick; so is the beauty of the face in ripe age.

18 As the golden pillars are upon the sockets of silver; so are the fair feet with a constant heart.

19 My son, keep the flower of thine age sound; and give not thy strength to strangers.

20 When thou hast gotten a fruitful possession through all the field, sow it with thine own seed, trusting in the goodness of thy stock.

21 So thy race which thou leavest shall be magnified, having the confidence of their good descent.

22 An harlot shall be accounted as spittle; but a married woman is a tower against death to her husband.

23 A wicked woman is given as a portion to a wicked man: but a godly woman is given to him that feareth the Lord.

24 A dishonest woman contemneth shame: but an honest woman will reverence her husband.

25 A shameless woman shall be counted as a dog; but she that is shamefaced will fear the Lord.

26 A woman that honoureth her husband shall be judged wise of all; but she that dishonoureth him in her pride shall be counted ungodly of all.

27 A loud crying woman and a scold shall be sought out to drive away the enemies.

28 There be two things that grieve my heart; and the third maketh me angry: a man of war that suffereth poverty;

and men of understanding that are not set by; and one that returneth from righteousness to sin; the Lord prepareth such an one for the sword.

29 A merchant shall hardly keep himself from doing wrong; and an huckster shall not be freed from sin.

CHAPTER XXVII

MANY have sinned for a small matter; and he that seeketh for abundance will turn his eyes away.

2 As a nail sticketh fast between the joinings of the stones; so doth sin stick close between buying and selling.

3 Unless a man hold himself diligently in the fear of the Lord, his house shall soon be overthrown.

4 As when one sifteth with a sieve, the refuse remaineth; so the filth of man in his talk.

5 The furnace proveth the potter's vessels; so the trial of man is in his reasoning.

6 The fruit declareth if the tree have been dressed; so is the utterance of a conceit in the heart of man.

7 Praise no man before thou hearest him speak; for this is the trial of men.

8 If thou followest righteousness, thou shalt obtain her, and put her on, as a glorious long robe.

9 The birds will resort unto their like; so will truth return unto them that practise in her.

10 As the lion lieth in wait for the prey; so sin for them that work iniquity.

11 The discourse of a godly man is always with wisdom; but a fool changeth as the moon.

12 If thou be among the indiscreet, observe the time; but be continually among men of understanding.

13 The discourse of fools is irksome, and their sport is the wantonness of sin.

14 The talk of him that sweareth much maketh the hair stand upright; and their brawls make one stop his ears.

15 The strife of the proud is bloodshedding, and their revilings are grievous to the ear.

16 Whoso discovereth secrets loseth his credit; and shall never find friend to his mind.

17 Love thy friend, and be faithful unto him: but if thou bewrayest his secrets, follow no more after him.

18 For as a man hath destroyed his enemy; so hast thou lost the love of thy neighbour.

19 As one that letteth a bird go out of his hand, so hast thou let thy neighbour go, and shalt not get him again.

20 Follow after him no more, for he is too far off; he is as a roe escaped out of the snare.

21 As for a wound, it may be bound up; and after reviling there may be reconcilement: but he that bewrayeth secrets is without hope.

22 He that winketh with the eyes worketh evil: and he that knoweth him will depart from him.

23 When thou art present, he will speak sweetly, and will admire thy words: but at the last he will writhe his mouth, and slander thy sayings.

24 I have hated many things, but nothing like him; for the Lord will hate him.

25 Whoso casteth a stone on high casteth it on his own head; and a deceitful stroke shall make wounds.

26 Whoso diggeth a pit shall fall therein: and he that setteth a trap shall be taken therein.

27 He that worketh mischief, it shall fall upon him, and he shall not know whence it cometh.

28 Mockery and reproach are from the proud; but vengeance, as a lion, shall lie in wait for them.

29 They that rejoice at the fall of the righteous shall be taken in the snare; and anguish shall consume them before they die.

30 Malice and wrath, even these are abominations; and the sinful man shall have them both.

CHAPTER XXVIII

HE that revengeth shall find vengeance from the Lord, and he will surely keep his sins [in remembrance.]

2 Forgive thy neighbour the hurt that he hath done unto thee, so shall thy sins also be forgiven when thou prayest.

3 One man beareth hatred against another, and doth he seek pardon from the Lord?

4 He sheweth no mercy to a man, which is like himself: and doth he ask forgiveness of his own sins?

5 If he that is but flesh nourish hatred, who will intreat for pardon of his sins?

6 Remember thy end, and let enmity cease; [remember] corruption and death, and abide in the commandments.

7 Remember the commandments, and bear no malice to thy neighbour: [remember] the

covenant of the Highest, and wink at ignorance.

8 Abstain from strife, and thou shalt diminish thy sins: for a furious man will kindle strife.

9 A sinful man disquieteth friends, and maketh debate among them that be at peace.

10 As the matter of the fire is, so it burneth: and as a man's strength is, so is his wrath; and according to his riches his anger riseth; and the stronger they are which contend, the more they will be inflamed.

11 An hasty contention kindleth a fire: and an hasty fighting sheddeth blood.

12 If thou blow the spark, it shall burn: if thou spit upon it, it shall be quenched: and both these come out of thy mouth.

13 Curse the whisperer and doubletongued: for such have destroyed many that were at peace.

14 A backbiting tongue hath disquieted many, and driven them from nation to nation: strong cities hath it pulled down, and overthrown the houses of great men.

15 A backbiting tongue hath cast out virtuous women, and deprived them of their labours.

16 Whoso hearkeneth unto it shall never find rest, and never dwell quietly.

17 The stroke of the whip maketh marks in the flesh: but the stroke of the tongue breaketh the bones.

18 Many have fallen by the edge of the sword: but not so many as have fallen by the tongue.

19 Well is he that is defended from it, and hath not passed through the venom thereof; who hath not drawn the yoke thereof, nor hath been bound in her bands.

20 For the yoke thereof is a yoke of iron, and the bands thereof are bands of brass.

21 The death thereof is an evil death, the grave were better than it.

22 It shall not have rule over them that fear God, neither shall they be burned with the flame thereof.

23 Such as forsake the Lord shall fall into it; and it shall burn in them, and not be quenched; it shall be sent upon them as a lion, and devour them as a leopard.

24 Look that thou hedge thy possession about with thorns, and bind up thy silver and gold,

25 And weigh thy words in a balance, and make a door and bar for thy mouth.

26 Beware thou slide not by it, lest thou fall before him that lieth in wait.

CHAPTER XXIX

HE that is merciful will lend unto his neighbour; and he that strengtheneth his hand keepeth the commandments.

2 Lend to thy neighbour in time of his need, and pay thou thy neighbour again in due season.

3 Keep thy word, and deal faithfully with him, and thou shalt always find the thing that is necessary for thee.

4 Many, when a thing was lent them, reckoned it to be found, and put them to trouble that helped them.

5 Till he hath received, he will kiss a man's hand; and for his neighbour's money he will speak submissly: but when he

should repay, he will prolong the time, and return words of grief, and complain of the time.

6 If he prevail, he shall hardly receive the half, and he will count as if he had found it: if not, he hath deprived him of his money, and he hath gotten him an enemy without cause: he payeth him with cursings and railings; and for honour he will pay him disgrace.

7 Many therefore have refused to lend for other men's ill dealing, fearing to be defrauded.

8 Yet have thou patience with a man in poor estate, and delay not to shew him mercy.

9 Help the poor for the commandment's sake, and turn him not away because of his poverty.

10 Lose thy money for thy brother and thy friend, and let it not rust under a stone to be lost.

11 Lay up thy treasure according to the commandments of the most High, and it shall bring thee more profit than gold.

12 Shut up alms in thy storehouses: and it shall deliver thee from all affliction.

13 It shall fight for thee against thine enemies better than a mighty shield and strong spear.

14 An honest man is surety for his neighbour: but he that is impudent will forsake him.

15 Forget not the friendship of thy surety, for he hath given his life for thee.

16 A sinner will overthrow the good estate of his surety:

17 And he that is of an unthankful mind will leave him [in danger] that delivered him.

18 Suretiship hath undone many of good estate, and shaken them as a wave of the sea: mighty men hath it driven from their houses, so that they wandered among strange nations.

19 A wicked man transgressing the commandments of the Lord shall fall into suretiship: and he that undertaketh and followeth other men's business for gain shall fall into suits.

20 Help thy neighbour according to thy power, and beware that thou thyself fall not into the same.

21 The chief thing for life is water, and bread, and clothing, and an house to cover shame.

22 Better is the life of a poor man in a mean cottage, than delicate fare in another man's house.

23 Be it little or much, hold thee contented, that thou hear not the reproach of thy house.

24 For it is a miserable life to go from house to house: for where thou art a stranger, thou darest not open thy mouth.

25 Thou shalt entertain, and feast, and have no thanks: moreover thou shalt hear bitter words:

26 Come, thou stranger, and furnish a table, and feed me of that thou hast ready.

27 Give place, thou stranger, to an honourable man; my brother cometh to be lodged, and I have need of mine house.

28 These things are grievous to a man of understanding; the upbraiding of houseroom, and reproaching of the lender.

CHAPTER XXX

HE that loveth his son causeth him oft to feel the

166

rod, that he may have joy of him in the end.

2 He that chastiseth his son shall have joy in him, and shall rejoice of him among his acquaintance.

3 He that teacheth his son grieveth the enemy: and before his friends he shall rejoice of him.

4 Though his father die, yet he is as though he were not dead: for he hath left one behind him that is like himself.

5 While he lived, he saw and rejoiced in him: and when he died, he was not sorrowful.

6 He left behind him an avenger against his enemies, and one that shall requite kindness to his friends.

7 He that maketh too much of his son shall bind up his wounds; and his bowels will be troubled at every cry.

8 An horse not broken becometh headstrong: and a child left to himself will be wilful.

9 Cocker thy child, and he shall make thee afraid: play with him, and he will bring thee to heaviness.

10 Laugh not with him, lest thou have sorrow with him, and lest thou gnash thy teeth in the end.

11 Give him no liberty in his youth, and wink not at his follies.

12 Bow down his neck while he is young, and beat him on the sides while he is a child, lest he wax stubborn, and be disobedient unto thee, and so bring sorrow to thine heart.

13 Chastise thy son, and hold him to labour, lest his lewd behaviour be an offence unto thee.

14 Better is the poor, being sound and strong of constitution, than a rich man that is afflicted in his body.

15 Health and good estate of body are above all gold, and a strong body above infinite wealth.

16 There is no riches above a sound body, and no joy above the joy of the heart.

17 Death is better than a bitter life or continual sickness.

18 Delicates poured upon a mouth shut up are as messes of meat set upon a grave.

19 What good doeth the offering unto an idol? for neither can it eat nor smell: so is he that is persecuted of the Lord.

20 He seeth with his eyes and groaneth, as an eunuch that embraceth a virgin and sigheth.

21 Give not over thy mind to heaviness, and afflict not thyself in thine own counsel.

22 The gladness of the heart is the life of man, and the joyfulness of a man prolongeth his days.

23 Love thine own soul, and comfort thy heart, remove sorrow far from thee: for sorrow hath killed many, and there is no profit therein.

24 Envy and wrath shorten the life, and carefulness bringeth age before the time.

25 A cheerful and good heart will have a care of his meat and diet.

CHAPTER XXXI

WATCHING for riches consumeth the flesh, and the care thereof driveth away sleep.

2 Watching care will not let a man slumber, as a sore disease breaketh sleep.

3 The rich hath great labour in gathering riches together; and when he resteth, he is filled with his delicates.

4 The poor laboureth in his poor estate; and when he leaveth off, he is still needy.

5 He that loveth gold shall not be justified, and he that followeth corruption shall have enough thereof.

6 Gold hath been the ruin of many, and their destruction was present.

7 It is a stumbling block unto them that sacrifice unto it, and every fool shall be taken therewith.

8 Blessed is the rich that is found without blemish, and hath not gone after gold.

9 Who is he? and we will call him blessed: for wonderful things hath he done among his people.

10 Who hath been tried thereby, and found perfect? then let him glory. Who might offend, and hath not offended? or done evil, and hath not done it?

11 His goods shall be established, and the congregation shall declare his alms.

12 If thou sit at a bountiful table, be not greedy upon it, and say not, There is much meat on it.

13 Remember that a wicked eye is an evil thing: and what is created more wicked than an eye? therefore it weepeth upon every occasion.

14 Stretch not thine hand whithersoever it looketh, and thrust it not with him into the dish.

15 Judge of thy neighbour by thyself: and be discreet in every point.

16 Eat, as it becometh a man, those things which are set before thee; and devour not, lest thou be hated.

17 Leave off first for manners' sake; and be not unsatiable, lest thou offend.

18 When thou sittest among many, reach not thine hand out first of all.

19 A very little is sufficient for a man well nurtured, and he fetcheth not his wind short upon his bed.

20 Sound sleep cometh of moderate eating: he riseth early, and his wits are with him: but the pain of watching, and choler, and pangs of the belly, are with an unsatiable man.

21 And if thou hast been forced to eat, arise, go forth, vomit, and thou shalt have rest.

22 My son, hear me, and despise me not, and at the last thou shalt find as I told thee: in all thy works be quick, so shall there no sickness come unto thee.

23 Whoso is liberal of his meat, men shall speak well of him; and the report of his good housekeeping will be believed.

24 But against him that is a niggard of his meat the whole city shall murmur; and the testimonies of his niggardness shall not be doubted of.

25 Shew not thy valiantness in wine; for wine hath destroyed many.

26 The furnace proveth the edge by dipping: so doth wine the hearts of the proud by drunkenness.

27 Wine is as good as life to a man, if it be drunk moderately: what life is then to a man that is without wine? for it was made to make men glad.

28 Wine measurably drunk and in season bringeth gladness of the heart, and cheerfulness of the mind:

29 But wine drunken with excess maketh bitterness of the mind, with brawling and quarrelling.

30 Drunkenness increaseth the rage of a fool till he offend: it diminisheth strength, and maketh wounds.

31 Rebuke not thy neighbour at the wine, and despise him not in his mirth: give him no despiteful words, and press not upon him with urging him [to drink.]

CHAPTER XXXII

IF thou be made the master [of a feast,] lift not thyself up, but be among them as one of the rest; take diligent care for them, and so sit down.

2 And when thou hast done all thy office, take thy place, that thou mayest be merry with them, and receive a crown for thy well ordering of the feast.

3 Speak, thou that art the elder, for it becometh thee, but with sound judgment; and hinder not musick.

4 Pour not out words where there is a musician, and shew not forth wisdom out of time.

5 A concert of musick in a banquet of wine is as a signet of carbuncle set in gold.

6 As a signet of an emerald set in a work of gold, so is the melody of musick with pleasant wine.

7 Speak, young man, if there be need of thee: and yet scarcely when thou art twice asked.

8 Let thy speech be short, comprehending much in few words; be as one that knoweth and yet holdeth his tongue.

9 If thou be among great men, make not thyself equal with them; and when ancient men are in place, use not many words.

10 Before the thunder goeth lightning; and before a shamefaced man shall go favour.

11 Rise up betimes, and be not the last; but get thee home without delay.

12 There take thy pastime, and do what thou wilt: but sin not by proud speech.

13 And for these things bless him that made thee, and hath replenished thee with his good things.

14 Whoso feareth the Lord will receive his discipline; and they that seek him early shall find favour.

15 He that seeketh the law shall be filled therewith: but the hypocrite will be offended thereat.

16 They that fear the Lord shall find judgment, and shall kindle justice as a light.

17 A sinful man will not be reproved, but findeth an excuse according to his will.

18 A man of counsel will be considerate; but a strange and proud man is not daunted with fear, even when of himself he hath done without counsel.

19 Do nothing without advice; and when thou hast once done, repent not.

20 Go not in a way wherein thou mayest fall, and stumble not among the stones.

21 Be not confident in a plain way.

22 And beware of thine own children.

23 In every good work trust

169

thy own soul; for this is the keeping of the commandments.

24 He that believeth in the Lord taketh heed to the commandment; and he that trusteth in him shall fare never the worse.

CHAPTER XXXIII

THERE shall no evil happen unto him that feareth the Lord; but in temptation even again he will deliver him.

2 A wise man hateth not the law; but he that is an hypocrite therein is as a ship in a storm.

3 A man of understanding trusteth in the law; and the law is faithful unto him, as an oracle.

4 Prepare what to say, and so thou shalt be heard: and bind up instruction, and then make answer.

5 The heart of the foolish is like a cartwheel; and his thoughts are like a rolling axletree.

6 A stallion horse is as a mocking friend, he neigheth under every one that sitteth upon him.

7 Why doth one day excel another, when as all the light of every day in the year is of the sun?

8 By the knowledge of the Lord they were distinguished: and he altered seasons and feasts.

9 Some of them hath he made high days, and hallowed *them*, and some of them hath he made ordinary days.

10 And all men are from the ground, and Adam was created of earth.

11 In much knowledge the Lord hath divided them, and made their ways diverse.

12 Some of them hath he blessed and exalted, and some of them hath he sanctified, and set near himself: but some of them hath he cursed and brought low, and turned out of their places.

13 As the clay is in the potter's hand, to fashion it at his pleasure: so man is in the hand of him that made him, to render to them as liketh him best.

14 Good is set against evil, and life against death: so is the godly against the sinner, and the sinner against the godly.

15 So look upon all the works of the most High; and there are two and two, one against another.

16 I awaked up last of all, as one that gathereth after the grapegatherers: by the blessing of the Lord I profited, and filled my winepress like a gatherer of grapes.

17 Consider that I laboured not for myself only, but for all them that seek learning.

18 Hear me, O ye great men of the people, and hearken with your ears, ye rulers of the congregation.

19 Give not thy son and wife, thy brother and friend, power over thee while thou livest, and give not thy goods to another: lest it repent thee, and thou intreat for the same again.

20 As long as thou livest and hast breath in thee, give not thyself over to any.

21 For better it is that thy children should seek to thee, than that thou shouldest stand to their courtesy.

22 In all thy works keep to thyself the preeminence; leave not a stain in thine honour.

23 At the time when thou shalt end thy days, and finish

thy life, distribute thine inheritance.

24 Fodder, a wand, and burdens, *are* for the ass; and bread, correction, and work, for a servant.

25 If thou set thy servant to labour, thou shalt find rest: but if thou let him go idle, he shall seek liberty.

26 A yoke and a collar do bow the neck: so are tortures and torments for an evil servant.

27 Send him to labour, that he be not idle; for idleness teacheth much evil.

28 Set him to work, as is fit for him: if he be not obedient, put on more heavy fetters.

29 But be not excessive toward any; and without discretion do nothing.

30 If thou have a servant, let him be unto thee as thyself, because thou hast bought him with a price.

31 If thou have a servant, entreat him as a brother: for thou hast need of him, as of thine own soul: if thou entreat him evil, and he run from thee, which way wilt thou go to seek him?

CHAPTER XXXIV

THE hopes of a man void of understanding are vain and false: and dreams lift up fools.

2 Whoso regardeth dreams is like him that catcheth at a shadow, and followeth after the wind.

3 The vision of dreams is the resemblance of one thing to another, even as the likeness of a face to a face.

4 Of an unclean thing what can be cleansed? and from that thing which is false what truth can come?

5 Divinations, and soothsayings, and dreams, are vain: and the heart fancieth, as a woman's heart in travail.

6 If they be not sent from the most High in thy visitation, set not thy heart upon them.

7 For dreams have deceived many, and they have failed that put their trust in them.

8 The law shall be found perfect without lies: and wisdom is perfection to a faithful mouth.

9 A man that hath travelled knoweth many things; and he that hath much experience will declare wisdom.

10 He that hath no experience knoweth little: but he that hath travelled is full of prudence.

11 When I travelled, I saw many things; and I understand more than I can express.

12 I was ofttimes in danger of death: yet I was delivered because of these things.

13 The spirit of those that fear the Lord shall live; for their hope is in him that saveth them.

14 Whoso feareth the Lord shall not fear nor be afraid; for he is his hope.

15 Blessed is the soul of him that feareth the Lord: to whom doth he look? and who is his strength?

16 For the eyes of the Lord are upon them that love him, he is their mighty protection and strong stay, a defence from heat, and a cover from the sun at noon, a preservation from stumbling, and an help from falling.

17 He raiseth up the soul, and lighteneth the eyes: he giveth health, life, and blessing.

18 He that sacrificeth of a

thing wrongfully gotten, his offering is ridiculous; and the gifts of unjust men are not accepted.

19 The most High is not pleased with the offerings of the wicked; neither is he pacified for sin by the multitude of sacrifices.

20 Whoso bringeth an offering of the goods of the poor doeth as one that killeth the son before his father's eyes.

21 The bread of the needy is their life: he that defraudeth him thereof is a man of blood.

22 He that taketh away his neighbour's living slayeth him; and he that defraudeth the labourer of his hire is a bloodshedder.

23 When one buildeth, and another pulleth down, what profit have they then but labour?

24 When one prayeth, and another curseth, whose voice will the Lord hear?

25 He that washeth himself after the touching of a dead body, if he touch it again, what availeth his washing?

26 So is it with a man that fasteth for his sins, and goeth again, and doeth the same: who will hear his prayer? or what doth his humbling profit him?

CHAPTER XXXV

HE that keepeth the law bringeth offerings enough: he that taketh heed to the commandment offereth a peace offering.

2 He that requiteth a good turn offereth fine flour; and he that giveth alms sacrificeth praise.

3 To depart from wickedness is a thing pleasing to the Lord;

and to forsake unrighteousness is a propitiation.

4 Thou shalt not appear empty before the Lord.

5 For all these things [are to be done] because of the commandment.

6 The offering of the righteous maketh the altar fat, and the sweet savour thereof *is* before the most High.

7 The sacrifice of a just man is acceptable, and the memorial thereof shall never be forgotten.

8 Give the Lord his honour with a good eye, and diminish not the firstfruits of thine hands.

9 In all thy gifts shew a cheerful countenance, and dedicate thy tithes with gladness.

10 Give unto the most High according as he hath enriched thee; and as thou hast gotten, give with a cheerful eye.

11 For the Lord recompenseth, and will give thee seven times as much.

12 Do not think to corrupt with gifts; for such he will not receive: and trust not to unrighteous sacrifices; for the Lord is judge, and with him is no respect of persons.

13 He will not accept any person against a poor man, but will hear the prayer of the oppressed.

14 He will not despise the supplication of the fatherless; nor the widow, when she poureth out her complaint.

15 Do not the tears run down the widow's cheeks? and is not her cry against him that causeth them to fall?

16 He that serveth the Lord shall be accepted with favour, and his prayer shall reach unto the clouds.

17 The prayer of the humble pierceth the clouds: and till it come nigh, he will not be comforted; and will not depart, till the most High shall behold to judge righteously, and execute judgment.

18 For the Lord will not be slack, neither will the Mighty be patient toward them, till he have smitten in sunder the loins of the unmerciful, and repayed vengeance to the heathen; till he have taken away the multitude of the proud, and broken the sceptre of the unrighteous;

19 Till he have rendered to every man according to his deeds, and to the works of men according to their devices; till he have judged the cause of his people, and made them to rejoice in his mercy.

20 Mercy is seasonable in the time of affliction, as clouds of rain in the time of drought.

CHAPTER XXXVI

HAVE mercy upon us, O Lord God of all, and behold us:

2 And send thy fear upon all the nations that seek not after thee.

3 Lift up thy hand against the strange nations, and let them see thy power.

4 As thou wast sanctified in us before them: so be thou magnified among them before us.

5 And let them know thee, as we have known thee, that there is no God but only thou, O God.

6 Shew new signs, and make other strange wonders: glorify thy hand and thy right arm, that they may set forth thy wondrous works.

7 Raise up indignation, and pour out wrath: take away the adversary, and destroy the enemy.

8 Make the time short, remember the covenant, and let them declare thy wonderful works.

9 Let him that escapeth be consumed by the rage of the fire; and let them perish that oppress the people.

10 Smite in sunder the heads of the rulers of the heathen, that say, There is none other but we.

11 Gather all the tribes of Jacob together, and inherit thou them, as from the beginning.

12 O Lord, have mercy upon the people that is called by thy name, and upon Israel, whom thou hast named thy firstborn.

13 O be merciful unto Jerusalem, thy holy city, the place of thy rest.

14 Fill Sion with thine unspeakable oracles, and thy people with thy glory.

15 Give testimony unto those that thou hast possessed from the beginning, and raise up prophets that have been in thy name.

16 Reward them that wait for thee, and let thy prophets be found faithful.

17 O Lord, hear the prayer of thy servants, according to the blessing of Aaron over thy people, that all they which dwell upon the earth may know that thou art the Lord, the eternal God.

18 The belly devoureth all meats, yet is one meat better than another.

19 As the palate tasteth divers kinds of venison: so

doth an heart of understanding false speeches.

20 A froward heart causeth heaviness: but a man of experience will recompense him.

21 A woman will receive every man, yet is one daughter better than another.

22 The beauty of a woman cheereth the countenance, and a man loveth nothing better.

23 If there be kindness, meekness, and comfort, in her tongue, then is not her husband like other men.

24 He that getteth a wife beginneth a possession, a help like unto himself, and a pillar of rest.

25 Where no hedge is, there the possession is spoiled: and he that hath no wife will wander up and down mourning.

26 Who will trust a thief well appointed, that skippeth from city to city? so [who will believe] a man that hath no house, and lodgeth wheresoever the night taketh him?

CHAPTER XXXVII

EVERY friend saith, I am his friend also: but there is a friend, which is only a friend in name.

2 Is it not a grief unto death, when a companion and friend is turned to an enemy?

3 O wicked imagination, whence camest thou in to cover the earth with deceit?

4 There is a companion, which rejoiceth in the prosperity of a friend, but in the time of trouble will be against him.

5 There is a companion, which helpeth his friend for the belly, and taketh up the buckler against the enemy.

6 Forget not thy friend in thy

mind, and be not unmindful of him in thy riches.

7 Every counsellor extolleth counsel; but there is some that counselleth for himself.

8 Beware of a counsellor, and know before what need he hath; for he will counsel for himself; lest he cast the lot upon thee,

9 And say unto thee, Thy way is good: and afterward he stand on the other side, to see what shall befall thee.

10 Consult not with one that suspecteth thee: and hide thy counsel from such as envy thee.

11 Neither consult with a woman touching her of whom she is jealous; neither with a coward in matters of war; nor with a merchant concerning exchange; nor with a buyer of selling; nor with an envious man of thankfulness; nor with an unmerciful man touching kindness; nor with the slothful for any work; nor with an hireling for a year of finishing work; nor with an idle servant of much business: hearken not unto these in any matter of counsel.

12 But be continually with a godly man, whom thou knowest to keep the commandments of the Lord, whose mind is according to thy mind, and will sorrow with thee, if thou shalt miscarry.

13 And let the counsel of thine own heart stand: for there is no man more faithful unto thee than it.

14 For a man's mind is sometime wont to tell him more than seven watchmen, that sit above in an high tower.

15 And above all this pray to the most High, that he will direct thy way in truth.

16 Let reason go before every enterprize, and counsel before every action.

17 The countenance is a sign of changing of the heart.

18 Four manner of things appear: good and evil, life and death: but the tongue ruleth over them continually.

19 There is one that is wise and teacheth many, and yet is unprofitable to himself.

20 There is one that sheweth wisdom in words, and is hated: he shall be destitute of all food.

21 For grace is not given him from the Lord; because he is deprived of all wisdom.

22 Another is wise to himself; and the fruits of understanding are commendable in his mouth.

23 A wise man instructeth his people; and the fruits of his understanding fail not.

24 A wise man shall be filled with blessing; and all they that see him shall count him happy.

25 The days of the life of man may be numbered: but the days of Israel are innumerable.

26 A wise man shall inherit glory among his people, and his name shall be perpetual.

27 My son, prove thy soul in thy life, and see what is evil for it, and give not that unto it.

28 For all things are not profitable for all men, neither hath every soul pleasure in every thing.

29 Be not unsatiable in any dainty thing, nor too greedy upon meats:

30 For excess of meats bringeth sickness, and surfeiting will turn into choler.

31 By surfeiting have many perished; but he that taketh heed prolongeth his life.

CHAPTER XXXVIII

HONOUR a physician with the honour due unto him for the uses which ye may have of him: for the Lord hath created him.

2 For of the most High cometh healing, and he shall receive honour of the king.

3 The skill of the physician shall lift up his head: and in the sight of great men he shall be in admiration.

4 The Lord hath created medicines out of the earth; and he that is wise will not abhor them.

5 Was not the water made sweet with wood, that the virtue thereof might be known?

6 And he hath given men skill, that he might be honoured in his marvellous works.

7 With such doth he heal [men,] and taketh away their pains.

8 Of such doth the apothecary make a confection; and of his works there is no end; and from him is peace over all the earth.

9 My son, in thy sickness be not negligent: but pray unto the Lord, and he will make thee whole.

10 Leave off from sin, and order thine hands aright, and cleanse thy heart from all wickedness.

11 Give a sweet savour, and a memorial of fine flour; and make a fat offering, as not being.

12 Then give place to the physician, for the Lord hath created him: let him not go from thee, for thou hast need of him.

13 There is a time when in their hands there is good success.

14 For they shall also pray unto the Lord, that he would prosper that, which they give for ease and remedy to prolong life.

15 He that sinneth before his Maker, let him fall into the hand of the physician.

16 My son, let tears fall down over the dead, and begin to lament, as if thou hadst suffered great harm thyself; and then cover his body according to the custom, and neglect not his burial.

17 Weep bitterly, and make great moan, and use lamentation, as he is worthy, and that a day or two, lest thou be evil spoken of: and then comfort thyself for thy heaviness.

18 For of heaviness cometh death, and the heaviness of the heart breaketh strength.

19 In affliction also sorrow remaineth: and the life of the poor is the curse of the heart.

20 Take no heaviness to heart: drive it away, and remember the last end.

21 Forget it not, for there is no turning again: thou shalt not do him good, but hurt thyself.

22 Remember my judgment: for thine also shall be so; yesterday for me, and to day for thee.

23 When the dead is at rest, let his remembrance rest; and be comforted for him, when his spirit is departed from him.

24 The wisdom of a learned man cometh by opportunity of leisure: and he that hath little business shall become wise.

25 How can he get wisdom that holdeth the plough, and that glorieth in the goad, that driveth oxen, and is occupied in their labours, and whose talk is of bullocks?

26 He giveth his mind to make furrows; and is diligent to give the kine fodder.

27 So every carpenter and workmaster, that laboureth night and day; and they that cut and grave seals, and are diligent to make great variety, and give themselves to counterfeit imagery, and watch to finish a work:

28 The smith also sitting by the anvil, and considering the iron work, the vapour of the fire wasteth his flesh, and he fighteth with the heat of the furnace: the noise of the hammer and the anvil is ever in his ears, and his eyes look still upon the pattern of the thing that he maketh; he setteth his mind to finish his work, and watcheth to polish it perfectly:

29 So doth the potter sitting at his work, and turning the wheel about with his feet, who is alway carefully set at his work, and maketh all his work by number;

30 He fashioneth the clay with his arm, and boweth down his strength before his feet; he applieth himself to lead it over; and he is diligent to make clean the furnace:

31 All these trust to their hands: and every one is wise in his work.

32 Without these cannot a city be inhabited: and they shall not dwell where they will, nor go up and down:

33 They shall not be sought for in publick counsel, nor sit high in the congregation: they shall not sit on the judges' seat, nor understand the sentence of judgment: they cannot declare justice and judgment; and they shall not be

found where parables are spoken.

34 But they will maintain the state of the world, and [all] their desire is in the work of their craft.

CHAPTER XXXIX

BUT he that giveth his mind to the law of the most High, and is occupied in the meditation thereof, will seek out the wisdom of all the ancient, and be occupied in prophecies.

2 He will keep the sayings of the renowned men: and where subtil parables are, he will be there also.

3 He will seek out the secrets of grave sentences, and be conversant in dark parables.

4 He shall serve among great men, and appear before princes: he will travel through strange countries; for he hath tried the good and the evil among men.

5 He will give his heart to resort early to the Lord that made him, and will pray before the most High, and will open his mouth in prayer, and make supplication for his sins.

6 When the great Lord will, he shall be filled with the spirit of understanding: he shall pour out wise sentences, and give thanks unto the Lord in his prayer.

7 He shall direct his counsel and knowledge, and in his secrets shall he meditate.

8 He shall shew forth that which he hath learned, and shall glory in the law of the covenant of the Lord.

9 Many shall commend his understanding; and so long as the world endureth, it shall not be blotted out; his memorial shall not depart away, and his name shall live from generation to generation.

10 Nations shall shew forth his wisdom, and the congregation shall declare his praise.

11 If he die, he shall leave a greater name than a thousand: and if he live, he shall increase it.

12 Yet have I more to say, which I have thought upon; for I am filled as the moon at the full.

13 Hearken unto me, ye holy children, and bud forth as a rose growing by the brook of the field:

14 And give ye a sweet savour as frankincense, and flourish as a lily, send forth a smell, and sing a song of praise, bless the Lord in all his works.

15 Magnify his name, and shew forth his praise with the songs of your lips, and with harps, and in praising him ye shall say after this manner:

16 All the works of the Lord are exceeding good, and whatsoever he commandeth shall be *accomplished* in due season.

17 And none may say, What is this? wherefore is that? for at time convenient they shall all be sought out: at his commandment the waters stood as an heap, and at the words of his mouth the receptacles of waters.

18 At his commandment is done whatsoever pleaseth him; and none can hinder, when he will save.

19 The works of all flesh are before him, and nothing can be hid from his eyes.

20 He seeth from everlasting to everlasting; and there is nothing wonderful before him.

21 A man need not to say, What is this? wherefore is that? for he hath made all things for their uses.

22 His blessing covered the dry land as a river, and watered it as a flood.

23 As he hath turned the waters into saltness: so shall the heathen inherit his wrath.

24 As his ways are plain unto the holy; so are they stumbling-blocks unto the wicked.

25 For the good are good things created from the beginning: so evil things for sinners.

26 The principal things for the whole use of man's life are water, fire, iron, and salt, flour of wheat, honey, milk, and the blood of the grape, and oil, and clothing.

27 All these things are for good to the godly: so to the sinners they are turned into evil.

28 There be spirits that are created for vengeance, which in their fury lay on sore strokes; in the time of destruction they pour out their force, and appease the wrath of him that made them.

29 Fire, and hail, and famine, and death, all these were created for vengeance;

30 Teeth of wild beasts, and scorpions, serpents, and the sword, punishing the wicked to destruction.

31 They shall rejoice in his commandment, and they shall be ready upon earth, when need is; and when their time is come, they shall not transgress his word.

32 Therefore from the beginning I was resolved, and thought upon these things, and have left them in writing.

33 All the works of the Lord
178

are good: and he will give every needful thing in due season.

34 So that a man cannot say, This is worse than that: for in time they shall all be well approved.

35 And therefore praise ye the Lord with the whole heart and mouth, and bless the name of the Lord.

CHAPTER XL

GREAT travail is created for every man, and an heavy yoke is upon the sons of Adam, from the day that they go out of their mother's womb, till the day that they return to the mother of all things.

2 Their imagination of things to come, and the day of death, [trouble] their thoughts, and [cause] fear of heart;

3 From him that sitteth on a throne of glory, unto him that is humbled in earth and ashes;

4 From him that weareth purple and a crown, unto *him that is clothed with a linen* frock.

5 Wrath, and envy, trouble, and unquietness, fear of death, and anger, and strife, and in the time of rest upon his bed his night sleep, do change his knowledge.

6 A little or nothing is his rest, and afterward he is in his sleep, as in a day of keeping watch, troubled in the vision of his heart, as if he were escaped out of a battle.

7 When all is safe, he awaketh, and marvelleth that the fear was nothing.

8 [Such things happen] unto all flesh, both man and beast, and that is sevenfold more upon sinners.

9 Death, and bloodshed, strife, and sword, calamities,

famine, tribulation, and the scourge;

10 These things are created for the wicked, and for their sakes came the flood.

11 All things that are of the earth shall turn to the earth again: and that which is of the waters doth return into the sea.

12 All bribery and injustice shall be blotted out: but true dealing shall endure for ever.

13 The goods of the unjust shall be dried up like a river, and shall vanish with noise, like a great thunder in rain.

14 While he openeth his hand he shall rejoice: so shall transgressors come to nought.

15 The children of the ungodly shall not bring forth many branches: but are as unclean roots upon a hard rock.

16 The weed growing upon every water and bank of a river shall be pulled up before all grass.

17 Bountifulness is as a most fruitful garden, and mercifulness endureth for ever.

18 To labour, and to be content with that a man hath, is a sweet life: but he that findeth a treasure is above them both.

19 Children and the building of a city continue a man's name: but a blameless wife is counted above them both.

20 Wine and musick rejoice the heart: but the love of wisdom is above them both.

21 The pipe and the psaltery make sweet melody: but a pleasant tongue is above them both.

22 Thine eye desireth favour and beauty: but more than both corn while it is green.

23 A friend and companion never meet amiss: but above both is a wife with her husband.

24 Brethren and help are against time of trouble: but alms shall deliver more than them both.

25 Gold and silver make the foot stand sure: but counsel is esteemed above them both.

26 Riches and strength lift up the heart: but the fear of the Lord is above them both: there is no want in the fear of the Lord, and it needeth not to seek help.

27 The fear of the Lord is a fruitful garden, and covereth him above all glory.

28 My son, lead not a beggar's life; for better it is to die than to beg.

29 The life of him that dependeth on another man's table is not to be counted for a life; for he polluteth himself with other men's meat: but a wise man well nurtured will beware thereof.

30 Begging is sweet in the mouth of the shameless: but in his belly there shall burn a fire.

CHAPTER XLI

O DEATH, how bitter is the remembrance of thee to a man that liveth at rest in his possessions, unto the man that hath nothing to vex him, and that hath prosperity in all things: yea, unto him that is yet able to receive meat!

2 O death, acceptable is thy sentence unto the needy, and unto him whose strength faileth, that is now in the last age, and is vexed with all things, and to him that despaireth, and hath lost patience!

3 Fear not the sentence of death, remember them that

have been before thee, and that come after; for this is the sentence of the Lord over all flesh.

4 And why art thou against the pleasure of the most High? there is no inquisition in the grave, whether thou have lived ten, or an hundred, or a thousand years.

5 The children of sinners are abominable children, and they that are conversant in the dwelling of the ungodly.

6 The inheritance of sinners' children shall perish, and their posterity shall have a perpetual reproach.

7 The children will complain of an ungodly father, because they shall be reproached for his sake.

8 Woe be unto you, ungodly men, which have forsaken the law of the most high God! for if ye increase, it shall be to your destruction:

9 And if ye be born, ye shall be born to a curse: and if ye die, a curse shall be your portion.

10 All that are of the earth shall turn to earth again: so the ungodly shall go from a curse to destruction.

11 The mourning of men is about their bodies: but an ill name of sinners shall be blotted out.

12 Have regard to thy name; for that shall continue with thee above a thousand great treasures of gold.

13 A good life hath but few days: but a good name endureth for ever.

14 My children, keep discipline in peace: for wisdom that is hid, and a treasure that is not seen, what profit is in them both?

15 A man that hideth his 180

foolishness is better than a man that hideth his wisdom.

16 Therefore be shamefaced according to my word: for it is not good to retain all shamefacedness; neither is it altogether approved in every thing.

17 Be ashamed of whoredom before father and mother: and of a lie before a prince and a mighty man;

18 Of an offence before a judge and ruler; of iniquity before a congregation and people; of unjust dealing before thy partner and friend;

19 And of theft in regard of the place where thou sojournest, and in regard of the truth of God and his covenant; and to lean with thine elbow upon the meat; and of scorning to give and take;

20 And of silence before them that salute thee; and to look upon an harlot;

21 And to turn away thy face from thy kinsman; or to take away a portion or a gift; or to gaze upon another man's wife;

22 Or to be overbusy with his maid, and come not near her bed; or of upbraiding speeches before friends; and after thou hast given, upbraid not;

23 Or of iterating and speaking again that which thou hast heard; and of revealing of secrets.

24 So shalt thou be truly shamefaced, and find favour before all men.

CHAPTER XLII

OF these things be not thou ashamed, and accept no person to sin thereby:

2 Of the law of the most High,

and his covenant; and of judgment to justify the ungodly;

3 Of reckoning with thy partners and travellers; or of the gift of the heritage of friends;

4 Of exactness of balance and weights; or of getting much or little;

5 And of merchants' indifferent selling; of much correction of children; and to make the side of an evil servant to bleed.

6 Sure keeping is good, where an evil wife is; and shut up, where many hands are.

7 Deliver all things in number and weight; and put all in writing that thou givest out, or receivest in.

8 Be not ashamed to inform the unwise and foolish, and the extreme aged that contendeth with those that are young: thus shalt thou be truly learned, and approved of all men living.

9 The father waketh for the daughter, when no man knoweth; and the care for her taketh away sleep: when she is young, lest she pass away the flower of her age; and being married, lest she should be hated:

10 In her virginity, lest she should be defiled and gotten with child in her father's house; and having an husband, lest she should misbehave herself; and when she is married, lest she should be barren.

11 Keep a sure watch over a shameless daughter, lest she make thee a laughingstock to thine enemies, and a byword in the city, and a reproach among the people, and make thee ashamed before the multitude.

12 Behold not every body's beauty, and sit not in the midst of women.

13 For from garments cometh a moth, and from women wickedness.

14 Better is the churlishness of a man than a courteous woman, a woman, *I say*, which bringeth shame and reproach.

15 I will now remember the works of the Lord, and declare the things that I have seen: In the words of the Lord are his works.

16 The sun that giveth light looketh upon all things, and the work thereof *is* full of the glory of the Lord.

17 The Lord hath not given power to the saints to declare all his marvellous works, which the Almighty Lord firmly settled, that whatsoever is might be established for his glory.

18 He seeketh out the deep, and the heart, and considereth their crafty devices: for the Lord knoweth all that may be known, and he beholdeth the signs of the world.

19 He declareth the things that are past, and for to come, and revealeth the steps of hidden things.

20 No thought escapeth him, neither any word is hidden from him.

21 He hath garnished the excellent works of his wisdom, and he is from everlasting to everlasting: unto him may nothing be added, neither can he be diminished, and he hath no need of any counsellor.

22 Oh how desirable are all his works! and that a man may see even to a spark.

23 All these things live and remain for ever for all uses, and they are all obedient.

24 All things are double one

against another: and he hath made nothing imperfect.

25 One thing establisheth the good of another: and who shall be filled with beholding his glory?

CHAPTER XLIII

THE pride of the height, the clear firmament, the beauty of heaven, with his glorious shew;

2 The sun when it appeareth, declaring at his rising a marvellous instrument, the work of the most High:

3 At noon it parcheth the country, and who can abide the burning heat thereof?

4 A man blowing a furnace is in works of heat, but the sun burneth the mountains three times more; breathing out fiery vapours, and sending forth bright beams, it dimmeth the eyes.

5 Great is the Lord that made it; and at his commandment it runneth hastily.

6 He made the moon also to serve in her season for a declaration of times, and a sign of the world.

7 From the moon is the sign of feasts, a light that decreaseth in her perfection.

8 The month is called after her name, increasing wonderfully in her changing, being an instrument of the armies above, shining in the firmament of heaven;

9 The beauty of heaven, the glory of the stars, an ornament giving light in the highest places of the Lord.

10 At the commandment of the Holy One they will stand in their order, and never faint in their watches.

11 Look upon the rainbow, and praise him that made it; very beautiful it is in the brightness thereof.

12 It compasseth the heaven about with a glorious circle, and the hands of the most High have bended it.

13 By his commandment he maketh the snow to fall apace, and sendeth swiftly the lightnings of his judgment.

14 Through this the treasures are opened: and clouds fly forth as fowls.

15 By his great power he maketh the clouds firm, and the hailstones are broken small.

16 At his sight the mountains are shaken, and at his will the south wind bloweth.

17 The noise of the thunder maketh the earth to tremble: so doth the northern storm and the whirlwind: as birds flying he scattereth the snow, and the falling down thereof is as the lighting of grasshoppers:

18 The eye marvelleth at the beauty of the whiteness thereof, and the heart is astonished at the raining of it.

19 The hoarfrost also as salt he poureth on the earth, and being congealed, it lieth on the top of sharp stakes.

20 When the cold north wind bloweth, and the water is congealed into ice, it abideth upon every gathering together of water, and clotheth the water as with a breastplate.

21 It devoureth the mountains, and burneth the wilderness, and consumeth the grass as fire.

22 A present remedy of all is a mist *coming speedily:* a dew coming after heat refresheth.

23 By his counsel he appeas-

eth the deep, and planteth islands therein.

24 They that sail on the sea tell of the danger thereof; and when we hear it with our ears, we marvel thereat.

25 For therein be strange and wondrous works, variety of all kinds of beasts and whales created.

26 By him the end of them hath prosperous success, and by his word all things consist.

27 We may speak much, and yet come short: wherefore in sum, he is all.

28 How shall we be able to magnify him? for he is great above all his works.

29 The Lord is terrible and very great, and marvellous is his power.

30 When ye glorify the Lord, exalt him as much as ye can; for even yet will he far exceed: and when ye exalt him, put forth all your strength, and be not weary; for ye can never go far enough.

31 Who hath seen him, that he might tell us? and who can magnify him as he is?

32 There are yet hid greater things than these be, for we have seen but a few of his works.

33 For the Lord hath made all things; and to the godly hath he given wisdom.

CHAPTER XLIV

LET us now praise famous men, and our fathers that begat us.

2 The Lord hath wrought great glory by them through his great power from the beginning.

3 Such as did bear rule in their kingdoms, men renowned for their power, giving counsel by their understanding, and declaring prophecies:

4 Leaders of the people by their counsels, and by their knowledge of learning meet for the people, wise and eloquent in their instructions:

5 Such as found out musical tunes, and recited verses in writing:

6 Rich men furnished with ability, living peaceably in their habitations:

7 All these were honoured in their generations, and were the glory of their times.

8 There be of them, that have left a name behind them, that their praises might be reported.

9 And some there be, which have no memorial; who are perished, as though they had never been; and are become as though they had never been born; and their children after them.

10 But these were merciful men, whose righteousness hath not been forgotten.

11 With their seed shall continually remain a good inheritance, and their children are within the covenant.

12 Their seed standeth fast, and their children for their sakes.

13 Their seed shall remain for ever, and their glory shall not be blotted out.

14 Their bodies are buried in peace; but their name liveth for evermore.

15 The people will tell of their wisdom, and the congregation will shew forth their praise.

16 Enoch pleased the Lord, and was translated, being an example of repentance to all generations.

17 Noah was found perfect

and righteous; in the time of wrath he was taken in exchange [for the world;] therefore was he left as a remnant unto the earth, when the flood came.

18 An everlasting covenant was made with him, that all flesh should perish no more by the flood.

19 Abraham was a great father of many people: in glory was there none like unto him;

20 Who kept the law of the most High, and was in covenant with him: he established the covenant in his flesh; and when he was proved, he was found faithful.

21 Therefore he assured him by an oath, that he would bless the nations in his seed, and that he would multiply him as the dust of the earth, and exalt his seed as the stars, and cause them to inherit from sea to sea, and from the river unto the utmost part of the land.

22 With Isaac did he establish likewise [for Abraham his father's sake] the blessing of all men, and the covenant,

23 And made it rest upon the head of Jacob. He acknowledged him in his blessing, and gave him an heritage, and divided his portions; among the twelve tribes did he part them.

CHAPTER XLV

AND he brought out of him a merciful man, which found favour in the sight of all flesh, even Moses, beloved of God and men, whose memorial is blessed.

2 He made him like to the glorious saints, and magnified
184

him, so that his enemies stood in fear of him.

3 By his words he caused the wonders to cease, and he made him glorious in the sight of kings, and gave him a commandment for his people, and shewed him part of his glory.

4 He sanctified him in his faithfulness and meekness, and chose him out of all men.

5 He made him to hear his voice, and brought him into the dark cloud, and gave him commandments before his face, even the law of life and knowledge, that he might teach Jacob his covenants, and Israel his judgments.

6 He exalted Aaron, an holy man like unto him, even his brother, of the tribe of Levi.

7 An everlasting covenant he made with him, and gave him the priesthood among the people; he beautified him with comely ornaments, and clothed him with a robe of glory.

8 He put upon him perfect glory; and strengthened him with rich garments, with breeches, with a long robe, and the ephod.

9 And he compassed him with pomegranates, and with many golden bells round about, that as he went there might be a sound, and a noise made that might be heard in the temple, for a memorial to the children of his people;

10 With an holy garment, with gold, and blue silk, and purple, the work of the embroiderer, with a breastplate of judgment, and with Ū′-rīm and Thummim;

11 With twisted scarlet, the work of the cunning workman, with precious stones graven like seals, and set in gold, the

work of the jeweller, with a writing engraved for a memorial, after the number of the tribes of Israel.

12 He set a crown of gold upon the mitre, wherein was engraved Holiness, an ornament of honour, a costly work, the desires of the eyes, goodly and beautiful.

13 Before him there were none such, neither did ever any stranger put them on, but only his children and his children's children perpetually.

14 Their sacrifices shall be wholly consumed every day twice continually.

15 Moses consecrated him, and anointed him with holy oil: this was appointed unto him by an everlasting covenant, and to his seed, so long as the heavens should remain, that they should minister unto him, and execute the office of the priesthood, and bless the people in his name.

16 He chose him out of all men living to offer sacrifices to the Lord, incense, and a sweet savour, for a memorial, to make reconciliation for his people.

17 He gave unto him his commandments, and authority in the statutes of judgments, that he should teach Jacob the testimonies, and inform Israel in his laws.

18 Strangers conspired together against him, and maligned him in the wilderness, even the men that were of Dā'-thăn's and Ă-bī'-rŏn's side, and the congregation of Core, with fury and wrath.

19 This the Lord saw, and it displeased him, and in his wrathful indignation were they consumed: he did wonders upon them, to consume them with the fiery flame.

20 But he made Aaron more honourable, and gave him an heritage, and divided unto him the firstfruits of the increase; especially he prepared bread in abundance:

21 For they eat of the sacrifices of the Lord, which he gave unto him and his seed.

22 Howbeit in the land of the people he had no inheritance, neither had he any portion among the people: for the Lord himself is his portion and inheritance.

23 The third in glory is Phĭn'-ĕ-ĕs the son of Ĕl-ĕ-ā'-zăr, because he had zeal in the fear of the Lord, and stood up with good courage of heart when the people were turned back, and made reconciliation for Israel.

24 Therefore was there a covenant of peace made with him, that he should be the chief of the sanctuary and of his people, and that he and his posterity should have the dignity of the priesthood for ever:

25 According to the covenant made with David son of Jesse, of the tribe of Juda, that the inheritance of the king should be to his posterity alone: so the inheritance of Aaron should also be unto his seed.

26 God give you wisdom in your heart to judge his people in righteousness, that their good things be not abolished, and that their glory may endure for ever.

CHAPTER XLVI

JESUS the son of Nā'-vĕ was valiant in the wars, and was the successor of Moses in prophecies, who according to his name was made great for the saving of the elect of God, and taking vengeance of the enemies that rose up against them, that he might set Israel in their inheritance.

2 How great glory gat he, when he did lift up his hands, and stretched out his sword against the cities!

3 Who before him so stood to it? for the Lord himself brought his enemies unto him.

4 Did not the sun go back by his means? and was not one day as long as two?

5 He called upon the most high Lord, when the enemies pressed upon him on every side; and the great Lord heard him.

6 And with hailstones of mighty power he made the battle to fall violently upon the nations, and in the descent [of Bĕth-hō´-ron] he destroyed them that resisted, that the nations might know all their strength, because he fought in the sight of the Lord, and he followed the Mighty One.

7 In the time of Moses also he did a work of mercy, he and Caleb the son of Jĕ-phŭn´-nĕ, in that they withstood the congregation, and withheld the people from sin, and appeased the wicked murmuring.

8 And of six hundred thousand people on foot, they two were preserved to bring them into the heritage, even unto the land that floweth with milk and honey.

9 The Lord gave strength also unto Caleb, which remained with him unto his old age: so that he entered upon the high places of the land, and his seed obtained it for an heritage:

186

10 That all the children of Israel might see that it is good to follow the Lord.

11 And concerning the judges, every one by name, whose heart went not a whoring, nor departed from the Lord, let their memory be blessed.

12 Let their bones flourish out of their place, and let the name of them that were honoured be continued upon their children.

13 Samuel, the prophet of the Lord, beloved of his Lord, established a kingdom, and anointed princes over his people.

14 By the law of the Lord he judged the congregation, and the Lord had respect unto Jacob.

15 By his faithfulness he was found a true prophet, and by his word he was known to be faithful in vision.

16 He called upon the mighty Lord, when his enemies pressed upon him on every side, when he offered the sucking lamb.

17 And the Lord thundered from heaven, and with a great noise made his voice to be heard.

18 And he destroyed the rulers of the Tȳr´-ĭ-ăns, and all the princes of the Phĭ-lĭs´-tĭnes.

19 And before his long sleep he made protestations in the sight of the Lord and his anointed, I have not taken any man's goods, so much as a shoe: and no man did accuse him.

20 And after his death he prophesied, and shewed the king his end, and lifted up his voice from the earth in prophecy, to blot out the wickedness of the people.

CHAPTER XLVII

AND after him rose up Nathan to prophesy in the time of David.

2 As is the fat taken away from the peace offering, so was David chosen out of the children of Israel.

3 He played with lions as with kids, and with bears as with lambs.

4 Slew he not a giant, when he was yet but young? and did he not take away reproach from the people, when he lifted up his hand with the stone in the sling, and beat down the boasting of Goliath?

5 For he called upon the most high Lord; and he gave him strength in his right hand to slay that mighty warrior, and set up the horn of his people.

6 So the people honoured him with ten thousands, and praised him in the blessings of the Lord, in that he gave him a crown of glory.

7 For he destroyed the enemies on every side, and brought to nought the Phi-lis'-tines his adversaries, and brake their horn in sunder unto this day.

8 In all his works he praised the Holy One most high with words of glory; with his whole heart he sung songs, and loved him that made him.

9 He set singers also before the altar, that by their voices they might make sweet melody, and daily sing praises in their songs.

10 He beautified their feasts, and set in order the solemn times until the end, that they might praise his holy name, and that the temple might sound from morning.

11 The Lord took away his sins, and exalted his horn for ever: he gave him a covenant of kings, and a throne of glory in Israel.

12 After him rose up a wise son, and for his sake he dwelt at large.

13 Solomon reigned in a peaceable time, and was honoured; for God made all quiet round about him, that he might build an house in his name, and prepare his sanctuary for ever.

14 How wise wast thou in thy youth, and, as a flood, filled with understanding!

15 Thy soul covered the whole earth, and thou filledst it with dark parables.

16 Thy name went far unto the islands; and for thy peace thou wast beloved.

17 The countries marvelled at thee for thy songs, and proverbs, and parables, and interpretations.

18 By the name of the Lord God, which is called the Lord God of Israel, thou didst gather gold as tin, and didst multiply silver as lead.

19 Thou didst bow thy loins unto women, and by thy body thou wast brought into subjection.

20 Thou didst stain thy honour, and pollute thy seed: so that thou broughtest wrath upon thy children, and wast grieved for thy folly.

21 So the kingdom was divided, and out of Ephraim ruled a rebellious kingdom.

22 But the Lord will never leave off his mercy, neither shall any of his works perish, neither will he abolish the posterity of his elect, and the seed of him that loveth him he

will not take away: wherefore he gave a remnant unto Jacob, and out of him a root unto David.

23 Thus rested Solomon with his fathers, and of his seed he left behind him Rŏ-bŏ'-ăm, even the foolishness of the people, and one that had no understanding, who turned away the people through his counsel. There was also Jĕr-ŏ-bŏ'-ăm the son of Nē'-băt, who caused Israel to sin, and shewed Ephraim the way of sin:

24 And their sins were multiplied exceedingly, that they were driven out of the land.

25 For they sought out all wickedness, till the vengeance came upon them.

CHAPTER XLVIII

THEN stood up Ĕ-lī'-ăs the prophet as fire, and his word burned like a lamp.

2 He brought a sore famine upon them, and by his zeal he diminished their number.

3 By the word of the Lord he shut up the heaven, and also three times brought down fire.

4 O Ĕlī'-ăs, how wast thou honoured in thy wondrous deeds! and who may glory like unto thee!

5 Who didst raise up a dead man from death, and his soul from the place of the dead, by the word of the most High:

6 Who broughtest kings to destruction, and honourable men from their bed:

7 Who heardest the rebuke o the Lord in Sī'-nâi, and in Hō'-rĕb the judgment of vengeance:

8 Who anointedst kings to take revenge, and prophets to succeed after him:

9 Who wast taken up in a whirlwind of fire, and in a chariot of fiery horses:

10 Who wast ordained for reproofs in their times, to pacify the wrath of the Lord's judgment, before it brake forth into fury, and to turn the heart of the father unto the son, and to restore the tribes of Jacob.

11 Blessed are they that saw thee, and slept in love; for we shall surely live.

12 Ĕ-lī'-ăs it was, who was covered with a whirlwind: and Ĕl-ĭ-sē'-ŭs was filled with his spirit: whilst he lived, he was not moved *with the presence* of any prince, neither could any bring him into subjection.

13 No word could overcome him; and after his death his body prophesied.

14 He did wonders in his life, and at his death were his works marvellous.

15 For all this the people repented not, neither departed they from their sins, till they were spoiled and carried out of their land, and were scattered through all the earth: yet there remained a small people, and a ruler in the house of David:

16 Of whom some did that which was pleasing *to God,* and some multiplied sins.

17 Ĕz-ĕ-kī'-ăs fortified his city, and brought in water into the midst thereof: he digged the hard rock with iron, and made wells for waters.

18 In his time Sĕn-năch'-ĕr-ĭb came up, and sent Răb'-să-çēs, and lifted up his hand against Sion, and boasted proudly.

19 Then trembled their hearts and hands, and they were in pain, as women in travail.

20 But they called upon the Lord which is merciful, and stretched out their hands toward him: and immediately the Holy One heard them out of heaven, and delivered them by the ministry of Ē'-say.

21 He smote the host of the Assyrians, and his angel destroyed them.

22 For Ĕz-ĕ-kī'-ăs had done the thing that pleased the Lord, and was strong in the ways of David his father, as Ē'-say the prophet, who was great and faithful in his vision, had commanded him.

23 In his time the sun went backward, and he lengthened the king's life.

24 He saw by an excellent spirit what should come to pass at the last, and he comforted them that mourned in Sion.

25 He shewed what should come to pass for ever, and secret things or ever they came.

CHAPTER XLIX

THE remembrance of Jŏ-sī'-ăs is like the composition of the perfume that is made by the art of the apothecary: it is sweet as honey in all mouths, and as musick at a banquet of wine.

2 He behaved himself uprightly in the conversion of the people, and took away the abominations of iniquity.

3 He directed his heart unto the Lord, and in the time of the ungodly he established the worship of God.

4 All, except David and Ĕz-ĕ-kī'-ăs and Jŏ-sī'-ăs, were defective: for they forsook the law of the most High, *even* the kings of Juda failed.

5 Therefore he gave their power unto others, and their glory to a strange nation.

6 They burnt the chosen city of the sanctuary, and made the streets desolate, according to the prophecy of Jeremias.

7 For they entreated him evil, who nevertheless was a prophet, sanctified in his mother's womb, that he might root out, and afflict, and destroy; and that he might build up also, and plant.

8 It was Ē-zē'-kĭ-ĕl who saw the glorious vision, which was shewed him upon the chariot of the cherubims.

9 For he made mention of the enemies under *the figure of* the rain, and directed them that went right.

10 And of the twelve prophets let the memorial be blessed, and let their bones flourish again out of their place: for they comforted Jacob, and delivered them by assured hope.

11 How shall we magnify Zō-rŏb'-ă-bĕl? even he was as a signet on the right hand:

12 So was Jesus the son of Jŏs'-ĕ-dĕc: who in their time builded the house, and set up an holy temple to the Lord, which was prepared for everlasting glory.

13 And among the elect was Nē-ĕ-mī'-ăs, whose renown is great, who raised up for us the walls that were fallen, and set up the gates and the bars, and raised up our ruins again.

14 But upon the earth was no man created like Enoch; for he was taken from the earth.

15 Neither was there a man born like unto Joseph, a governor of his brethren, a stay of the people, whose bones

were regarded of the Lord.

16 Sem and Seth were in great honour among men, and so was Adam above every living thing in the creation.

CHAPTER L

SIMON the high priest, the son of Ŏ-nī´-ăs, who in his life repaired the house again, and in his days fortified the temple:

2 And by him was built from the foundation the double height, the high fortress of the wall about the temple:

3 In his days the cistern to receive water, being in compass as the sea, was covered with plates of brass:

4 He took care of the temple that it should not fall, and fortified the city against besieging:

5 How was he honoured in the midst of the people in his coming out of the sanctuary!

6 He was as the morning star in the midst of a cloud, and as the moon at the full:

7 As the sun shining upon the temple of the most High, and as the rainbow giving light in the bright clouds:

8 And as the flower of roses in the spring of the year, as lilies by the rivers of waters, and as the branches of the frankincense tree in the time of summer:

9 As fire and incense in the censer, and as a vessel of beaten gold set with all manner of precious stones:

10 And as a fair olive tree budding forth fruit, and as a cypress tree which groweth up to the clouds.

11 When he put on the robe of honour, and was clothed with the perfection of glory, when he went up to the holy altar, he made the garment of holiness honourable.

12 When he took the portions out of the priests' hands, he himself stood by the hearth of the altar, compassed with his brethren round about, as a young cedar in Lĭb´-ă-nŭs; and as palm trees compassed they him round about.

13 So were all the sons of Aaron in their glory, and the oblations of the Lord in their hands, before all the congregation of Israel.

14 And finishing the service at the altar, that he might adorn the offering of the most high Almighty,

15 He stretched out his hand to the cup, and poured of the blood of the grape, he poured out at the foot of the altar a sweetsmelling savour unto the most high King of all.

16 Then shouted the sons of Aaron, and sounded the silver trumpets, and made a great noise to be heard, for a remembrance before the most High.

17 Then all the people together hasted, and fell down to the earth upon their faces to worship their Lord God Almighty, the most High.

18 The singers also sang praises with their voices, with great variety of sounds was there made sweet melody.

19 And the people besought the Lord, the most High, by prayer before him that is merciful, till the solemnity of the Lord was ended, and they had finished his service.

20 Then he went down, and lifted up his hands over the whole congregation of the children of Israel, to give

the blessing of the Lord with his lips, and to rejoice in his name.

21 And they bowed themselves down to worship the second time, that they might receive a blessing from the most High.

22 Now therefore bless ye the God of all, which only doeth wondrous things every where, which exalteth our days from the womb, and dealeth with us according to his mercy.

23 He grant us joyfulness of heart, and that peace may be in our days in Israel for ever:

24 That he would confirm his mercy with us, and deliver us at his time!

25 There be two manner of nations which my heart abhorreth, and the third is no nation:

26 They that sit upon the mountain of Samaria, and they that dwell among the Phĭ-lĭs'-tĭnes, and that foolish people that dwell in Sĭ'-chĕm.

27 Jesus the son of Sĭ'-răch of Jerusalem hath written in this book the instruction of understanding and knowledge, who out of his heart poured forth wisdom.

28 Blessed is he that shall be exercised in these things; and he that layeth them up in his heart shall become wise.

29 For if he do them, he shall be strong to all things: for the light of the Lord leadeth him, who giveth wisdom to the godly. Blessed be the Lord for ever. Amen, Amen.

CHAPTER LI

I WILL thank thee, O Lord and King, and praise thee, O God my Saviour: I do give praise unto thy name:

2 For thou art my defender and helper, and hast preserved my body from destruction, and from the snare of the slanderous tongue, and from the lips that forge lies, and hast been mine helper against mine adversaries:

3 And hast delivered me, according to the multitude of thy mercies and greatness of thy name, from the teeth of them that were ready to devour me, and out of the hands of such as sought after my life, and from the manifold afflictions which I had;

4 From the choking of fire on every side, and from the midst of the fire which I kindled not;

5 From the depth of the belly of hell, from an unclean tongue, and from lying words.

6 By an accusation to the king from an unrighteous tongue my soul drew near even unto death, my life was near to the hell beneath.

7 They compassed me on every side, and there was no man to help me: I looked for the succour of men, but there was none.

8 Then thought I upon thy mercy, O Lord, and upon thy acts of old, how thou deliverest such as wait for thee, and savest them out of the hands of the enemies.

9 Then lifted I up my supplication from the earth, and prayed for deliverance from death.

10 I called upon the Lord, the Father of my Lord, that he would not leave me in the days of my trouble, and in the time of the proud, when there was no help.

11 I will praise thy name continually, and will sing praise

with thanksgiving; and so my prayer was heard:

12 For thou savedst me from destruction, and deliveredst me from the evil time: therefore will I give thanks, and praise thee, and bless thy name, O Lord.

13 When I was yet young, or ever I went abroad, I desired wisdom openly in my prayer.

14 I prayed for her before the temple, and will seek her out even to the end.

15 Even from the flower till the grape was ripe hath my heart delighted in her: my foot went the right way, from my youth up sought I after her.

16 I bowed down mine ear a little, and received her, and gat much learning.

17 I profited therein, *therefore* will I ascribe the glory unto him that giveth me wisdom.

18 For I purposed to do after her, and earnestly I followed that which is good; so shall I not be confounded.

19 My soul hath wrestled with her, and in my doings I was exact: I stretched forth my hands to the heaven above, and bewailed my ignorances of her.

20 I directed my soul unto her, and I found her in pureness: I have had my heart joined with her from the beginning, therefore shall I not be forsaken.

21 My heart was troubled in seeking her: therefore have I gotten a good possession.

22 The Lord hath given me a tongue for my reward, and I will praise him therewith.

23 Draw near unto me, ye unlearned, and dwell in the house of learning.

24 Wherefore are ye slow, and what say ye of these things, seeing your souls are very thirsty?

25 I opened my mouth, and said, Buy her for yourselves without money.

26 Put your neck under the yoke, and let your soul receive instruction: she is hard at hand to find.

27 Behold with your eyes, how that I have had but little labour, and have gotten unto me much rest.

28 Get learning with a great sum of money, and get much gold by her.

29 Let your soul rejoice in his mercy, and be not ashamed of his praise.

30 Work your work betimes, and in his time he will give you your reward.

BARUCH

CHAPTER 1

AND these are the words of the book, which Bâr'-ŭch the son of Nĕ-rī'-ăs, the son of Mă-ă-sī'-ăs, the son of Sĕd-ĕ-cī'-ăs, the son of Ăs-ă-dī'-ăs, the son of Chĕl-çī'-ăs, wrote in Babylon,

2 In the fifth year, and in the seventh day of the month, what time as the Chăl-dē'-ăns took Jerusalem, and burnt it with fire.

3 And Bâr'-ŭch did read the words of this book in the hearing of Jĕch-ŏ-nī'-ăs the son of Jō'-ă-chĭm king of Juda, and in

the ears of all the people that came to hear the book,

4 And in the hearing of the nobles, and of the king's sons, and in the hearing of the elders, and of all the people, from the lowest unto the highest, even of all them that dwelt at Babylon by the river Süd.

5 Whereupon they wept, fasted, and prayed before the Lord.

6 They made also a collection of money according to every man's power:

7 And they sent it to Jerusalem unto Jō'-ă-chīm the high priest, the son of Chĕl-çī'-ăs, son of Sā'-lŏm, and to the priests, and to all the people which were found with him at Jerusalem,

8 At the same time when he received the vessels of the house of the Lord, that were carried out of the temple, to return them into the land of Juda, the tenth day of *the month* Sī-vän', *namely*, silver vessels, which Sĕd-ĕ-cī'-ăs the son of Jŏ-sī'-ăs king of Juda had made,

9 After that Năb'-ŭ-chŏ-dŏn'-ŏ-sôr king of Babylon had carried away Jĕch-ŏ-nī'-ăs, and the princes, and the captives, and the mighty men, and the people of the land, from Jerusalem, and brought them unto Babylon.

10 And they said, Behold, we have sent you money to buy you burnt offerings, and sin offerings, and incense, and prepare ye manna, and offer upon the altar of the Lord our God;

11 And pray for the life of Năb'-ŭ-chŏ-dŏn'-ŏ-sôr king of Babylon, and for the life of Băl-thăs'-är his son, that their days may be upon earth as the days of heaven:

12 And the Lord will give us strength, and lighten our eyes, and we shall live under the shadow of Năb'-ŭ-chŏ-dŏn'-ŏ-sôr king of Babylon, and under the shadow of Băl-thăs'-är his son, and we shall serve them many days, and find favour in their sight.

13 Pray for us also unto the Lord our God, for we have sinned against the Lord our God; and unto this day the fury of the Lord and his wrath is not turned from us.

14 And ye shall read this book which we have sent unto you, to make confession in the house of the Lord, upon the feasts and solemn days.

15 And ye shall say, To the Lord our God *belongeth* righteousness, but unto us the confusion of faces, as *it is come to pass* this day, unto them of Juda, and to the inhabitants of Jerusalem,

16 And to our kings, and to our princes, and to our priests, and to our prophets, and to our fathers:

17 For we have sinned before the Lord,

18 And disobeyed him, and have not hearkened unto the voice of the Lord our God, to walk in the commandments that he gave us openly:

19 Since the day that the Lord brought our forefathers out of the land of Egypt, unto this present day, we have been disobedient unto the Lord our God, and we have been negligent in not hearing his voice.

20 Wherefore the evils cleaved unto us, and the curse, which the Lord appointed by Moses his servant at the time

G

that he brought our fathers out of the land of Egypt, to give us a land that floweth with milk and honey, like as *it is to see* this day.

21 Nevertheless we have not hearkened unto the voice of the Lord our God, according unto all the words of the prophets, whom he sent unto us:

22 But every man followed the imagination of his own wicked heart, to serve strange gods, and to do evil in the sight of the Lord our God.

CHAPTER II

THEREFORE the Lord hath made good his word, which he pronounced against us, and against our judges that judged Israel, and against our kings, and against our princes, and against the men of Israel and Juda,

2 To bring upon us great plagues, such as never happened under the whole heaven, as it came to pass in Jerusalem, according to the things that were written in the law of Moses;

3 That a man should eat the flesh of his own son, and the flesh of his own daughter.

4 Moreover he hath delivered them to be in subjection to all the kingdoms that are round about us, to be as a reproach and desolation among all the people round about, where the Lord hath scattered them.

5 Thus we were cast down, and not exalted, because we have sinned against the Lord our God, and have not been obedient unto his voice.

6 To the Lord our God *appertaineth* righteousness: but unto

194

us and to our fathers open shame, as *appeareth* this day.

7 For all these plagues are come upon us, which the Lord hath pronounced against us.

8 Yet have we not prayed before the Lord, that we might turn every one from the imaginations of his wicked heart.

9 Wherefore the Lord watched over us for evil, and the Lord hath brought it upon us: for the Lord is righteous in all his works which he hath commanded us.

10 Yet we have not hearkened unto his voice, to walk in the commandments of the Lord, that he hath set before us.

11 And now, O Lord God of Israel, that hast brought thy people out of the land of Egypt with a mighty hand, and high arm, and with signs, and with wonders, and with great power, and hast gotten thyself a name, as *appeareth* this day:

12 O Lord our God, we have sinned, we have done ungodly, we have dealt unrighteously in all thine ordinances.

13 Let thy wrath turn from us: for we are but a few left among the heathen, where thou hast scattered us.

14 Hear our prayers, O Lord, and our petitions, and deliver us for thine own sake, and give us favour in the sight of them which have led us away:

15 That all the earth may know that thou art the Lord our God, because Israel and his posterity is called by thy name.

16 O Lord, look down from thine holy house, and consider us: bow down thine ear, O Lord, to hear us.

17 Open thine eyes, and behold; for the dead that are in the graves, whose souls are taken from their bodies, will give unto the Lord neither praise nor righteousness:

18 But the soul that is greatly vexed, which goeth stooping and feeble, and the eyes that fail, and the hungry soul, will give thee praise and righteousness, O Lord.

19 Therefore we do not make our humble supplication before thee, O Lord our God, for the righteousness of our fathers, and of our kings.

20 For thou hast sent out thy wrath and indignation upon us, as thou hast spoken by thy servants the prophets, saying,

21 Thus saith the Lord, Bow down your shoulders to serve the king of Babylon: so shall ye remain in the land that I gave unto your fathers.

22 But if ye will not hear the voice of the Lord, to serve the king of Babylon,

23 I will cause to cease out of the cities of Juda, and from without Jerusalem, the voice of mirth, and the voice of joy, the voice of the bridegroom, and the voice of the bride: and the whole land shall be desolate of inhabitants.

24 But we would not hearken unto thy voice, to serve the king of Babylon: therefore hast thou made good the words that thou spakest by thy servants the prophets, namely, that the bones of our kings, and the bones of our fathers, should be taken out of their places.

25 And, lo, they are cast out to the heat of the day, and to the frost of the night, and they died in great miseries by famine, by sword, and by pestilence.

26 And the house which is called by thy name hast thou laid waste, as *it is to be seen* this day, for the wickedness of the house of Israel and the house of Juda.

27 O Lord our God, thou hast dealt with us after all thy goodness, and according to all that great mercy of thine,

28 As thou spakest by thy servant Moses in the day when thou didst command him to write thy law before the children of Israel, saying,

29 If ye will not hear my voice, surely this very great multitude shall be turned into a small *number* among the nations, where I will scatter them.

30 For I knew that they would not hear me, because it is a stiffnecked people: but in the land of their captivities they shall remember themselves,

31 And shall know that I am the Lord their God: for I will give them an heart, and ears to hear:

32 And they shall praise me in the land of their captivity, and think upon my name,

33 And return from their stiff neck, and from their wicked deeds: for they shall remember the way of their fathers, which sinned before the Lord.

34 And I will bring them again into the land which I promised with an oath unto their fathers, Abraham, Isaac, and Jacob, and they shall be lords of it: and I will increase them, and they shall not be diminished.

35 And I will make an everlasting covenant with them to

be their God, and they shall be my people: and I will no more drive my people of Israel out of the land that I have given them.

CHAPTER III

O LORD Almighty, God of Israel, the soul in anguish, the troubled spirit, crieth unto thee.

2 Hear, O Lord, and have mercy; for thou art merciful: and have pity upon us, because we have sinned before thee.

3 For thou endurest for ever, and we perish utterly.

4 O Lord Almighty, thou God of Israel, hear now the prayers of the dead Israelites, and of their children, which have sinned before thee, and not hearkened unto the voice of thee their God: for the which cause these plagues cleave unto us.

5 Remember not the iniquities of our forefathers: but think upon thy power and thy name now at this time.

6 For thou art the Lord our God, and thee, O Lord, will we praise.

7 And for this cause thou hast put thy fear in our hearts, to the intent that we should call upon thy name, and praise thee in our captivity: for we have called to mind all the iniquity of our forefathers, that sinned before thee.

8 Behold, we are yet this day in our captivity, where thou hast scattered us, for a reproach and a curse, and to be subject to payments, according to all the iniquities of our fathers, which departed from the Lord our God.

9 Hear, Israel, the commandments of life: give ear to understand wisdom.

10 How happeneth it, Israel, that thou art in thine enemies' land, that thou art waxen old in a strange country, that thou art defiled with the dead,

11 That thou art counted with them that go down into the grave?

12 Thou hast forsaken the fountain of wisdom.

13 For if thou hadst walked in the way of God, thou shouldest have dwelled in peace for ever.

14 Learn where is wisdom, where is strength, where is understanding; that thou mayest know also where is length of days, and life, where is the light of the eyes, and peace.

15 Who hath found out her place? or who hath come into her treasures?

16 Where are the princes of the heathen become, and such as ruled the beasts upon the earth;

17 They that had their pastime with the fowls of the air, and they that hoarded up silver and gold, wherein men trust, and made no end of their getting?

18 For they that wrought in silver, and were so careful, and whose works are unsearchable,

19 They are vanished and gone down to the grave, and others are come up in their steads.

20 Young men have seen light, and dwelt upon the earth: but the way of knowledge have they not known,

21 Nor understood the paths thereof, nor laid hold of it: their children were far off from that way.

22 It hath not been heard of in Chā'-nāan, neither hath it been seen in Thē'-măn.

23 The Ăg'-ă-rēnes that seek wisdom upon earth, the merchants of Mē'-răn and of Thē'-măn, the authors of fables, and searchers out of understanding; none of these have known the way of wisdom, or remember her paths.

24 O Israel, how great is the house of God! and how large is the place of his possession!

25 Great, and hath none end; high, and unmeasurable.

26 There were the giants famous from the beginning, that were of so great stature, and so expert in war.

27 Those did not the Lord choose, neither gave he the way of knowledge unto them:

28 But they were destroyed, because they had no wisdom, and perished through their own foolishness.

29 Who hath gone up into heaven, and taken her, and brought her down from the clouds?

30 Who hath gone over the sea, and found her, and will bring her for pure gold?

31 No man knoweth her way, nor thinketh of her path.

32 But he that knoweth all things knoweth her, and hath found her out with his understanding: he that prepared the earth for evermore hath filled it with fourfooted beasts:

33 He that sendeth forth light, and it goeth, calleth it *again*, and it obeyeth him with fear.

34 The stars shined in their watches, and rejoiced: when he calleth them, they say, Here we be; and so with cheerfulness they shewed light unto him that made them.

35 This is our God, and there shall none other be accounted of in comparison of him.

36 He hath found out all the way of knowledge, and hath given it unto Jacob his servant, and to Israel his beloved.

37 Afterward did he shew himself upon earth, and conversed with men.

CHAPTER IV

THIS is the book of the commandments of God, and the law that endureth for ever: all they that keep it *shall come* to life; but such as leave it shall die.

2 Turn thee, O Jacob, and take hold of it: walk in the presence of the light thereof, that thou mayest be illuminated.

3 Give not thine honour to another, nor the things that are profitable unto thee to a strange nation.

4 O Israel, happy are we: for things that are pleasing to God are made known unto us.

5 Be of good cheer, my people, the memorial of Israel.

6 Ye were sold to the nations, not for [your] destruction: but because ye moved God to wrath, ye were delivered unto the enemies.

7 For ye provoked him that made you by sacrificing unto devils, and not to God.

8 Ye have forgotten the everlasting God, that brought you up; and ye have grieved Jerusalem, that nursed you.

9 For when she saw the wrath of God coming upon you, she said, Hearken, O ye that dwell about Sion: God hath brought upon me great mourning;

10 For I saw the captivity of my sons and daughters, which the Everlasting brought upon them.

11 With joy did I nourish them; but sent them away with weeping and mourning.

12 Let no man rejoice over me, a widow, and forsaken of many, who for the sins of my children am left desolate; because they departed from the law of God.

13 They knew not his statutes, nor walked in the ways of his commandments, nor trod in the paths of discipline in his righteousness.

14 Let them that dwell about Sion come, and remember ye the captivity of my sons and daughters, which the Everlasting hath brought upon them.

15 For he hath brought a nation upon them from far, a shameless nation, and of a strange language, who neither reverenced old man, nor pitied child.

16 These have carried away the dear beloved children of the widow, and left her that was alone desolate without daughters.

17 But what can I help you?

18 For he that brought these plagues upon you will deliver you from the hands of your enemies.

19 Go your way, O my children, go your way: for I am left desolate.

20 I have put off the clothing of peace, and put upon me the sackcloth of my prayer: I will cry unto the Everlasting in my days.

21 Be of good cheer, O my children, cry unto the Lord, and he shall deliver you from the power and hand of the enemies.

22 For my hope is in the Everlasting, that he will save you; and joy is come unto me from the Holy One, because of the mercy which shall soon come unto you from the Everlasting our Saviour.

23 For I sent you out with mourning and weeping: but God will give you to me again with joy and gladness for ever.

24 Like as now the neighbours of Sion have seen your captivity: so shall they see shortly your salvation from our God, which shall come upon you with great glory, and brightness of the Everlasting.

25 My children, suffer patiently the wrath that is come upon you from God: for thine enemy hath persecuted thee; but shortly thou shalt see his destruction, and shalt tread upon his neck.

26 My delicate ones have gone rough ways, and were taken away as a flock caught of the enemies.

27 Be of good comfort, O my children, and cry unto God: for ye shall be remembered of him that brought these things upon you.

28 For as it was your mind to go astray from God: so, being returned, seek him ten times more.

29 For he that hath brought these plagues upon you shall bring you everlasting joy again with your salvation.

30 Take a good heart, O Jerusalem: for he that gave thee that name will comfort thee.

31 Miserable are they that afflicted thee, and rejoiced at thy fall.

32 Miserable are the cities which thy children served: miserable is she that received thy sons.

33 For as she rejoiced at thy ruin, and was glad of thy fall: so shall she be grieved for her own desolation.

34 For I will take away the rejoicing of her great multitude, and her pride shall be turned into mourning.

35 For fire shall come upon her from the Everlasting, long to endure; and she shall be inhabited of devils for a great time.

36 O Jerusalem, look about thee toward the east, and behold the joy that cometh unto thee from God.

37 Lo, thy sons come, whom thou sentest away, they come gathered together from the east to the west by the word of the Holy One, rejoicing in the glory of God.

CHAPTER V

PUT off, O Jerusalem, the garment of thy mourning and affliction, and put on the comeliness of the glory that cometh from God for ever.

2 Cast about thee a double garment of the righteousness which cometh from God; and set a diadem on thine head of the glory of the Everlasting.

3 For God will shew thy brightness unto every country under heaven.

4 For thy name shall be called of God for ever The peace of righteousness, and The glory of God's worship.

5 Arise, O Jerusalem, and stand on high, and look about toward the east, and behold thy children gathered from the west unto the east by the word of the Holy One, rejoicing in the remembrance of God.

6 For they departed from thee on foot, and were led away of their enemies: but God bringeth them unto thee exalted with glory, as children of the kingdom.

7 For God hath appointed that every high hill, and banks of long continuance, should be cast down, and valleys filled up, to make even the ground, that Israel may go safely in the glory of God.

8 Moreover even the woods and every sweetsmelling tree shall overshadow Israel by the commandment of God.

9 For God shall lead Israel with joy in the light of his glory with the mercy and righteousness that cometh from him.

THE EPISTLE OF JEREMY

CHAPTER VI

A copy of an epistle, which Jeremy sent unto them which were to be led captives into Babylon by the king of the Babylonians, to certify them, as it was commanded him of God.

BECAUSE of the sins which ye have committed before God, ye shall be led away captives into Babylon by Năb′-ŭ-chŏ-dŏn′-ŏ-sŏr king of the Babylonians.

3 So when ye be come unto Babylon, ye shall remain there many years, and for a long season, namely, seven generations: and after that I will bring you away peaceably from thence.

4 Now shall ye see in Babylon gods of silver, and of gold, and of wood, borne upon shoulders, which cause the nations to fear.

5 Beware therefore that ye in no wise be like to strangers, neither be ye afraid of them, when ye see the multitude before them and behind them, worshipping them.

6 But say ye in your hearts, O Lord, we must worship thee.

7 For mine angel is with you, and I myself caring for your souls.

8 As for their tongue, it is polished by the workman, and they themselves are gilded and laid over with silver; yet are they but false, and cannot speak.

9 And taking gold, as it were for a virgin that loveth to go gay, they make crowns for the heads of their gods.

10 Sometimes also the priests convey from their gods gold and silver, and bestow it upon themselves.

11 Yea, they will give thereof to the common harlots, and deck them as men with garments, [being] gods of silver, and gods of gold, and wood.

12 Yet cannot these gods save themselves from rust and moths, though they be covered with purple raiment.

13 They wipe their faces because of the dust of the temple, when there is much upon them.

14 And he that cannot put to death one that offendeth him holdeth a sceptre, as though he were a judge of the country.

15 He hath also in his right hand a dagger and an axe: but cannot deliver himself from war and thieves.

16 Whereby they are known

not to be gods: therefore fear them not.

17 For like as a vessel that a man useth is nothing worth when it is broken; even so it is with their gods: when they be set up in the temple, their eyes be full of dust through the feet of them that come in.

18 And as the doors are made sure on every side upon him that offendeth the king, as being committed to suffer death: even so the priests make fast their temples with doors, with locks, and bars, lest *their gods* be spoiled with robbers.

19 They light them candles, yea, more than for themselves, whereof they cannot see one.

20 They are as one of the beams of the temple, yet they say their hearts are gnawed upon by things creeping out of the earth; and when they eat them and their clothes, they feel it not.

21 Their faces are blacked through the smoke that cometh out of the temple.

22 Upon their bodies and heads sit bats, swallows, and birds, and the cats also.

23 By this ye may know that they are no gods: therefore fear them not.

24 Notwithstanding the gold that is about them to make them beautiful, except they wipe off the rust, they will not shine: for neither when they were molten did they feel it.

25 The things wherein there is no breath are bought for a most high price.

26 They are borne upon shoulders, having no feet, whereby they declare unto men that they be nothing worth.

27 They also that serve them

are ashamed: for if they fall to the ground at any time, they cannot rise up again of themselves: neither, if one set them upright, can they move of themselves: neither, if they be bowed down, can they make themselves straight: but they set gifts before them, as unto dead men.

28 As for the things that are sacrificed unto them, their priests sell and abuse; in like manner their wives lay up part thereof in salt; but unto the poor and impotent they give nothing of it.

29 Menstruous women and women in childbed eat their sacrifices: by these things ye may know that they are no gods: fear them not.

30 For how can they be called gods? because women set meat before the gods of silver, gold, and wood.

31 And the priests sit in their temples, having their clothes rent, and their heads and beards shaven, and nothing upon their heads.

32 They roar and cry before their gods, as men do at the feast when one is dead.

33 The priests also take off their garments, and clothe their wives and children.

34 Whether it be evil that one doeth unto them, or good, they are not able to recompense it: they can neither set up a king, nor put him down.

35 In like manner, they can neither give riches nor money: though a man make a vow unto them, and keep it not, they will not require it.

36 They can save no man from death, neither deliver the weak from the mighty.

37 They cannot restore a blind man to his sight, nor help any man in his distress.

38 They can shew no mercy to the widow, nor do good to the fatherless.

39 Their gods of wood, and which are overlaid with gold and silver, are like the stones that be hewn out of the mountain: they that worship them shall be confounded.

40 How should a man then think and say that they are gods, when even the Chăl-dē'-ăns themselves dishonour them?

41 Who if they shall see one dumb that cannot speak, they bring him, and intreat Bel that he may speak, as though he were able to understand.

42 Yet they cannot understand this themselves, and leave them: for they have no knowledge.

43 The women also with cords about them, sitting in the ways, burn bran for perfume: but if any of them, drawn by some that passeth by, lie with him, she reproacheth her fellow, that she was not thought as worthy as herself, nor her cord broken.

44 Whatsoever is done among them is false: how may it then be thought or said that they are gods?

45 They are made of carpenters and goldsmiths: they can be nothing else than the workmen will have them to be.

46 And they themselves that made them can never continue long; how should then the things that are made of them be gods?

47 For they left lies and reproaches to them that come after.

48 For when there cometh

any war or plague upon them, the priests consult with themselves, where they may be hidden with them.

49 How then cannot men perceive that they be no gods, which can neither save themselves from war, nor from plague?

50 For seeing they be but of wood, and overlaid with silver and gold, it shall be known hereafter that they are false:

51 And it shall manifestly appear to all nations and kings that they are no gods, but the works of men's hands, and that there is no work of God in them.

52 Who then may not know that they are no gods?

53 For neither can they set up a king in the land, nor give rain unto men.

54 Neither can they judge their own cause, nor redress a wrong, being unable: for they are as crows between heaven and earth.

55 Whereupon when fire falleth upon the house of gods of wood, or laid over with gold or silver, their priests will flee away, and escape; but they themselves shall be burned asunder like beams.

56 Moreover they cannot withstand any king or enemies: how can it then be thought or said that they be gods?

57 Neither are those gods of wood, and laid over with silver or gold, able to escape either from thieves or robbers.

58 Whose gold, and silver, and garments wherewith they are clothed, they that are strong do take, and go away withal: neither are they able to help themselves.

59 Therefore it is better to be

a king that sheweth his power, or else a profitable vessel in an house, which the owner shall have use of, than such false gods; or to be a door in an house, to keep such things safe as be therein, than such false gods; or a pillar of wood in a palace, than such false gods.

60 For sun, moon, and stars, being bright, and sent to do their offices, are obedient.

61 In like manner the lightning when it breaketh forth is easy to be seen; and after the same manner the wind bloweth in every country.

62 And when God commandeth the clouds to go over the whole world, they do as they are bidden.

63 And the fire sent from above to consume hills and woods doeth as it is commanded: but these are like unto them neither in shew nor power.

64 Wherefore it is neither to be supposed nor said that they are gods, seeing they are able neither to judge causes, nor to do good unto men.

65 Knowing therefore that they are no gods, fear them not.

66 For they can neither curse nor bless kings:

67 Neither can they shew signs in the heavens among the heathen, nor shine as the sun, nor give light as the moon.

68 The beasts are better than they: for they can get under a covert, and help themselves.

69 It is then by no means manifest unto us that they are gods: therefore fear them not.

70 For as a scarecrow in a garden of cucumbers keepeth nothing: so are their gods of wood, and laid over with silver and gold.

71 And likewise their gods of wood, and laid over with silver and gold, are like to a white thorn in an orchard, that every bird sitteth upon; as also to a dead body, that is cast into the dark.

72 And ye shall know them to be no gods by the bright purple that rotteth upon them: and they themselves afterward shall be eaten, and shall be a reproach in the country.

73 Better therefore is the just man that hath none idols: for he shall be far from reproach.

THE SONG OF THE

THREE HOLY CHILDREN

Which followeth in the third Chapter of DANIEL after this place,—*fell down bound into the midst of the burning fiery furnace.*—Verse 23. That which followeth is not in the Hebrew, to wit, *And they walked*—unto these words, *Then Nebuchadnezzar*—verse 24.

AND they walked in the midst of the fire, praising God, and blessing the Lord.

2 Then Ăz-ă-rī´-ăs stood up, and prayed on this manner; and opening his mouth in the midst of the fire said,

3 Blessed art thou, O Lord God of our fathers: thy name is worthy to be praised and glorified for evermore:

4 For thou art righteous in all the things that thou hast done to us: yea, true are all thy works, thy ways are right, and all thy judgments truth.

5 In all the things that thou hast brought upon us, and upon the holy city of our fathers, *even* Jerusalem, thou hast executed true judgment: for according to truth and judgment didst thou bring all these things upon us because of our sins.

6 For we have sinned and committed iniquity, departing from thee.

7 In all things have we trespassed, and not obeyed thy commandments, nor kept them, neither done as thou hast commanded us, that it might go well with us.

8 Wherefore all that thou hast brought upon us, and every thing that thou hast done to us, thou hast done in true judgment.

9 And thou didst deliver us into the hands of lawless enemies, most hateful forsakers *of God,* and to an unjust king, and the most wicked in all the world.

10 And now we cannot open our mouths, we are become a shame and reproach to thy servants, and to them that worship thee.

11 Yet deliver us not up wholly, for thy name's sake, neither disannul thou thy covenant:

12 And cause not thy mercy to depart from us, for thy beloved Abraham's sake, for thy servant Isaac's sake, and for thy holy Israel's sake;

13 To whom thou hast spoken

203

and promised, that thou wouldest multiply their seed as the stars of heaven, and as the sand that lieth upon the sea-shore.

14 For we, O Lord, are become less than any nation, and be kept under this day in all the world because of our sins.

15 Neither is there at this time prince, or prophet, or leader, or burnt offering, or sacrifice, or oblation, or incense, or place to sacrifice before thee, and to find mercy.

16 Nevertheless in a contrite heart and an humble spirit let us be accepted.

17 Like as in the burnt offerings of rams and bullocks, and like as in ten thousands of fat lambs: so let our sacrifice be in thy sight this day, and *grant* that we may wholly go after thee: for they shall not be confounded that put their trust in thee.

18 And now we follow thee with all our heart, we fear thee, and seek thy face.

19 Put us not to shame: but deal with us after thy lovingkindness, and according to the multitude of thy mercies.

20 Deliver us also according to thy marvellous works, and give glory to thy name, O Lord: and let all them that do thy servants hurt be ashamed;

21 And let them be confounded in all their power and might, and let their strength be broken;

22 And let them know that thou art Lord, the only God, and glorious over the whole world.

23 And the king's servants, that put them in, ceased not to make the oven hot with rosin, pitch, tow, and small wood;

24 So that the flame streamed forth above the furnace forty and nine cubits.

25 And it passed through, and burned those Chăl-dē'-ăns it found about the furnace.

26 But the angel of the Lord came down into the oven together with Ăz-ă-rī'-ăs and his fellows, and smote the flame of the fire out of the oven;

27 And made the midst of the furnace as it had been a moist whistling wind, so that the fire touched them not at all, neither hurt nor troubled them.

28 Then the three, as out of one mouth, praised, glorified, and blessed God in the furnace, saying,

29 Blessed art thou, O Lord God of our fathers: and to be praised and exalted above all for ever.

30 And blessed is thy glorious and holy name: and to be praised and exalted above all for ever.

31 Blessed art thou in the temple of thine holy glory: and to be praised and glorified above all for ever.

32 Blessed art thou that beholdest the depths, and sittest upon the cherubims: and to be praised and exalted above all for ever.

33 Blessed art thou on the glorious throne of thy kingdom: and to be praised and glorified above all for ever.

34 Blessed art thou in the firmament of heaven: and above all to be praised and glorified for ever.

35 O all ye works of the Lord, bless ye the Lord: praise and exalt him above all for ever.

36 O ye heavens, bless ye the

Lord: praise and exalt him above all for ever.

37 O ye angels of the Lord, bless ye the Lord: praise and exalt him above all for ever.

38 O all ye waters that be above the heaven, bless ye the Lord: praise and exalt him above all for ever.

39 O all ye powers of the Lord, bless ye the Lord: praise and exalt him above all for ever.

40 O ye sun and moon, bless ye the Lord: praise and exalt him above all for ever.

41 O ye stars of heaven, bless ye the Lord: praise and exalt him above all for ever.

42 O every shower and dew, bless ye the Lord: praise and exalt him above all for ever.

43 O all ye winds, bless ye the Lord: praise and exalt him above all for ever.

44 O ye fire and heat, bless ye the Lord: praise and exalt him above all for ever.

45 O ye winter and summer, bless ye the Lord: praise and exalt him above all for ever.

46 O ye dews and storms of snow, bless ye the Lord: praise and exalt him above all for ever.

47 O ye nights and days, bless ye the Lord: praise and exalt him above all for ever.

48 O ye light and darkness, bless ye the Lord: praise and exalt him above all for ever.

49 O ye ice and cold, bless ye the Lord: praise and exalt him above all for ever.

50 O ye frost and snow, bless ye the Lord: praise and exalt him above all for ever.

51 O ye lightnings and clouds, bless ye the Lord: praise and exalt him above all for ever.

52 O let the earth bless the Lord: praise and exalt him above all for ever.

53 O ye mountains and little hills, bless ye the Lord: praise and exalt him above all for ever.

54 O all ye things that grow on the earth, bless ye the Lord: praise and exalt him above all for ever.

55 O ye fountains, bless ye the Lord: praise and exalt him above all for ever.

56 O ye seas and rivers, bless ye the Lord: praise and exalt him above all for ever.

57 O ye whales, and all that move in the waters, bless ye the Lord: praise and exalt him above all for ever.

58 O all ye fowls of the air, bless ye the Lord: praise and exalt him above all for ever.

59 O all ye beasts and cattle, bless ye the Lord: praise and exalt him above all for ever.

60 O ye children of men, bless ye the Lord: praise and exalt him above all for ever.

61 O Israel, bless ye the Lord: praise and exalt him above all for ever.

62 O ye priests of the Lord, bless ye the Lord: praise and exalt him above all for ever.

63 O ye servants of the Lord, bless ye the Lord: praise and exalt him above all for ever.

64 O ye spirits and souls of the righteous, bless ye the Lord: praise and exalt him above all for ever.

65 O ye holy and humble men of heart, bless ye the Lord: praise and exalt him above all for ever.

66 O Ăn-ă-nī′-ăs, Ăz-ă-rī′-ăs, and Mĭs′-ă-ĕl, bless ye the Lord: praise and exalt him above all for ever: for he hath delivered us from hell, and saved us from

the hand of death, and delivered us out of the midst of the furnace *and* burning flame: even out of the midst of the fire hath he delivered us.

67 O give thanks unto the Lord, because he is gracious: for his mercy *endureth* for ever.

68 O all ye that worship the Lord, bless the God of gods, praise him, and give him thanks: for his mercy *endureth* for ever.

THE
HISTORY OF SUSANNA

Set apart from the beginning of *Daniel*, because it is not in the Hebrew, as neither the Narration of *Bel and the Dragon*.

THERE dwelt a man in Babylon, called Jŏ́-ă-cĭm;

2 And he took a wife, whose name was Susanna, the daughter of Chĕl-çĭ́-ăs, a very fair woman, and one that feared the Lord.

3 Her parents also were righteous, and taught their daughter according to the law of Moses.

4 Now Jŏ́-ă-cĭm was a great rich man, and had a fair garden joining unto his house: and to him resorted the Jews; because he was more honourable than all others.

5 The same year were appointed two of the ancients of the people to be judges, such as the Lord spake of, that wickedness came from Babylon from ancient judges, who seemed to govern the people.

6 These kept much at Jŏ́-ă-cĭm's house: and all that had any suits in law came unto them.

7 Now when the people departed away at noon, Susanna went into her husband's garden to walk.

8 And the two elders saw her going in every day, and walking; so that their lust was inflamed toward her.

9 And they perverted their own mind, and turned away their eyes, that they might not look unto heaven, nor remember just judgments.

10 And albeit they both were wounded with her love, yet durst not one shew another his grief.

11 For they were ashamed to declare their lust, that they desired to have to do with her.

12 Yet they watched diligently from day to day to see her.

13 And the one said to the other, Let us now go home: for it is dinner time.

14 So when they were gone out, they parted the one from the other, and turning back again they came to the same place; and after that they had asked one another the cause, they acknowledged their lust: then appointed they a time both together, when they might find her alone.

15 And it fell out, as they watched a fit time, she went in as before with two maids only, and she was desirous to wash

herself in the garden: for it was hot.

16 And there was no body there save the two elders, that had hid themselves, and watched her.

17 Then she said to her maids, Bring me oil and washing balls, and shut the garden doors, that I may wash me.

18 And they did as she bade them, and shut the garden doors, and went out themselves at privy doors to fetch the things that she had commanded them: but they saw not the elders, because they were hid.

19 Now when the maids were gone forth, the two elders rose up, and ran unto her, saying,

20 Behold, the garden doors are shut, that no man can see us, and we are in love with thee; therefore consent unto us, and lie with us.

21 If thou wilt not, we will bear witness against thee, that a young man was with thee: and therefore thou didst send away thy maids from thee.

22 Then Susanna sighed, and said, I am straitened on every side: for if I do this thing, it is death unto me: and if I do it not, I cannot escape your hands.

23 It is better for me to fall into your hands, and not do it, than to sin in the sight of the Lord.

24 With that Susanna cried with a loud voice: and the two elders cried out against her.

25 Then ran the one, and opened the garden door.

26 So when the servants of the house heard the cry in the garden, they rushed in at a privy door, to see what was done unto her.

27 But when the elders had declared their matter, the servants were greatly ashamed: for there was never such a report made of Susanna.

28 And it came to pass the next day, when the people were assembled to her husband Jō-ă-cĭm, the two elders came also full of mischievous imagination against Susanna to put her to death;

29 And said before the people, Send for Susanna, the daughter of Chĕl-çĭ'-ăs, Jō-ă-cĭm's wife. And so they sent.

30 So she came with her father and mother, her children, and all her kindred.

31 Now Susanna was a very delicate woman, and beauteous to behold.

32 And these wicked men commanded to uncover her *face*, (for she was covered) that they might be filled with her beauty.

33 Therefore her friends and all that saw her wept.

34 Then the two elders stood up in the midst of the people, and laid their hands upon her head.

35 And she weeping looked up toward heaven: for her heart trusted in the Lord.

36 And the elders said, As we walked in the garden alone, this woman came in with two maids, and shut the garden doors, and sent the maids away.

37 Then a young man, who there was hid, came unto her, and lay with her.

38 Then we that stood in a corner of the garden, seeing this wickedness, ran unto them.

39 And when we saw them together, the man we could not

hold: for he was stronger than we, and opened the door, and leaped out.

40 But having taken this woman, we asked who the young man was, but she would not tell us: these things do we testify.

41 Then the assembly believed them, as those that were the elders and judges of the people: so they condemned her to death.

42 Then Susanna cried out with a loud voice, and said, O everlasting God, that knowest the secrets, and knowest all things before they be:

43 Thou knowest that they have borne false witness against me, and, behold, I must die; whereas I never did such things as these men have maliciously invented against me.

44 And the Lord heard her voice.

45 Therefore when she was led to be put to death, the Lord raised up the holy spirit of a young youth, whose name was Daniel:

46 Who cried with a loud voice, I am clear from the blood of this woman.

47 Then all the people turned them toward him, and said, What mean these words that thou hast spoken?

48 So he standing in the midst of them said, Are ye such fools, ye sons of Israel, that without examination or knowledge of the truth ye have condemned a daughter of Israel?

49 Return again to the place of judgment: for they have borne false witness against her.

50 Wherefore all the people turned again in haste, and the

elders said unto him, Come, sit down among us, and shew it us, seeing God hath given thee the honour of an elder.

51 Then said Daniel unto them, Put these two aside one far from another, and I will examine them.

52 So when they were put asunder one from another, he called one of them, and said unto him, O thou that art waxen old in wickedness, now thy sins which thou hast committed aforetime are come *to light:*

53 For thou hast pronounced false judgment, and hast condemned the innocent, and hast let the guilty go free; albeit the Lord saith, The innocent and righteous shalt thou not slay.

54 Now then, if thou hast seen her, tell me, Under what tree sawest thou them companying together? Who answered, Under a mastick tree.

55 And Daniel said, Very well; thou hast lied against thine own head; for even now the angel of God hath received the sentence of God to cut thee in two.

56 So he put him aside, and commanded to bring the other, and said unto him, O thou seed of Chā'-nāān, and not of Juda, beauty hath deceived thee, and lust hath perverted thine heart.

57 Thus have ye dealt with the daughters of Israel, and they for fear companied with you: but the daughter of Juda would not abide your wickedness.

58 Now therefore tell me, Under what tree didst thou take them companying together? Who answered, Under an holm tree.

59 Then said Daniel unto him, Well; thou hast also lied against thine own head: for the angel of God waiteth with the sword to cut thee in two, that he may destroy you.

60 With that all the assembly cried out with a loud voice, and praised God, who saveth them that trust in him.

61 And they arose against the two elders, for Daniel had convicted them of false witness by their own mouth:

62 And according to the law of Moses they did unto them in such sort as they maliciously intended to do to their neighbour: and they put them to death. Thus the innocent blood was saved the same day.

63 Therefore Chĕl-cī-ăs and his wife praised God for their daughter Susanna, with Jō-ă-cĭm her husband, and all the kindred, because there was no dishonesty found in her.

64 From that day forth was Daniel had in great reputation in the sight of the people.

THE HISTORY OF THE DESTRUCTION OF

BEL AND THE DRAGON

CUT OFF FROM THE END OF DANIEL

AND king Ăs-tȳ-ă-ġēs was gathered to his fathers, and Cyrus of Persia received his kingdom.

2 And Daniel conversed with the king, and was honoured above all his friends.

3 Now the Babylonians had an idol, called Bel, and there were spent upon him every day twelve great measures of fine flour, and forty sheep, and six vessels of wine.

4 And the king worshipped it, and went daily to adore it: but Daniel worshipped his own God. And the king said unto him, Why dost not thou worship Bel?

5 Who answered and said, Because I may not worship idols made with hands, but the living God, who hath created the heaven and the earth, and hath sovereignty over all flesh.

6 Then said the king unto him, Thinkest thou not that Bel is a living God? seest thou not how much he eateth and drinketh every day?

7 Then Daniel smiled, and said, O king, be not deceived: for this is but clay within, and brass without, and did never eat or drink any thing.

8 So the king was wroth, and called for his priests, and said unto them, If ye tell me not who this is that devoureth these expences, ye shall die.

9 But if ye can certify me that Bel devoureth them, then Daniel shall die: for he hath spoken blasphemy against Bel. And Daniel said unto the king, Let it be according to thy word.

10 Now the priests of Bel were threescore and ten, beside their wives and children. And the king went with Daniel into the temple of Bel.

11 So Bel's priests said, Lo, we go out: but thou, O king,

set on the meat, and make ready the wine, and shut the door fast, and seal it with thine own signet;

12 And to morrow when thou comest in, if thou findest not that Bel hath eaten up all, we will suffer death: or else Daniel, that speaketh falsely against us.

13 And they little regarded it: for under the table they had made a privy entrance, whereby they entered in continually, and consumed those things.

14 So when they were gone forth, the king set meats before Bel. Now Daniel had commanded his servants to bring ashes, and those they strewed throughout all the temple in the presence of the king alone: then went they out, and shut the door, and sealed it with the king's signet, and so departed.

15 Now in the night came the priests with their wives and children, as they were wont to do, and did eat and drink up all.

16 In the morning betime the king arose, and Daniel with him.

17 And the king said, Daniel, are the seals whole? And he said, Yea, O king, they be whole.

18 And as soon as he had opened the door, the king looked upon the table, and cried with a loud voice, Great art thou, O Bel, and with thee is no deceit at all.

19 Then laughed Daniel, and held the king that he should not go in, and said, Behold now the pavement, and mark well whose footsteps are these.

20 And the king said, I see the footsteps of men, women, and children. And then the king was angry,

21 And took the priests with their wives and children, who shewed him the privy doors, where they came in, and consumed such things as were upon the table.

22 Therefore the king slew them, and delivered Bel into Daniel's power, who destroyed him and his temple.

23 And in that same place there was a great dragon, which they of Babylon worshipped.

24 And the king said unto Daniel, Wilt thou also say that this is of brass? lo, he liveth, he eateth and drinketh; thou canst not say that he is no living god: therefore worship him.

25 Then said Daniel unto the king, I will worship the Lord my God: for he is the living God.

26 But give me leave, O king, and I shall slay this dragon without sword or staff. The king said, I give thee leave.

27 Then Daniel took pitch, and fat, and hair, and did seethe them together, and made lumps thereof: this he put in the dragon's mouth, and so the dragon burst in sunder: and Daniel said, Lo, these are the gods ye worship.

28 When they of Babylon heard that, they took great indignation, and conspired against the king, saying, The king is become a Jew, and he hath destroyed Bel, he hath slain the dragon, and put the priests to death.

29 So they came to the king, and said, Deliver us Daniel, or else we will destroy thee and thine house.

30 Now when the king saw that they pressed him sore, being constrained, he delivered Daniel unto them:

31 Who cast him into the lions' den: where he was six days.

32 And in the den there were seven lions, and they had given them every day two carcases, and two sheep: which then were not given to them, to the intent they might devour Daniel.

33 Now there was in Jewry a prophet, called Hăb′-bă-cŭc, who had made pottage, and had broken bread in a bowl, and was going into the field, for to bring it to the reapers.

34 But the angel of the Lord said unto Hăb′-bă-cŭc, Go, carry the dinner that thou hast into Babylon unto Daniel, who is in the lions' den.

35 And Hăb′-bă-cŭc said, Lord, I never saw Babylon; neither do I know where the den is.

36 Then the angel of the Lord took him by the crown, and bare him by the hair of his head, and through the vehemency of his spirit set him in Babylon over the den.

37 And Hăb′-bă-cŭc cried, saying, O Daniel, Daniel, take the dinner which God hath sent thee.

38 And Daniel said, Thou hast remembered me, O God: neither hast thou forsaken them that seek thee and love thee.

39 So Daniel arose, and did eat: and the angel of the Lord set Hăb′-bă-cŭc in his own place again immediately.

40 Upon the seventh day the king went to bewail Daniel: and when he came to the den, he looked in, and, behold, Daniel was sitting.

41 Then cried the king with a loud voice, saying, Great art thou, O Lord God of Daniel, and there is none other beside thee.

42 And he drew him out, and cast those that were the cause of his destruction into the den: and they were devoured in a moment before his face.

THE
PRAYER OF MANASSES
KING OF JUDAH
WHEN HE WAS HOLDEN CAPTIVE IN BABYLON

O LORD, Almighty God of our fathers, Abraham, Isaac, and Jacob, and of their righteous seed; who hast made heaven and earth, with all the ornament thereof; who hast bound the sea by the word of thy commandment; who hast shut up the deep, and sealed it by thy terrible and glorious name; whom all men fear, and tremble before thy power; for the majesty of thy glory cannot be borne, and thine angry threatening toward sinners is importable: but thy merciful promise is unmeasurable and unsearchable; for thou art the most high Lord, of great compassion, longsuffering, very merciful, and repentest of the evils of men. Thou, O Lord, according to thy great goodness hast promised repentance and forgiveness to them that have sinned against thee: and of thine infinite mercies hast appointed repentance unto sinners, that they may be saved. Thou therefore, O Lord, that art the God of the just, hast not appointed repentance to the just, as to Abraham, and Isaac, and Jacob, which have not sinned against thee; but thou hast appointed repentance unto me that am a sinner: for I have sinned above the number of the sands of the sea. My transgressions, O Lord, are multiplied: my transgressions are multiplied, and I am not worthy to behold and see the height of heaven for the multitude of mine iniquities. I am bowed down with many iron bands, that I cannot lift up mine head, neither have any

release: for I have provoked thy wrath, and done evil before thee: I did not thy will, neither kept I thy commandments: I have set up abominations, and have multiplied offences. Now therefore I bow the knee of mine heart, beseeching thee of grace. I have sinned, O Lord, I have sinned, and I acknowledge mine iniquities: wherefore, I humbly beseech thee, forgive me, O Lord, forgive me, and destroy me not with mine iniquities. Be not angry with me for ever, by reserving evil for me; neither condemn me into the lower parts of the earth. For thou art the God, *even* the God of them that repent; and in me thou wilt shew all thy goodness: for thou wilt save me, that am unworthy, according to thy great mercy. Therefore I will praise thee for ever all the days of my life: for all the powers of the heavens do praise thee, and thine is the glory for ever and ever. Amen.

THE FIRST BOOK OF THE

MACCABEES

CHAPTER I

AND it happened, after that Alexander *son* of Philip, the Macedonian, who came out of the land of Chĕt-tī-'ĭm, had smitten Dă-rī-ŭs king of the Persians and Medes, that he reigned in his stead, the first over Greece.

2 And made many wars, and won many strong holds, and slew the kings of the earth,

3 And went through to the ends of the earth, and took spoils of many nations, insomuch that the earth was quiet before him; whereupon he was exalted, and his heart was lifted up.

4 And he gathered a mighty strong host, and ruled over countries, and nations, and kings, who became tributaries unto him.

5 And after these things he

fell sick, and perceived that he should die.

6 Wherefore he called his servants, such as were honourable, and had been brought up with him from his youth, and parted his kingdom among them, while he was yet alive.

7 So Alexander reigned twelve years, and *then* died.

8 And his servants bare rule every one in his place.

9 And after his death they all put crowns *upon themselves*; so did their sons after them many years: and evils were multiplied in the earth.

10 And there came out of them a wicked root, Ăn-tī'-ŏ-chŭs surnamed Ē-pĭph'-ă-nēs, son of Antiochus the king, who had been an hostage at Rome, and he reigned in the hundred and thirty and seventh year of the kingdom of the Greeks.

11 In those days went there out of Israel wicked men, who persuaded many, saying, Let us go and make a covenant with the heathen that are round about us: for since we departed from them we have had much sorrow.

12 So this device pleased them well.

13 Then certain of the people were so forward herein, that they went to the king, who gave them licence to do after the ordinances of the heathen:

14 Whereupon they built a place of exercise at Jerusalem according to the customs of the heathen:

15 And made themselves uncircumcised, and forsook the holy covenant, and joined themselves to the heathen, and were sold to do mischief.

16 Now when the kingdom was established before Ăn-tī'-ŏ-chŭs, he thought to reign over Egypt, that he might have the dominion of two realms.

17 Wherefore he entered into Egypt with a great multitude, with chariots, and elephants, and horsemen, and a great navy,

18 And made war against Ptŏl'-ĕ-mēē king of Egypt: but Ptolemee was afraid of him, and fled; and many were wounded to death.

19 Thus they got the strong cities in the land of Egypt, and he took the spoils thereof.

20 And after that Ăn-tī'-ŏ-chŭs had smitten Egypt, he returned again in the hundred forty and third year, and went up against Israel and Jerusalem with a great multitude,

21 And entered proudly into the sanctuary, and took away the golden altar, and the candlestick of light, and all the vessels thereof,

22 And the table of the shewbread, and the pouring vessels, and the vials, and the censers of gold, and the veil, and the crowns, and the golden ornaments that were before the temple, all which he pulled off.

23 He took also the silver and the gold, and the precious vessels: also he took the hidden treasures which he found.

24 And when he had taken all away, he went into his own land, having made a great massacre, and spoken very proudly.

25 Therefore there was great mourning in Israel, in every place where they were;

26 So that the princes and elders mourned, the virgins and young men were made

feeble, and the beauty of women was changed.

27 Every bridegroom took up lamentation, and she that sat in the marriage chamber was in heaviness.

28 The land also was moved for the inhabitants thereof, and all the house of Jacob was covered with confusion.

29 And after two years fully expired the king sent his chief collector of tribute unto the cities of Juda, who came unto Jerusalem with a great multitude,

30 And spake peaceable words unto them, but *all was* deceit: for when they had given him credence, he fell suddenly upon the city, and smote it very sore, and destroyed much people of Israel.

31 And when he had taken the spoils of the city, he set it on fire, and pulled down the houses and walls thereof on every side.

32 But the women and children took they captive, and possessed the cattle.

33 Then builded they the city of David with a great and strong wall, *and* with mighty towers, and made it a strong hold for them.

34 And they put therein a sinful nation, wicked men, and fortified *themselves* therein.

35 They stored it also with armour and victuals, and when they had gathered together the spoils of Jerusalem, they laid them up there, and so they became a sore snare:

36 For it was a place to lie in wait against the sanctuary, and an evil adversary to Israel.

37 Thus they shed innocent blood on every side of the sanctuary, and defiled it:

38 Insomuch that the inhabitants of Jerusalem fled because of them: whereupon *the city* was made an habitation of strangers, and became strange to those that were born in her; and her own children left her.

39 Her sanctuary was laid waste like a wilderness, her feasts were turned into mourning, her sabbaths into reproach, her honour into contempt.

40 As had been her glory, so was her dishonour increased, and her excellency was turned into mourning.

41 Moreover king Ăn-tī′-ŏ-chŭs wrote to his whole kingdom, that all should be one people,

42 And every one should leave his laws: so all the heathen agreed according to the commandment of the king.

43 Yea, many also of the Israelites consented to his religion, and sacrificed unto idols, and profaned the sabbath.

44 For the king had sent letters by messengers unto Jerusalem and the cities of Juda, that they should follow the strange laws of the land,

45 And forbid burnt offerings, and sacrifice, and drink offerings, in the temple; and that they should profane the sabbaths and festival days:

46 And pollute the sanctuary and holy people:

47 Set up altars, and groves, and chapels of idols, and sacrifice swine's flesh, and unclean beasts:

48 That they should also leave their children uncircumcised, and make their souls abominable with all manner of uncleanness and profanation:

49 To the end they might forget the law, and change all the ordinances.

50 And whosoever would not do according to the commandment of the king, *he said*, he should die.

51 In the selfsame manner wrote he to his whole kingdom, and appointed overseers over all the people, commanding the cities of Juda to sacrifice, city by city.

52 Then many of the people were gathered unto them, to wit, every one that forsook the law; and so they committed evils in the land;

53 And drove the Israelites into secret places, even wheresoever they could flee for succour.

54 Now the fifteenth day of *the month* Căs'-lĕū, in the hundred forty and fifth year, they set up the abomination of desolation upon the altar, and builded idol altars throughout the cities of Juda on every side;

55 And burnt incense at the doors of their houses, and in the streets.

56 And when they had rent in pieces the books of the law which they found, they burnt them with fire.

57 And wheresoever was found with any the book of the testament, or if any consented to the law, the king's commandment was, that they should put him to death.

58 Thus did they by their authority unto the Israelites every month, to as many as were found in the cities.

59 Now the five and twentieth day of the month they did sacrifice upon the idol altar, which was upon the altar of God.

60 At which time according to the commandment they put to death certain women, that had caused their children to be circumcised.

61 And they hanged the infants about their necks, and rifled their houses, and slew them that had circumcised them.

62 Howbeit many in Israel were fully resolved and confirmed in themselves not to eat any unclean thing.

63 Wherefore they chose rather to die, that they might not be defiled with meats, and that they might not profane the holy covenant: so then they died.

64 And there was very great wrath upon Israel.

CHAPTER II

IN those days arose Măt-tă-thī'-ăs *the son* of John, *the son* of Simeon, a priest of the sons of Jō'-ă-rĭb, from Jerusalem, and dwelt in Mō'-dĭn.

2 And he had five sons, Jŏ-ăn'-năn, called Caddis:

3 Simon, called Thăs'-sī:

4 Judas, who was called Măc-că-bē'-ŭs:

5 Ĕl-ĕ-ā'-zăr, called Ăv'-ă-răn: and Jonathan, whose surname was Apphus.

6 And when he saw the blasphemies that were committed in Juda and Jerusalem,

7 He said, Woe is me! wherefore was I born to see this misery of my people, and of the holy city, and to dwell there, when it was delivered into the hand of the enemy, and the sanctuary into the hand of strangers?

8 Her temple is become as a man without glory.

9 Her glorious vessels are carried away into captivity, her infants are slain in the streets, her young men with the sword of the enemy.

10 What nation hath not had a part in *her* kingdom, and gotten of her spoils?

11 All her ornaments are taken away; of a free woman she is become a bondslave.

12 And, behold, our sanctuary, even our beauty and our glory, is laid waste, and the Gentiles have profaned it.

13 To what end therefore shall we live any longer?

14 Then Măt-tă-thī'-ăs and his sons rent their clothes, and put on sackcloth, and mourned very sore.

15 In the mean while the king's officers, such as compelled the people to revolt, came into the city Mō'-dĭn, to make them sacrifice.

16 And when many of Israel came unto them, Măt-tă-thī'-ăs also and his sons came together.

17 Then answered the king's officers, and said to Măt-tă-thī'-ăs on this wise, Thou art a ruler, and an honourable and great man in this city, and strengthened with sons and brethren:

18 Now therefore come thou first, and fulfil the king's commandment, like as all the heathen have done, yea, and the men of Juda also, and such as remain at Jerusalem: so shalt thou and thy house be in the number of the king's friends, and thou and thy children shall be honoured with silver and gold, and many rewards.

19 Then Măt-tă-thī'-ăs answered and spake with a loud voice, Though all the nations that are under the king's dominion obey him, and fall away every one from the religion of their fathers, and give consent to his commandments:

20 Yet will I and my sons and my brethren walk in the covenant of our fathers.

21 God forbid that we should forsake the law and the ordinances.

22 We will not hearken to the king's words, to go from our religion, either on the right hand, or the left.

23 Now when he had left speaking these words, there came one of the Jews in the sight of all to sacrifice on the altar which was at Mō'-dĭn, according to the king's commandment.

24 Which thing when Măt-tă-thī'-ăs saw, he was inflamed with zeal, and his reins trembled, neither could he forbear to shew his anger according to judgment: wherefore he ran, and slew him upon the altar.

25 Also the king's commissioner, who compelled men to sacrifice, he killed at that time, and the altar he pulled down.

26 Thus dealt he zealously for the law of God, like as Phĭn'-ĕ-ĕs did unto Zăm'-brī the son of Sā'-lŏm.

27 And Măt-tă-thī'-ăs cried throughout the city with a loud voice, saying, Whosoever is zealous of the law, and maintaineth the covenant, let him follow me.

28 So he and his sons fled into the mountains, and left all that ever they had in the city.

29 Then many that sought after justice and judgment

went down into the wilderness, to dwell there:

30 Both they, and their children, and their wives, and their cattle; because afflictions increased sore upon them.

31 Now when it was told the king's servants, and the host that was at Jerusalem, in the city of David, that certain men, who had broken the king's commandment, were gone down into the secret places in the wilderness,

32 They pursued after them a great number, and having overtaken them, they camped against them, and made war against them on the sabbath day.

33 And they said unto them, Let that which ye have done hitherto suffice; come forth, and do according to the commandment of the king, and ye shall live.

34 But they said, We will not come forth, neither will we do the king's commandment, to profane the sabbath day.

35 So then they gave them the battle with all speed.

36 Howbeit they answered them not, neither cast they a stone at them, nor stopped the places where they lay hid;

37 But said, Let us die all in our innocency: heaven and earth shall testify for us, that ye put us to death wrongfully.

38 So they rose up against them in battle on the sabbath, and they slew them, with their wives and children, and their cattle, to the number of a thousand people.

39 Now when Măt-tă-thī′-ăs and his friends understood hereof, they mourned for them right sore.

40 And one of them said to another, If we all do as our brethren have done, and fight not for our lives and laws against the heathen, they will now quickly root us out of the earth.

41 At that time therefore they decreed, saying, Whosoever shall come to make battle with us on the sabbath day, we will fight against him; neither will we die all, as our brethren that were murdered in the secret places.

42 Then came there unto him a company of Ăs-sĭ-dē′-ăns, who were mighty men of Israel, even all such as were voluntarily devoted unto the law.

43 Also all they that fled for persecution joined themselves unto them, and were a stay unto them.

44 So they joined their forces, and smote sinful men in their anger, and wicked men in their wrath: but the rest fled to the heathen for succour.

45 Then Măt-tă-thī′-ăs and his friends went round about, and pulled down the altars:

46 And what children soever they found within the coast of Israel uncircumcised, those they circumcised valiantly.

47 They pursued also after the proud men, and the work prospered in their hand.

48 So they recovered the law out of the hand of the Gentiles, and out of the hand of kings, neither suffered they the sinner to triumph.

49 Now when the time drew near that Măt-tă-thī′-ăs should die, he said unto his sons, Now hath pride and rebuke gotten strength, and the time of destruction, and the wrath of indignation:

50 Now therefore, my sons, be ye zealous for the law, and give your lives for the covenant of your fathers.

51 Call to remembrance what acts our fathers did in their time; so shall ye receive great honour and an everlasting name.

52 Was not Abraham found faithful in temptation, and it was imputed unto him for righteousness?

53 Joseph in the time of his distress kept the commandment, and was made lord of Egypt.

54 Phĭn´-ĕ-ĕs our father in being zealous and fervent obtained the covenant of an everlasting priesthood.

55 Jesus for fulfilling the word was made a judge in Israel.

56 Caleb for bearing witness before the congregation received the heritage of the land.

57 David for being merciful possessed the throne of an everlasting kingdom.

58 Elias for being zealous and fervent for the law was taken up into heaven.

59 Ăn-ă-nī´-ăs, Ăz-ă-rī´-ăs, and Mīs´-ă-ĕl, by believing were saved out of the flame.

60 Daniel for his innocency was delivered from the mouth of lions.

61 And thus consider ye throughout all ages, that none that put their trust in him shall be overcome.

62 Fear not then the words of a sinful man: for his glory shall be dung and worms.

63 To day he shall be lifted up, and to morrow he shall not be found, because he is returned into his dust, and his thought is come to nothing.

64 Wherefore, ye my sons, be valiant, and shew yourselves men in the behalf of the law; for by it shall ye obtain glory.

65 And, behold, I know that your brother Simon is a man of counsel, give ear unto him alway: he shall be a father unto you.

66 As for Judas Măc-că-bē´-ŭs, he hath been mighty and strong, even from his youth up: let him be your captain, and fight the battle of the people.

67 Take also unto you all those that observe the law, and avenge ye the wrong of your people.

68 Recompense fully the heathen, and take heed to the commandments of the law.

69 So he blessed them, and was gathered to his fathers.

70 And he died in the hundred forty and sixth year, and his sons buried him in the sepulchres of his fathers at Mŏ´-dĭn, and all Israel made great lamentation for him.

CHAPTER III

THEN his son Judas, called Măc-că-bē´-ŭs, rose up in his stead.

2 And all his brethren helped him, and so did all they that held with his father, and they fought with cheerfulness the battle of Israel.

3 So he gat his people great honour, and put on a breastplate as a giant, and girt his warlike harness about him, and he made battles, protecting the host with his sword.

4 In his acts he was like a lion, and like a lion's whelp roaring for his prey.

5 For he pursued the wicked,

and sought them out, and burnt up those that vexed his people.

6 Wherefore the wicked shrunk for fear of him, and all the workers of iniquity were troubled, because salvation prospered in his hand.

7 He grieved also many kings, and made Jacob glad with his acts, and his memorial is blessed for ever.

8 Moreover he went through the cities of Juda, destroying the ungodly out of them, and turning away wrath from Israel:

9 So that he was renowned unto the utmost part of the earth, and he received unto him such as were ready to perish.

10 Then Ăp'-ŏl-lō'-nĭ-ŭs gathered the Gentiles together, and a great host out of Samaria, to fight against Israel.

11 Which thing when Judas perceived, he went forth to meet him, and so he smote him, and slew him: many also fell down slain, but the rest fled.

12 Wherefore Judas took their spoils, and Ăp'-ŏl-lō'-nĭ-ŭs' sword also, and therewith he fought all his life long.

13 Now when Sē'-rŏn, a prince of the army of Syria, heard say that Judas had gathered unto him a multitude and company of the faithful to go out with him to war;

14 He said, I will get me a name and honour in the kingdom; for I will go fight with Judas and them that are with him, who despise the king's commandment.

15 So he made him ready to go up, and there went with him a mighty host of the un-godly to help him, and to be avenged of the children of Israel.

16 And when he came near to the going up of Bĕth-hō'-rŏn, Judas went forth to meet him with a small company:

17 Who, when they saw the host coming to meet them, said unto Judas, How shall we be able, being so few, to fight against so great a multitude *and* so strong, seeing we are ready to faint with fasting all this day?

18 Unto whom Judas answered, It is no hard matter for many to be shut up in the hands of a few; and with *the God of* heaven it is all one, to deliver with a great multitude, or a small company:

19 For the victory of battle standeth not in the multitude of an host; but strength cometh from heaven.

20 They come against us in much pride and iniquity to destroy us, and our wives and children, and to spoil us:

21 But we fight for our lives and our laws.

22 Wherefore the Lord himself will overthrow them before our face: and as for you, be ye not afraid of them.

23 Now as soon as he had left off speaking, he leapt suddenly upon them, and so Sē'-rŏn and his host was overthrown before him.

24 And they pursued them from the going down of Bĕth-hō'-rŏn unto the plain, where were slain about eight hundred men of them; and the residue fled into the land of the Phĭ-lĭs'-tĭnes.

25 Then began the fear of Judas and his brethren, and an exceeding great dread, to fall

upon the nations round about them:

26 Insomuch as his fame came unto the king, and all nations talked of the battles of Judas.

27 Now when king Ăn-tī'-ŏ-chŭs heard these things, he was full of indignation: wherefore he sent and gathered together all the forces of his realm, *even* a very strong army.

28 He opened also his treasure, and gave his soldiers pay for a year, commanding them to be ready whensoever he should need them.

29 Nevertheless, when he saw that the money of his treasures failed, and that the tributes in the country were small, because of the dissension and plague, which he had brought upon the land in taking away the laws which had been of old time;

30 He feared that he should not be able to bear the charges any longer, nor to have such gifts to give so liberally as he did before: for he had abounded above the kings that were before him.

31 Wherefore, being greatly perplexed in his mind, he determined to go into Persia, there to take the tributes of the countries, and to gather much money.

32 So he left Lўs'-ĭ-ăs, a nobleman, and one of the blood royal, to oversee the affairs of the king from the river Eū-phrā'-tēs unto the borders of Egypt:

33 And to bring up his son Ăn-tī'-ŏ-chŭs, until he came again.

34 Moreover he delivered unto him the half of his forces, and the elephants, and gave

him charge of all things that he would have done, as also concerning them that dwelt in Juda and Jerusalem:

35 *To wit*, that he should send an army against them, to destroy and root out the strength of Israel, and the remnant of Jerusalem, and to take away their memorial from that place;

36 And that he should place strangers in all their quarters, and divide their land by lot.

37 So the king took the half of the forces that remained, and departed from Antioch, his royal city, the hundred forty and seventh year; and having passed the river Eū-phrā'-tēs, he went through the high countries.

38 Then Lўs'-ĭ-ăs chose Ptŏl'-ŏ-mēē the *son* of Dŏ-rŷm'-ŏ-nēs, and Nī-cā'-nôr, and Gôr'-ġi-ăs, mighty men of the king's friends:

39 And with them he sent forty thousand footmen, and seven thousand horsemen, to go into the land of Juda, and to destroy it, as the king commanded.

40 So they went forth with all their power, and came and pitched by Ĕm-mā'-ŭs in the plain country.

41 And the merchants of the country, hearing the fame of them, took silver and gold very much, with servants, and came into the camp to buy the children of Israel for slaves: a power also of Syria and of the land of the Phĭ-lis'-tĭnes joined themselves unto them.

42 Now when Judas and his brethren saw that miseries were multiplied, and that the forces did encamp themselves in their borders; for they knew

how the king had given commandment to destroy the the people, and utterly abolish them;

43 They said one to another, Let us restore the decayed estate of our people, and let us fight for our people and the sanctuary.

44 Then was the congregation gathered together, that they might be ready for battle, and that they might pray, and ask mercy and compassion.

45 Now Jerusalem lay void as a wilderness, there was none of her children that went in or out: the sanctuary also was trodden down, and aliens kept the strong hold; the heathen had their habitation in that place; and joy was taken from Jacob, and the pipe with the harp ceased.

46 Wherefore the Israelites assembled themselves together, and came to Mas'-phá, over against Jerusalem; for in Maspha was the place where they prayed aforetime in Israel.

47 Then they fasted that day, and put on sackcloth, and cast ashes upon their heads, and rent their clothes,

48 And laid open the book of the law, wherein the heathen had sought to paint the likeness of their images.

49 They brought also the priests' garments, and the firstfruits, and the tithes: and the Nazarites they stirred up, who had accomplished their days.

50 Then cried they with a loud voice toward heaven, saying, What shall we do with these, and whither shall we carry them away?

51 For thy sanctuary is trodden down and profaned, and thy priests are in heaviness, and brought low.

52 And, lo, the heathen are assembled together against us to destroy us: what things they imagine against us, thou knowest.

53 How shall we be able to stand against them, except thou, O God, be our help?

54 Then sounded they with trumpets, and cried with a loud voice.

55 And after this Judas ordained captains over the people, *even* captains over thousands, and over hundreds, and over fifties, and over tens.

56 But as for such as were building houses, or had betrothed wives, or were planting vineyards, or were fearful, those he commanded that they should return, every man to his own house, according to the law.

57 So the camp removed, and pitched upon the south side of Ĕm-mā'-ŭs.

58 And Judas said, Arm yourselves, and be valiant men, and see that ye be in readiness against the morning, that ye may fight with these nations, that are assembled together against us to destroy us and our sanctuary:

59 For it is better for us to die in battle, than to behold the calamities of our people and our sanctuary.

60 Nevertheless, as the will *of* God is in heaven, so let him do.

CHAPTER IV

THEN took Gôr'-ġi-ăs five thousand footmen, and a thousand of the best horsemen, and removed out of the camp by night;

2 To the end he might rush in upon the camp of the Jews, and smite them suddenly. And the men of the fortress were his guides.

3 Now when Judas heard thereof, he himself removed, and the valiant men with him, that he might smite the king's army which was at Ĕm-mā'-ŭs,

4 While as yet the forces were dispersed from the camp.

5 In the mean season came Gôr'-ġi-ăs by night into the camp of Judas: and when he found no man there, he sought them in the mountains: for said he, These fellows flee from us.

6 But as soon as it was day, Judas shewed himself in the plain with three thousand men, who nevertheless had neither armour nor swords to their minds.

7 And they saw the camp of the heathen, that it was strong and well harnessed, and compassed round about with horsemen; and these were expert of war.

8 Then said Judas to the men that were with him, Fear ye not their multitude, neither be ye afraid of their assault.

9 Remember how our fathers were delivered in the Red sea, when Phā'-rāōh pursued them with an army.

10 Now therefore let us cry unto heaven, if peradventure the Lord will have mercy upon us, and remember the covenant of our fathers, and destroy this host before our face this day:

11 That so all the heathen may know that there is one who delivereth and saveth Israel.

12 Then the strangers lifted up their eyes, and saw them coming over against them.

13 Wherefore they went out of the camp to battle; but they that were with Judas sounded their trumpets.

14 So they joined battle, and the heathen being discomfited fled into the plain.

15 Howbeit all the hindmost of them were slain with the sword: for they pursued them unto Gă-zē'-ră, and unto the plains of Ĭd-ŭ-mē'-ă, and Ă-zō'-tŭs, and Jăm'-nĭ-ă, so that there were slain of them upon a three thousand men.

16 This done, Judas returned again with his host from pursuing them,

17 And said to the people, Be not greedy of the spoils, inasmuch as there is a battle before us,

18 And Gôr'-ġi-ăs and his host are here by us in the mountain: but stand ye now against our enemies, and overcome them, and after this ye may boldly take the spoils.

19 As Judas was yet speaking these words, there appeared a part of them looking out of the mountain:

20 Who when they perceived that the Jews had put their host to flight, and were burning the tents; for the smoke that was seen declared what was done:

21 When therefore they perceived these things, they were sore afraid, and seeing also the host of Judas in the plain ready to fight,

22 They fled every one into the land of strangers.

23 Then Judas returned to spoil the tents, where they got much gold, and silver, and blue

silk, and purple of the sea, and great riches.

24 After this they went home, and sung a song of thanksgiving, and praised the Lord in heaven: because it is good, because his mercy *endureth* for ever.

25 Thus Israel had a great deliverance that day.

26 Now all the strangers that had escaped came and told Lўs'-ĭ-ăs what had happened:

27 Who, when he heard thereof, was confounded and discouraged, because neither such things as he would were done unto Israel, nor such things as the king commanded him were come to pass.

28 The next year therefore following Lўs'-ĭ-ăs gathered together threescore thousand choice men *of foot*, and five thousand horsemen, that he might subdue them.

29 So they came into Ĭd-ŭ-mē'-ă, and pitched their tents at Bĕth-sū'-ră, and Judas met them with ten thousand men.

30 And when he saw that mighty army, he prayed and said, Blessed art thou, O Saviour of Israel, who didst quell the violence of the mighty man by the hand of thy servant David, and gavest the host of strangers into the hands of Jonathan the son of Saul, and his armourbearer;

31 Shut up this army in the hand of thy people Israel, and let them be confounded in their power and horsemen:

32 Make them to be of no courage, and cause the boldness of their strength to fall away, and let them quake at their destruction:

33 Cast them down with the sword of them that love thee,

and let all those that know thy name praise thee with thanksgiving.

34 So they joined battle; and there were slain of the host of Lўs'-ĭ-ăs about five thousand men, even before them were they slain.

35 Now when Lўs'-ĭ-ăs saw his army put to flight, and the manliness of Judas' soldiers, and how they were ready either to live or die valiantly, he went into Ăn'-tĭ-ŏ'-chĭ-ă, and gathered together a company of strangers, and having made his army greater than it was, he purposed to come again into Judea.

36 Then said Judas and his brethren, Behold, our enemies are discomfited: let us go up to cleanse and dedicate the sanctuary.

37 Upon this all the host assembled themselves together, and went up into mount Sion.

38 And when they saw the sanctuary desolate, and the altar profaned, and the gates burned up, and shrubs growing in the courts as in a forest, or in one of the mountains, yea, and the priests' chambers pulled down;

39 They rent their clothes, and made great lamentation, and cast ashes upon their heads,

40 And fell down flat to the ground upon their faces, and blew an alarm with the trumpets, and cried toward heaven.

41 Then Judas appointed certain men to fight against those that were in the fortress, until he had cleansed the sanctuary.

42 So he chose priests of blameless conversation, such as had pleasure in the law:

43 Who cleansed the sanctuary, and bare out the defiled stones into an unclean place.

44 And when as they consulted what to do with the altar of burnt offerings, which was profaned;

45 They thought it best to pull it down, lest it should be a reproach to them, because the heathen had defiled it: wherefore they pulled it down,

46 And laid up the stones in the mountain of the temple in a convenient place, until there should come a prophet to shew what should be done with them.

47 Then they took whole stones according to the law, and built a new altar according to the former;

48 And made up the sanctuary, and the things that were within the temple, and hallowed the courts.

49 They made also new holy vessels, and into the temple they brought the candlestick, and the altar of burnt offerings, and of incense, and the table.

50 And upon the altar they burned incense, and the lamps that were upon the candlestick they lighted, that they might give light in the temple.

51 Furthermore they set the loaves upon the table, and spread out the veils, and finished all the works which they had begun to make.

52 Now on the five and twentieth day of the ninth month, which *is called* the month Căs´-lĕu, in the hundred forty and eighth year, they rose up betimes in the morning,

53 And offered sacrifice according to the law upon the new altar of burnt offerings, which they had made.

54 Look, at what time and what day the heathen had profaned it, even in that was it dedicated with songs, and citherns, and harps, and cymbals.

55 Then all the people fell upon their faces, worshipping and praising the God of heaven, who had given them good success.

56 And so they kept the dedication of the altar eight days, and offered burnt offerings with gladness, and sacrificed the sacrifice of deliverance and praise.

57 They decked also the forefront of the temple with crowns of gold, and with shields; and the gates and the chambers they renewed, and hanged doors upon them.

58 Thus was there very great gladness among the people, for that the reproach of the heathen was put away.

59 Moreover Judas and his brethren with the whole congregation of Israel ordained, that the days of the dedication of the altar should be kept in their season from year to year by the space of eight days, from the five and twentieth day of the month Căs´-lĕu, with mirth and gladness.

60 At that time also they builded up the mount Sion with high walls and strong towers round about, lest the Gentiles should come and tread it down, as they had done before.

61 And they set there a garrison to keep it, and fortified Bĕth-sū´-ră to preserve it; that the people might have a defence against Ĭd-ū-mē´-ă.

224

CHAPTER V

NOW when the nations round about heard that the altar was built, and the sanctuary renewed as before, it displeased them very much.

2 Wherefore they thought to destroy the generation of Jacob that was among them, and thereupon they began to slay and destroy the people.

3 Then Judas fought against the children of Esau in Ĭd-ŭ-mē'-ă at Ăr'-ă-băt'-tĭ-nĕ, because they besieged Israel: and he gave them a great overthrow, and abated their courage, and took their spoils.

4 Also he remembered the injury of the children of Bē'-ăn, who had been a snare and an offence unto the people, in that they lay in wait for them in the ways.

5 He shut them up therefore in the towers, and encamped against them, and destroyed them utterly, and burned the towers of that *place* with fire, and all that were therein.

6 Afterward he passed over to the children of Ammon, where he found a mighty power, and much people, with Tĭ-mō'-thĕ-ŭs their captain.

7 So he fought many battles with them, till at length they were discomfited before him; and he smote them.

8 And when he had taken Jā'-zăr, with the towns belonging thereto, he returned into Judea.

9 Then the heathen that were at Găl'-ă-ăd assembled themselves together against the Israelites that were in their quarters, to destroy them; but they fled to the fortress of Dăth'-ĕ-mă,

10 And sent letters unto Judas and his brethren, The heathen that are round about us are assembled together against us to destroy us:

11 And they are preparing to come and take the fortress whereunto we are fled, Tĭ-mō'-thĕ-ŭs being captain of their host.

12 Come now therefore, and deliver us from their hands, for many of us are slain:

13 Yea, all our brethren that were in the places of Tŏ'-bīē are put to death: their wives and their children also they have carried away captives, and borne away their stuff; and they have destroyed there about a thousand men.

14 While these letters were yet reading, behold, there came other messengers from Galilee with their clothes rent, who reported on this wise,

15 And said, They of Ptŏl-ĕ-mā'-ĭs, and of Tyrus, and Sidon, and all Galilee of the Gentiles, are assembled together against us to consume us.

16 Now when Judas and the people heard these words, there assembled a great congregation together, to consult what they should do for their brethren, that were in trouble, and assaulted of them.

17 Then said Judas unto Simon his brother, Choose thee out men, and go and deliver thy brethren that are in Galilee, for I and Jonathan my brother will go into the country of Găl'-ă-ăd.

18 So he left Joseph the *son* of Zăch-ă-rī'-ăs, and Ăz-ă-rī'-ăs, captains of the people, with the remnant of the host in Judea to keep it.

19 Unto whom he gave

H

commandment, saying, Take ye the charge of this people, and see that ye make not war against the heathen until the time that we come again.

20 Now unto Simon were given three thousand men to go into Galilee, and unto Judas eight thousand men for the country of Găl´-ă-ăd.

21 Then went Simon into Galilee, where he fought many battles with the heathen, so that the heathen were discomfited by him.

22 And he pursued them unto the gate of Ptŏl-ĕ-mā´-ĭs; and there were slain of the heathen about three thousand men, whose spoils he took.

23 And those that were in Galilee, and in Är-băt´-tĭs, with their wives and their children, and all that they had, took he away *with him*, and brought them into Judea with great joy.

24 Judas Măc-că-bē´-ŭs also and his brother Jonathan went over Jordan, and travelled three days' journey in the wilderness,

25 Where they met with the Năb´-ă-thītes, who came unto them in a peaceable manner, and told them every thing that had happened to their brethren in the land of Găl´-ă-ăd:

26 And how that many of them were shut up in Bŏs´-ŏ-ră, and Bō´-sôr, and Ăl´-ĕ-mă, Căs´-phôr, Mā´-kĕd, and Cär´-nă-ĭm; all these cities are strong and great:

27 And that they were shut up in the rest of the cities of the country of Găl´-ă-ăd, and that against to morrow they had appointed to bring their host against the forts, and to take them, and to destroy them all in one day.

28 Hereupon Judas and his host turned suddenly by the way of the wilderness unto Bŏs´-ŏ-ră; and when he had won the city, he slew all the males with the edge of the sword, and took all their spoils, and burned the city with fire.

29 From whence he removed by night, and went till he came to the fortress.

30 And betimes in the morning they looked up, and, behold, there was an innumerable people bearing ladders and other engines of war, to take the fortress: for they assaulted them.

31 When Judas therefore saw that the battle was begun, and that the cry of the city went up to heaven, with trumpets, and a great sound,

32 He said unto his host, Fight this day for your brethren.

33 So he went forth behind them in three companies, who sounded their trumpets, and cried with prayer.

34 Then the host of Tĭ-mō´-thĕ-ŭs, knowing that it was Măc-că-bē´-ŭs, fled from him: wherefore he smote them with a great slaughter; so that there were killed of them that day about eight thousand men.

35 This done, Judas turned aside to Măs´-phă; and after he had assaulted it, he took it, and slew all the males therein, and received the spoils thereof, and burnt it with fire.

36 From thence went he, and took Căs´-phŏn, Mā´-gĕd, Bō´-sôr, and the other cities of the country of Găl´-ă-ăd.

37 After these things gathered Tĭ-mō´-thĕ-ŭs another host, and encamped against Rā´-phŏn beyond the brook.

38 So Judas sent *men* to espy the host, who brought him word, saying, All the heathen that be round about us are assembled unto them, even a very great host.

39 He hath also hired the Arabians to help them, and they have pitched their tents beyond the brook, ready to come and fight against thee. Upon this Judas went to meet them.

40 Then Tĭ-mō'-thĕ-ŭs said unto the captains of his host, When Judas and his host come near the brook, if he pass over first unto us, we shall not be able to withstand him; for he will mightily prevail against us:

41 But if he be afraid, and camp beyond the river, we shall go over unto him, and prevail against him.

42 Now when Judas came near the brook, he caused the scribes of the people to remain by the brook: unto whom he gave commandment, saying, Suffer no man to remain in the camp, but let all come to the battle.

43 So he went first over unto them, and all the people after him: then all the heathen, being discomfited before him, cast away their weapons, and fled unto the temple that was at Cär'-nă-ĭm.

44 But they took the city, and burned the temple with all that were therein. Thus was Cär'-nă-ĭm subdued, neither could they stand any longer before Judas.

45 Then Judas gathered together all the Israelites that were in the country of Găl'-ă-ăd, from the least unto the greatest, even their wives, and their children, and their stuff, a very great host, to the end they might come into the land of Judea.

46 Now when they came unto E'-phrŏn, (this was a great city in the way as they should go, very well fortified) they could not turn from it, either on the right hand or the left, but must needs pass through the midst of it.

47 Then they of the city shut them out, and stopped up the gates with stones.

48 Whereupon Judas sent unto them in peaceable manner, saying, Let us pass through your land to go into our own country, and none shall do you any hurt; we will only pass through on foot: howbeit they would not open unto him.

49 Wherefore Judas commanded a proclamation to be made throughout the host, that every man should pitch his tent in the place where he was.

50 So the soldiers pitched, and assaulted the city all that day and all that night, till at the length the city was delivered into his hands:

51 Who then slew all the males with the edge of the sword, and rased the city, and took the spoils thereof, and passed through the city over them that were slain.

52 After this went they over Jordan into the great plain before Bĕth-săn'.

53 And Judas gathered together those that came behind, and exhorted the people all the way through, till they came into the land of Judea.

54 So they went up to mount Sion with joy and gladness, where they offered burnt

offerings, because not one of them were slain until they had returned in peace.

55 Now what time as Judas and Jonathan were in the land of Găl-ă-ăd, and Simon his brother in Galilee before Ptŏl-ĕ-mā'-ĭs,

56 Joseph the *son* of Zăch-ă-rī'-ăs, and Ăz-ă-rī'-ăs, captains of the garrisons, heard of the valiant acts and warlike deeds which they had done.

57 Wherefore they said, Let us also get us a name, and go fight against the heathen that are round about us.

58 So when they had given charge unto the garrison that was with them, they went toward Jăm'-nĭ-a.

59 Then came Gôr'-gĭ-ăs and his men out of the city to fight against them.

60 And so it was, that Joseph and Ăz-ă-rī'-ăs were put to flight, and pursued unto the borders of Judea: and there were slain that day of the people of Israel about two thousand men.

61 Thus was there a great overthrow among the children of Israel, because they were not obedient unto Judas and his brethren, but thought to do some valiant act.

62 Moreover these men came not of the seed of those, by whose hand deliverance was given unto Israel.

63 Howbeit the man Judas and his brethren were greatly renowned in the sight of all Israel, and of all the heathen, wheresoever their name was heard of;

64 Insomuch as the people assembled unto them with joyful acclamations.

65 Afterward went Judas

forth with his brethren, and fought against the children of Esau in the land toward the south, where he smote Hē'-brŏn, and the towns thereof, and pulled down the fortress of it, and burned the towers thereof round about.

66 From thence he removed to go into the land of the Phĭ-lĭs'-tīnes, and passed through Samaria.

67 At that time certain priests, desirous to shew their valour, were slain in battle, for that they went out to fight unadvisedly.

68 So Judas turned to Ă-zō'-tŭs in the land of the Phĭ-lĭs'-tīnes, and when he had pulled down their altars, and burned their carved images with fire, and spoiled their cities, he returned into the land of Judea.

CHAPTER VI

ABOUT that time king Ăn-tī'-ŏ-chŭs travelling through the high countries heard say, that Ĕl-ȳ-mā'-ĭs in the country of Persia was a city greatly renowned for riches, silver, and gold;

2 And that there was in it a very rich temple, wherein were coverings of gold, and breastplates, and shields, which Alexander, *son* of Philip, the Macedonian king, who reigned first among the Grecians, had left there.

3 Wherefore he came and sought to take the city, and to spoil it; but he was not able, because they of the city, having had warning thereof,

4 Rose up against him in battle: so he fled, and departed thence with great heaviness, and returned to Babylon.

5 Moreover there came one who brought him tidings into Persia, that the armies, which went against the land of Judea, were put to flight:

6 And that Lўs'-ị-ăs, who went forth first with a great power, was driven away of the Jews; and that they were made strong by the armour, and power, and store of spoils, which they had gotten of the armies, whom they had destroyed:

7 Also that they had pulled down the abomination, which he had set up upon the altar in Jerusalem, and that they had compassed about the sanctuary with high walls, as before, and his city Běth-sū'-rȧ.

8 Now when the king heard these words, he was astonished and sore moved: whereupon he laid him down upon his bed, and fell sick for grief, because it had not befallen him as he looked for.

9 And there he continued many days: for his grief was ever more and more, and he made account that he should die.

10 Wherefore he called for all his friends, and said unto them, The sleep is gone from mine eyes, and my heart faileth for very care.

11 And I thought with myself, Into what tribulation am I come, and how great a flood *of misery* is it, wherein now I am! for I was bountiful and beloved in my power.

12 But now I remember the evils that I did at Jerusalem, and that I took all the vessels of gold and silver that were therein, and sent to destroy the inhabitants of Judea without a cause.

13 I perceive therefore that for this cause these troubles are come upon me, and, behold, I perish through great grief in a strange land.

14 Then called he for Philip, one of his friends, whom he made ruler over all his realm,

15 And gave him the crown, and his robe, and his signet, to the end he should bring up his son Ăn-tī'-ȯ-chŭs, and nourish him up for the kingdom.

16 So king Ăn-tī'-ȯ-chŭs died there in the hundred forty and ninth year.

17 Now when Lўs'-ị-ăs knew that the king was dead, he set up Ăn-tī'-ȯ-chŭs his son, whom he had brought up being young, to reign in his stead, and his name he called Ēu-pā'-tôr.

18 About this time they that were in the tower shut up the Israelites round about the sanctuary, and sought always their hurt, and the strengthening of the heathen.

19 Wherefore Judas, purposing to destroy them, called all the people together to besiege them.

20 So they came together, and besieged them in the hundred and fiftieth year, and he made mounts for shot against them, and *other* engines.

21 Howbeit certain of them that were besieged got forth, unto whom some ungodly men of Israel joined themselves:

22 And they went unto the king, and said, How long will it be ere thou execute judgment, and avenge our brethren?

23 We have been willing to serve thy father, and to do as he would have us, and to obey his commandments;

24 For which cause they of our nation besiege the tower, and are alienated from us: moreover as many of us as they could light on they slew, and spoiled our inheritance.

25 Neither have they stretched out their hand against us only, but also against all their borders.

26 And, behold, this day are they besieging the tower at Jerusalem, to take it: the sanctuary also and Bĕth-sū′-ră have they fortified.

27 Wherefore if thou dost not prevent them quickly, they will do greater things than these, neither shalt thou be able to rule them.

28 Now when the king heard this, he was angry, and gathered together all his friends, and the captains of his army, and those that had charge of the horse.

29 There came also unto him from other kingdoms, and from isles of the sea, bands of hired soldiers.

30 So that the number of his army was an hundred thousand footmen, and twenty thousand horsemen, and two and thirty elephants exercised in battle.

31 These went through Ĭd-ŭ-mē′-ă, and pitched against Bĕth-sū′-ră, which they assaulted many days, making engines of war; but they *of Bethsura* came out, and burned them with fire, and fought valiantly.

32 Upon this Judas removed from the tower, and pitched in Băth-zăch-ă-rī′-ăs, over against the king's camp.

33 Then the king rising very early marched fiercely with his host toward Băth-zăch-ă-rī′-ăs,

where his armies made them ready to battle, and sounded the trumpets.

34 And to the end they might provoke the elephants to fight, they shewed them the blood of grapes and mulberries.

35 Moreover they divided the beasts among the armies, and for every elephant they appointed a thousand men, armed with coats of mail, and with helmets of brass on their heads; and beside this, for every beast were ordained five hundred horsemen of the best.

36 These were ready at every occasion: wheresoever the beast was, and whithersoever the beast went, they went also, neither departed they from him.

37 And upon the beasts were there strong towers of wood, which covered every one of them, and were girt fast unto them with devices: there were also upon every one two and thirty strong men, that fought upon them, beside the Indian that ruled him.

38 As for the remnant of the horsemen, they set them on this side and that side at the two parts of the host, giving them signs what to do, and being harnessed all over amidst the ranks.

39 Now when the sun shone upon the shields of gold and brass, the mountains glistered therewith, and shined like lamps of fire.

40 So part of the king's army being spread upon the high mountains, and part on the valleys below, they marched on safely and in order.

41 Wherefore all that heard the noise of their multitude, and the marching of the

company, and the rattling of the harness, were moved: for the army was very great and mighty.

42 Then Judas and his host drew near, and entered into battle, and there were slain of the king's army six hundred men.

43 ¶ Ĕl-ē-ā'-zär also, *surnamed* Săv'-ă-răn, perceiving that one of the beasts, armed with royal harness, was higher than all the rest, and supposing that the king was upon him,

44 Put himself in jeopardy, to the end he might deliver his people, and get him a perpetual name:

45 Wherefore he ran upon him courageously through the midst of the battle, slaying on the right hand and on the left, so that they were divided from him on both sides.

46 Which done, he crept under the elephant, and thrust him under, and slew him: whereupon the elephant fell down upon him, and there he died.

47 Howbeit *the rest of the Jews* seeing the strength of the king, and the violence of his forces, turned away from them.

48 ¶ Then the king's army went up to Jerusalem to meet them, and the king pitched his tents against Judea, and against mount Sion.

49 But with them that were in Bĕth-sū'-rā he made peace: for they came out of the city, because they had no victuals there to endure the siege, it being a year of rest to the land.

50 So the king took Bĕth-sū'-rā, and set a garrison there to keep it.

51 As for the sanctuary, he besieged it many days: and set there artillery with engines and instruments to cast fire and stones, and pieces to cast darts and slings.

52 Whereupon they also made engines against their engines, and held them battle a long season.

53 Yet at the last, their vessels being without victuals, (for that it was the seventh year, and they in Judea, that were delivered from the Gentiles, had eaten up the residue of the store;)

54 There were but a few left in the sanctuary, because the famine did so prevail against them, that they were fain to disperse themselves, every man to his own place.

55 At that time Lўs'-į-ăs heard say, that Philip, whom Ăn-tī'-ŏ-chŭs the king, whiles he lived, had appointed to bring up his son Antiochus, that he might be king,

56 Was returned out of Persia and Mē'-dį-ă, and the king's host also that went with him, and that he sought to take unto him the ruling of the affairs.

57 Wherefore he went in all haste, and said to the king and the captains of the host and the company, We decay daily, and our victuals are but small, and the place we lay siege unto is strong, and the affairs of the kingdom lie upon us:

58 Now therefore let us be friends with these men, and make peace with them, and with all their nation;

59 And covenant with them, that they shall live after their laws, as they did before: for they are therefore displeased, and have done all these things, because we abolished their laws.

60 So the king and the princes were content: wherefore he sent unto them to make peace; and they accepted thereof.

61 Also the king and the princes made an oath unto them: whereupon they went out of the strong hold.

62 Then the king entered into mount Sion; but when he saw the strength of the place, he brake his oath that he had made, and gave commandment to pull down the wall round about.

63 Afterward departed he in all haste, and returned unto Ăn-tĭ-ŏ′-chĭ-ă, where he found Philip to be master of the city: so he fought against him, and took the city by force.

CHAPTER VII

IN the hundred and one and fiftieth year Dĕ-mē′-trĭ-ŭs the *son* of Sĕ-leū′-cŭs departed from Rome, and came up with a few men unto a city of the sea coast, and reigned there.

2 And as he entered into the palace of his ancestors, so it was, that his forces had taken Ăn-tĭ′-ŏ-chŭs and Lўs′-ĭ-ăs, to bring them unto him.

3 Wherefore, when he knew it, he said, Let me not see their faces.

4 So his host slew them. Now when Dĕ-mē′-trĭ-ŭs was set upon the throne of his kingdom,

5 There came unto him all the wicked and ungodly men of Israel, having Ăl′-çĭ-mŭs, who was desirous to be high priest, for their captain:

6 And they accused the people to the king, saying, Judas and his brethren have slain all thy friends, and driven us out of our own land.

7 Now therefore send some man whom thou trustest, and let him go and see what havock he hath made among us, and in the king's land, and let him punish them with all them that aid them.

8 Then the king chose Băc′-chĭ-dēs, a friend of the king, who ruled beyond the flood, and was a great man in the kingdom, and faithful to the king.

9 And him he sent with that wicked Ăl′-çĭ-mŭs, whom he made high priest, and commanded that he should take vengeance of the children of Israel.

10 So they departed, and came with a great power into the land of Judea, where they sent messengers to Judas and his brethren with peaceable words deceitfully.

11 But they gave no heed to their words; for they saw that they were come with a great power.

12 Then did there assemble unto Ăl′-çĭ-mŭs and Băc′-chĭ-dēs a company of scribes, to require justice.

13 Now the Ăs′-sĭ-dē′-ăns were the first among the children of Israel that sought peace of them:

14 For said they, One that is a priest of the seed of Aaron is come with this army, and he will do us no wrong.

15 So he spake unto them peaceably, and sware unto them, saying, We will procure the harm neither of you nor your friends.

16 Whereupon they believed him: howbeit he took of them threescore men, and slew them

232

in one day, according to the words which he wrote,

17 The flesh of thy saints *have they cast out*, and their blood have they shed round about Jerusalem, and there was none to bury them.

18 Wherefore the fear and dread of them fell upon all the people, who said, There is neither truth nor righteousness in them; for they have broken the covenant and oath that they made.

19 After this removed Băc'-chī-dēs from Jerusalem, and pitched his tents in Bē'-zĕth, where he sent and took many of the men that had forsaken him, and certain of the people also, and when he had slain them, *he cast them* into the great pit.

20 Then committed he the country to Ăl'-çĭ-mŭs, and left with him a power to aid him: so Băc'-chī-dēs went to the king.

21 But Ăl'-çĭ-mŭs contended for the high priesthood.

22 And unto him resorted all such as troubled the people, who, after they had gotten the land of Juda into their power, did much hurt in Israel.

23 Now when Judas saw all the mischief that Ăl'-çĭ-mŭs and his company had done among the Israelites, even above the heathen,

24 He went out into all the coasts of Judea round about, and took vengeance of them that had revolted from him, so that they durst no more go forth into the country.

25 On the other side, when Ăl'-çĭ-mŭs saw that Judas and his company had gotten the upper hand, and knew that he was not able to abide their

force, he went again to the king, and said all the worst of them that he could.

26 Then the king sent Nī-cā'-nôr, one of his honourable princes, a man that bare deadly hate unto Israel, with commandment to destroy the people.

27 So Nī-cā'-nôr came to Jerusalem with a great force; and sent unto Judas and his brethren deceitfully with friendly words, saying,

28 Let there be no battle between me and you; I will come with a few men, that I may see you in peace.

29 He came therefore to Judas, and they saluted one another peaceably. Howbeit the enemies were prepared to take away Judas by violence.

30 Which thing after it was known to Judas, *to wit*, that he came unto him with deceit, he was sore afraid of him, and would see his face no more.

31 Nī-cā'-nôr also, when he saw that his counsel was discovered, went out to fight against Judas beside Căph'-ăr-săl'-ă-mă:

32 Where there were slain of Nī-cā'-nôr's side about five thousand men, and *the rest* fled into the city of David.

33 After this went Nī-cā'-nôr up to mount Sion, and there came out of the sanctuary certain of the priests and certain of the elders of the people, to salute him peaceably, and to shew him the burnt sacrifice that was offered for the king.

34 But he mocked them, and laughed at them, and abused them shamefully, and spake proudly,

35 And sware in his wrath, saying, Unless Judas and his

host be now delivered into my hands, if ever I come again in safety, I will burn up this house: and with that he went out in a great rage.

36 Then the priests entered in, and stood before the altar and the temple, weeping, and saying,

37 Thou, O Lord, didst choose this house to be called by thy name, and to be a house of prayer and petition for thy people:

38 Be avenged of this man and his host, and let them fall by the sword: remember their blasphemies, and suffer them not to continue any longer.

39 So Nĭ-cā′-nôr went out of Jerusalem, and pitched his tents in Bĕth-hŏ′-rŏn, where an host out of Syria met him.

40 But Judas pitched in Ăd′-ă-să with three thousand men, and there he prayed, saying,

41 O Lord, when they that were sent from the king of the Assyrians blasphemed, thine angel went out, and smote an hundred fourscore and five thousand of them.

42 Even so destroy thou this host before us this day, that the rest may know that he hath spoken blasphemously against thy sanctuary, and judge thou him according to his wickedness.

43 So the thirteenth day of the month Ă-där′ the hosts joined battle: but Nĭ-cā′-nôr's host was discomfited, and he himself was first slain in the battle.

44 Now when Nĭ-cā′-nôr's host saw that he was slain, they cast away their weapons, and fled.

45 Then they pursued after

them a day's journey, from Ăd′-ă-să unto Gă-zē′-ră, sounding an alarm after them with their trumpets.

46 Whereupon they came forth out of all the towns of Judea round about, and closed them in; so that they, turning back upon them that pursued them, were all slain with the sword, and not one of them was left.

47 Afterwards they took the spoils, and the prey, and smote off Nĭ-cā′-nôr's head, and his right hand, which he stretched out so proudly, and brought them away, and hanged them up toward Jerusalem.

48 For this cause the people rejoiced greatly, and they kept that day a day of great gladness.

49 Moreover they ordained to keep yearly this day, being the thirteenth of Ă-där′.

50 Thus the land of Juda was in rest a little while.

CHAPTER VIII

NOW Judas had heard of the fame of the Romans, that they were mighty and valiant men, and such as would lovingly accept all that joined themselves unto them, and make a league of amity with all that came unto them;

2 And that they were men of great valour. It was told him also of their wars and noble acts which they had done among the Galatians, and how they had conquered them, and brought them under tribute;

3 And what they had done in the country of Spain, for the winning of the mines of the silver and gold which is there;

4 And that by their policy

and patience they had conquered all the place, though it were very far from them; and the kings also that came against them from the uttermost part of the earth, till they had discomfited them, and given them a great overthrow, so that the rest did give them tribute every year:

5 Beside this, how they had discomfited in battle Philip, and Pĕr'-sĕus, king of the Cĭt'-ĭms, with others that lifted up themselves against them, and had overcome them:

6 How also Ăn-tī'-ŏ-chŭs the great king of Asia, that came against them in battle, having an hundred and twenty elephants, with horsemen, and chariots, and a very great army, was discomfited by them;

7 And how they took him alive, and covenanted that he and such as reigned after him should pay a great tribute, and give hostages, and that which was agreed upon,

8 And the country of India, and Mē'-dĭ-ă, and Lydia, and of the goodliest countries, which they took of him, and gave to king Eū-mē'-nēs:

9 Moreover how the Grecians had determined to come and destroy them;

10 And that they, having knowledge thereof, sent against them a certain captain, and fighting with them slew many of them, and carried away captives their wives and their children, and spoiled them, and took possession of their lands, and pulled down their strong holds, and brought them to be their servants unto this day:

11 It *was* told him besides, how they destroyed and brought under their dominion all other kingdoms and isles that at any time resisted them;

12 But with their friends and such as relied upon them they kept amity: and that they had conquered kingdoms both far and nigh, insomuch as all that heard of their name were afraid of them:

13 Also that, whom they would help to a kingdom, those reign; and whom again they would, they displace: finally, that they were greatly exalted:

14 Yet for all this none of them wore a crown, or was clothed in purple, to be magnified thereby:

15 Moreover how they had made for themselves a senate house, wherein three hundred and twenty men sat in council daily, consulting alway for the people, to the end they might be well ordered:

16 And that they committed their government to one man every year, who ruled over all their country, and that all were obedient to that one, and that there was neither envy nor emulation among them.

17 In consideration of these things, Judas chose Eū-pŏl'-ĕ-mŭs the son of John, *the son of* Ăc'-cos, and Jason the son of Ĕl-ĕ-ā'-zăr, and sent them to Rome, to make a league of amity and confederacy with them,

18 *And to intreat them* that they would take the yoke from them; for they saw that the kingdom of the Grecians did oppress Israel with servitude.

19 They went therefore to Rome, which was a very great journey, and came into the

235

senate, where they spake and said,

20 Judas Măc-că-bē´-ŭs with his brethren, and the people of the Jews, have sent us unto you, to make a confederacy and peace with you, and that we might be registered your confederates and friends.

21 So that matter pleased the Romans well.

22 And this is the copy of the epistle which *the senate* wrote back again in tables of brass, and sent to Jerusalem, that there they might have by them a memorial of peace and confederacy:

23 Good success be to the Romans, and to the people of the Jews, by sea and by land for ever: the sword also and enemy be far from them.

24 If there come first any war upon the Romans or any of their confederates throughout all their dominion,

25 The people of the Jews shall help them, as the time shall be appointed, with all their heart:

26 Neither shall they give any thing unto them that make war upon them, or aid them with victuals, weapons, money, or ships, as it hath seemed good unto the Romans; but they shall keep their covenants without taking any thing therefore.

27 In the same manner also, if war come first upon the nation of the Jews, the Romans shall help them with all their heart, according as the time shall be appointed them:

28 Neither shall victuals be given to them that take part against them, or weapons, or money, or ships, as it hath seemed good to the Romans;

but they shall keep their covenants, and that without deceit.

29 According to these articles did the Romans make a covenant with the people of the Jews.

30 Howbeit if hereafter the one party or the other shall think meet to add or diminish any thing, they may do it at their pleasures, and whatsoever they shall add or take away shall be ratified.

31 And as touching the evils that Dĕ-mē´-trĭ-ŭs doeth to the Jews, we have written unto him, saying, Wherefore hast thou made thy yoke heavy upon our friends and confederates the Jews?

32 If therefore they complain any more against thee, we will do them justice, and fight with thee by sea and by land.

CHAPTER IX

FURTHERMORE when Dĕ-mē´-trĭ-ŭs heard that Nĭ-cā´-nôr and his host were slain in battle, he sent Băc´-chĭ-dēs and Ăl´-çĭ-mŭs into the land of Judea the second time, and with them the chief strength of his host:

2 Who went forth by the way that leadeth to Găl´-gă-lă, and pitched their tents before Măs´-ă-lŏth, which is in Är-bē´-lă, and after they had won it, they slew much people.

3 Also the first month of the hundred fifty and second year they encamped before Jerusalem:

4 From whence they removed, and went to Bē´-rĕ-ă, with twenty thousand footmen and two thousand horsemen.

5 Now Judas had pitched his tents at Ĕl-ĕ-ā´-să, and three

thousand chosen men with him:

6 Who seeing the multitude of the other army to be so great were sore afraid; whereupon many conveyed themselves out of the host, insomuch as there abode of them no more but eight hundred men.

7 When Judas therefore saw that his host slipt away, and that the battle pressed upon him, he was sore troubled in mind, and much distressed, for that he had no time to gather them together.

8 Nevertheless unto them that remained he said, Let us arise and go up against our enemies, if peradventure we may be able to fight with them.

9 But they dehorted him, saying, We shall never be able: let us now rather save our lives, and hereafter we will return with our brethren, and fight against them: for we are but few.

10 Then Judas said, God forbid that I should do this thing, and flee away from them: if our time be come, let us die manfully for our brethren, and let us not stain our honour.

11 With that the host of Băc'-chĭ-dēs removed out of their tents, and stood over against them, their horsemen being divided into two troops, and their slingers and archers going before the host, and they that marched in the foreward were all mighty men.

12 As for Băc'-chĭ-dēs, he was in the right wing: so the host drew near on the two parts, and sounded their trumpets.

13 They also of Judas' side, even they sounded their trumpets also, so that the earth shook at the noise of the armies, and the battle continued from morning till night.

14 Now when Judas perceived that Băc'-chĭ-dēs and the strength of his army were on the right side, he took with him all the hardy men,

15 Who discomfited the right wing, and pursued them unto the mount Ā-zō'-tŭs.

16 But when they of the left wing saw that they of the right wing were discomfited, they followed upon Judas and those that were with him hard at the heels from behind:

17 Whereupon there was a sore battle, insomuch as many were slain on both parts.

18 Judas also was killed, and the remnant fled.

19 Then Jonathan and Simon took Judas their brother, and buried him in the sepulchre of his fathers in Mō'-dĭn.

20 Moreover they bewailed him, and all Israel made great lamentation for him, and mourned many days, saying,

21 How is the valiant man fallen, that delivered Israel!

22 As for the other things concerning Judas and his wars, and the noble acts which he did, and his greatness, they are not written: for they were very many.

23 ¶ Now after the death of Judas the wicked began to put forth their heads in all the coasts of Israel, and there arose up all such as wrought iniquity.

24 In those days also was there a very great famine, by reason whereof the country revolted, and went with them.

25 Then Băc'-chĭ-dēs chose the wicked men, and made them lords of the country.

26 And they made enquiry and search for Judas' friends, and brought them unto Băc'-chĭ-dēs, who took vengeance of them, and used them despitefully.

27 So was there a great affliction in Israel, the like whereof was not since the time that a prophet was not seen among them.

28 For this cause all Judas' friends came together, and said unto Jonathan,

29 Since thy brother Judas died, we have no man like him to go forth against our enemies, and Băc'-chĭ-dēs, and against them of our nation that are adversaries to us.

30 Now therefore we have chosen thee this day to be our prince and captain in his stead, that thou mayest fight our battles.

31 Upon this Jonathan took the governance upon him at that time, and rose up instead of his brother Judas.

32 But when Băc'-chĭ-dēs gat knowledge thereof, he sought for to slay him.

33 Then Jonathan, and Simon his brother, and all that were with him, perceiving that, fled into the wilderness of Thē-cŏ'-ĕ, and pitched their tents by the water of the pool Ăs'-phär.

34 Which when Băc'-chĭ-dēs understood, he came near to Jordan with all his host upon the sabbath day.

35 Now Jonathan had sent his brother John, a captain of the people, to pray his friends the Năb'-ă-thītes, that they might leave with them their carriage, which was much.

36 But the children of Jăm'-brī came out of Mĕd'-ă-bă, and 238

took John, and all that he had, and went their way with it.

37 After this came word to Jonathan and Simon his brother, that the children of Jăm'-brī made a great marriage, and were bringing the bride from Nă-dăb'-ă-thă with a great train, as being the daughter of one of the great princes of Chā'-nāan.

38 Therefore they remembered John their brother, and went up, and hid themselves under the covert of the mountain:

39 Where they lifted up their eyes, and looked, and, behold, there was much ado and great carriage: and the bridegroom came forth, and his friends and brethren, to meet them with drums, and instruments of musick, and many weapons.

40 Then Jonathan and they that were with him rose up against them from the place where they lay in ambush, and made a slaughter of them in such sort, as many fell down dead, and the remnant fled into the mountain, and they took all their spoils.

41 Thus was the marriage turned into mourning, and the noise of their melody into lamentation.

42 So when they had avenged fully the blood of their brother, they turned again to the marsh of Jordan.

43 Now when Băc'-chĭ-dēs heard hereof, he came on the sabbath day unto the banks of Jordan with a great power.

44 Then Jonathan said to his company, Let us go up now and fight for our lives, for it standeth not with us to day, as in time past:

45 For, behold, the battle is

before us and behind us, and the water of Jordan on this side and that side, the marsh likewise and wood, neither is there place for us to turn aside.

46 Wherefore cry ye now unto heaven, that ye may be delivered from the hand of your enemies.

47 With that they joined battle, and Jonathan stretched forth his hand to smite Băc̆-chĭ-dēs, but he turned back from him.

48 Then Jonathan and they that were with him leapt into Jordan, and swam over unto the farther bank: howbeit the other passed not over Jordan unto them.

49 So there were slain of Băc̆-chĭ-dēs' side that day about a thousand men.

50 Afterward returned *Băc̆-chĭ-dēs* to Jerusalem, and repaired the strong cities in Judea; the fort in Jericho, and Ĕm-mā'-ŭs, and Bĕth-hō'-ron, and Bethel, and Thăm'-nă-thă, Phăr'-ă-thō-nī, and Tā'-phon, *these did he strengthen* with high walls, with gates, and with bars.

51 And in them he set a garrison, that they might work malice upon Israel.

52 He fortified also the city Bĕth-sū'-ră, and Gă-zā'-ră, and the tower, and put forces in them, and provision of victuals.

53 Besides, he took the chief men's sons in the country for hostages, and put them into the tower at Jerusalem to be kept.

54 Moreover in the hundred fifty and third year, in the second month, Ăl'-çĭ-mŭs commanded that the wall of the inner court of the sanctuary should be pulled down; he pulled down also the works of the prophets.

55 And as he began to pull down, even at that time was Ăl'-çĭ-mŭs plagued, and his enterprizes hindered: for his mouth was stopped, and he was taken with a palsy, so that he could no more speak any thing, nor give order concerning his house.

56 So Ăl'-çĭ-mŭs died at that time with great torment.

57 Now when Băc̆'-chĭ-dēs saw that Ăl'-çĭ-mŭs was dead, he returned to the king: whereupon the land of Judea was in rest two years.

58 Then all the ungodly men held a council, saying, Behold, Jonathan and his company are at ease, and dwell without care: now therefore we will bring Băc̆'-chĭ-dēs hither, who shall take them all in one night.

59 So they went and consulted with him.

60 Then removed he, and came with a great host, and sent letters privily to his adherents in Judea, that they should take Jonathan and those that were with him: howbeit they could not, because their counsel was known unto them.

61 Wherefore they took of the men of the country, that were authors of that mischief, about fifty persons, and slew them.

62 Afterward Jonathan, and Simon, and they that were with him, got them away to Bĕth-bā'-sī, which is in the wilderness, and they repaired the decays thereof, and made it strong.

63 Which thing when Băc̆'-chĭ-dēs knew, he gathered

together all his host, and sent word to them that were of Judea.

64 Then went he and laid siege against Bĕth-bā´-sī; and they fought against it a long season, and made engines of war.

65 But Jonathan left his brother Simon in the city, and went forth himself into the country, and with a certain number went he forth.

66 And he smote Ŏd-ŏ-när´-kēs and his brethren, and the children of Phăs´-ĭ-ron in their tent.

67 And when he began to smite them, and came up with his forces, Simon and his company went out of the city, and burned up the engines of war,

68 And fought against Băc´-chī-dēs, who was discomfited by them, and they afflicted him sore: for his counsel and travail was in vain.

69 Wherefore he was very wroth at the wicked men that gave him counsel to come into the country, insomuch as he slew many of them, and purposed to return into his own country.

70 Whereof when Jonathan had knowledge, he sent ambassadors unto him, to the end he should make peace with him, and deliver them the prisoners.

71 Which thing he accepted, and did according to his demands, and sware unto him that he would never do him harm all the days of his life.

72 When therefore he had restored unto him the prisoners that he had taken aforetime out of the land of Judea, he returned and went his way into his own land, neither came

240

he any more into their borders.

73 Thus the sword ceased from Israel: but Jonathan dwelt at Măch´-măs, and began to govern the people; and he destroyed the ungodly men out of Israel.

CHAPTER X

IN the hundred and sixtieth year Alexander, the *son of* Ăn-tī´-ŏ-chŭs *surnamed* Ē-pĭph´-ă-nēs, went up and took Ptŏl-ē-mā´-ĭs: for the people had received him, by means whereof he reigned there.

2 Now when king Dĕ-mē´-trĭ-ŭs heard thereof, he gathered together an exceeding great host, and went forth against him to fight.

3 Moreover Dĕ-mē´-trĭ-ŭs sent letters unto Jonathan with loving words, so as he magnified him.

4 For said he, Let us first make peace with him, before he join with Alexander against us:

5 Else he will remember all the evils that we have done against him, and against his brethren and his people.

6 Wherefore he gave him authority to gather together an host, and to provide weapons, that he might aid him in battle: he commanded also that the hostages that were in the tower should be delivered him.

7 Then came Jonathan to Jerusalem, and read the letters in the audience of all the people, and of them that were in the tower:

8 Who were sore afraid, when they heard that the king had given him authority to gather together an host.

9 Whereupon they of the tower delivered their hostages unto Jonathan, and he delivered them unto their parents.

10 This done, Jonathan settled himself in Jerusalem, and began to build and repair the city.

11 And he commanded the workmen to build the walls and the mount Sion round about with square stones for fortification; and they did so.

12 Then the strangers, that were in the fortresses which Băc'-chĭ-dēs had built, fled away;

13 Insomuch as every man left his place, and went into his own country.

14 Only at Bĕth-sū'-rā certain of those that had forsaken the law and the commandments remained still: for it was their place of refuge.

15 Now when king Alexander had heard what promises Dĕ-mē'-trĭ-ŭs had sent unto Jonathan: when also it was told him of the battles and noble acts which he and his brethren had done, and of the pains that they had endured,

16 He said, Shall we find such another man? now therefore we will make him our friend and confederate.

17 Upon this he wrote a letter, and sent it unto him, according to these words, saying,

18 King Alexander to his brother Jonathan sendeth greeting:

19 We have heard of thee, that thou art a man of great power, and meet to be our friend.

20 Wherefore now this day we ordain thee to be the high priest of thy nation, and to be called the king's friend; (and

therewithal he sent him a purple robe and a crown of gold:) and *require thee* to take our part, and keep friendship with us.

21 So in the seventh month of the hundred and sixtieth year, at the feast of the tabernacles, Jonathan put on the holy robe, and gathered together forces, and provided much armour.

22 Whereof when Dĕ-mē'-trĭ-ŭs heard, he was very sorry, and said,

23 What have we done, that Alexander hath prevented us in making amity with the Jews to strengthen himself?

24 I also will write unto them words of encouragement, *and promise them* dignities and gifts, that I may have their aid.

25 He sent unto them therefore to this effect: King Dĕ-mē'-trĭ-ŭs unto the people of the Jews sendeth greeting:

26 Whereas ye have kept covenants with us, and continued in our friendship, not joining yourselves with our enemies, we have heard hereof, and are glad.

27 Wherefore now continue ye still to be faithful unto us, and we will well recompense you for the things ye do in our behalf,

28 And will grant you many immunities, and give you rewards.

29 And now do I free you, and for your sake I release all the Jews, from tributes, and from the customs of salt, and from crown taxes,

30 And from that which appertaineth unto me to receive for the third part of the seed, and the half of the fruit of the trees, I release it from

this day forth, so that they shall not be taken of the land of Judea, nor of the three governments which are added thereunto out of the country of Samaria and Galilee, from this day forth for evermore.

31 Let Jerusalem also be holy and free, with the borders thereof, both from tenths and tributes.

32 And as for the tower which is at Jerusalem, I yield up my authority over it, and give it to the high priest, that he may set in it such men as he shall choose to keep it.

33 Moreover I freely set at liberty every one of the Jews, that were carried captives out of the land of Judea into any part of my kingdom, and I *will* that all my officers remit the tributes even of their cattle.

34 Furthermore I *will* that all the feasts, and sabbaths, and new moons, and solemn days, and the three days before the feast, and the three days after the feast, shall be all days of immunity and freedom for all the Jews in my realm.

35 Also no man shall have authority to meddle *with them*, or to molest any of them in any matter.

36 I *will* further, that there be enrolled among the king's forces about thirty thousand men of the Jews, unto whom pay shall be given, as belongeth to all the king's forces.

37 And of them *some* shall be placed in the king's strong holds, of whom also *some* shall be set over the affairs of the kingdom, which are of trust: and I *will* that their overseers and governors be of themselves, and that they live after their own laws, even as the king hath commanded in the land of Judea.

38 And concerning the three governments that are added to Judea from the country of Samaria, let them be joined with Judea, that they may be reckoned to be under one, nor bound to obey other authority than the high priest's.

39 As for Ptŏl-ĕ-mā'-ĭs, and the land pertaining thereto, I give it as a free gift to the sanctuary at Jerusalem for the necessary expences of the sanctuary.

40 Moreover I give every year fifteen thousand shekels of silver out of the king's accounts from the places appertaining.

41 And all the overplus, which the officers payed not in as in former time, from henceforth shall be given toward the works of the temple.

42 And beside this, the five thousand shekels of silver, which they took from the uses of the temple out of the accounts year by year, even those things shall be released, because they appertain to the priests that minister.

43 And whosoever they be that flee unto the temple at Jerusalem, or be within the liberties thereof, being indebted unto the king, or for any other matter, let them be at liberty, and all that they have in my realm.

44 For the building also and repairing of the works of the sanctuary expences shall be given of the king's accounts.

45 Yea, and for the building of the walls of Jerusalem, and the fortifying thereof round about, expences shall be given out of the king's accounts, as

also for the building of the walls in Judea.

46 Now when Jonathan and the people heard these words, they gave no credit unto them, nor received them, because they remembered the great evil that he had done in Israel; for he had afflicted them very sore.

47 But with Alexander they were well pleased, because he was the first that entreated of true peace with them, and they were confederate with him always.

48 Then gathered king Alexander great forces, and camped over against Dĕ-mē'-trĭ-ŭs.

49 And after the two kings had joined battle, Dĕ-mē'-trĭ-ŭs' host fled: but Alexander followed after him, and prevailed against them.

50 And he continued the battle very sore until the sun went down: and that day was Dĕ-mē'-trĭ-ŭs slain.

51 Afterward Alexander sent ambassadors to Ptŏl'-ĕ-mee king of Egypt with a message to this effect:

52 Forasmuch as I am come again to my realm, and am set in the throne of my progenitors, and have gotten the dominion, and overthrown Dĕ-mē'-trĭ-ŭs, and recovered our country;

53 For after I had joined battle with him, both he and his host was discomfited by us, so that we sit in the throne of his kingdom:

54 Now therefore let us make a league of amity together, and give me now thy daughter to wife: and I will be thy son in law, and will give both thee and her gifts according to thy dignity.

55 Then Ptŏl'-ĕ-mee the king gave answer, saying, Happy be the day wherein thou didst return into the land of thy fathers, and satest in the throne of their kingdom.

56 And now will I do to thee, as thou hast written: meet me therefore at Ptŏl-ĕ-mā'-ĭs, that we may see one another; for I will marry my daughter to thee according to thy desire.

57 So Ptŏl'-ĕ-mee went out of Egypt with his daughter Cleopatra, and they came unto Ptŏl-ĕ-mā'-ĭs in the hundred threescore and second year:

58 Where king Alexander meeting him, he gave unto him his daughter Cleopatra, and celebrated her marriage at Ptŏl-ĕ-mā'-ĭs with great glory, as the manner of kings is.

59 Now king Alexander had written unto Jonathan, that he should come and meet him.

60 Who thereupon went honourably to Ptŏl-ĕ-mā'-ĭs, where he met the two kings, and gave them and their friends silver and gold, and many presents, and found favour in their sight.

61 At that time certain pestilent fellows of Israel, men of a wicked life, assembled themselves against him, to accuse him: but the king would not hear them.

62 Yea more than that, the king commanded to take off his garments, and clothe him in purple: and they did so.

63 Also he made him sit by himself, and said unto his princes, Go with him into the midst of the city, and make proclamation, that no man complain against him of any matter, and that no man

243

trouble him for any manner of cause.

64 Now when his accusers saw that he was honoured according to the proclamation, and clothed in purple, they fled all away.

65 So the king honoured him, and wrote him among his chief friends, and made him a duke, and partaker of his dominion.

66 Afterward Jonathan returned to . Jerusalem with peace and gladness.

67 Furthermore in the hundred threescore and fifth year came Dĕ-mē'-trĭ-ŭs son of Demetrius out of Crete into the land of his fathers:

68 Whereof when king Alexander heard tell, he was right sorry, and returned into Antioch.

69 Then Dĕ-mē'-trĭ-ŭs made Ăp'-ŏl-lō'-nĭ-ŭs the governor of Çē'-lŏ-sȳr'-ĭ-ă his general, who gathered together a great host, and camped in Jăm'-nĭ-ă, and sent unto Jonathan the high priest, saying,

70 Thou alone liftest up thyself against us, and I am laughed to scorn for thy sake, and reproached: and why dost thou vaunt thy power against us in the mountains?

71 Now therefore, if thou trustest in thine own strength, come down to us into the plain field, and there let us try the matter together: for with me is the power of the cities.

72 Ask and learn who I am, and the rest that take our part, and they shall tell thee that thy foot is not able to stand before our face; for thy fathers have been twice put to flight in their own land.

73 Wherefore now thou shalt not be able to abide the horse-

men and so great a power in the plain, where is neither stone nor flint, nor place to flee unto.

74 So when Jonathan heard these words of Ăp'-ŏl-lō'-nĭ-ŭs, he was moved in his mind, and choosing ten thousand men he went out of Jerusalem, where Simon his brother met him for to help him.

75 And he pitched his tents against Jŏp'-pĕ: but they of Joppe shut him out of the city, because Ăp'-ŏl-lō'-nĭ-ŭs had a garrison there.

76 Then Jonathan laid siege unto it: whereupon they of the city let him in for fear: and so Jonathan won Jŏp'-pĕ.

77 Whereof when Ăp'-ŏl-lō'-nĭ-ŭs heard, he took three thousand horsemen, with a great host *of footmen*, and went to Ă-zō'-tŭs as one that journeyed, and therewithal drew him forth into the plain, because he had a great number of horsemen, in whom he put his trust.

78 Then *Jonathan* followed after him into Ă-zō'-tŭs, where the armies joined battle.

79 Now Ăp'-ŏl-lō'-nĭ-ŭs had left a thousand horsemen in ambush.

80 And Jonathan knew that there was an ambushment behind him; for they had compassed in his host, and cast darts at the people, from morning till evening.

81 But the people stood still, as Jonathan had commanded them: and so the enemies' horses were tired.

82 Then brought Simon forth his host, and set them against the footmen, (for the horsemen were spent,) who were discomfited by him, and fled.

83 The horsemen also, being scattered in the field, fled to Ă-zō´-tŭs, and went into Bĕth-dă´-gon, their idol's temple, for safety.

84 But Jonathan set fire on Ă-zō´-tŭs, and the cities round about it, and took their spoils; and the temple of Dagon, with them that were fled into it, he burned with fire.

85 Thus there were burned and slain with the sword well nigh eight thousand men.

86 And from thence Jonathan removed his host, and camped against Ăs´-că-lon, where the men of the city came forth, and met him with great pomp.

87 After this returned Jonathan and his host unto Jerusalem, having many spoils.

88 Now when king Alexander heard these things, he honoured Jonathan yet more,

89 And sent him a buckle of gold, as the use is to be given to such as are of the king's blood: he gave him also Ăc´-că-ron with the borders thereof in possession.

CHAPTER XI

AND the king of Egypt gathered together a great host, like the sand that lieth upon the sea shore, and many ships, and went about through deceit to get Alexander's kingdom, and join it to his own.

2 Whereupon he took his journey into Syria in peaceable manner, so as they of the cities opened unto him, and met him: for king Alexander had commanded them so to do, because he was his father in law.

3 Now as Ptŏl´-ĕ-mēē entered into the cities, he set in every one of them a garrison of soldiers to keep it.

4 And when he came near to Ă-zō´-tŭs, they shewed him the temple of Dagon that was burnt, and Azotus and the suburbs thereof that were destroyed, and the bodies that were cast abroad, and them that he had burnt in the battle; for they had made heaps of them by the way where he should pass.

5 Also they told the king whatsoever Jonathan had done, to the intent he might blame him: but the king held his peace.

6 Then Jonathan met the king with great pomp at Jŏp´-pĕ, where they saluted one another, and lodged.

7 Afterward Jonathan, when he had gone with the king to the river called Ē-lēū´-thĕr-ŭs, returned again to Jerusalem.

8 King Ptŏl´-ĕ-mēē therefore, having gotten the dominion of the cities by the sea unto Sĕ-lēū´-çi-ă upon the sea coast, imagined wicked counsels against Alexander.

9 Whereupon he sent ambassadors unto king Dĕ-mē´-trĭ-ŭs, saying, Come, let us make a league betwixt us, and I will give thee my daughter whom Alexander hath, and thou shalt reign in thy father's kingdom:

10 For I repent that I gave my daughter unto him, for he sought to slay me.

11 Thus did he slander him, because he was desirous of his kingdom.

12 Wherefore he took his daughter from him, and gave her to Dĕ-mē´-trĭ-ŭs, and forsook Alexander, so that their hatred was openly known.

245

13 Then Ptŏl'-ĕ-mee entered into Antioch, where he set two crowns upon his head, the crown of Asia, and of Egypt.

14 In the mean season was king Alexander in Çi-lïi'-çi-ă, because those that dwelt in those parts had revolted from him.

15 But when Alexander heard of this, he came to war against him: whereupon *king* Ptŏl'-ĕ-mee brought forth *his host*, and met him with a mighty power, and put him to flight.

16 So Alexander fled into Arabia, there to be defended; but king Ptŏl'-ĕ-mee was exalted:

17 For Zăb'-dï-ĕl the Arabian took off Alexander's head, and sent it unto Ptŏl'-ĕ-mee.

18 King Ptŏl'-ĕ-mee also died the third day after, and they that were in the strong holds were slain one of another.

19 By this means Dĕ-mē'-trï-ŭs reigned in the hundred threescore and seventh year.

20 At the same time Jonathan gathered together them that were in Judea, to take the tower that was in Jerusalem: and he made many engines of war against it.

21 Then certain ungodly persons, who hated their own people, went unto the king, and told him that Jonathan besieged the tower.

22 Whereof when he heard, he was angry, and immediately removing, he came to Ptŏl-ĕ-mā'-ĭs, and wrote unto Jonathan, that he should not lay siege to the tower, but come and speak with him at Ptolemais in great haste.

23 Nevertheless Jonathan, when he heard this, command-ed to besiege it *still*: and he

chose certain of the elders of Israel and the priests, and put himself in peril;

24 And took silver and gold, and raiment, and divers presents besides, and went to Ptŏl-ĕ-mā'-ĭs unto the king, where he found favour in his sight.

25 And though certain ungodly men of the people had made complaints against him,

26 Yet the king entreated him as his predecessors had done before, and promoted him in the sight of all his friends,

27 And confirmed him in the high priesthood, and in all the honours that he had before, and gave him preeminence among his chief friends.

28 Then Jonathan desired the king, that he would make Judea free from tribute, as also the three governments, with the country of Samaria; and he promised him three hundred talents.

29 So the king consented, and wrote letters unto Jonathan of all these things after this manner:

30 King Dĕ-mē'-trï-ŭs unto his brother Jonathan, and unto the nation of the Jews, sendeth greeting:

31 We send you here a copy of the letter which we did write unto our cousin Lăs'-thĕ-nĕs concerning you, that ye might see it.

32 King Dĕ-mē'-trï-ŭs unto his father Lăs'-thĕ-nĕs sendeth greeting:

33 We are determined to do good to the people of the Jews, who are our friends, and keep covenants with us, because of their good will toward us.

34 Wherefore we have ratified unto them the borders of Judea, with the three govern-

ments of Ă-phĕr'-ĕ-mă and Lydda and Răm'-ă-thĕm, that are added unto Judea from the country of Samaria, and all things appertaining unto them, for all such as do sacrifice in Jerusalem, instead of the payments which the king received of them yearly aforetime out of the fruits of the earth and of trees.

35 And as for other things that belong unto us, of the tithes and customs pertaining unto us, as also the saltpits, and the crown taxes, which are unto us, we discharge them of them all for their relief.

36 And nothing hereof shall be revoked from this time forth for ever.

37 Now therefore see that thou make a copy of these things, and let it be delivered unto Jonathan, and set upon the holy mount in a conspicuous place.

38 After this, when king Dĕ-mē'-trĭ-ŭs saw that the land was quiet before him, and that no resistance was made against him, he sent away all his forces, every one to his own place, except certain bands of strangers, whom he had gathered from the isles of the heathen: wherefore all the forces of his fathers hated him.

39 Moreover there was one Tryphon, that had been of Alexander's part afore, who, seeing that all the host murmured against Dĕ-mē'-trĭ-ŭs, went to Sĭ-măl-cū'-ē the Arabian, that brought up Ăn-tī'-ŏ-chŭs the young son of Alexander,

40 And lay sore upon him to deliver him *this young* Ăn-tī'-ŏ-chŭs, that he might reign in his father's stead: he told him therefore all that Dĕ-mē'-trĭ-ŭs had done, and how his men of war were at enmity with him, and there he remained a long season.

41 In the mean time Jonathan sent unto king Dĕ-mē'-trĭ-ŭs, that he would cast those of the tower out of Jerusalem, and those also in the fortresses: for they fought against Israel.

42 So Dĕ-mē'-trĭ-ŭs sent unto Jonathan, saying, I will not only do this for thee and thy people, but I will greatly honour thee and thy nation, if opportunity serve.

43 Now therefore thou shalt do well, if thou send me men to help me; for all my forces are gone from me.

44 Upon this Jonathan sent him three thousand strong men unto Antioch: and when they came to the king, the king was very glad of their coming.

45 Howbeit they that were of the city gathered themselves together into the midst of the city, to the number of an hundred and twenty thousand men, and would have slain the king.

46 Wherefore the king fled into the court, but they of the city kept the passages of the city, and began to fight.

47 Then the king called to the Jews for help, who came unto him all at once, and dispersing themselves through the city slew that day in the city to the number of an hundred thousand.

48 Also they set fire on the city, and gat many spoils that day, and delivered the king.

49 So when they of the city

saw that the Jews had got the city as they would, their courage was abated: wherefore they made supplication to the king, and cried, saying,

50 Grant us peace, and let the Jews cease from assaulting us and the city.

51 With that they cast away their weapons, and made peace; and the Jews were honoured in the sight of the king, and in the sight of all that were in his realm; and they returned to Jerusalem, having great spoils.

52 So king Dĕ-mē'-trĭ-ŭs sat on the throne of his kingdom, and the land was quiet before him.

53 Nevertheless he dissembled in all that ever he spake, and estranged himself from Jonathan, neither rewarded he him according to the benefits which he had received of him, but troubled him very sore.

54 After this returned Tryphon, and with him the young child Ăn-tī'-ŏ-chŭs, who reigned, and was crowned.

55 Then there gathered unto him all the men of war, whom Dĕ-mē'-trĭ-ŭs had put away, and they fought against Demetrius, who turned his back and fled.

56 Moreover Tryphon took the elephants, and won Antioch.

57 At that time young Ăn-tī'-ŏ-chŭs wrote unto Jonathan, saying, I confirm thee in the high priesthood, and appoint thee ruler over the four governments, and to be one of the king's friends.

58 Upon this he sent him golden vessels to be served in, and gave him leave to drink in gold, and to be clothed in

248

purple, and to wear a golden buckle.

59 His brother Simon also he made captain from the place called The ladder of Tyrus unto the borders of Egypt.

60 Then Jonathan went forth, and passed through the cities beyond the water, and all the forces of Syria gathered themselves unto him for to help him: and when he came to Ăs'-că-lŏn, they of the city met him honourably.

61 From whence he went to Gaza, but they of Gaza shut him out; wherefore he laid siege unto it, and burned the suburbs thereof with fire, and spoiled them.

62 Afterward, when they of Gaza made supplication unto Jonathan, he made peace with them, and took the sons of their chief men for hostages, and sent them to Jerusalem, and passed through the country unto Damascus.

63 Now when Jonathan heard that Dĕ-mē'-trĭ-ŭs' princes were come to Cā'-dēs, which is in Galilee, with a great power, purposing to remove him out of the country,

64 He went to meet them, and left Simon his brother in the country.

65 Then Simon encamped against Bĕth-sū'-ră, and fought against it a long season, and shut it up:

66 But they desired to have peace with him, which he granted them, and then put them out from thence, and took the city, and set a garrison in it.

67 As for Jonathan and his host, they pitched at the water of Gĕn-nē'-sär, from whence betimes in the morning they gat

them to the plain of Nā′-sôr.

68 And, behold, the host of strangers met them in the plain, who, having laid men in ambush for him in the mountains, came themselves over against him.

69 So when they that lay in ambush rose out of their places, and joined battle, all that were of Jonathan's side fled;

70 Insomuch as there was not one of them left, except Măt-tă-thī′-ăs the *son* of Absalom, and Judas the *son* of Căl′-phī, the captains of the host.

71 Then Jonathan rent his clothes, and cast earth upon his head, and prayed.

72 Afterwards turning again to battle, he put them to flight, and so they ran away.

73 Now when his own men that were fled saw this, they turned again unto him, and with him pursued them to Cā′-dēs, even unto their own tents, and there they camped.

74 So there were slain of the heathen that day about three thousand men: but Jonathan returned to Jerusalem.

CHAPTER XII

NOW when Jonathan saw that the time served him, he chose certain men, and sent them to Rome, for to confirm and renew the friendship that they had with them.

2 He sent letters also to the Lăc′-ĕ-dĕ-mō′-nĭ-ăns, and to other places, for the same purpose.

3 So they went unto Rome, and entered into the senate, and said, Jonathan the high priest, and the people of the Jews, sent us unto you, to the end ye should renew the friendship, which ye had with them, and league, as in former time.

4 Upon this *the Romans* gave them letters unto the governors of every place, that they should bring them into the land of Judea peaceably.

5 And this is the copy of the letters which Jonathan wrote to the Lăc′-ĕ-dĕ-mō′-nĭ-ăns:

6 Jonathan the high priest, and the elders of the nation, and the priests, and the other people of the Jews, unto the Lăc′-ĕ-dĕ-mō′-nĭ-ăns their brethren send greeting:

7 There were letters sent in times past unto Ŏ-nī′-ăs the high priest from Dă-rī′-ŭs, who reigned then among you, to signify that ye are our brethren, as the copy here underwritten doth specify.

8 At which time Ŏ-nī′-ăs entreated the ambassador that was sent honourably, and received the letters, wherein declaration was made of the league and friendship.

9 Therefore we also, albeit we need none of these things, for that we have the holy books of scripture in our hands to comfort us,

10 Have nevertheless attempted to send unto you for the renewing of brotherhood and friendship, lest we should become strangers unto you altogether: for there is a long time passed since ye sent unto us.

11 We therefore at all times without ceasing, both in our feasts, and other convenient days, do remember you in the sacrifices which we offer, and in our prayers, as reason is, and as it becometh us to think upon our brethren:

12 And we are right glad of your honour.

13 As for ourselves, we have had great troubles and wars on every side, forsomuch as the kings that are round about us have fought against us.

14 Howbeit we would not be troublesome unto you, nor to others of our confederates and friends, in these wars:

15 For we have help from heaven that succoureth us, so as we are delivered from our enemies, and our enemies are brought under foot.

16 For this cause we chose Nŭ-mḗ-nĭ-ŭs *the son* of Ăn-tī́-ŏ-chŭs, and Ăn-tĭ́p'-ă-tēr *the son* of Jason, and sent them unto the Romans, to renew the amity that we had with them, and the former league.

17 We commanded them also to go unto you, and to salute you, and to deliver you our letters concerning the renewing of our brotherhood.

18 Wherefore now ye shall do well to give us an answer thereto.

19 And this is the copy of the letters which Ō-nī́-ă-rēs sent.

20 Ä-rḗ'-ŭs king of the Lăç'-ĕ-dĕ-mō'-nĭ-ăns to Ō-nī́-ăs the high priest, greeting:

21 It is found in writing, that the Lăç'-ĕ-dĕ-mō'-nĭ-ăns and Jews are brethren, and that they are of the stock of Abraham:

22 Now therefore, since this is come to our knowledge, ye shall do well to write unto us of your prosperity.

23 We do write back again to you, that your cattle and goods are ours, and ours are yours. We do command therefore *our ambassadors* to make report unto you on this wise.

24 Now when Jonathan heard that Dĕ-mḗ'-trĭ-ŭs' princes were come to fight against him with a greater host than afore,

25 He removed from Jerusalem, and met them in the land of Ăm'-ă-thĭs: for he gave them no respite to enter his country.

26 He sent spies also unto their tents, who came again, and told him that they were appointed to come upon them in the night season.

27 Wherefore so soon as the sun was down, Jonathan commanded his men to watch, and to be in arms, that all the night long they might be ready to fight: also he sent forth centinels round about the host.

28 But when the adversaries heard that Jonathan and his men were ready for battle, they feared, and trembled in their hearts, and they kindled fires in their camp.

29 Howbeit Jonathan and his company knew it not till the morning: for they saw the lights burning.

30 Then Jonathan pursued after them, but overtook them not: for they were gone over the river É-leü'-thĕr-ŭs.

31 Wherefore Jonathan turned to the Arabians, who were called Zăb-ă-dḗ'-ăns, and smote them, and took their spoils.

32 And removing thence, he came to Damascus, and so passed through all the country.

33 Simon also went forth, and passed through the country unto Ăs'-că-lọn, and the holds there adjoining, from whence he turned aside to Jŏp'-pĕ, and won it.

34 For he had heard that they would deliver the hold unto them that took Dĕ-mḗ'-trĭ-ŭs'

part; wherefore he set a garrison there to keep it.

35 After this came Jonathan home again, and calling the elders of the people together, he consulted with them about building strong holds in Judea,

36 And making the walls of Jerusalem higher, and raising a great mount between the tower and the city, for to separate it from the city, that so it might be alone, that men might neither sell nor buy in it.

37 Upon this they came together to build up the city, forasmuch as *part of* the wall toward the brook on the east side was fallen down, and they repaired that which was called Că-phĕn'-ă-thă.

38 Simon also set up Ăd'-ĭ-dă in Sĕ-phē'-lă, and made it strong with gates and bars.

39 Now Tryphon went about to get the kingdom of Asia, and to kill Ăn-tĭ'-ŏ-<u>ch</u>ŭs the king, that he might set the crown upon his own head.

40 Howbeit he was afraid that Jonathan would not suffer him, and that he would fight against him; wherefore he sought a way how to take Jonathan, that he might kill him. So he removed, and came to Bĕth-săn'.

41 Then Jonathan went out to meet him with forty thousand men chosen for the battle, and came to Bĕth-săn'.

42 Now when Tryphon saw that Jonathan came with so great a force, he durst not stretch his hand against him;

43 But received him honourably, and commended him unto all his friends, and gave him gifts, and commanded his men of war to be as obedient unto him, as to himself.

44 Unto Jonathan also he said, Why hast thou put all this people to so great trouble, seeing there is no war betwixt us?

45 Therefore send them now home again, and choose a few men to wait on thee, and come thou with me to Ptŏl-ĕ-mā'-ĭs, for I will give it thee, and the rest of the strong holds and forces, and all that have any charge: as for me, I will return and depart: for this is the cause of my coming.

46 So Jonathan believing him did as he bade him, and sent away his host, who went into the land of Judea.

47 And with himself he retained but three thousand men, of whom he sent two thousand into Galilee, and one thousand went with him.

48 Now as soon as Jonathan entered into Ptŏl-ĕ-mā'-ĭs, they of Ptolemais shut the gates, and took him, and all them that came with him they slew with the sword.

49 Then sent Tryphon an host of footmen and horsemen into Galilee, and into the great plain, to destroy all Jonathan's company.

50 But when they knew that Jonathan and they that were with him were taken and slain, they encouraged one another, and went close together, prepared to fight.

51 They therefore that followed upon them, perceiving that they were ready to fight for their lives, turned back again.

52 Whereupon they all came into the land of Judea peaceably, and there they bewailed Jonathan, and them that were with him, and they were sore

afraid; wherefore all Israel made great lamentation.

53 Then all the heathen that were round about them sought to destroy them: for said they, They have no captain, nor any to help them: now therefore let us make war upon them, and take away their memorial from among men.

CHAPTER XIII

NOW when Simon heard that Tryphon had gathered together a great host to invade the land of Judea, and destroy it,

2 And saw that the people was in great trembling and fear, he went up to Jerusalem, and gathered the people together,

3 And gave them exhortation, saying, Ye yourselves know what great things I, and my brethren, and my father's house, have done for the laws and the sanctuary, the battles also and troubles which we have seen,

4 By reason whereof all my brethren are slain for Israel's sake, and I am left alone.

5 Now therefore be it far from me, that I should spare mine own life in any time of trouble: for I am no better than my brethren.

6 Doubtless I will avenge my nation, and the sanctuary, and our wives, and our children: for all the heathen are gathered to destroy us of very malice.

7 Now as soon as the people heard these words, their spirit revived.

8 And they answered with a loud voice, saying, Thou shalt be our leader instead of Judas and Jonathan thy brother.

9 Fight thou our battles, and whatsoever thou commandest us, that will we do.

10 So then he gathered together all the men of war, and made haste to finish the walls of Jerusalem, and he fortified it round about.

11 Also he sent Jonathan the *son* of Absalom, and with him a great power, to Jŏṗ-pē̇: who casting out them that were therein remained there in it.

12 So Tryphon removed from Ptŏl-ē-mā̇-ĭs with a great power to invade the land of Judea, and Jonathan was with him in ward.

13 But Simon pitched his tents at Ăḋ-ĭ-dă̇, over against the plain.

14 Now when Tryphon knew that Simon was risen up instead of his brother Jonathan, and meant to join battle with him, he sent messengers unto him, saying,

15 Whereas we have Jonathan thy brother in hold, it is for money that he is owing unto the king's treasure, concerning the business that was committed unto him.

16 Wherefore now send an hundred talents of silver, and two of his sons for hostages, that when he is at liberty he may not revolt from us, and we will let him go.

17 Hereupon Simon, albeit he perceived that they spake deceitfully unto him, yet sent he the money and the children, lest peradventure he should procure to himself great hatred of the people:

18 Who might have said, Because I sent him not the money and the children, therefore is *Jonathan* dead.

19 So he sent them the child-

ren and the hundred talents: howbeit *Tryphon* dissembled, neither would he let Jonathan go.

20 And after this came Tryphon to invade the land, and destroy it, going round about by the way that leadeth unto Ă-dṓ-rӑ: but Simon and his host marched against him in every place, wheresoever he went.

21 Now they that were in the tower sent messengers unto Tryphon, to the end that he should hasten his coming unto them by the wilderness, and send them victuals.

22 Wherefore Tryphon made ready all his horsemen to come that night: but there fell a very great snow, by reason whereof he came not. So he departed, and came into the country of Găl-ă-ăd.

23 And when he came near to Băs-că-mă, he slew Jonathan, who was buried there.

24 Afterward Tryphon returned and went into his own land.

25 Then sent Simon, and took the bones of Jonathan his brother, and buried them in Mṓ-dĭn, the city of his fathers.

26 And all Israel made great lamentation for him, and bewailed him many days.

27 Simon also built a monument upon the sepulchre of his father and his brethren, and raised it aloft to the sight, with hewn stone behind and before.

28 Moreover he set up seven pyramids, one against another, for his father, and his mother, and his four brethren.

29 And in these he made cunning devices, about the which he set great pillars, and upon the pillars he made all

their armour for a perpetual memory, and by the armour ships carved, that they might be seen of all that sail on the sea.

30 This is the sepulchre which he made at Mṓ-dĭn, and it standeth yet unto this day.

31 Now Tryphon dealt deceitfully with the young king Ăn-tĭ́-ŏ-chŭs, and slew him.

32 And he reigned in his stead, and crowned himself king of Asia, and brought a great calamity upon the land.

33 Then Simon built up the strong holds in Judea, and fenced them about with high towers, and great walls, and gates, and bars, and laid up victuals therein.

34 Moreover Simon chose men, and sent to king Dĕ-mḗ́-trĭ-ŭs, to the end he should give the land an immunity, because all that Tryphon did was to spoil.

35 Unto whom king Dĕ-mḗ́-trĭ-ŭs answered and wrote after this manner:

36 King Dĕ-mḗ-trĭ-ŭs unto Simon the high priest, and friend of kings, as also unto the elders and nation of the Jews, sendeth greeting:

37 The golden crown, and the scarlet robe, which ye sent unto us, we have received: and we are ready to make a stedfast peace with you, yea, and to write unto our officers, to confirm the immunities which we have granted.

38 And whatsoever covenants we have made with you shall stand; and the strong holds, which ye have builded, shall be your own.

39 As for any oversight or fault committed unto this day, we forgive it, and the crown

tax also, which ye owe us: and if there were any other tribute paid in Jerusalem, it shall no more be paid.

40 And look who are meet among you to be in our court, let them be enrolled, and let there be peace betwixt us.

41 Thus the yoke of the heathen was taken away from Israel in the hundred and seventieth year.

42 Then the people of Israel began to write in their instruments and contracts, In the first year of Simon the high priest, the governor and leader of the Jews.

43 In those days Simon camped against Gaza, and besieged it round about; he made also an engine of war, and set it by the city, and battered a certain tower, and took it.

44 And they that were in the engine leaped into the city; whereupon there was a great uproar in the city:

45 Insomuch as the people of the city rent their clothes, and climbed upon the walls with their wives and children, and cried with a loud voice, beseeching Simon to grant them peace.

46 And they said, Deal not with us according to our wickedness, but according to thy mercy.

47 So Simon was appeased toward them, and fought no more against them, but put them out of the city, and cleansed the houses wherein the idols were, and so entered into it with songs and thanksgiving.

48 Yea, he put all uncleanness out of it, and placed such men there as would keep the law, and made it stronger than

254

it was before, and built therein a dwellingplace for himself.

49 They also of the tower in Jerusalem were kept so strait, that they could neither come forth, nor go into the country, nor buy, nor sell: wherefore they were in great distress for want of victuals, and a great number of them perished through famine.

50 Then cried they to Simon, beseeching him to be at one with them: which thing he granted them; and when he had put them out from thence, he cleansed the tower from pollutions:

51 And entered into it the three and twentieth day of the second month, in the hundred seventy and first year, with thanksgiving, and branches of palm trees, and with harps, and cymbals, and with viols, and hymns, and songs: because there was destroyed a great enemy out of Israel.

52 He ordained also that that day should be kept every year with gladness. Moreover the hill of the temple that was by the tower he made stronger than it was, and there he dwelt himself with his company.

53 And when Simon saw that John his son was a valiant man, he made him captain of all the hosts; and he dwelt in Gā-zā'-rā.

CHAPTER XIV

NOW in the hundred three-score and twelfth year king Dĕ-mē'-trĭ-ŭs gathered his forces together, and went into Mē'-dĭ-ă, to get him help to fight against Tryphon.

2 But when Är'-să-çēs, the king of Persia and Mē'-dĭ-ă,

heard that Dĕ-mē'-trĭ-ŭs was entered within his borders, he sent one of his princes to take him alive:

3 Who went and smote the host of Dĕ-mē'-trĭ-ŭs, and took him, and brought him to Ăr'-să-çēs, by whom he was put in ward.

4 As for the land *of Judea,* that was quiet all the days of Simon; for he sought the good of his nation in such wise, as that evermore his authority and honour pleased them well.

5 And as he was honourable in all his acts, so in this, that he took Jŏp'-pĕ for an haven, and made an entrance to the isles of the sea,

6 And enlarged the bounds of his nation, and recovered the country,

7 And gathered together a great number of captives, and had the dominion of Gă-zā'-ră, and Bĕth-sū'-ră, and the tower, out of the which he took all uncleanness, neither was there any that resisted him.

8 Then did they till their ground in peace, and the earth gave her increase, and the trees of the field their fruit.

9 The ancient men sat all in the streets, communing together of good things, and the young men put on glorious and warlike apparel.

10 He provided victuals for the cities, and set in them all manner of munition, so that his honourable name was renowned unto the end of the world.

11 He made peace in the land, and Israel rejoiced with great joy:

12 For every man sat under his vine and his fig tree, and there was none to fray them:

13 Neither was there any left in the land to fight against them: yea, the kings themselves were overthrown in those days.

14 Moreover he strengthened all those of his people that were brought low; the law he searched out; and every contemner of the law and wicked person he took away.

15 He beautified the sanctuary, and multiplied the vessels of the temple.

16 Now when it was heard at Rome, and as far as Sparta, that Jonathan was dead, they were very sorry.

17 But as soon as they heard that his brother Simon was made high priest in his stead, and ruled the country, and the cities therein:

18 They wrote unto him in tables of brass, to renew the friendship and league which they had made with Judas and Jonathan his brethren:

19 Which writings were read before the congregation at Jerusalem.

20 And this is the copy of the letters that the Lăç-ĕ-dĕ-mō'-nĭ-ăns sent; The rulers of the Lacedemonians, with the city, unto Simon the high priest, and the elders, and priests, and residue of the people of the Jews, our brethren, *send* greeting:

21 The ambassadors that were sent unto our people certified us of your glory and honour: wherefore we were glad of their coming,

22 And did register the things that they spake in the council of the people in this manner; Nŭ-mē'-nĭ-ŭs *son* of Ăn-tī'-ŏ-chŭs, and Ăn-tĭp'-ă-tēr *son of* Jason, the Jews' ambassadors,

came unto us to renew the friendship they had with us.

23 And it pleased the people to entertain the men honourably, and to put the copy of their ambassage in publick records, to the end the people of the Lăc̆-ĕ-dĕ-mō'-nj-ăns might have a memorial thereof: furthermore we have written a copy thereof unto Simon the high priest.

24 After this Simon sent Nŭ-mē'-nj-ŭs to Rome with a great shield of gold of a thousand pound weight, to confirm the league with them.

25 Whereof when the people heard, they said, What thanks shall we give to Simon and his sons?

26 For he and his brethren and the house of his father have established Israel, and chased away in fight their enemies from them, and confirmed their liberty.

27 So then they wrote *it* in tables of brass, which they set upon pillars in mount Sion: and this is the copy of the writing; The eighteenth day of *the month* Ĕ-lūl', in the hundred threescore and twelfth year, being the third year of Simon the high priest,

28 At Săr'-ă-mĕl in the great congregation of the priests, and people, and rulers of the nation, and elders of the country, were these things notified unto us.

29 Forasmuch as oftentimes there have been wars in the country, wherein for the maintenance of their sanctuary, and the law, Simon the son of Măt-tă-thī'-ăs, of the posterity of Jă'-rĭb, together with his brethren, put themselves in jeopardy, and resisting the

256

enemies of their nation did their nation great honour:

30 (For after that Jonathan, having gathered his nation together, and been their high priest, was added to his people,

31 Their enemies purposed to invade their country, that they might destroy it, and lay hands on the sanctuary:

32 At which time Simon rose up, and fought for his nation, and spent much of his own substance, and armed the valiant men of his nation, and gave them wages,

33 And fortified the cities of Judea, together with Bĕth-sū'-rȧ, that lieth upon the borders of Judea, where the armour of the enemies had been before; but he set a garrison of Jews there:

34 Moreover he fortified Jŏp'-pē, which lieth upon the sea, and Gă-zā'-rȧ, that bordereth upon Ȧ-zō'-tŭs, where the enemies had dwelt before: but he placed Jews there, and furnished them with all things convenient for the reparation thereof.)

35 The people therefore, seeing the acts of Simon, and unto what glory he thought to bring his nation, made him their governor and chief priest, because he had done all these things, and for the justice and faith which he kept to his nation, and for that he sought by all means to exalt his people.

36 For in his time things prospered in his hands, so that the heathen were taken out of their country, and they also that were in the city of David in Jerusalem, who had made themselves a tower, out of which they issued, and polluted all about the sanctuary,

and did much hurt in the holy place:

37 But he placed Jews therein, and fortified it for the safety of the country and the city, and raised up the walls of Jerusalem.

38 King Dĕ-mē'-trĭ-ŭs also confirmed him in the high priesthood according to those things,

39 And made him one of his friends, and honoured him with great honour.

40 For he had heard say, that the Romans had called the Jews their friends and confederates and brethren; and that they had entertained the ambassadors of Simon honourably;

41 Also that the Jews and priests were well pleased that Simon should be their governor and high priest for ever, until there should arise a faithful prophet;

42 Moreover that he should be their captain, and should take charge of the sanctuary, to set them over their works, and over the country, and over the armour, and over the fortresses, that, I say, he should take charge of the sanctuary:

43 Beside this, that he should be obeyed of every man, and that all the writings in the country should be made in his name, and that he should be clothed in purple, and wear gold:

44 Also that it should be lawful for none of the people or priests to break any of these things, or to gainsay his words, or to gather an assembly in the country without him, or to be clothed in purple, or wear a buckle of gold:

45 And whosoever should do otherwise, or break any of these things, he should be punished.

46 Thus it liked all the people to deal with Simon, and to do as hath been said.

47 Then Simon accepted hereof, and was well pleased to be high priest, and captain and governor of the Jews and priests, and to defend them all.

48 So they commanded that this writing should be put in tables of brass, and that they should be set up within the compass of the sanctuary in a conspicuous place;

49 Also that the copies thereof should be laid up in the treasury, to the end that Simon and his sons might have them.

CHAPTER XV

MOREOVER Ăn-tī'-ŏ-chŭs son of Dĕ-mē'-trĭ-ŭs the king sent letters from the isles of the sea unto Simon the priest and prince of the Jews, and to all the people;

2 The contents whereof were these: King Ăn-tī'-ŏ-chŭs to Simon the high priest and prince of his nation, and to the people of the Jews, greeting:

3 Forasmuch as certain pestilent men have usurped the kingdom of our fathers, and my purpose is to challenge it again, that I may restore it to the old estate, and to that end have gathered a multitude of foreign soldiers together, and prepared ships of war;

4 My meaning also being to go through the country, that I may be avenged of them that have destroyed it, and made many cities in the kingdom desolate:

I

5 Now therefore I confirm unto thee all the oblations which the kings before me granted thee, and whatsoever gifts besides they granted.

6 I give thee leave also to coin money for thy country with thine own stamp.

7 And as concerning Jerusalem and the sanctuary, let them be free; and all the armour that thou hast made, and fortresses that thou hast built, and keepest in thine hands, let them remain unto thee.

8 And if any thing be, or shall be, owing to the king, let it be forgiven thee from this time forth for evermore.

9 Furthermore, when we have obtained our kingdom, we will honour thee, and thy nation, and thy temple, with great honour, so that your honour shall be known throughout the world.

10 In the hundred threescore and fourteenth year went Ăn-tī'-ŏ-chŭs into the land of his fathers: at which time all the forces came together unto him, so that few were left with Tryphon.

11 Wherefore being pursued by king Ăn-tī'-ŏ-chŭs, he fled unto Dora, which lieth by the sea side:

12 For he saw that troubles came upon him all at once, and that his forces had forsaken him.

13 Then camped Ăn-tī'-ŏ-chŭs against Dora, having with him an hundred and twenty thousand men of war, and eight thousand horsemen.

14 And when he had compassed the city round about, and joined ships close to the town on the sea side, he vexed the city by land and by sea,

neither suffered he any to go out or in.

15 In the mean season came Nŭ-mē'-nĭ-ŭs and his company from Rome, having letters to the kings and countries; wherein were written these things:

16 Lū'-çĭ-ŭs, consul of the Romans unto king Ptŏl'-ĕ-mēē greeting:

17 The Jews' ambassadors, our friends and confederates, came unto us to renew the old friendship and league, being sent from Simon the high priest, and from the people of the Jews:

18 And they brought a shield of gold of a thousand pound.

19 We thought it good therefore to write unto the kings and countries, that they should do them no harm, nor fight against them, their cities, or countries, nor yet aid their enemies against them.

20 It seemed also good to us to receive the shield of them.

21 If therefore there be any pestilent fellows, that have fled from their country unto you, deliver them unto Simon the high priest, that he may punish them according to their own law.

22 The same things wrote he likewise unto Dĕ-mē'-trĭ-ŭs the king, and Ăt'-tă-lŭs, to Ăr'-ĭ-ă-rā'-thēs, and Ăr'-să-çēs,

23 And to all the countries, and to Sămp'-să-mēs, and the Lăç'-ĕ-dĕ-mō'-nĭ-ăns, and to Dē'-lŭs, and Myndus, and Sĭç'-ў-ŏn, and Cā'-rĭ-ă, and Sā'-mŏs, and Păm-phўl'-ĭ-ă, and Lўç'-ĭ-ă, and Hăl'-ĭ-cär-năs'-sŭs, and Rhodus, and Phă-sē'-lĭs, and Cŏs, and Sī'-dē, and Ăr'-ă-dŭs, and Gôr-tў'-nă, and Cnī'-dŭs, and Cyprus, and Çў-rē'-nĕ.

24 And the copy hereof

258

they wrote to Simon the high priest.

25 So Ăn-tī´-ŏ-chŭs the king camped against Dora the second *day*, assaulting it continually, and making engines, by which means he shut up Tryphon, that he could neither go out nor in.

26 At that time Simon sent him two thousand chosen men to aid him; silver also, and gold, and much armour.

27 Nevertheless he would not receive them, but brake all the covenants which he had made with him afore, and became strange unto him.

28 Furthermore he sent unto him Ăth´-ĕ-nō´-bĭ-ŭs, one of his friends, to commune with him, and say, Ye withhold Jŏp´-pĕ and Gă-zā´-ră, with the tower that is in Jerusalem, which are cities of my realm.

29 The borders thereof ye have wasted, and done great hurt in the land, and got the dominion of many places within my kingdom.

30 Now therefore deliver the cities which ye have taken, and the tributes of the places, whereof ye have gotten dominion without the borders of Judea:

31 Or else give me for them five hundred talents of silver; and for the harm that ye have done, and the tributes of the cities, other five hundred talents: if not, we will come and fight against you.

32 So Ăth´-ĕ-nō´-bĭ-ŭs the king's friend came to Jerusalem: and when he saw the glory of Simon, and the cupboard of gold and silver plate, and his great attendance, he was astonished, and told him the king's message.

33 Then answered Simon, and said unto him, We have neither taken other men's land, nor holden that which appertaineth to others, but the inheritance of our fathers, which our enemies had wrongfully in possession a certain time.

34 Wherefore we, having opportunity, hold the inheritance of our fathers.

35 And whereas thou demandest Jŏp´-pĕ and Gă-zā´-ră, albeit they did great harm unto the people in our country, yet will we give an hundred talents for them. Hereunto Ăth´-ĕ-nō´-bĭ-ŭs answered him not a word;

36 But returned in a rage to the king, and made report unto him of these speeches, and of the glory of Simon, and of all that he had seen: whereupon the king was exceeding wroth.

37 In the mean time fled Tryphon by ship unto Ŏr-thŏ-sī´-ăs.

38 Then the king made Çĕn-dĕ-bē´-ŭs captain of the sea coast, and gave him an host of footmen and horsemen,

39 And commanded him to remove his host toward Judea: also he commanded him to build up Çē´-drŏn, and to fortify the gates, and to war against the people; but as for the king *himself*, he pursued Tryphon.

40 So Çĕn-dĕ-bē´-ŭs came to Jamnia, and began to provoke the people, and to invade Judea, and to take the people prisoners, and to slay them.

41 And when he had built up Çē´-drŏn, he set horsemen there, and an host *of footmen*, to the end that issuing out they might make outroads upon the ways of Judea, as the king had commanded him.

CHAPTER XVI

THEN came up John from Gă-zā'-ră, and told Simon his father what Çĕn-dĕ-bē'-ŭs had done.

2 Wherefore Simon called his two eldest sons, Judas and John, and said unto them, I, and my brethren, and my father's house, have ever from our youth unto this day fought against the enemies of Israel; and things have prospered so well in our hands, that we have delivered Israel oftentimes.

3 But now I am old, and ye, by God's mercy, are of a sufficient age: be ye instead of me and my brother, and go and fight for our nation, and the help from heaven be with you.

4 So he chose out of the country twenty thousand men of war with horsemen, who went out against Çĕn-dĕ-bē'-ŭs, and rested that night at Mō'-dīn.

5 And when as they rose in the morning, and went into the plain, behold, a mighty great host both of footmen and horsemen came against them: howbeit there was a water brook betwixt them.

6 So he and his people pitched over against them: and when he saw that the people were afraid to go over the water brook, he went first over himself, and then the men seeing him passed through after him.

7 *That done*, he divided his men, and set the horsemen in the midst of the footmen: for the enemies' horsemen were very many.

8 Then sounded they with the holy trumpets: whereupon Çĕn-dĕ-bē'-ŭs and his host were put to flight, so that many of them were slain, and the remnant gat them to the strong hold.

9 At that time was Judas John's brother wounded; but John still followed after them, until he came to Çē'-dron, which Çĕn-dĕ-bē'-ŭs had built.

10 So they fled even unto the towers in the fields of Ă-zō'-tŭs; wherefore he burned it with fire: so that there were slain of them about two thousand men. Afterward he returned into the land of Judea in peace.

11 Moreover in the plain of Jericho was Ptŏl-ĕ-mē'-ŭs the son of Ă-bū'-bŭs made captain, and he had abundance of silver and gold:

12 For he was the high priest's son in law.

13 Wherefore his heart being lifted up, he thought to get the country to himself, and thereupon consulted deceitfully against Simon and his sons to destroy them.

14 Now Simon was visiting the cities that were in the country, and taking care for the good ordering of them; at which time he came down himself to Jericho with his sons, Măt-tă-thī'-ăs and Judas, in the hundred threescore and seventeenth year, in the eleventh month, called Sā'-băt:

15 Where the *son* of Ă-bū'-bŭs receiving them deceitfully into a little hold, called Docus, which he had built, made them a great banquet: howbeit he had hid men there.

16 So when Simon and his sons had drunk largely, Ptŏl'-ĕ-mēē and his men rose up, and took their weapons, and came upon Simon into the banqueting place, and slew him, and

260

his two sons, and certain of his servants.

17 In which doing he committed a great treachery, and recompensed evil for good.

18 Then Ptŏl'-ĕ-mēe wrote these things, and sent to the king, that he should send him an host to aid him, and he would deliver him the country and cities.

19 He sent others also to Gă-zā'-rä to kill John: and unto the tribunes he sent letters to come unto him, that he might give them silver, and gold, and rewards.

20 And others he sent to take Jerusalem, and the mountain of the temple.

21 Now one had run afore to

Gă-zā'-rä, and told John that his father and brethren were slain, and, *quoth he, Ptŏl'-ĕ-mēe* hath sent to slay thee also.

22 Hereof when he heard, he was sore astonished: so he laid hands on them that were come to destroy him, and slew them; for he knew that they sought to make him away.

23 As concerning the rest of the acts of John, and his wars, and worthy deeds which he did, and the building of the walls which he made, and his doings,

24 Behold, these are written in the chronicles of his priesthood, from the time he was made high priest after his father.

THE SECOND BOOK OF THE

MACCABEES

CHAPTER 1

THE brethren, the Jews that be at Jerusalem and in the land of Judea, wish unto the brethren, the Jews that are throughout Egypt, health and peace:

2 God be gracious unto you, and remember his covenant that he made with Abraham, Isaac, and Jacob, his faithful servants;

3 And give you all an heart to serve him, and to do his will, with a good courage and a willing mind;

4 And open your hearts in his law and commandments, and send you peace,

5 And hear your prayers, and be at one with you, and never forsake you in time of trouble.

6 And now we be here praying for you.

7 What time as Dĕ-mē'-tri-ŭs reigned, in the hundred threescore and ninth year, we the Jews wrote unto you in the extremity of trouble that came upon us in those years, from the time that Jason and his company revolted from the holy land and kingdom,

8 And burned the porch, and shed innocent blood: then we prayed unto the Lord, and were heard; we offered also sacrifices and fine flour, and lighted the lamps, and set forth the loaves.

9 And now see that ye keep the feast of tabernacles in the month Căs'-lĕū.

10 In the hundred fourscore and eighth year, the people that were at Jerusalem and in Judea, and the council, and Judas, sent greeting and health unto Ă-rĭs'-tŏ-bŭ'-lŭs, king Ptŏl-ĕ-mē'-ŭs' master, who was of

the stock of the anointed priests, and to the Jews that were in Egypt:

11 Insomuch as God hath delivered us from great perils, we thank him highly, as having been in battle against a king.

12 For he cast them out that fought within the holy city.

13 For when the leader was come into Persia, and the army with him that seemed invincible, they were slain in the temple of Nă-nĕ'-ă by the deceit of Nanea's priests.

14 For Ăn-tĭ'-ŏ-chŭs, as though he would marry her, came into the place, and his friends that were with him, to receive money in name of a dowry.

15 Which when the priests of Nă-nĕ'-ă had set forth, and he was entered with a small company into the compass of the temple, they shut the temple as soon as Ăn-tĭ'-ŏ-chŭs was come in:

16 And opening a privy door of the roof, they threw stones like thunderbolts, and struck down the captain, hewed them in pieces, smote off their heads, and cast them to those that were without.

17 Blessed be our God in all things, who hath delivered up the ungodly.

18 Therefore whereas we are now purposed to keep the purification of the temple upon the five and twentieth day of *the month* Căs'-lĕû, we thought it necessary to certify you thereof, that ye also might keep *it, as* the feast of the tabernacles, and of the fire, *which was given us* when Nĕ-ĕ-mĭ'-ăs offered sacrifice, after that he

262

had builded the temple and the altar.

19 For when our fathers were led into Persia, the priests that were then devout took the fire of the altar privily, and hid it in an hollow place of a pit without water, where they kept *it* sure, so that the place was unknown to all men.

20 Now after many years, when it pleased God, Nĕ-ĕ-mĭ'-ăs, being sent from the king of Persia, did send of the posterity of those priests that had hid it to the fire: but when they told us they found no fire, but thick water;

21 Then commanded he them to draw it up, and to bring it; and when the sacrifices were laid on, Nĕ-ĕ-mĭ'-ăs commanded the priests to sprinkle the wood and the things laid thereupon with the water.

22 When this was done, and the time came that the sun shone, which afore was hid in the cloud, there was a great fire kindled, so that every man marvelled.

23 And the priests made a prayer whilst the sacrifice was consuming, I *say,* both the priests, and all *the rest,* Jonathan beginning, and the rest answering thereunto, as Nĕ-ĕ-mĭ'-ăs did.

24 And the prayer was after this manner; O Lord, Lord God, Creator of all things, who art fearful and strong, and righteous, and merciful, and the only and gracious King,

25 The only giver of all things, the only just, almighty, and everlasting, thou that deliverest Israel from all trouble, and didst choose the fathers, and sanctify them:

26 Receive the sacrifice for

thy whole people Israel, and preserve thine own portion, and sanctify it.

27 Gather those together that are scattered from us, deliver them that serve among the heathen, look upon them that are despised and abhorred, and let the heathen know that thou art our God.

28 Punish them that oppress us, and with pride do us wrong.

29 Plant thy people again in thy holy place, as Moses hath spoken.

30 And the priests sung psalms of thanksgiving.

31 Now when the sacrifice was consumed, Nē-ĕ-mī'-ăs commanded the water that was left to be poured on the great stones.

32 When this was done, there was kindled a flame: but it was consumed by the light that shined from the altar.

33 So when this matter was known, it was told the king of Persia, that in the place, where the priests that were led away had hid the fire, there appeared water, and that Nē-ĕ-mī'-ăs had purified the sacrifices therewith.

34 Then the king, inclosing the place, made it holy, after he had tried the matter.

35 And the king took many gifts, and bestowed thereof on those whom he would gratify.

36 And Nē-ĕ-mī'-ăs called this thing Năph'-thär, which is as much as to say, a cleansing: but many men call it Nē'-phi.

CHAPTER II

IT is also found in the records, that Jeremy the prophet commanded them that were carried away to take of the fire, as it hath been signified:

2 And how that the prophet, having given them the law, charged them not to forget the commandments of the Lord, and that they should not err in their minds, when they see images of silver and gold, with their ornaments.

3 And with other such speeches exhorted he them, that the law should not depart from their hearts.

4 It was also contained in the same writing, that the prophet, being warned of God, commanded the tabernacle and the ark to go with him, as he went forth into the mountain, where Moses climbed up, and saw the heritage of God.

5 And when Jeremy came thither, he found an hollow cave, wherein he laid the tabernacle, and the ark, and the altar of incense, and so stopped the door.

6 And some of those that followed him came to mark the way, but they could not find it.

7 Which when Jeremy perceived, he blamed them, saying, As for that place, it shall be unknown until the time that God gather his people again together, and receive them unto mercy.

8 Then shall the Lord shew them these things, and the glory of the Lord shall appear, and the cloud also, as it was shewed under Moses, and as when Solomon desired that the place might be honourably sanctified.

9 It was also declared, that he being wise offered the sacrifice of dedication, and of the finishing of the temple.

10 And as when Moses prayed

263

unto the Lord, the fire came down from heaven, and consumed the sacrifices: even so prayed Solomon also, and the fire came down from heaven, and consumed the burnt offerings.

11 And Moses said, Because the sin offering was not to be eaten, it was consumed.

12 So Solomon kept those eight days.

13 The same things also were reported in the writings and commentaries of Nē-ē-mī'-ās; and how he founding a library gathered together the acts of the kings, and the prophets, and of David, and the epistles of the kings concerning the holy gifts.

14 In like manner also Judas gathered together all those things that were lost by reason of the war we had, and they remain with us.

15 Wherefore if ye have need thereof, send some to fetch them unto you.

16 Whereas we then are about to celebrate the purification, we have written unto you, and ye shall do well, if ye keep the same days.

17 We hope also, that the God, that delivered all his people, and gave them all an heritage, and the kingdom, and the priesthood, and the sanctuary,

18 As he promised in the law, will shortly have mercy upon us, and gather us together out of every land under heaven into the holy place: for he hath delivered us out of great troubles, and hath purified the place.

19 Now as concerning Judas Măc-că-bē'-ŭs, and his brethren, and the purification of the great temple, and the dedication of the altar,

20 And the wars against Ăn-tī'-ŏ-chŭs Ē-pĭph'-ä-nēs, and Ēu-pā'-tôr his son,

21 And the manifest signs that came from heaven unto those that behaved themselves manfully to their honour for Judaism: so that, being but a few, they overcame the whole country, and chased barbarous multitudes,

22 And recovered again the temple renowned all the world over, and freed the city, and upheld the laws which were going down, the Lord being gracious unto them with all favour:

23 *All these things, I say,* being declared by Jason of Çȳ-rē'-nĕ in five books, we will assay to abridge in one volume.

24 For considering the infinite number, and the difficulty which they find that desire to look into the narrations of the story, for the variety of the matter,

25 We have been careful, that they that will read may have delight, and that they that are desirous to commit to memory might have ease, and that all into whose hands it comes might have profit.

26 Therefore to us, that have taken upon us this painful labour of abridging, it was not easy, but a matter of sweat and watching;

27 Even as it is no ease unto him that prepareth a banquet, and seeketh the benefit of others: yet for the pleasuring of many we will undertake gladly this great pains;

28 Leaving to the author the exact handling of every particular, and labouring to follow

264

the rules of an abridgement.

29 For as the master builder of a new house must care for the whole building; but he that undertaketh to set it out, and paint it, must seek out fit things for the adorning thereof: even so I think it is with us.

30 To stand upon every point, and go over things at large, and to be curious in particulars, belongeth to the first author of the story:

31 But to use brevity, and avoid much labouring of the work, is to be granted to him that will make an abridgement.

32 Here then will we begin the story: only adding thus much to that which hath been said, that it is a foolish thing to make a long prologue, and to be short in the story itself.

CHAPTER III

NOW when the holy city was inhabited with all peace, and the laws were kept very well, because of the godliness of Ŏ-nī'-ăs the high priest, and his hatred of wickedness,

2 It came to pass that even the kings themselves did honour the place, and magnify the temple with their best gifts;

3 Insomuch that Sĕ-leú'-cŭs king of Asia of his own revenues bare all the costs belonging to the service of the sacrifices.

4 But one Simon of the tribe of Benjamin, who was made governor of the temple, fell out with the high priest about disorder in the city.

5 And when he could not overcome Ŏ-nī'-ăs, he gat him to Ăp'-ŏl-lō'-nĭ-ŭs *the son of* Thrā-sē'-ăs, who then was governor of Çē'-lŏ-sўr'-ĭ-ă and Phē-nī'-çĕ,

6 And told him that the treasury in Jerusalem was full of infinite sums of money, so that the multitude of their riches, which did not pertain to the account of the sacrifices, was innumerable, and that it was possible to bring all into the king's hand.

7 Now when Ăp'-ŏl-lō'-nĭ-ŭs came to the king, and had shewed him of the money whereof he was told, the king chose out Hĕ'-lĭ-ŏ-dō'-rŭs his treasurer, and sent him with a commandment to bring him the foresaid money.

8 So forthwith Hĕ'-lĭ-ŏ-dō'-rŭs took his journey, under a colour of visiting the cities of Çē'-lŏ-sўr'-ĭ-ă and Phē-nī'-çĕ, but indeed to fulfil the king's purpose.

9 And when he was come to Jerusalem, and had been courteously received of the high priest of the city, he told him what intelligence was given of the money, and declared wherefore he came, and asked if these things were so indeed.

10 Then the high priest told him that there was such money laid up for the relief of widows and fatherless children:

11 And that some of it belonged to Hĭr-cā'-nŭs *son* of Tŏ-bī'-ăs, a man of great dignity, and not as that wicked Simon had misinformed: the sum whereof in all was four hundred talents of silver, and two hundred of gold:

12 And that it was altogether impossible that such wrongs should be done unto them, that had committed it to the holiness of the place, and to the

265

majesty and inviolable sanctity of the temple, honoured over all the world.

13 But Hĕ'-lĭ-ŏ-dō'-rŭs, because of the king's commandment given him, said, That in any wise it must be brought into the king's treasury.

14 So at the day which he appointed he entered in to order this matter: wherefore there was no small agony throughout the whole city.

15 But the priests, prostrating themselves before the altar in their priests' vestments, called unto heaven upon him that made a law concerning things given to be kept, that they should safely be preserved for such as had committed them to be kept.

16 Then whoso had looked the high priest in the face, it would have wounded his heart: for his countenance and the changing of his colour declared the inward agony of his mind.

17 For the man was so compassed with fear and horror of the body, that it was manifest to them that looked upon him, what sorrow he had now in his heart.

18 Others ran flocking out of their houses to the general supplication, because the place was like to come into contempt.

19 And the women, girt with sackcloth under their breasts, abounded in the streets, and the virgins that were kept in ran, some to the gates, and some to the walls, and others looked out of the windows.

20 And all, holding their hands toward heaven, made supplication.

21 Then it would have pitied

a man to see the falling down of the multitude of all sorts, and the fear of the high priest, being in such an agony.

22 They then called upon the Almighty Lord to keep the things committed of trust safe and sure for those that had committed them.

23 Nevertheless Hĕ'-lĭ-ŏ-dō'-rŭs executed that which was decreed.

24 Now as he was there present himself with his guard about the treasury, the Lord of spirits, and the Prince of all power, caused a great apparition, so that all that presumed to come in with him were astonished at the power of God, and fainted, and were sore afraid.

25 For there appeared unto them an horse with a terrible rider upon him, and adorned with a very fair covering, and he ran fiercely, and smote at Hĕ'-lĭ-ŏ-dō'-rŭs with his forefeet, and it seemed that he that sat upon the horse had complete harness of gold.

26 Moreover two other young men appeared before him, notable in strength, excellent in beauty, and comely in apparel, who stood by him on either side, and scourged him continually, and gave him many sore stripes.

27 And Hĕ'-lĭ-ŏ-dō'-rŭs fell suddenly unto the ground, and was compassed with great darkness: but they that were with him took him up, and put him into a litter.

28 Thus him, that lately came with a great train and with all his guard into the said treasury, they carried out, being unable to help himself with his weapons: and manifestly they

acknowledged the power of God:

29 For he by the hand of God was cast down, and lay speechless without all hope of life.

30 But they praised the Lord, that had miraculously honoured his own place: for the temple, which a little afore was full of fear and trouble, when the Almighty Lord appeared, was filled with joy and gladness.

31 Then straightways certain of Hĕ'-lĭ-ŏ-dō'-rŭs' friends prayed Ŏ-nī'-ăs, that he would call upon the most High to grant him his life, who lay ready to give up the ghost.

32 So the high priest, suspecting lest the king should misconceive that some treachery had been done to Hĕ'-lĭ-ŏ-dō'-rŭs by the Jews, offered a sacrifice for the health of the man.

33 Now as the high priest was making an atonement, the same young men in the same clothing appeared and stood beside Hĕ'-lĭ-ŏ-dō'-rŭs, saying, Give Ŏ-nī'-ăs the high priest great thanks, insomuch as for his sake the Lord hath granted thee life:

34 And seeing that thou hast been scourged from heaven, declare unto all men the mighty power of God. And when they had spoken these words, they appeared no more.

35 So Hĕ'-lĭ-ŏ-dō'-rŭs, after he had offered sacrifice unto the Lord, and made great vows unto him that had saved his life, and saluted Ŏ-nī'-ăs, returned with his host to the king.

36 Then testified he to all men the works of the great God, which he had seen with his eyes.

37 And when the king asked Hĕ'-lĭ-ŏ-dō'-rŭs, who might be a fit man to be sent yet once again to Jerusalem, he said,

38 If thou hast any enemy or traitor, send him thither, and thou shalt receive him well scourged, if he escape with his life: for in that place, no doubt, there is an especial power of God.

39 For he that dwelleth in heaven hath his eye on that place, and defendeth it; and he beateth and destroyeth them that come to hurt it.

40 And the things concerning Hĕ'-lĭ-ŏ-dō'-rŭs, and the keeping of the treasury, fell out on this sort.

CHAPTER IV

THIS Simon now, of whom we spake afore, having been a bewrayer of the money, and of his country, slandered Ŏ-nī'-ăs, as if he had terrified Hĕ'-lĭ-ŏ-dō'-rŭs, and been the worker of these evils.

2 Thus was he bold to call him a traitor, that had deserved well of the city, and tendered his own nation, and was so zealous of the laws.

3 But when their hatred went so far, that by one of Simon's faction murders were committed,

4 Ŏ-nī'-ăs seeing the danger of this contention, and that Ăp'-ŏl-lō'-nĭ-ŭs, as being the governor of Cē'-lŏ-sўr'-ĭ-ă and Phē-nī'-çē, did rage, and increase Simon's malice,

5 He went to the king, not to be an accuser of his countrymen, but seeking the good of all, both publick and private:

6 For he saw that it was impossible that the state should

continue quiet, and Simon leave his folly, unless the king did look thereunto.

7 But after the death of Sĕ-lĕū'-cŭs, when Ăn-tī'-ŏ-chŭs, called Ē-pīph'-ă-nēs, took the kingdom, Jason the brother of Ŏ-nī'-ăs laboured underhand to be high priest,

8 Promising unto the king by intercession three hundred and threescore talents of silver, and of another revenue eighty talents:

9 Beside this, he promised to assign an hundred and fifty more, if he might have licence to set him up a place for exercise, and for the training up of youth in the fashions of the heathen, and to write them of Jerusalem *by the name of* Ăn'-tī-ō'-chī-ăns.

10 Which when the king had granted, and he had gotten into his hand the rule, he forthwith brought his own nation to the Greekish fashion.

11 And the royal privileges granted of special favour to the Jews by the means of John the father of Eu-pŏl'-ĕ-mŭs, who went ambassador to Rome for amity and aid, he took away; and putting down the governments which were according to the law, he brought up new customs against the law:

12 For he built gladly a place of exercise under the tower itself, and brought the chief young men under his subjection, and made them wear a hat.

13 Now such was the height of Greek fashions, and increase of heathenish manners, through the exceeding profaneness of Jason, that ungodly wretch, and no high priest;

14 That the priests had no

courage to serve any more at the altar, but despising the temple, and neglecting the sacrifices, hastened to be partakers of the unlawful allowance in the place of exercise, after the game of Discus called them forth;

15 Not setting by the honours of their fathers, but liking the glory of the Grecians best of all.

16 By reason whereof sore calamity came upon them: for they had them to be their enemies and avengers, whose custom they followed so earnestly, and unto whom they desired to be like in all things.

17 For it is not a light thing to do wickedly against the laws of God: but the time following shall declare these things.

18 Now when the game that was used every fifth year was kept at Tyrus, the king being present,

19 This ungracious Jason sent special messengers from Jerusalem, who were Ăn'-tī-ō'-chī-ăns, to carry three hundred drachms of silver to the sacrifice of Hēr'-cŭ-lēs, which even the bearers thereof thought fit not to bestow upon the sacrifice, because it was not convenient, but to be reserved for other charges.

20 This money then, in regard of the sender, was appointed to Hēr'-cŭ-lēs' sacrifice; but because of the bearers thereof, it was employed to the making of galleys.

21 Now when Ăp'-ŏl-lō'-nǐ-ŭs the *son* of Mĕ-nĕs'-thĕ-ŭs was sent into Egypt for the coronation of king Ptŏl-ĕ-mē'-ŭs Phī-lŏ-mē'-tôr, Ăn'-tī-ō'-chŭs, understanding him not to be well affected to his affairs, provided

for his own safety: whereupon he came to Jŏp'-pĕ, and from thence to Jerusalem:

22 Where he was honourably received of Jason, and of the city, and was brought in with torch light, and with great shoutings: and so afterward went with his host unto Phĕ-nī'-çĕ.

23 Three years afterward Jason sent Mĕn-ē-lā'-ŭs, the aforesaid Simon's brother, to bear the money unto the king, and to put him in mind of certain necessary matters.

24 But he being brought to the presence of the king, when he had magnified him for the glorious appearance of his power, got the priesthood to himself, offering more than Jason by three hundred talents of silver.

25 So he came with the king's mandate, bringing nothing worthy the high priesthood, but having the fury of a cruel tyrant, and the rage of a savage beast.

26 Then Jason, who had undermined his own brother, being undermined by another, was compelled to flee into the country of the Ammonites.

27 So Mĕn-ē-lā'-ŭs got the principality: but as for the money that he had promised unto the king, he took no good order for it, albeit Sŏs-trā'-tŭs the ruler of the castle required it:

28 For unto him appertained the gathering of the customs. Wherefore they were both called before the king.

29 Now Mĕn-ē-lā'-ŭs left his brother Lȳ-sĭm'-ă-chŭs in his stead in the priesthood; and Sŏs-trā'-tŭs *left* Crā'-tēs, who was governor of the Çȳp'-rĭ-ăns.

30 While those things were in doing, they of Tarsus and Mallos made insurrection, because they were given to the king's concubine, called Ăn-tī'-ŏ-chĭs.

31 Then came the king in all haste to appease matters, leaving Ăn-drŏn'-ĭ-cŭs, a man in authority, for his deputy.

32 Now Mĕn-ē-lā'-ŭs, supposing that he had gotten a convenient time, stole certain vessels of gold out of the temple, and gave some of them to Ăn-drŏn'-ĭ-cŭs, and some he sold into Tyrus and the cities round about.

33 Which when Ŏ-nī'-ăs knew of a surety, he reproved him, and withdrew himself into a sanctuary at Daphne, that lieth by Ăn-tĭ-ŏ'-chĭ-ă.

34 Wherefore Mĕn-ē-lā'-ŭs, taking Ăn-drŏn'-ĭ-cŭs apart, prayed him to get Ŏ-nī'-ăs into his hands; who being persuaded thereunto, and coming to Onias in deceit, gave him his right hand with oaths; and though he were suspected *by him*, yet persuaded he him to come forth of the sanctuary: whom forthwith he shut up without regard of justice.

35 For the which cause not only the Jews, but many also of other nations, took great indignation, and were much grieved for the unjust murder of the man.

36 And when the king was come again from the places about Çĭ-lĭ'-çĭ-a, the Jews that were in the city, and certain of the Greeks that abhorred the fact also, complained because Ŏ-nī'-ăs was slain without cause.

37 Therefore Ăn-tī'-ŏ-chŭs was heartily sorry, and moved

to pity, and wept, because of the sober and modest behaviour of him that was dead.

38 And being kindled with anger, forthwith he took away Ăn-drŏn'-ĭ-cŭs his purple, and rent off his clothes, and leading him through the whole city unto that very place, where he had committed impiety against Ŏ-nī'-ăs, there slew he the cursed murderer. Thus the Lord rewarded him his punishment, as he had deserved.

39 Now when many sacrileges had been committed in the city by Lў-sĭm'-ă-chŭs with the consent of Mĕn-ĕ-lā'-ŭs, and the bruit thereof was spread abroad, the multitude gathered themselves together against Lysimachus, many vessels of gold being already carried away.

40 Whereupon the common people rising, and being filled with rage, Lў-sĭm'-ă-chŭs armed about three thousand men, and began first to offer violence; one Ău-rā'-nŭs being the leader, a man far gone in years, and no less in folly.

41 They then seeing the attempt of Lў-sĭm'-ă-chŭs, some of them caught stones, some clubs, others taking handfuls of dust, that was next at hand, cast them all together upon Lysimachus, and those that set upon them.

42 Thus many of them they wounded, and some they struck to the ground, and all *of them* they forced to flee: but as for the churchrobber himself, him they killed beside the treasury.

43 Of these matters therefore there was an accusation laid against Mĕn-ĕ-lā'-ŭs.
270

44 Now when the king came to Tyrus, three men that were sent from the senate pleaded the cause before him:

45 But Mĕn-ĕ-lā'-ŭs, being now convicted, promised Ptŏl'-ĕ-mēē the *son* of Dŏ-rŷm'-ĕ-nēs to give him much money, if he would pacify the king toward him.

46 Whereupon Ptŏl'-ĕ-mēē taking the king aside into a certain gallery, as it were to take the air, brought him to be of another mind:

47 Insomuch that he discharged Mĕn-ĕ-lā'-ŭs from the accusations, who notwithstanding was cause of all the mischief: and those poor men, who, if they had told their cause, yea, before the Scythians, should have been judged innocent, them he condemned to death.

48 Thus they that followed the matter for the city, and for the people, and for the holy vessels, did soon suffer unjust punishment.

49 Wherefore even they of Tyrus, moved with hatred of that wicked deed, caused them to be honourably buried.

50 And so through the covetousness of them that were of power Mĕn-ĕ-lā'-ŭs remained still in authority, increasing in malice, and being a great traitor to the citizens.

CHAPTER V

ABOUT the same time Ăn-tī'-ŏ-chŭs prepared his second voyage into Egypt:

2 And then it happened, that through all the city, for the space almost of forty days, there were seen horsemen running in the air, in cloth of gold,

and armed with lances, like a band of soldiers,

3 And troops of horsemen in array, encountering and running one against another, with shaking of shields, and multitude of pikes, and drawing of swords, and casting of darts, and glittering of golden ornaments, and harness of all sorts.

4 Wherefore every man prayed that that apparition might turn to good.

5 Now when there was gone forth a false rumour, as though Ăn-tī́-ŏ-<u>ch</u>ŭs had been dead, Jason took at the least a thousand men, and suddenly made an assault upon the city; and they that were upon the walls being put back, and the city at length taken, Mĕn-ĕ-lā́-ŭs fled into the castle:

6 But Jason slew his own citizens without mercy, not considering that to get the day of them of his own nation would be a most unhappy day for him; but thinking they had been *his* enemies, and not *his* countrymen, whom he conquered.

7 Howbeit for all this he obtained not the principality, but at the last received shame for the reward of his treason, and fled again into the country of the Ammonites.

8 In the end therefore he had an unhappy return, being accused before Ăŕ-ĕ-tăs the king of the Arabians, fleeing from city to city, pursued of all men, hated as a forsaker of the laws, and being had in abomination as an open enemy of his country and countrymen, he was cast out into Egypt.

9 Thus he that had driven many out of their country perished in a strange land, retiring to the Lăḉ-ĕ-dĕ-mṓ-nĭ-ăns, and thinking *there* to find succour by reason of his kindred:

10 And he that had cast out many unburied had none to mourn for him, nor any solemn funerals at all, nor sepulchre with his fathers.

11 Now when this that was done came to the king's ear, he thought that Judea had revolted: whereupon removing out of Egypt in a furious mind, he took the city by force of arms,

12 And commanded his men of war not to spare such as they met, and to slay such as went up upon the houses.

13 Thus there was killing of young and old, making away of men, women, and children, slaying of virgins and infants.

14 And there were destroyed within the space of three whole days fourscore thousand, whereof forty thousand were slain in the conflict; and no fewer sold than slain.

15 Yet was he not content with this, but presumed to go into the most holy temple of all the world; Mĕn-ĕ-lā́-ŭs, that traitor to the laws, and to his own country, being his guide:

16 And taking the holy vessels with polluted hands, and with profane hands pulling down the things that were dedicated by other kings to the augmentation and glory and honour of the place, he gave them away.

17 And so haughty was Ăn-tī́-ŏ-<u>ch</u>ŭs in mind, that he considered not that the Lord was angry for a while for the sins of them that dwelt in the city, and therefore his eye was not upon the place.

18 For had they not been formerly wrapped in many sins, this man, as soon as he had come, had forthwith been scourged, and put back from his presumption, as Hĕ́-lĭ-ŏ-dṓ-rŭs was, whom Sĕ-leú́-cŭs the king sent to view the treasury.

19 Nevertheless God did not choose the people for the place's sake, but the place for the people's sake.

20 And therefore the place itself, that was partaker with them of the adversity that happened to the nation, did afterward communicate in the benefits sent from the Lord: and as it was forsaken in the wrath of the Almighty, so again, the great Lord being reconciled, it was set up with all glory.

21 So when Ān-tī́-ŏ-chŭs had carried out of the temple a thousand and eight hundred talents, he departed in all haste unto Ān-tĭ-ŏ́-chĭ-ă, weening in his pride to make the land navigable, and the sea passable by foot: such was the haughtiness of his mind.

22 And he left governors to vex the nation: at Jerusalem, Philip, for his country a Phrẏ́g̈-ĭ-ăn, and for manners more barbarous than he that set him there;

23 And at Găŕ-ĭ-zim, Ăn-drŏń-ĭ-cŭs; and besides, Mĕn-ĕ-lā́-ŭs, who worse than all the rest bare an heavy hand over the citizens, having a malicious mind against his countrymen the Jews.

24 He sent also that detestable ringleader Ăṕ-ŏl-lṓ-nĭ-ŭs with an army of two and twenty thousand, commanding him to slay all those that were in
272

their best age, and to sell the women and the younger sort:

25 Who coming to Jerusalem, and pretending peace, did forbear till the holy day of the sabbath, when taking the Jews keeping holy day, he commanded his men to arm themselves.

26 And so he slew all them that were gone to the celebrating of the sabbath, and running through the city with weapons slew great multitudes.

27 But Judas Măc-că-bḗ-ŭs with nine others, or thereabout, withdrew himself into the wilderness, and lived in the mountains after the manner of beasts, with his company, who fed on herbs continually, lest they should be partakers of the pollution.

CHAPTER VI

NOT long after this the king sent an old man of Athens to compel the Jews to depart from the laws of their fathers, and not to live after the laws of God:

2 And to pollute also the temple in Jerusalem, and to call it the temple of Jupiter Olympius; and that in Găŕ-ĭ-zim, of Jupiter the Defender of strangers, as they did desire that dwelt in the place.

3 The coming in of this mischief was sore and grievous to the people:

4 For the temple was filled with riot and revelling by the Gentiles, who dallied with harlots, and had to do with women within the circuit of the holy places, and besides that brought in things that were not lawful.

5 The altar also was filled with profane things, which the law forbiddeth.

6 Neither was it lawful for a man to keep sabbath days or ancient feasts, or to profess himself at all to be a Jew.

7 And in the day of the king's birth every month they were brought by bitter constraint to eat of the sacrifices; and when the feast of Bacchus was kept, the Jews were compelled to go in procession to Bacchus, carrying ivy.

8 Moreover there went out a decree to the neighbour cities of the heathen, by the suggestion of Ptŏl'-ĕ-mēē, against the Jews, that they should observe the same fashions, and be partakers of their sacrifices:

9 And whoso would not conform themselves to the manners of the Gentiles should be put to death. Then might a man have seen the present misery.

10 For there were two women brought, who had circumcised their children; whom when they had openly led round about the city, the babes hanging at their breasts, they cast them down headlong from the wall.

11 And others, that had run together into caves near by, to keep the sabbath day secretly, being discovered to Philip, were all burnt together, because they made a conscience to help themselves for the honour of the most sacred day.

12 Now I beseech those that read this book, that they be not discouraged for these calamities, but that they judge those punishments not to be for destruction, but for a chastening of our nation.

13 For it is a token of his great goodness, when wicked doers are not suffered any long time, but forthwith punished.

14 For not as with other nations, whom the Lord patiently forbeareth to punish, till they be come to the fulness of their sins, so dealeth he with us,

15 Lest that, being come to the height of sin, afterwards he should take vengeance of us.

16 And therefore he never withdraweth his mercy from us: and though he punish with adversity, yet doth he never forsake his people.

17 But let this that we have spoken be for a warning unto us. And now will we come to the declaring of the matter in few words.

18 Ĕl-ĕ-ā'-zăr, one of the principal scribes, an aged man, and of a wellfavoured countenance, was constrained to open his mouth, and to eat swine's flesh.

19 But he, choosing rather to die gloriously, than to live stained with such an abomination, spit it forth, and came of his own accord to the torment,

20 As it behoved them to come, that are resolute to stand out against such things, as are not lawful for love of life to be tasted.

21 But they that had the charge of that wicked feast, for the old acquaintance they had with the man, taking him aside, besought him to bring flesh of his own provision, such as was lawful for him to use, and make as if he did eat of the flesh taken from the sacrifice commanded by the king;

22 That in so doing he might be delivered from death, and

for the old friendship with them find favour.

23 But he began to consider discreetly, and as became his age, and the excellency of his ancient years, and the honour of his gray head, whereunto he was come, and his most honest education from a child, or rather the holy law made and given by God: therefore he answered accordingly, and willed them straightways to send him to the grave.

24 For it becometh not our age, *said he,* in any wise to dissemble, whereby many young persons might think that Ĕl-ĕ-ā'-zär, being fourscore years old and ten, were now gone to a strange religion;

25 And so they through mine hypocrisy, and desire to live a little time and a moment longer, should be deceived by me, and I get a stain to mine old age, and make it abominable.

26 For though for the present time I should be delivered from the punishment of men: yet should I not escape the hand of the Almighty, neither alive, nor dead.

27 Wherefore now, manfully changing this life, I will shew myself such an one as mine age requireth,

28 And leave a notable example to such as be young to die willingly and courageously for the honourable and holy laws. And when he had said these words, immediately he went to the torment:

29 They that led him changing the good will they bare him a little before into hatred, because the foresaid speeches proceeded, as they thought, from a desperate mind.

30 But when he was ready to die with stripes, he groaned, and said, It is manifest unto the Lord, that hath the holy knowledge, that whereas I might have been delivered from death, I *now* endure sore pains in body by being beaten: but in soul am well content to suffer these things, because I fear him.

31 And thus this man died, leaving his death for an example of a noble courage, and a memorial of virtue, not only unto young men, but unto all his nation.

CHAPTER VII

IT came to pass also, that seven brethren with their mother were taken, and compelled by the king against the law to taste swine's flesh, and were tormented with scourges and whips.

2 But one of them that spake first said thus, What wouldest thou ask or learn of us? we are ready to die, rather than to transgress the laws of our fathers.

3 Then the king, being in a rage, commanded pans and caldrons to be made hot:

4 Which forthwith being heated, he commanded to cut out the tongue of him that spake first, and to cut off the utmost parts of his body, the rest of his brethren and his mother looking on.

5 Now when he was thus maimed in all his members, he commanded him being yet alive to be brought to the fire, and to be fried in the pan: and as the vapour of the pan was for a good space dispersed, they exhorted one another

with the mother to die manfully, saying thus,

6 The Lord God looketh upon us, and in truth hath comfort in us, as Moses in his song, which witnessed to their faces, declared, saying, And he shall be comforted in his servants.

7 So when the first was dead after this manner, they brought the second to make him a mocking stock: and when they had pulled off the skin of his head with the hair, they asked him, Wilt thou eat, before thou be punished throughout every member of thy body?

8 But he answered in his own language, and said, No. Wherefore he also received the next torment in order, as the former did.

9 And when he was at the last gasp, he said, Thou like a fury takest us out of this present life, but the King of the world shall raise us up, who have died for his laws, unto everlasting life.

10 After him was the third made a mocking stock: and when he was required, he put out his tongue, and that right soon, holding forth his hands manfully,

11 And said courageously, These I had from heaven; and for his laws I despise them; and from him I hope to receive them again.

12 Insomuch that the king, and they that were with him, marvelled at the young man's courage, for that he nothing regarded the pains.

13 Now when this man was dead also, they tormented and mangled the fourth in like manner.

14 So when he was ready to

die he said thus, It is good, being put to death by men, to look for hope from God to be raised up again by him: as for thee, thou shalt have no resurrection to life.

15 Afterward they brought the fifth also, and mangled him.

16 Then looked he unto the king, and said, Thou hast power over men, thou art corruptible, thou doest what thou wilt; yet think not that our nation is forsaken of God;

17 But abide a while, and behold his great power, how he will torment thee and thy seed.

18 After him also they brought the sixth, who being ready to die said, Be not deceived without cause: for we suffer these things for ourselves, having sinned against our God: therefore marvellous things are done *unto us.*

19 But think not thou, that takest in hand to strive against God, that thou shalt escape unpunished.

20 But the mother was marvellous above all, and worthy of honourable memory: for when she saw her seven sons slain within the space of one day, she bare it with a good courage, because of the hope that she had in the Lord.

21 Yea, she exhorted every one of them in her own language, filled with courageous spirits; and stirring up her womanish thoughts with a manly stomach, she said unto them,

22 I cannot tell how ye came into my womb; for I neither gave you breath nor life, neither was it I that formed the members of every one of you;

23 But doubtless the Creator of the world, who formed the generation of man, and found out the beginning of all things, will also of his own mercy give you breath and life again, as ye now regard not your own selves for his laws' sake.

24 Now Ăn-tī'-ŏ-chŭs, thinking himself despised, and suspecting it to be a reproachful speech, whilst the youngest was yet alive, did not only exhort him by words, but also assured him with oaths, that he would make him both a rich and a happy man, if he would turn from the laws of his fathers; and that also he would take him for his friend, and trust him with affairs.

25 But when the young man would in no case hearken unto him, the king called his mother, and exhorted her that she would counsel the young man to save his life.

26 And when he had exhorted her with many words, she promised him that she would counsel her son.

27 But she bowing herself toward him, laughing the cruel tyrant to scorn, spake in her country language on this manner; O my son, have pity upon me that bare thee nine months in my womb, and gave thee suck three years, and nourished thee, and brought thee up unto this age, and endured the troubles of education.

28 I beseech thee, my son, look upon the heaven and the earth, and all that is therein, and consider that God made them of things that were not; and so was mankind made likewise.

29 Fear not this tormentor, but, being worthy of thy breth-

ren, take thy death, that I may receive thee again in mercy with thy brethren.

30 Whiles she was yet speaking these words, the young man said, Whom wait ye for? I will not obey the king's commandment: but I will obey the commandment of the law that was given unto our fathers by Moses.

31 And thou, that hast been the author of all mischief against the Hebrews, shalt not escape the hands of God.

32 For we suffer because of our sins.

33 And though the living Lord be angry with us a little while for our chastening and correction, yet shall he be at one again with his servants.

34 But thou, O godless man, and of all other most wicked, be not lifted up without a cause, nor puffed up with uncertain hopes, lifting up thy hand against the servants of God:

35 For thou hast not yet escaped the judgment of Almighty God, who seeth all things.

36 For our brethren, who now have suffered a short pain, are dead under God's covenant of everlasting life: but thou, through the judgment of God, shalt receive just punishment for thy pride.

37 But I, as my brethren, offer up my body and life for the laws of our fathers, beseeching God that he would speedily be merciful unto our nation; and that thou by torments and plagues mayest confess, that he alone is God;

38 And that in me and my brethren the wrath of the Almighty, which is justly brought

upon all our nation, may cease.

39 Then the king, being in a rage, handled him worse than all the rest, and took it grievously that he was mocked.

40 So this man died undefiled, and put his whole trust in the Lord.

41 Last of all after the sons the mother died.

42 Let this be enough now to have spoken concerning the idolatrous feasts, and the extreme tortures.

CHAPTER VIII

THEN Judas Măc-că-bē'-ŭs, and they that were with him, went privily into the towns, and called their kinsfolks together, and took unto them all such as continued in the Jews' religion, and assembled about six thousand men.

2 And they called upon the Lord, that he would look upon the people that was trodden down of all; and also pity the temple profaned of ungodly men;

3 And that he would have compassion upon the city, sore defaced, and ready to be made even with the ground; and hear the blood that cried unto him,

4 And remember the wicked slaughter of harmless infants, and the blasphemies committed against his name; and that he would shew his hatred against the wicked.

5 Now when Măc-că-bē'-ŭs had his company about him, he could not be withstood by the heathen: for the wrath of the Lord was turned into mercy.

6 Therefore he came at un-

awares, and burnt up towns and cities, and got into his hands the most commodious places, and overcame and put to flight no small number of his enemies.

7 But specially took he advantage of the night for such privy attempts, insomuch that the bruit of his manliness was spread every where.

8 So when Philip saw that this man increased by little and little, and that things prospered with him still more and more, he wrote unto Ptŏl-ĕ-mē'-ŭs, the governor of Çē'-lŏ-sў̈r'-ḭ-ă and Phē-nī'-çĕ, to yield more aid to the king's affairs.

9 Then forthwith choosing Nī-că'-nôr the *son* of Pă-trŏ'-clŭs, one of his special friends, he sent him with no fewer than twenty thousand of all nations under him, to root out the whole generation of the Jews; and with him he joined also Gôr'-ġḭ-ăs a captain, who in matters of war had great experience.

10 So Nī-că'-nôr undertook to make so much money of the captive Jews, as should defray the tribute of two thousand talents, which the king was to pay to the Romans.

11 Wherefore immediately he sent to the cities upon the sea coast, proclaiming a sale of the captive Jews, and promising that they should have fourscore and ten bodies for one talent, not expecting the vengeance that was to follow upon him from the Almighty God.

12 Now when word was brought unto Judas of Nī-că'-nôr's coming, and he had imparted unto those that were with him that the army was at hand,

13 They that were fearful, and distrusted the justice of God, fled, and conveyed themselves away.

14 Others sold all that they had left, and withal besought the Lord to deliver them, being sold by the wicked Nĭ-cā'-nôr before they met together:

15 And if not for their own sakes, yet for the covenants he had made with their fathers, and for his holy and glorious name's sake, by which they were called.

16 So Măc-că-bē'-ŭs called his men together unto the number of six thousand, and exhorted them not to be stricken with terror of the enemy, nor to fear the great multitude of the heathen, who came wrongfully against them; but to fight manfully,

17 And to set before their eyes the injury that they had unjustly done to the holy place, and the cruel handling of the city, whereof they made a mockery, and also the taking away of the government of their forefathers:

18 For they, said he, trust in their weapons and boldness; but our confidence is in the Almighty God, who at a beck can cast down both them that come against us, and also all the world.

19 Moreover he recounted unto them what helps their forefathers had found, and how they were delivered, when under Sĕn-năch'-ĕr-ĭb an hundred fourscore and five thousand perished.

20 And he told them of the battle that they had in Babylon with the Galatians, how they came but eight thousand in all to the business, with four thousand Macedonians, and that the Macedonians being perplexed, the eight thousand destroyed an hundred and twenty thousand because of the help that they had from heaven, and so received a great booty.

21 Thus when he had made them bold with these words, and ready to die for the laws and the country, he divided his army into four parts;

22 And joined with himself his own brethren, leaders of each band, *to wit,* Simon, and Joseph, and Jonathan, giving each one fifteen hundred men.

23 Also *he appointed* Ĕl-ĕ-ā'-zăr to read the holy book: and when he had given them this watchword, The help of God; himself leading the first band, he joined battle with Nĭ-cā'-nôr.

24 And by the help of the Almighty they slew above nine thousand of their enemies, and wounded and maimed the most part of Nĭ-cā'-nôr's host, and so put all to flight;

25 And took their money that came to buy them, and pursued them far: but lacking time they returned:

26 For it was the day before the sabbath, and therefore they would no longer pursue them.

27 So when they had gathered their armour together, and spoiled their enemies, they occupied themselves about the sabbath, yielding exceeding praise and thanks to the Lord, who had preserved them unto that day, which was the beginning of mercy distilling upon them.

28 And after the sabbath, when they had given part of

the spoils to the maimed, and the widows, and orphans, the residue they divided among themselves and their servants.

29 When this was done, and they had made a common supplication, they besought the merciful Lord to be reconciled with his servants for ever.

30 Moreover of those that were with Tĭ-mō'-thĕ-ŭs and Băc'-chĭ-dēs, who fought against them, they slew above twenty thousand, and very easily got high and strong holds, and divided among themselves many spoils more, and made the maimed, orphans, widows, yea, and the aged also, equal in spoils with themselves.

31 And when they had gathered their armour together, they laid them up all carefully in convenient places, and the remnant of the spoils they brought to Jerusalem.

32 They slew also Phĭ-lär'-chēs, that wicked person, who was with Tĭ-mō'-thĕ-ŭs, and had annoyed the Jews many ways.

33 Furthermore at such time as they kept the feast for the victory in their country they burnt Căl-lĭs'-thĕ-nēs, that had set fire upon the holy gates, who had fled into a little house; and so he received a reward meet for his wickedness.

34 As for that most ungracious Nĭ-cā'-nôr, who had brought a thousand merchants to buy the Jews,

35 He was through the help of the Lord brought down by them, of whom he made least account; and putting off his glorious apparel, and discharging his company, he came like a fugitive servant through the midland unto Antioch, having very great dishonour, for that his host was destroyed.

36 Thus he, that took upon him to make good to the Romans their tribute by means of the captives in Jerusalem, told abroad, that the Jews had God to fight for them, and therefore they could not be hurt, because they followed the laws that he gave them.

CHAPTER IX

ABOUT that time came Ăn-tī'-ŏ-chŭs with dishonour out of the country of Persia.

2 For he had entered the *city* called Pĕr-sĕp'-ŏ-lĭs, and went about to rob the temple, and to hold the city; whereupon the multitude running to defend themselves with their weapons put them to flight; and so it happened, that Ăn-tī'-ŏ-chŭs being put to flight of the inhabitants returned with shame.

3 Now when he came to Ĕc-băt'-ă-nĕ, news was brought him what had happened unto Nĭ-cā'-nôr and Tĭ-mō'-thĕ-ŭs.

4 Then swelling with anger, he thought to avenge upon the Jews the disgrace done unto him by those that made him flee. Therefore commanded he his chariotman to drive without ceasing, and to dispatch the journey, the judgment of God now following him. For he had spoken proudly in this sort, That he would come to Jerusalem, and make it a common buryingplace of the Jews.

5 But the Lord Almighty, the God of Israel, smote him with an incurable and invisible plague: for as soon as he had

279

spoken these words, a pain of the bowels that was remediless came upon him, and sore torments of the inner parts;

6 And that most justly: for he had tormented other men's bowels with many and strange torments.

7 Howbeit he nothing at all ceased from his bragging, but still was filled with pride, breathing out fire in his rage against the Jews, and commanding to haste the journey: but it came to pass that he fell down from his chariot, carried violently; so that having a sore fall, all the members of his body were much pained.

8 And thus he that a little afore thought he might command the waves of the sea, (so proud was he beyond the condition of man) and weigh the high mountains in a balance, was now cast on the ground, and carried in an horselitter, shewing forth unto all the manifest power of God.

9 So that the worms rose up out of the body of this wicked man, and whiles he lived in sorrow and pain, his flesh fell away, and the filthiness of his smell was noisome to all his army.

10 And the man, that thought a little afore he could reach to the stars of heaven, no man could endure to carry for his intolerable stink.

11 Here therefore, being plagued, he began to leave off his great pride, and to come to the knowledge *of himself* by the scourge of God, his pain increasing every moment.

12 And when he himself could not abide his own smell, he said these words, It is meet to be subject unto God, and that

280

a man that is mortal should not proudly think of himself, as if he were God.

13 This wicked person vowed also unto the Lord, who now no more would have mercy upon him, saying thus,

14 That the holy city (to the which he was going in haste, to lay it even with the ground, and to make it a common buryingplace,) he would set at liberty:

15 And as touching the Jews, whom he had judged not worthy so much as to be buried, but to be cast out with their children to be devoured of the fowls and wild beasts, he would make them all equals to the citizens of Athens:

16 And the holy temple, which before he had spoiled, he would garnish with goodly gifts, and restore all the holy vessels with many more, and out of his own revenue defray the charges belonging to the sacrifices:

17 Yea, and that also he would become a Jew himself, and go through all the world that was inhabited, and declare the power of God.

18 But for all this his pains would not cease: for the just judgment of God was come upon him: therefore despairing of his health, he wrote unto the Jews the letter underwritten, containing the form of a supplication, after this manner:

19 Ăn-tī-ŏ-chŭs, king and governor, to the good Jews his citizens wisheth much joy, health, and prosperity:

20 If ye and your children fare well, and your affairs be to your contentment, I give very great thanks to God, having my hope in heaven.

21 As for me, I was weak, or else I would have remembered kindly your honour and good will. Returning out of Persia, and being taken with a grievous disease, I thought it necessary to care for the common safety of all:

22 Not distrusting mine health, but having great hope to escape this sickness.

23 But considering that even my father, at what time he led an army into the high countries, appointed a successor,

24 To the end that, if any thing fell out contrary to expectation, or if any tidings were brought that were grievous, they of the land, knowing to whom the state was left, might not be troubled:

25 Again, considering how that the princes that are borderers and neighbours unto my kingdom wait for opportunities, and expect what shall be the event, I have appointed my son Ăn-tī´-ŏ-chŭs king, whom I often committed and commended unto many of you, when I went up into the high provinces; to whom I have written as followeth:

26 Therefore I pray and request you to remember the benefits that I have done unto you generally, and in special, and that every man will be still faithful to me and my son.

27 For I am persuaded that he understanding my mind will favourably and graciously yield to your desires.

28 Thus the murderer and blasphemer having suffered most grievously, as he entreated other men, so died he a miserable death in a strange country in the mountains.

29 And Philip, that was brought up with him, carried away his body, who also fearing the son of Ăn-tī´-ŏ-chŭs went into Egypt to Ptŏl-ĕ-mē´-ŭs Phī-lŏ-mē´-tôr.

CHAPTER X

NOW Măc-că-bē´-ŭs and his company, the Lord guiding them, recovered the temple and the city:

2 But the altars which the heathen had built in the open street, and also the chapels, they pulled down.

3 And having cleansed the temple they made another altar, and striking stones they took fire out of them, and offered a sacrifice after two years, and set forth incense, and lights, and shewbread.

4 When that was done, they fell flat down, and besought the Lord that they might come no more into such troubles; but if they sinned any more against him, that he himself would chasten them with mercy, and that they might not be delivered unto the blasphemous and barbarous nations.

5 Now upon the same day that the strangers profaned the temple, on the very same day it was cleansed again, even the five and twentieth day of the same month, which is Căs´-lĕū.

6 And they kept eight days with gladness, as in the feast of the tabernacles, remembering that not long afore they had held the feast of the tabernacles, when as they wandered in the mountains and dens like beasts.

7 Therefore they bare branches, and fair boughs, and palms also, and sang psalms unto him that had given them good

success in cleansing his place.

8 They ordained also by a common statute and decree, That every year those days should be kept of the whole nation of the Jews.

9 And this was the end of Ăn-tī´-ŏ-chŭs, called Ē-pĭph´-ă-nēs.

10 Now will we declare the acts of Ăn-tī´-ŏ-chŭs Ēu-pā´-tôr, who was the son of this wicked man, gathering briefly the calamities of the wars.

11 So when he was come to the crown, he set one Lўs´-į-ăs over the affairs of his realm, and *appointed him* chief governor of Çē´-lŏ-sўr´-į-ă and Phē-nī´-çē.

12 For Ptŏl-ē-mē´-ŭs, that was called Mā´-crŏn, choosing rather to do justice unto the Jews for the wrong that had been done unto them, endeavoured to continue peace with them.

13 Whereupon being accused of *the king's* friends before Ēu-pā´-tôr, and called traitor at every word, because he had left Cyprus, that Phĭ-lŏ-mē´-tôr had committed unto him, and departed to Ăn-tī´-ŏ-chŭs Ē-pĭph´-ă-nēs, and seeing that he was in no honourable place, he was so discouraged, that he poisoned himself and died.

14 But when Gôr´-gį-ăs was governor of the holds, he hired soldiers, and nourished war continually with the Jews:

15 And therewithal the Ĭd-ŭ-mē´-ăns, having gotten into their hands the most commodious holds, kept the Jews occupied, and receiving those that were banished from Jerusalem, they went about to nourish war.

16 Then they that were with Măc-că-bē´-ŭs made supplication, and besought God that he

would be their helper; and so they ran with violence upon the strong holds of the Ĭd-ŭ-mē´-ăns,

17 And assaulting them strongly, they won the holds, and kept off all that fought upon the wall, and slew all that fell into their hands, and killed no fewer than twenty thousand.

18 And because certain, who were no less than nine thousand, were fled together into two very strong castles, having all manner of things convenient to *sustain* the siege,

19 Măc-că-bē´-ŭs left Simon and Joseph, and Zăc-chē´-ŭs also, and them that were with him, who were enough to besiege them, and departed himself unto those places which more needed his help.

20 Now they that were with Simon, being led with covetousness, were persuaded for money through certain of those that were in the castle, and took seventy thousand drachms, and let some of them escape.

21 But when it was told Măc-că-bē´-ŭs what was done, he called the governors of the people together, and accused those men, that they had sold their brethren for money, and set their enemies free to fight against them.

22 So he slew those that were found traitors, and immediately took the two castles.

23 And having good success with his weapons in all things he took in hand, he slew in the two holds more than twenty thousand.

24 Now Tĭ-mō´-thē-ŭs, whom the Jews had overcome before, when he had gathered a great

multitude of foreign forces, and horses out of Asia not a few, came as though he would take Jewry by force of arms.

25 But when he drew near, they that were with Măc-că-bē'-ŭs turned themselves to pray unto God, and sprinkled earth upon their heads, and girded their loins with sackcloth,

26 And fell down at the foot of the altar, and besought him to be merciful to them, and to be an enemy to their enemies, and an adversary to their adversaries, as the law declareth.

27 So after the prayer they took their weapons, and went on further from the city: and when they drew near to their enemies, they kept by themselves.

28 Now the sun being newly risen, they joined both together; the one part having together with their virtue their refuge also unto the Lord for a pledge of their success and victory: the other side making their rage leader of their battle.

29 But when the battle waxed strong, there appeared unto the enemies from heaven five comely men upon horses, with bridles of gold, and two of them led the Jews,

30 And took Măc-că-bē'-ŭs betwixt them, and covered him on every side with their weapons, and kept him safe, but shot arrows and lightnings against the enemies: so that being confounded with blindness, and full of trouble, they were killed.

31 And there were slain *of footmen* twenty thousand and five hundred, and six hundred horsemen.

32 As for Tĭ-mō'-thĕ-ŭs himself, he fled into a very strong hold, called Gă-zā'-ră, where Chē'-rĕ-ăs was governor.

33 But they that were with Măc-că-bē'-ŭs laid siege against the fortress courageously four days.

34 And they that were within, trusting to the strength of the place, blasphemed exceedingly, and uttered wicked words.

35 Nevertheless upon the fifth day early twenty young men of Măc-că-bē'-ŭs' company, inflamed with anger because of the blasphemies, assaulted the wall manly, and with a fierce courage killed all that they met withal.

36 Others likewise ascending after them, whiles they were busied with them that were within, burnt the towers, and kindling fires burnt the blasphemers alive; and others broke open the gates, and, having received in the rest of the army, took the city,

37 And killed Tĭ-mō'-thĕ-ŭs, that was hid in a certain pit, and Chē'-rĕ-ăs his brother, with Ăp'-ŏl-lŏph'-ă-nēs.

38 When this was done, they praised the Lord with psalms and thanksgiving, who had done so great things for Israel, and given them the victory.

CHAPTER XI

NOT long after this, Lўs'-ĭ-ăs the king's protector and cousin, who also managed the affairs, took sore displeasure for the things that were done.

2 And when he had gathered about fourscore thousand with all the horsemen, he came against the Jews, thinking to

make the city an habitation of the Gentiles,

3 And to make a gain of the temple, as of the other chapels of the heathen, and to set the high priesthood to sale every year:

4 Not at all considering the power of God, but puffed up with his ten thousands of footmen, and his thousands of horsemen, and his fourscore elephants.

5 So he came to Judea, and drew near to Bĕth-sŭ´-rā, which was a strong town, but distant from Jerusalem about five furlongs, and he laid sore siege unto it.

6 Now when they that were with Măc-că-bē´-ŭs heard that he besieged the holds, they and all the people with lamentation and tears besought the Lord that he would send a good angel to deliver Israel.

7 Then Măc-că-bē´-ŭs himself first of all took weapons, exhorting the other that they would jeopard themselves together with him to help their brethren: so they went forth together with a willing mind.

8 And as they were at Jerusalem, there appeared before them on horseback one in white clothing, shaking his armour of gold.

9 Then they praised the merciful God all together, and took heart, insomuch that they were ready not only to fight with men, but with most cruel beasts, and to pierce through walls of iron.

10 Thus they marched forward in their armour, having an helper from heaven: for the Lord was merciful unto them.

11 And giving a charge upon their enemies like lions, they

284

slew eleven thousand *footmen*, and sixteen hundred horsemen, and put all the other to flight.

12 Many of them also being wounded escaped naked; and Lўs´-ị-ăs himself fled away shamefully, and so escaped.

13 Who, as he was a man of understanding, casting with himself what loss he had had, and considering that the Hebrews could not be overcome, because the Almighty God helped them, he sent unto them,

14 And persuaded them to agree to all reasonable *conditions*, and *promised* that he would persuade the king that he must needs be a friend unto them.

15 Then Măc-că-bē´-ŭs consented to all that Lўs´-ị-ăs desired, being careful of the common good; and whatsoever Maccabeus wrote unto Lysias concerning the Jews, the king granted it.

16 For there were letters written unto the Jews from Lўs´-ị-ăs to this effect: Lysias unto the people of the Jews *sendeth* greeting:

17 John and Absalon, who were sent from you, delivered me the petition subscribed, and made request for the performance of the contents thereof.

18 Therefore what things soever were meet to be reported to the king, I have declared them, and he hath granted as much as might be.

19 If then ye will keep yourselves loyal to the state, hereafter also will I endeavour to be a means of your good.

20 But of the particulars I have given order both to these,

and the other that came from me, to commune with you.

21 Fare ye well. The hundred and eight and fortieth year, the four and twentieth day of *the month* Dĭ´-ŏs-cŏ-rĭn´-thĭ-ŭs.

22 Now the king's letter contained these words: King Ăn-tĭ´-ŏ-chŭs unto his brother Lўs´-ĭ-ăs *sendeth* greeting:

23 Since our father is translated unto the gods, our will is, that they that are in our realm live quietly, that every one may attend upon his own affairs.

24 We understand also that the Jews would not consent to our father, for to be brought unto the custom of the Gentiles, but had rather keep their own manner of living: for the which cause they require of us, that we should suffer them to live after their own laws.

25 Wherefore our mind is, that this nation shall be in rest, and we have determined to restore them their temple, that they may live according to the customs of their forefathers.

26 Thou shalt do well therefore to send unto them, and grant them peace, that when they are certified of our mind, they may be of good comfort, and ever go cheerfully about their own affairs.

27 And the letter of the king unto the nation of the Jews was after this manner: King Ăn-tĭ´-ŏ-chŭs *sendeth* greeting unto the council, and the rest of the Jews:

28 If ye fare well, we have our desire; we are also in good health.

29 Mĕn-ĕ-lā´-ŭs declared unto us, that your desire was to return home, and to follow your own business:

30 Wherefore they that will depart shall have safe conduct till the thirtieth day of Xăn´-thĭ-cŭs with security.

31 And the Jews shall use their own kind of meats and laws, as before; and none of them any manner of ways shall be molested for things ignorantly done.

32 I have sent also Mĕn-ĕ-lā´-ŭs, that he may comfort you.

33 Fare ye well. In the hundred forty and eighth year, *and* the fifteenth day of *the month* Xăn´-thĭ-cŭs.

34 The Romans also sent unto them a letter containing these words: Quintus Mĕm´-mĭ-ŭs and Titus Manlius, ambassadors of the Romans, *send* greeting unto the people of the Jews.

35 Whatsoever Lўs´-ĭ-ăs the king's cousin hath granted, therewith we also are well pleased.

36 But touching such things as he judged to be referred to the king, after ye have advised thereof, send one forthwith, that we may declare as it is convenient for you: for we are now going to Antioch.

37 Therefore send some with speed, that we may know what is your mind.

38 Farewell. This hundred and eight and fortieth year, the fifteenth day of *the month* Xăn´-thĭ-cŭs.

CHAPTER XII

WHEN these covenants were made, Lўs´-ĭ-ăs went unto the king, and the Jews were about their husbandry.

2 But of the governors of several places, Tĭ-mṓ-thē-ŭs, and Ăp̓-ŏl-lṓ-nĭ-ŭs the *son of* Gĕn-nḗ-ŭs, also Hĭ́-ĕr-ŏn̓-ў̆-mŭs, and Dĕm̓-ŏ-phŏn, and beside them Nĭ-cā́-nôr the governor of Cyprus, would not suffer them to be quiet, and live in peace.

3 The men of Jŏp̓-pĕ also did such an ungodly deed: they prayed the Jews that dwelt among them to go with their wives and children into the boats which they had prepared, as though they had meant them no hurt.

4 Who accepted of it according to the common decree of the city, as being desirous to live in peace, and suspecting nothing: but when they were gone forth into the deep, they drowned no less than two hundred of them.

5 When Judas heard of this cruelty done unto his countrymen, he commanded those that were with him *to make them ready.*

6 And calling upon God the righteous Judge, he came against those murderers of his brethren, and burnt the haven by night, and set the boats on fire, and those that fled thither he slew.

7 And when the town was shut up, he went backward, as if he would return to root out all them of the city of Jŏp̓-pĕ.

8 But when he heard that the Jamnites were minded to do in like manner unto the Jews that dwelt among them,

9 He came upon the Jamnites also by night, and set fire on the haven and the navy, so that the light of fire was seen at Jerusalem two hundred and forty furlongs off.

10 Now when they were gone from thence nine furlongs in their journey toward Tĭ-mṓ-thē-ŭs, no fewer than five thousand *men on foot* and five hundred horsemen of the Arabians set upon him.

11 Whereupon there was a very sore battle; but Judas' side by the help of God got the victory; so that the Nṓ-mādes of Arabia, being overcome, besought Judas for peace, promising both to give him cattle, and to pleasure him otherwise.

12 Then Judas, thinking indeed that they would be profitable in many things, granted them peace: whereupon they shook hands, and so they departed to their tents.

13 He went also about to make a bridge to a certain strong city, which was fenced about with walls, and inhabited by people of divers countries; and the name of it was Caspis.

14 But they that were within it put such trust in the strength of the walls and provision of victuals, that they behaved themselves rudely toward them that were with Judas, railing and blaspheming, and uttering such words as were not to be spoken.

15 Wherefore Judas with his company, calling upon the great Lord of the world, who without any rams or engines of war did cast down Jericho in the time of Joshua, gave a fierce assault against the walls,

16 And took the city by the will of God, and made unspeakable slaughters, insomuch that a lake two furlongs broad near adjoining thereunto, being filled full, was seen running with blood.

17 Then departed they from thence seven hundred and fifty furlongs, and came to Chăr´-ă-că unto the Jews that are called Tū´-bĭ-ē´-nĭ.

18 But as for Tĭ-mŏ´-thē-ŭs, they found him not in the places: for before he had dispatched any thing, he departed from thence, having left a very strong garrison in a certain hold.

19 Howbeit Dŏ-sĭth´-ĕ-ŭs and Sŏ-sĭp´-ă-tēr, who were of Măc-că-bē´-ŭs' captains, went forth, and slew those that Tĭ-mŏ´-thē-ŭs had left in the fortress, above ten thousand men.

20 And Măc-că-bē´-ŭs ranged his army by bands, and set them over the bands, and went against Tĭ-mŏ´-thē-ŭs, who had about him an hundred and twenty thousand men of foot, and two thousand and five hundred horsemen.

21 Now when Tĭ-mŏ´-thē-ŭs had knowledge of Judas' coming, he sent the women and children and the other baggage unto a fortress called Căr´-nĭ-on: for the town was hard to besiege, and uneasy to come unto, by reason of the straitness of all the places.

22 But when Judas his first band came in sight, the enemies, being smitten with fear and terror through the appearing of him that seeth all things, fled amain, one running this way, another that way, so as that they were often hurt of their own men, and wounded with the points of their own swords.

23 Judas also was very earnest in pursuing them, killing those wicked wretches, of whom he slew about thirty thousand men.

24 Moreover Tĭ-mŏ´-thē-ŭs himself fell into the hands of Dŏ-sĭth´-ĕ-ŭs and Sŏ-sĭp´-ă-tēr, whom he besought with much craft to let him go with his life, because he had many of the Jews' parents, and the brethren of some of them, who, if they put him to death, should not be regarded.

25 So when he had assured them with many words that he would restore them without hurt, according to the agreement, they let him go for the saving of their brethren.

26 Then Măc-că-bē´-ŭs marched forth to Căr´-nĭ-on, and to the temple of Ă-tär´-gă-tĭs, and there he slew five and twenty thousand persons.

27 And after he had put to flight and destroyed them, Judas removed the host toward E´-phrôn, a strong city, wherein Lўs´-ĭ-ăs abode, and a great multitude of divers nations, and the strong young men kept the walls, and defended them mightily: wherein also was great provision of engines and darts.

28 But when Judas and his company had called upon Almighty God, who with his power breaketh the strength of his enemies, they won the city, and slew twenty and five thousand of them that were within.

29 From thence they departed to Scў-thŏp´-ŏ-lĭs, which lieth six hundred furlongs from Jerusalem.

30 But when the Jews that dwelt there had testified that the Scўth´-ŏ-pŏl´-ĭ-tăns dealt lovingly with them, and entreated them kindly in the time of their adversity;

31 They gave them thanks,

desiring them to be friendly still unto them: and so they came to Jerusalem, the feast of the weeks approaching.

32 And after the *feast*, called Pentecost, they went forth against Gôr'-gi-ăs the governor of Ĭd-ŭ-mē'-ă,

33 Who came out with three thousand men of foot and four hundred horsemen.

34 And it happened that in their fighting together a few of the Jews were slain.

35 At which time Dŏ-sĭth'-ĕ-ŭs, one of Bă-çē'-nôr's company, who was on horseback, and a strong man, was still upon Gôr'-gi-ăs, and taking hold of his coat drew him by force; and when he would have taken that cursed man alive, a horseman of Thracia coming upon him smote off his shoulder, so that Gorgias fled unto Măr'-ĭ-să.

36 Now when they that were with Gôr'-gi-ăs had fought long, and were weary, Judas called upon the Lord, that he would shew himself to be their helper and leader of the battle.

37 And with that he began in his own language, and sung psalms with a loud voice, and rushing unawares upon Gôr'-gi-ăs' men, he put them to flight.

38 So Judas gathered his host, and came into the city of Ŏ-dŏl'-lăm. And when the seventh day came, they purified themselves, as the custom was, and kept the sabbath in the same place.

39 And upon the day following, as the use had been, Judas and his company came to take up the bodies of them that were slain, and to bury them with their kinsmen in their fathers' graves.

288

40 Now under the coats of every one that was slain they found things consecrated to the idols of the Jamnites, which is forbidden the Jews by the law. Then every man saw that this was the cause wherefore they were slain.

41 All men therefore praising the Lord, the righteous Judge, who had opened the things that were hid,

42 Betook themselves unto prayer, and besought him that the sin committed might wholly be put out of remembrance. Besides, that noble Judas exhorted the people to keep themselves from sin, forsomuch as they saw before their eyes the things that came to pass for the sins of those that were slain.

43 And when he had made a gathering throughout the company to the sum of two thousand drachms of silver, he sent it to Jerusalem to offer a sin offering, doing therein very well and honestly, in that he was mindful of the resurrection:

44 For if he had not hoped that they that were slain should have risen again, it had been superfluous and vain to pray for the dead.

45 And also in that he perceived that there was great favour laid up for those that died godly, it was an holy and good thought. Whereupon he made a reconciliation for the dead, that they might be delivered from sin.

CHAPTER XIII

IN the hundred forty and ninth year it was told Judas. that Ăn-tī'-ŏ-chŭs Eū-pā'-tôr was coming with a great power into Judea,

2 And with him Lўs'-ĭ-ăs his protector, and ruler of his affairs, having either of them a Grecian power of footmen, an hundred and ten thousand, and horsemen five thousand and three hundred, and elephants two and twenty, and three hundred chariots armed with hooks.

3 Mĕn-ĕ-lā'-ŭs also joined himself with them, and with great dissimulation encouraged Ăn-tĭ'-ŏ-chŭs, not for the safeguard of the country, but because he thought to have been made governor.

4 But the King of kings moved Ăn-tĭ'-ŏ-chŭs' mind against this wicked wretch, and Lўs'-ĭ-ăs informed the king that this man was the cause of all mischief, so that the king commanded to bring him unto Bē'-rĕ-ă, and to put him to death, as the manner is in that place.

5 Now there was in that place a tower of fifty cubits high, full of ashes, and it had a round instrument, which on every side hanged down into the ashes.

6 And whosoever was condemned of sacrilege, or had committed any other grievous crime, there did all men thrust him unto death.

7 Such a death it happened that wicked man to die, not having so much as burial in the earth; and that most justly:

8 For inasmuch as he had committed many sins about the altar, whose fire and ashes were holy, he received his death in ashes.

9 Now the king came with a barbarous and haughty mind to do far worse to the Jews,

than had been done in his father's time.

10 Which things when Judas perceived, he commanded the multitude to call upon the Lord night and day, that if ever at any other time, he would now also help them, being at the point to be put from their law, from their country, and from the holy temple:

11 And that he would not suffer the people, that had even now been but a little refreshed, to be in subjection to the blasphemous nations.

12 So when they had all done this together, and besought the merciful Lord with weeping and fasting, and lying flat upon the ground three days long, Judas, having exhorted them, commanded they should be in a readiness.

13 And Judas, being apart with the elders, determined, before the king's host should enter into Judea, and get the city, to go forth and try the matter *in fight* by the help of the Lord.

14 So when he had committed *all* to the Creator of the world, and exhorted his soldiers to fight manfully, even unto death, for the laws, the temple, the city, the country, and the commonwealth, he camped by Mō'-dĭn:

15 And having given the watchword to them that were about him, Victory is of God; with the most valiant and choice young men he went in into the king's tent by night, and slew in the camp about four thousand men, and the chiefest of the elephants, with all that were upon him.

16 And at last they filled the

camp with fear and tumult, and departed with good success.

17 This was done in the break of the day, because the protection of the Lord did help him.

18 Now when the king had taken a taste of the manliness of the Jews, he went about to take the holds by policy,

19 And marched toward Běth-sū'-rǎ, which was a strong hold of the Jews: but he was put to flight, failed, and lost of his men:

20 For Judas had conveyed unto them that were in it such things as were necessary.

21 But Rhŏd'-ŏ-cŭs, who was in the Jews' host, disclosed the secrets to the enemies; therefore he was sought out, and when they had gotten him, they put him in prison.

22 The king treated with them in Běth-sū'-rǎ the second time, gave his hand, took theirs, departed, fought with Judas, was overcome;

23 Heard that Philip, who was left over the affairs in Antioch, was desperately bent, confounded, intreated the Jews, submitted himself, and sware to all equal conditions, agreed with them, and offered sacrifice, honoured the temple, and dealt kindly with the place,

24 And accepted well of Măc-că-bē'-ŭs, made him principal governor from Ptŏl-ĕ-mā'-ĭs unto the Gĕr-rhē'-nĭ-ăns;

25 Came to Ptŏl-ĕ-mā'-ĭs: the people there were grieved for the covenants; for they stormed, because they would make their covenants void:

26 Lȳs'-ĭ-ăs went up to the judgment seat, said as much as could be in defence of the

cause, persuaded, pacified, made them well affected, returned to Antioch. Thus it went touching the king's coming and departing.

CHAPTER XIV

AFTER three years was Judas informed, that Dĕ-mē'-trĭ-ŭs the *son* of Sĕ-lĕu'-cŭs, having entered in by the haven of Trĭp'-ŏ-lĭs with a great power and navy,

2 Had taken the country, and killed Ăn-tī'-ŏ-<u>ch</u>ŭs, and Lȳs'-ĭ-ăs his protector.

3 Now one Ăl'-çĭ-mŭs, who had been high priest, and had defiled himself wilfully in the times of their mingling *with the Gentiles*, seeing that by no means he could save himself, nor have any more access to the holy altar,

4 Came to king Dĕ-mē'-trĭ-ŭs in the hundred and one and fiftieth year, presenting unto him a crown of gold, and a palm, and also of the boughs which were used solemnly in the temple: and so that day he held his peace.

5 Howbeit, having gotten opportunity to further his foolish enterprize, *and* being called into counsel by Dĕ-mē'-trĭ-ŭs, and asked how the Jews stood affected, and what they intended, he answered thereunto:

6 Those of the Jews that be called Ăs-sĭ-dē'-ăns, whose captain is Judas Măc-că-bē'-ŭs, nourish war, and are seditious, and will not let the realm be in peace.

7 Therefore I, being deprived of mine ancestors' honour, I mean the high priesthood, am now come hither:

8 First, verily for the unfeigned care I have of things pertaining to the king; and secondly, even for that I intend the good of mine own countrymen: for all our nation is in no small misery through the unadvised dealing of them aforesaid.

9 Wherefore, O king, seeing thou knowest all these things, be careful for the country, and our nation, which is pressed on every side, according to the clemency that thou readily shewest unto all.

10 For as long as Judas liveth, it is not possible that the state should be quiet.

11 This was no sooner spoken of him, but others of the king's friends, being maliciously set against Judas, did more incense Dĕ-mē´-trĭ-ŭs.

12 And forthwith calling Nĭ-cā´-nôr, who had been master of the elephants, and making him governor over Judea, he sent him forth,

13 Commanding him to slay Judas, and to scatter them that were with him, and to make Ăl´-çĭ-mŭs high priest of the great temple.

14 Then the heathen, that had fled out of Judea from Judas, came to Nĭ-cā´-nôr by flocks, thinking the harm and calamities of the Jews to be their welfare.

15 Now when the Jews heard of Nĭ-cā´-nôr's coming, and that the heathen were up against them, they cast earth upon their heads, and made supplication to him that had established his people for ever, and who always helpeth his portion with manifestation of his presence.

16 So at the commandment of the captain they removed straightways from thence, and came near unto them at the town of Dĕs´-saū.

17 Now Simon, Judas' brother, had joined battle with Nĭ-cā´-nôr, but was somewhat discomfited through the sudden silence of his enemies.

18 Nevertheless Nĭ-cā´-nôr, hearing of the manliness of them that were with Judas, and the courageousness that they had to fight for their country, durst not try the matter by the sword.

19 Wherefore he sent Pŏs´-ĭ-dō´-nĭ-ŭs, and Thĕ-ŏd´-ŏ-tŭs, and Măt-tă-thī´-ăs, to make peace.

20 So when they had taken long advisement thereupon, and the captain had made the multitude acquainted therewith, and it appeared that they were all of one mind, they consented to the covenants,

21 And appointed a day to meet in together by themselves: and when the day came, and stools were set for either of them,

22 Judas placed armed men ready in convenient places, lest some treachery should be suddenly practised by the enemies: so they made a peaceable conference.

23 Now Nĭ-cā´-nôr abode in Jerusalem, and did no hurt, but sent away the people that came flocking unto him.

24 And he would not willingly have Judas out of his sight: for he loved the man from his heart.

25 He prayed him also to take a wife, and to beget children: so he married, was quiet, and took part of this life.

26 But Ăl´-çĭ-mŭs, perceiving

291

the love that was betwixt them, and considering the covenants that were made, came to Dĕ-mē'-trĭ-ŭs, and told him that Nĭ-cā'-nôr was not well affected toward the state; for that he had ordained Judas, a traitor to his realm, to be the king's successor.

27 Then the king being in a rage, and provoked with the accusations of the most wicked man, wrote to Nĭ-cā'-nôr, signifying that he was much displeased with the covenants, and commanding him that he should send Măc-că-bē'-ŭs prisoner in all haste unto Antioch.

28 When this came to Nĭ-cā'-nôr's hearing, he was much confounded in himself, and took it grievously that he should make void the articles which were agreed upon, the man being in no fault.

29 But because there was no dealing against the king, he watched his time to accomplish this thing by policy.

30 Notwithstanding, when Măc-că-bē'-ŭs saw that Nĭ-cā'-nôr began to be churlish unto him, and that he entreated him more roughly than he was wont, perceiving that such sour behaviour came not of good, he gathered together not a few of his men, and withdrew himself from Nicanor.

31 But the other, knowing that he was notably prevented by Judas' policy, came into the great and holy temple, and commanded the priests, that were offering their usual sacrifices, to deliver him the man.

32 And when they sware that they could not tell where the man was whom he sought,

33 He stretched out his right hand toward the temple, and made an oath in this manner: If ye will not deliver me Judas as a prisoner, I will lay this temple of God even with the ground, and I will break down the altar, and erect a notable temple unto Bacchus.

34 After these words he departed. Then the priests lifted up their hands toward heaven, and besought him that was ever a defender of their nation, saying in this manner;

35 Thou, O Lord of all things, who hast need of nothing, wast pleased that the temple of thine habitation should be among us:

36 Therefore now, O holy Lord of all holiness, keep this house ever undefiled, which lately was cleansed, and stop every unrighteous mouth.

37 Now was there accused unto Nĭ-cā'-nôr one Rā'-zĭs, one of the elders of Jerusalem, a lover of his countrymen, and a man of very good report, who for his kindness was called a father of the Jews.

38 For in the former times, when they mingled not themselves with the Gentiles, he had been accused of Judaism, and did boldly jeopard his body and life with all vehemency for the religion of the Jews.

39 So Nĭ-cā'-nôr, willing to declare the hate that he bare unto the Jews, sent above five hundred men of war to take him:

40 For he thought by taking him to do the Jews much hurt.

41 Now when the multitude would have taken the tower, and violently broken into the outer door, and bade that fire should be brought to burn it, he being ready to be taken on every side fell upon his sword;

42 Choosing rather to die

manfully, than to come into the hands of the wicked, to be abused otherwise than beseemed his noble birth:

43 But missing his stroke through haste, the multitude also rushing within the doors, he ran boldly up to the wall, and cast himself down manfully among the thickest of them.

44 But they quickly giving back, and a space being made, he fell down into the midst of the void place.

45 Nevertheless, while there was yet breath within him, being inflamed with anger, he rose up; and though his blood gushed out like spouts of water, and his wounds were grievous, yet he ran through the midst of the throng; and standing upon a steep rock,

46 When as his blood was now quite gone, he plucked out his bowels, and taking them in both his hands, he cast them upon the throng, and calling upon the Lord of life and spirit to restore him those again, he thus died.

CHAPTER XV

BUT Nĭ-cā'-nôr, hearing that Judas and his company were in the strong places about Samaria, resolved without any danger to set upon them on the sabbath day.

2 Nevertheless the Jews that were compelled to go with him said, O destroy not so cruelly and barbarously, but give honour to that day, which he, that seeth all things, hath honoured with holiness above *other days*.

3 Then the most ungracious wretch demanded, if there were a Mighty one in heaven, that had commanded the sabbath day to be kept.

4 And when they said, There is in heaven a living Lord, and mighty, who commanded the seventh day to be kept:

5 Then said the other, And I also am mighty upon earth, and I command to take arms, and to do the king's business. Yet he obtained not to have his wicked will done.

6 So Nĭ-cā'-nôr in exceeding pride and haughtiness determined to set up a publick monument of his victory over Judas and them that were with him.

7 But Măc-că-bē'-ŭs had ever sure confidence that the Lord would help him:

8 Wherefore he exhorted his people not to fear the coming of the heathen against them, but to remember the help which in former times they had received from heaven, and now to expect the victory and aid, which should come unto them from the Almighty.

9 And so comforting them out of the law and the prophets, and withal putting them in mind of the battles that they won afore, he made them more cheerful.

10 And when he had stirred up their minds, he gave them their charge, shewing them therewithal the falsehood of the heathen, and the breach of oaths.

11 Thus he armed every one of them, not so much with defence of shields and spears, as with comfortable and good words: and beside that, he told them a dream worthy to be believed, as if it had been so indeed, which did not a little rejoice them.

293

12 And this was his vision: That Ō-nī'-ăs, who had been high priest, a virtuous and a good man, reverend in conversation, gentle in condition, well spoken also, and exercised from a child in all points of virtue, holding up his hands prayed for the whole body of the Jews.

13 This done, in like manner there appeared a man with gray hairs, and exceeding glorious, who was of a wonderful and excellent majesty.

14 Then Ō-nī'-ăs answered, saying, This is a lover of the brethren, who prayeth much for the people, and for the holy city, *to wit*, Jeremias the prophet of God.

15 Whereupon Jeremias holding forth his right hand gave to Judas a sword of gold, and in giving it spake thus,

16 Take this holy sword, a gift from God, with the which thou shalt wound the adversaries.

17 Thus being well comforted by the words of Judas, which were very good, and able to stir them up to valour, and to encourage the hearts of the young men, they determined not to pitch camp, but courageously to set upon them, and manfully to try the matter by conflict, because the city and the sanctuary and the temple were in danger.

18 For the care that they took for their wives, and their children, their brethren, and kinsfolks, was in least account with them: but the greatest and principal fear was for the holy temple.

19 Also they that were in the city took not the least care, being troubled for the conflict abroad.

20 And now, when as all looked what should be the trial, and the enemies were already come near, and the army was set in array, and the beasts conveniently placed, and the horsemen set in wings,

21 Măc-că-bē'-ŭs seeing the coming of the multitude, and the divers preparations of armour, and the fierceness of the beasts, stretched out his hands toward heaven, and called upon the Lord that worketh wonders, knowing that victory cometh not by arms, but even as it seemeth good to him, he giveth it to such as are worthy:

22 Therefore in his prayer he said after this manner; O Lord, thou didst send thine angel in the time of Ěz-ě-kī'-ăs king of Judea, and didst slay in the host of Sěn-năch'-ěr-ĭb an hundred fourscore and five thousand:

23 Wherefore now also, O Lord of heaven, send a good angel before us for a fear and dread unto them;

24 And through the might of thine arm let those be stricken with terror, that come against thy holy people to blaspheme. And he ended thus.

25 Then Nĭ-că'-nôr and they that were with him came forward with trumpets and songs.

26 But Judas and his company encountered the enemies with invocation and prayer.

27 So that fighting with their hands, and praying unto God with their hearts, they slew no less than thirty and five thousand men: for through the appearance of God they were greatly cheered.

28 Now when the battle was done, returning again with joy,

they knew that Nĭ-cā́-nôr lay dead in his harness.

29 Then they made a great shout and a noise, praising the Almighty in their own language.

30 And *Judas*, who was ever the chief defender of the citizens both in body and mind, and who continued his love toward his countrymen all his life, commanded to strike off Nĭ-cā́-nôr's head, and his hand with his shoulder, and bring them to Jerusalem.

31 So when he was there, and had called them of his nation together, and set the priests before the altar, he sent for them that were of the tower,

32 And shewed them vile Nĭ-cā́-nôr's head, and the hand of that blasphemer, which with proud brags he had stretched out against the holy temple of the Almighty.

33 And when he had cut out the tongue of that ungodly Nĭ-cā́-nôr, he commanded that they should give it by pieces unto the fowls, and hang up the reward of his madness before the temple.

34 So every man praised toward the heaven the glorious Lord, saying, Blessed be he that hath kept his own place undefiled.

35 He hanged also Nĭ-cā́-nôr's head upon the tower, an evident and manifest sign unto all of the help of the Lord.

36 And they ordained all with a common decree in no case to let that day pass without solemnity, but to celebrate the thirteenth day of the twelfth month, which in the Syrian tongue is called Ă-däŕ, the day before Mär-dŏ-chḗ-ŭs' day.

37 Thus went it with Nĭ-cā́-nôr: and from that time forth the Hebrews had the city in their power. And here will I make an end.

38 And if *I have done* well, and as is fitting the story, it is that which I desired: but if slenderly and meanly, it is that which I could attain unto.

39 For as it is hurtful to drink wine or water alone; and as wine mingled with water is pleasant, and delighteth the taste: even so speech finely framed delighteth the ears of them that read the story. And here shall be an end.

THE END OF THE APOCRYPHA

PRINTED IN GREAT BRITAIN BY
EYRE AND SPOTTISWOODE LIMITED
HER MAJESTY'S PRINTERS, LONDON